Intelligent Optimization Techniques for Business Analytics

Sanjeev Bansal
Amity Business School, Amity University, Noida, India

Nitendra Kumar
Amity Business School, Amity University, Noida, India

Priyanka Agarwal
Amity Business School, Amity University, Noida, India

A volume in the Advances in Business Information Systems and Analytics (ABISA) Book Series

IGI Global
PUBLISHER of TIMELY KNOWLEDGE

Published in the United States of America by
IGI Global
Business Science Reference (an imprint of IGI Global)
701 E. Chocolate Avenue
Hershey PA, USA 17033
Tel: 717-533-8845
Fax: 717-533-8661
E-mail: cust@igi-global.com
Web site: http://www.igi-global.com

Library of Congress Cataloging-in-Publication Data

Names: Bansal, Sanjeev, 1967- editor. | Kumar, Nitendra, 1989- editor. | Agarwal, Priyanka, editor.
Title: Intelligent optimization techniques for business analytics / edited by Sanjeev Bansal, Nitendra Kumar, Priyanka Agarwal.
Description: Hershey, PA : Business Science Reference, [2024] | Includes bibliographical references and index. | Summary: "The primary objective of this edited book is to present a comprehensive compilation of cutting-edge research and practical applications focusing on the synergy between learning algorithms and intelligent optimization techniques for business analytics"-- Provided by publisher.
Identifiers: LCCN 2024002243 (print) | LCCN 2024002244 (ebook) | ISBN 9798369315989 (hardcover) | ISBN 9798369315996 (ebook)
Subjects: LCSH: Business--Technological innovations. | Mathematical optimization.
Classification: LCC HD45 .I5535 2024 (print) | LCC HD45 (ebook) | DDC 658.4/063--dc23/eng/20240429
LC record available at https://lccn.loc.gov/2024002243
LC ebook record available at https://lccn.loc.gov/2024002244

This book is published in the IGI Global book series Advances in Business Information Systems and Analytics (ABISA) (ISSN: 2327-3275; eISSN: 2327-3283)

British Cataloguing in Publication Data
A Cataloguing in Publication record for this book is available from the British Library.

Advances in Business Information Systems and Analytics (ABISA) Book Series

ISSN:2327-3275
EISSN:2327-3283

MISSION

The successful development and management of information systems and business analytics is crucial to the success of an organization. New technological developments and methods for data analysis have allowed organizations to not only improve their processes and allow for greater productivity, but have also provided businesses with a venue through which to cut costs, plan for the future, and maintain competitive advantage in the information age.

The **Advances in Business Information Systems and Analytics (ABISA) Book Series** aims to present diverse and timely research in the development, deployment, and management of business information systems and business analytics for continued organizational development and improved business value.

COVERAGE

- Management Information Systems
- Statistics
- Performance Metrics
- Business Systems Engineering
- Business Decision Making
- Algorithms
- Data Strategy
- Forecasting
- Business Information Security
- Decision Support Systems

The Advances in Business Information Systems and Analytics (ABISA) Book Series (ISSN 2327-3275) is published by IGI Global, 701 E. Chocolate Avenue, Hershey, PA 17033-1240, USA, www.igi-global.com. This series is composed of titles available for purchase individually; each title is edited to be contextually exclusive from any other title within the series. For pricing and ordering information please visit http://www.igi-global.com/book-series/advances-business-information-systems-analytics/37155. Postmaster: Send all address changes to above address.

Titles in this Series

For a list of additional titles in this series, please visit:
http://www.igi-global.com/book-series/advances-business-information-systems-analytics/37155

Utilizing AI and Smart Technology to Improve Sustainability in Entrepreneurship
Syed Far Abid Hossain (BRAC University, Bangladesh)
Business Science Reference • © 2024 • 370pp • H/C (ISBN: 9798369318423) • US $290.00

Strengthening Industrial Cybersecurity to Protect Business Intelligence
Saqib Saeed (Department of Computer Information Systems, College of Computer Science and Information Technology, Imam Abdulrahman Bin Faisal University, Saudi Arabia) Neda Azizi (Torrens University, Australia) Shahzaib Tahir (Department of Information Security, College of Signals, Pakistan & National University of Sciences and Technology, Islamabad, Pakistan) Munir Ahmad (School of Computer Science, National College of Business Administration and Economics, Lahore, Pakistan) and Abdullah M. Almuhaideb (Department of Networks and Communications, College of Computer Science and Information Technology, Imam Abdulrahman Bin Faisal University, Saudi Arabia)
Business Science Reference • © 2024 • 373pp • H/C (ISBN: 9798369308394) • US $275.00

AI and Data Analytics Applications in Organizational Management
Tereza Raquel Merlo (University of North Texas, USA & Merlo Management Consulting, USA)
Business Science Reference • © 2024 • 317pp • H/C (ISBN: 9798369310588) • US $300.00

Evolution of Cross-Sector Cyber Intelligent Markets
Eugene J. Lewis (Capitol Technology University, USA)
Business Science Reference • © 2024 • 469pp • H/C (ISBN: 9798369319703) • US $275.00

Leveraging ChatGPT and Artificial Intelligence for Effective Customer Engagement
Rohit Bansal (Department of Management Studies, Vaish College of Engineering, Rohtak, India) Abdul Hafaz Ngah (Faculty of Business Economics and Social DevelopmentUniversiti Malaysia Terenganu, Malaysia) Aziza Chakir (FSJES AC, Hassan II University, Casablanca, Morocco) and Nishita Pruthi (Maharshi Dayanand University, India)
Business Science Reference • © 2024 • 349pp • H/C (ISBN: 9798369308158) • US $265.00

For an entire list of titles in this series, please visit:
http://www.igi-global.com/book-series/advances-business-information-systems-analytics/37155

IGI Global
PUBLISHER of TIMELY KNOWLEDGE

701 East Chocolate Avenue, Hershey, PA 17033, USA
Tel: 717-533-8845 x100 • Fax: 717-533-8661
E-Mail: cust@igi-global.com • www.igi-global.com

Table of Contents

Detailed Table of Contents

This chapter provides a thorough insight to the dynamic field of intelligent optimization techniques in the context of business analytics. It begins by explaining the fundamental concepts of optimization, evolution of optimization techniques, tracking their evolution from traditional procedures to the emergence of intelligent optimization techniques, and their application in modern business environments. In addition, it demonstrates the integration of intelligent optimization with data analytics techniques and technologies, emphasizes the possible obstacles and ethical dilemmas to use intelligent optimization, encouraging readers to consider responsible AI use. Ultimately, it provides a perspective on the role of intelligent optimization in creating the future of business analytics, paving the way for more efficient, data-driven, and competitive organizations. This chapter is an excellent resource for researchers, practitioners, and students interested in using intelligent optimization strategies to promote innovation and success in the ever-changing field of business analytics.

This chapter focuses on providing a complete grasp of the foundations of machine learning (ML). Machine learning is a rapidly evolving domain with wide-ranging applications, from natural language processing to autonomous vehicles. This chapter explores the basic ideas, techniques, and methodologies that underpin ML, laying the groundwork for a deeper dive into more advanced topics. Machine learning is a pivotal technology that has revolutionized numerous industries and continues to shape the future of artificial intelligence. Understanding its fundamental concepts is essential for anyone looking to explore the vast landscape of ML applications. This chapter will serve as a crucial reference point for readers embarking on their journey into the world of machine learning.

This study envisions the future trajectory of intelligent optimization and machine learning (ML) in the realm of business analytics, introducing novel perspectives. It investigates the synergy between big data analytics and ML, underscoring the effectiveness of deep learning architectures in unravelling complex patterns. Emphasizing interpretability, the study explores the development of ML models tailored for business contexts and delves into decentralized model training and data privacy through edge computing and federated learning. In the optimization domain, it addresses the ascendancy of customized meta-heuristic algorithms and explores the convergence of optimization and ML for heightened operational efficiency. This research contributes to a nuanced understanding, fostering innovative applications in the dynamic landscape of business analytics. It has been observed that machine learning and intelligent optimization techniques are very useful for business analytics.

In today's dynamic and complex financial landscape, accurate and reliable financial forecasting is crucial for businesses to make informed decisions, manage risks, and achieve long-term success. Artificial intelligence (AI) has emerged as a transformative force in the financial industry, offering a powerful set of tools and techniques for enhancing financial forecasting capabilities. This chapter delves into the realm of AI-driven financial forecasting, exploring the role of soft computing techniques in harnessing the power of AI for data-driven financial insights. Soft computing, a branch of computational intelligence, encompasses a suite of methodologies that mimic human reasoning and learning processes to handle complex and uncertain data. A comprehensive overview of AI-driven financial forecasting, highlighting the strengths and applications of soft computing techniques in this domain, has been envisaged beginning by introducing the fundamental concepts of AI in financial forecasting, including data pre-processing, feature selection, and model evaluation. It then delves into the specific applications of soft computing techniques in financial forecasting, exploring their use in various forecasting tasks, such as stock price prediction, exchange rate forecasting, and credit risk assessment. The transformative potential of AI-driven financial forecasting, empowered by the power of soft computing techniques, have also been underscored. The effectiveness of soft computing techniques has been shown through real-world examples and case studies, demonstrating their ability to outperform traditional forecasting methods in various financial scenarios. It also discusses the challenges and limitations of using AI in financial forecasting, emphasizing the importance of data quality, model interpretability, and ethical considerations.

As the stock market is an intricate, complex activity influenced by hundreds of factors, predicting such prices with accuracy or absolute conviction is quite difficult. This chapter focuses on the potential use of support vector machines (SVM), decision tree algorithm, and ARIMA model for predicting stock market prices using specific data obtained from Yahoo Finance. The authors train the model using daily price data derived from Yahoo Finance and make great efforts to estimate how well the model predicts market prices. The chapter adds value to the existing knowledge by showing that algorithms tend to work in this field. Insights from the study will help investors and traders take a better course of action in the market.

Credit card frauds are drastically increasing in number as compared to earlier days. Criminals are using fake identities and make use of various technologies to trap the users and get the money out from them. Therefore, it is essential to find a solution to these types of frauds. In the chapter, a model is planned to perceive the fraud in the credit card transactions. The model provides most of the important features required to detect illegal and illicit transactions.

One of the biggest challenges facing the industry today lies in the assignment of robots to the workstations of production processes in order to perform tasks collaboratively between robots and human labor; this is known as Cobots. This document proposes to minimize the number of workstations by assigning robots, to reduce production costs. Additionally, it seeks to minimize the number of workers by assigning Cobots to a percentage of workstations. Due to the above, in this research, the Assembly Line Balancing Problem Type I (SALBP-1) is adapted with a Cobot assignment problem. This problem is considered NP-hard, so the use of a hybrid heuristic is proposed in the search to minimize the number of workers and the number of workstations. The hybrid consists of a modified genetic algorithm applying a local search within the genetic selection operator. The results demonstrate a decrease in the assignment of workstations, as well as a decrease in assignment of workers when using Cobots in some workstations using the proposed algorithm for the benefit of organizations.

This chapter explores the intricate domain of enhancing customer service through strategically employing chatbots. It thoroughly investigates diverse optimization techniques, underscoring the vital role of refining chatbot responses and implementing efficiency metrics. The chapter dissects the challenges inherent in chatbot optimization, presenting innovative solutions that highlight the interconnected nature of these challenges. It illuminates the profound impact of well-optimized chatbots on customer service, demonstrating their capability to streamline tasks, improve accessibility, handle routine inquiries, and foster customer loyalty. Looking ahead, the chapter offers insights into upcoming trends and opportunities, such as integrating emotional intelligence and expanding multilingual functionalities. Essentially, this chapter functions as a comprehensive guide for practitioners and researchers, providing a nuanced comprehension of the pivotal role chatbots play in shaping the future landscape of customer service.

In the digital age, call centers remain a pivotal touchpoint between businesses and their clientele. They offer direct human interaction that shapes customer experience. One of the primary pain points in this interaction is the wait time a customer endures before being attended to. This research delves into the challenge of minimizing customer wait times in call centers. The authors experiment a blend of traditional optimization techniques and contemporary machine learning methods for the same. By leveraging integer programming, they formulate an optimization problem to efficiently allocate calls to agents. The main objective of the chapter is to reduce the cumulative waiting time while maintaining the customer satisfaction. The authors harness the predictive power of machine learning to forecast call durations based on various parameters as well. Preliminary results indicate a significant potential in combining these approaches. It offers a robust framework for call centers to enhance their operational efficiency. This elevates the customer experience in a very competitive environment as well.

Mental stress affects performance. With regard to farming, it has been more dangerous with greater fatality rates than any other occupation. The farmers often work on their own for long hours with untrustworthy equipment and in hard climates, with hazardous chemicals and livestock. In addition, they make large financial commitments that expose them to higher levels of financial risks giving them higher levels of mental stress. Thus, an attempt was made in this chapter to identify the key risk factors in farming workplaces in addition to the levels of depression, anxiety, and work stress of farmers of Indian agriculture leading to mental ill health among them, and further to develop a fuzzy-based model considering both these cases in the fuzzy-environment for the evaluation of mental-stress.

Preface

In today's dynamic business landscape, where data reigns supreme and decisions are increasingly driven by insights gleaned from analytics, the role of optimization techniques has never been more critical. The fusion of optimization techniques with business analytics represents a powerful synergy, enabling organizations to unlock hidden patterns, identify optimal solutions, and make data-driven decisions with confidence. From streamlining operations to enhancing customer experiences, from maximizing profitability to mitigating risks, the applications of intelligent optimization are vast and far-reaching.

In recent years, the field of business analytics has transformed dramatically due to advancements in artificial intelligence and machine learning technologies. The ability to interpret vast amounts of data, make predictions, and provide intelligent solutions to complex problems has resulted in improved decision-making, greater operational efficiencies, and enhanced competitive advantage for businesses. Despite these advancements, there remains a gap in understanding and implementing these technologies effectively across various business sectors. This book aims to bridge that gap by presenting a detailed examination of the principles, techniques, and real-world applications of machine learning and intelligent optimization systems in business analytics.

Intelligent Optimization Techniques for Business Analytics serves as a comprehensive guide for navigating the complexities of leveraging intelligent optimization methodologies to extract maximum value from business data. The book explores the intersection of optimization methodologies and business analytics, offering a comprehensive guide to harnessing the power of intelligent algorithms to solve complex business problems.

The book begins by laying the groundwork with an overview of optimization principles, providing readers with a solid foundation upon which to build their understanding. From there, we explore a diverse array of optimization algorithms, ranging from classical methods to cutting-edge approaches inspired by nature and artificial intelligence. Through a combination of theoretical foundations, practical applications, and hands-on examples, readers will gain a deep understanding of how these techniques can be applied to address diverse challenges across different industries and domains.

Whether you are a business professional, data scientist, researcher, or student, this book will serve a valuable resource for unlocking the potential of optimization techniques in driving business innovation and achieving sustainable growth. By mastering the principles outlined in the pages, readers will be equipped with the tools and insights needed to tackle the complexities of modern business environments and make informed decisions that lead to success.

The book contains 13 chapters. A brief description of each of the chapters is as follows:

1. The chapter titled "Introduction to Intelligent Optimization Techniques in Business Analytics" provides a thorough insight to the dynamic field of intelligent optimization techniques in the context of business analytics and provides a perspective on the role of intelligent optimization in creating the future of business analytics, paving the way for more efficient, data-driven, and competitive organizations. It also demonstrates the integration of intelligent optimization with data analytics techniques and technologies, emphasizes the possible obstacles and ethical dilemmas to use intelligent optimization, encouraging readers to consider responsible AI use.
2. The chapter titled "Foundations of Machine Learning" focuses on providing a complete grasp of the foundations of machine learning (ML). Machine learning is a rapidly evolving domain with wide-ranging applications, from natural language processing to autonomous vehicles. This chapter explores the basic ideas, techniques, and methodologies that underpin ML, laying the groundwork for a deeper dive into more advanced topics.
3. The third chapter titled "Future Directions in the Application of Machine Learning and Intelligent Optimization in Business Analytics" envisions the future trajectory of intelligent optimization and machine learning (ML) in the realm of business analytics, introducing novel perspectives. It investigates the synergy between big data analytics and ML, underscoring the effectiveness of deep learning architectures in unravelling complex patterns. Emphasizing interpretability, the chapter explores the development of ML models tailored for business contexts and delves into decentralized model training and data privacy through edge computing and federated learning.
4. The chapter titled "Deciphering the Realities of Deep Learning in Business Analytics: A Bibliometric Analysis" delves into the complexities surrounding the integration of DL into business analytics, highlighting computational complexities, infrastructure limitations, skill shortages, and the inherent black-box nature of DL models as key barriers. Furthermore, empirical evidence

suggests that DL may not consistently outperform traditional ML models, particularly in scenarios involving structured datasets with fixed-length feature vectors. The chapter provides insights into navigating the complexities of integrating DL into business analytics and outlines a roadmap for future research in this rapidly evolving field.

5. The chapter titled "Exploring the Impact of Deep Learning and Neural Networks on Business Analytics" explores the substantial uses of deep learning and neural networks in scientific business analytics, as well as how they are transforming the field. The chapters takes the readers through the incorporation of data science into scientific business analytics, starting with an overview of the fundamental ideas and technological history of these tools since an in-depth examination of neural network topologies is necessary before delving into their use in various commercial contexts.
6. "AI-Driven Financial Forecasting: The Power of Soft Computing" delves into the realm of AI-driven financial forecasting, exploring the role of soft computing techniques in harnessing the power of AI for data-driven financial insights. A comprehensive overview of AI-driven financial forecasting, highlighting the strengths and applications of soft computing techniques in this domain have been envisaged beginning by introducing the fundamental concepts of AI in financial forecasting, including data pre-processing, feature selection, and model evaluation.
7. The chapter titled "An Analysis of Stock Price Prediction Techniques" focuses on the potential use of Support Vector Machines (SVM), Decision Tree Algorithm and ARIMA model for predicting Stock Market Prices using specific data obtained from Yahoo Finance and adds value to the existing knowledge by showing that algorithms tend to work in this field.
8. The eighth chapter titled "Credit Card Fraud Detection and Analysis With Blend of Machine Learning and Blockchain" proposed a project design, a model planned to perceive the fraud bustle in the credit card transactions. The Model provides most of the important features required to detect illegal and illicit transactions.
9. The chapter titled "Genetic Crossover Operator in Local Search of the Assembly Line Balancing Problem" proposes to minimize the number of workstations by assigning robots, to reduce production costs. Additionally, it seeks to minimize the number of workers by assigning Cobots to a percentage of workstations.
10. The chapter titled "Optimizing Customer Service With Chatbots" explores the intricate domain of enhancing customer service through strategically employing chatbots. It thoroughly investigates diverse optimization techniques, underscoring the vital role of refining chatbot responses and implementing efficiency metrics. The chapter dissects the challenges inherent in chatbot

optimization, presenting innovative solutions that highlight the interconnected nature of these challenges. It illuminates the profound impact of well-optimized chatbots on customer service, demonstrating their capability to streamline tasks, improve accessibility, handle routine inquiries, and foster customer loyalty. Looking ahead, the section offers insights into upcoming trends and opportunities, such as integrating emotional intelligence and expanding multilingual functionalities.

11. The chapter titled "Tackling Customer Wait Times: Advanced Techniques for Call Centre Optimization" delves into the challenge of minimizing customer wait times in call centers and experimented a blend of traditional optimization techniques and contemporary machine learning methods for the same. By leveraging Integer Programming, the chapter tried to formulate an optimization problem to efficiently allocate calls to agents. Main objective is to reduce the cumulative waiting time while maintaining the customer satisfaction by harnessing the predictive power of machine learning to forecast call durations based on various parameters as well.
12. In the chapter titled "Fuzzy Logic Modelling-Based Measurement Approach for Mental Stress Measurement" an attempt was made in this study to identify the key risk-factors in farming work-places in addition to the levels of depressions, anxieties and work-stresses of farmers of Indian agriculture leading to mental ill-health among them, and further to develop a fuzzy-based models considering both these cases in the fuzzy-environment " for the evaluation of mental-stress.
13. The last chapter titled "Deep Learning, Neural Networks, and Their Applications in Business Analytics" provides an overview of deep learning and neural networks, delving into their fundamental principles, architectures, and training methodologies. It focusses on their real-world applications in various aspects of business analytics, such as customer behaviour analysis, demand forecasting, fraud detection, recommendation systems, and more.

We would like to express our gratitude to the contributors, researchers, practitioners, and educators who have helped shape the content of this book. It is our hope that *Intelligent Optimization Techniques for Business Analytics* will serve as a valuable resource for anyone seeking to harness the power of optimization to drive business success in the digital age.

Sanjeev Bansal
Amity Business School, Amity University, Noida, India

Nitendra Kumar

Amity Business School, Amity University, Noida, India

Priyanka Agarwal
Amity Business School, Amity University, Noida, India

Chapter 1
Introduction to Intelligent Optimization Techniques in Business Analytics

Amrita
https://orcid.org/0000-0001-6922-3403
Sharda University, India

Utkarsh
Sharda University, India

Ishu Gaur
Sharda University, India

Srishti Rai
Sharda University, India

ABSTRACT

This chapter provides a thorough insight to the dynamic field of intelligent optimization techniques in the context of business analytics. It begins by explaining the fundamental concepts of optimization, evolution of optimization techniques, tracking their evolution from traditional procedures to the emergence of intelligent optimization techniques, and their application in modern business environments. In addition, it demonstrates the integration of intelligent optimization with data analytics techniques and technologies, emphasizes the possible obstacles and ethical dilemmas to use intelligent optimization, encouraging readers to consider responsible AI use. Ultimately, it provides a perspective on the role of intelligent optimization in creating the future of business analytics, paving the way for more efficient, data-driven, and competitive organizations. This chapter is an excellent resource for researchers, practitioners, and students interested in using intelligent optimization strategies to promote innovation and success in the ever-changing field of business analytics.

DOI: 10.4018/979-8-3693-1598-9.ch001

1. INTRODUCTION

In the ever-evolving world of technology and corporate business, it's a fundamental requirement to utilize data and analytics in a strategic manner. Organizations all around the world are levering and using the power of information to enhance their decision-making processes, searching for every possible advantage in today's ever-changing market. The science of optimization, i.e., a dynamic and pivotal discipline that tries to improve efficiency, maximize output, and streamline operations, is at the heart of this data-driven resolution (Akkara & Selvakumar, 2023).

The use of optimization techniques in the field of business analytics is the key to unlocking this potential. This chapter provides a thorough introduction to this crucial intersection, where intelligence and analytics merge to construct a path for the future of decision-making in businesses of various sizes and domains (Albright & Winston, 2020).

In the upcoming sections, we will dive deep into the fundamentals and concepts of optimization, tracking its historical origins and revealing the exceptional evolution of classical methodologies into today's intelligent, sophisticated, and data-driven approaches. We will have a better understanding of the powerful tools available to modern businesses by learning the principles, paradigms, and practical applications of intelligent optimization strategies (Akkara & Selvakumar, 2023).

In an age dominated by data, our examination of the intersection between intelligent optimization and business analytics is not merely a theoretical and conceptual venture but also a practical requirement. We will observe how these techniques, when utilized strategically, can redefine the decision-making process, modify resource allocation, elevate resource chain management, and advance predictive modelling.

As we course through this complex landscape, we will not evade away from the challenges and ethical considerations that come along with the integration of intelligent optimization with business analytics (Niu et al., 2021). Rather, we will embrace them, understanding that with great power comes great responsibility. It is with this mindset that we address the moral aspects of responsible AI use in the context of business analytics.

Finally, this chapter goes beyond just academic exercise; it is a guiding mechanism for researchers, practitioners, and students towards a future where intelligent optimization plays a crucial role in making enterprises more efficient, data-driven, and competitive (Olaniyi et al., 2023). It is a journey into the core of business analytics, where the combined power of intelligence and data fosters innovation and success.

2. OPTIMIZATION FUNDAMENTALS

The essence of every efficient and effective decision-making process is the concept of optimization. To begin a thorough exploration of intelligent optimization techniques in business analytics, it is a must to understand the underlying fundamental principles of optimization and its importance in the modern decision-making process (Albright & Winston, 2020; Akkara & Selvakumar, 2023).

2.1 Understanding Optimization

Optimization is defined as the art and science of selecting the optimum solution from a set of viable options. It is the pursuit of perfection, the precise adjustment of systems, and the process of maximizing favorable outcomes while minimizing the unfavorable ones. Optimization addresses questions such as: What is the most efficient way of allocating resources? What combination of factors will produce the highest returns? How can we make optimal decisions when faced with constraints and uncertainties?

2.2 The Importance of Optimization in Decision-Making

Optimization is more than just a theoretical concept; it is a necessary tool for businesses seeking to thrive in today's data-driven world. Optimization is important in decision-making and resource-allocation processes for the following reasons:

a) **Efficiency**: Optimization ensures that resources are used efficiently. By identifying the best allocation of resources, it minimizes waste and maximizes productivity.
b) **Cost Reduction:** In a world where cost control is paramount, optimization helps in minimizing costs across various aspects of business operations.
c) **Competitive Advantage:** Businesses that excel in optimizing their processes and strategies gain a significant competitive advantage. They can deliver better products and services at lower costs.
d) **Complex Decision-Making:** In scenarios where decisions involve numerous variables and constraints, optimization provides a systematic framework for making the best choices.
e) **Risk Management:** Optimizing strategies can help mitigate risks by identifying the best ways to allocate resources while considering uncertainty.
f) **Resource Allocation:** From workforce management to budget allocation, optimization aids in efficient resource distribution.

In the rapidly changing landscape of modern businesses, optimization is an essential component of successful and impactful decision-making and the foundation of resource allocation (Li et al., 2022). As we move forward in this chapter, we will uncover the evolution of classical optimization techniques to intelligent, data-driven, and sophisticated methodologies that are transforming the way business' function and flourish (Olaniyi et al., 2023).

3. EVOLUTION OF OPTIMIZATION TECHNIQUES

The evolution of optimization techniques is marked by an endless pursuit of higher efficiency, optimality, precision, and adaptability. This journey is fueled by the ever-growing complexities of the modern business landscape (Albright & Winston, 2020). In this section, we will explore this historical path, tracking the growth of classical optimization methods and their shift to intelligent approaches.

3.1 From Classical to Intelligent Approaches

The origin of optimization can be traced back to the beginning of civilization, when ancient societies faced challenges regarding resource allocation, predating the formal coining of the term "optimization." Various traditional optimization techniques have been developed and enhanced throughout history, such as linear programming, mathematical optimization, and linear and nonlinear optimization (Akkara & Selvakumar, 2023).

Nevertheless, the 21st century has brought about a new era of optimization. With the abundance of data and the emergence of newly developed, powerful computational tools, classical approaches have proven to be insufficient to address the complex difficulties faced by modern businesses. As a result, this gives rise to intelligent optimization techniques, which combine the power of modern technologies, advanced algorithms, machine learning (ML), and artificial intelligence (AI) to enhance decision-making processes by tackling the problems faced by businesses, shown in Figure 1 (Bharadiya, 2023).

Figure 1. Evolution of optimization methods in business analytics (indicative timeline)

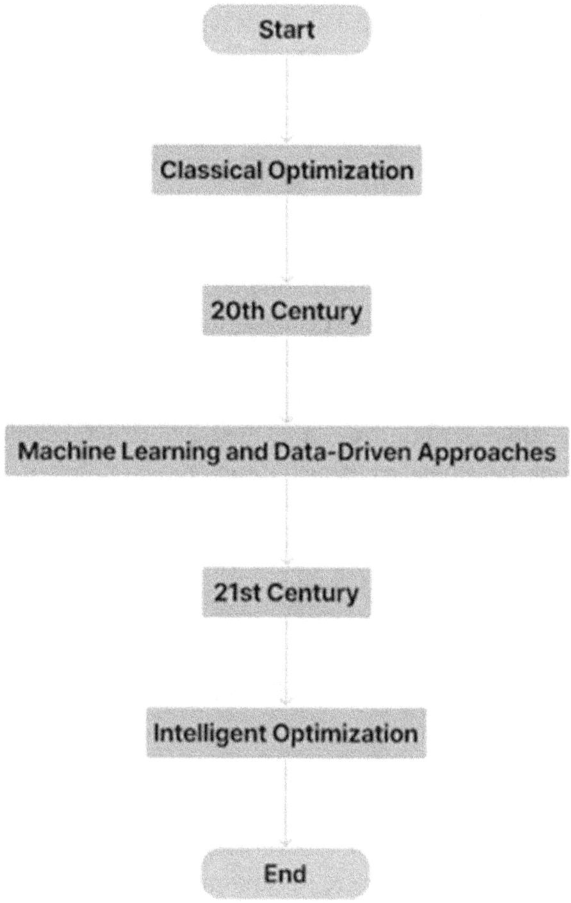

3.2 Limitations of Classical Optimization Methods

While classical optimization methods have their benefits, they also come with their own limitations, which have prompted the need for intelligent optimization approaches and accelerated their development. Some of the key limitations that led to the development of intelligent optimization techniques are:

a) **Complexity Handling:** Classical methods struggle to handle highly complex problems with numerous variables and constraints. They often require simplifications that may not reflect real-world intricacies.

b) **Sensitivity to Initial Conditions:** Classical optimization is often sensitive to initial conditions and may converge to local optima, missing global solutions.
c) **Lack of Adaptability:** Classical methods typically rely on fixed mathematical models, making them less adaptable to changing environments and dynamic systems.
d) **Data-Driven Insights:** In an era where data is abundant, classical optimization techniques can miss the valuable insights that data-driven approaches can provide.
e) **Computational Intensity:** As the scope and complexity of problems grow, classical methods may require vast computational resources and time, making them less practical for real-time decision-making.

The limitations of classical optimization methods have encouraged the development of intelligent optimization techniques. These techniques effectively tackle the limitations mentioned by using the combined strength of data, algorithms, and ML. In the following sections, we will go further into the details and specifics of key intelligent optimization paradigms, revealing their potential as well as practical applications in the field of business analytics.

4. INTELLIGENT OPTIMIZATION PARADIGMS

The transition towards intelligent optimizations paradigms has unlocked new exciting possibilities for solving complex problems, addressing difficult challenges, and making data-driven decisions in the ever-changing world of business analytics (Albright & Winston, 2020; Akkara & Selvakumar, 2023). In this section, we will identify and understand major intelligent optimization techniques, along with their principles and applications.

4.1 Genetic Algorithms

Genetic algorithm (GA) is optimization techniques inspired by the process of natural selection and evolution. They operate by mimicking the survival-of-the-fittest concept, where solutions evolve and improve over generations. GAs work by creating a population of potential solutions to a problem and using evolutionary operations such as selection, crossover, and mutation to generate new generations of solutions, shown in Figure 2. These iterations continue until an optimal or near-optimal solution is found. GAs are well-suited for optimization problems with a large search space and complex, non-linear relationships. They are often used in fields like logistics, engineering design, and finance.

Figure 2. Genetic algorithm

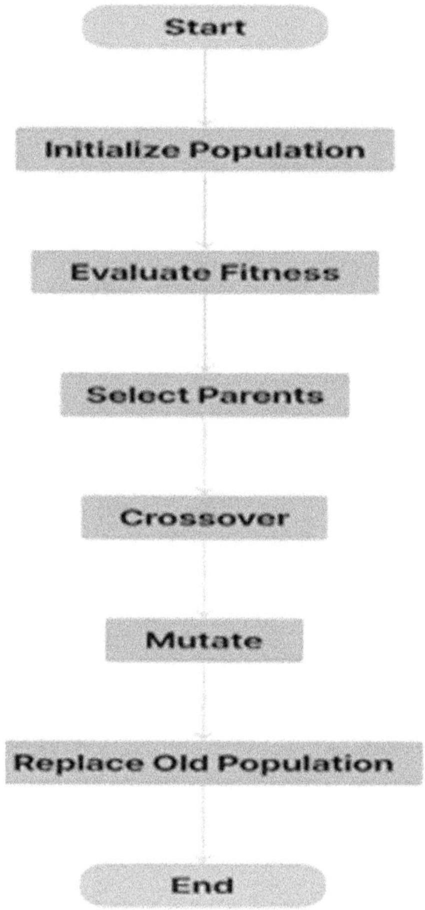

4.2 Simulated Annealing

Simulated annealing is a probabilistic optimization technique inspired by the annealing process in metallurgy. It aims to find the global optimum of a complex problem by gradually exploring the solution space. Simulated annealing involves a simulated "cooling" process where the algorithm accepts worse solutions initially and gradually becomes more selective, increasing the likelihood of finding the global optimum, as shown in Figure 3 (Barrere, 1997). Simulated annealing is effective in situations where an exact solution is difficult to find. It is commonly used in combinatorial optimization problems, such as the traveling salesman problem and resource scheduling.

Figure 3. Simulated annealing

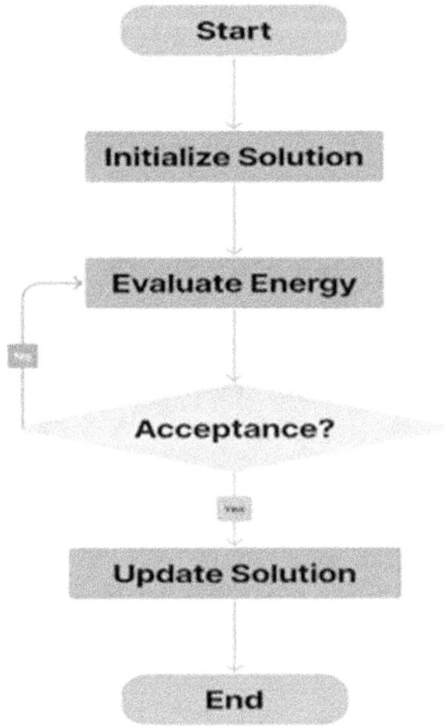

4.3 Particle Swarm Optimization

Particle Swarm Optimization (PSO) is a population-based optimization technique inspired by the social behavior of birds or fish. It models individuals as particles in a search space that cooperate to find the optimal solution (Eberhart & Kennedy, 1995). In PSO, particles adjust their positions based on their own experience and the experience of their neighbors. The goal is to converge on the best solution by iteratively updating particle positions. The steps involved in PSO algorithm is shown in Figure 4 (Kumar & Reddy, 2007). PSO is particularly effective for continuous optimization problems and dynamic optimization scenarios. It finds applications in areas such as robotics, image processing, business analytics, and data clustering (Duan et al., 2020).

Figure 4. Particle swarm optimization

4.4 Machine Learning-Driven Techniques

ML-driven optimization techniques involve integrating ML algorithms with optimization approaches to enhance decision-making. These techniques leverage data-driven insights to improve the optimization process (Tang & Meng, 2020). ML-driven techniques combine the power of ML models, such as neural networks, with optimization algorithms. They use historical data to make predictions and guide the optimization process. ML-driven techniques are versatile and can be applied to a wide range of business analytics problems, including predictive modeling, recommendation systems, and anomaly detection. The steps are presented in Figure 5.

Figure 5. Machine learning-driven optimization

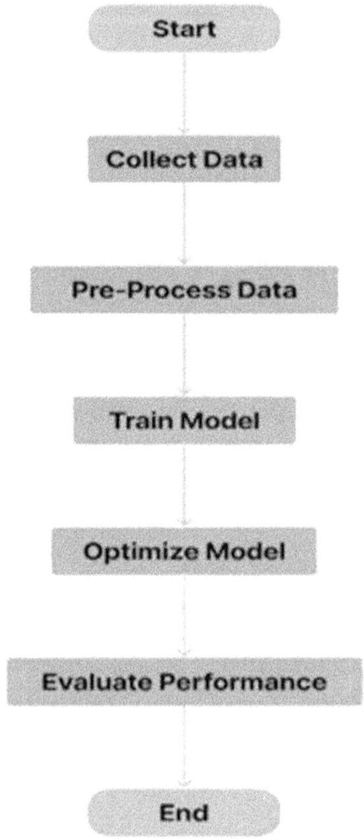

Intelligent optimization paradigms are at the forefront of optimization in the field of business analytics. As their principles and applicability differ from one another, they are invaluable tools for addressing the diverse variety of difficult challenges currently faced by enterprises. In the following sections, we will examine how these tools can be effectively put to use in the business field, demonstrating their potential for data-driven decision-making and resource optimization (Olaniyi et al., 2023).

5. APPLICATIONS IN BUSINESS ANALYTICS

The genuine effectiveness of intelligent optimization techniques becomes more noticeable once they are applied to real-world business challenges. In this section, we will thoroughly examine various domains where these techniques have been practically implemented, revolutionizing decision-making processes, resource allocation, and strategic planning (Lu et al., 2019; Li et al., 2022).

5.1 Decision Support and Optimization in Finance

In the field of finance, intelligent optimization techniques are pivotal in portfolio optimization, risk management, and trading strategies. They assist in identifying an optimal portfolio mix by taking into account various factors such as risk tolerance, market dynamics, and expected returns (Niu et al., 2021). They also improve trading algorithms that aim to execute orders efficiently while minimizing market impact. By utilizing these techniques, financial enterprises and institutions can make data-driven investment decisions, improve portfolio performance, and manage risks more effectively. This affects individual investors, asset managers, and even algorithmic trading firms (Sarker, 2021).

Case Study 1: Portfolio Optimization

A well-known example of portfolio optimization is the use of intelligent optimization techniques by investment firms. With the skillful utilization of algorithms, these firms construct investment portfolios that balance risk and return, shown in Figure 6. An example of this is the application of Modern Portfolio Theory (MPT) in asset management. MPT relies on optimization, helping asset managers create diversified portfolios suited to an investor's risk profile and investment goals.

Figure 6. Portfolio optimization in finance

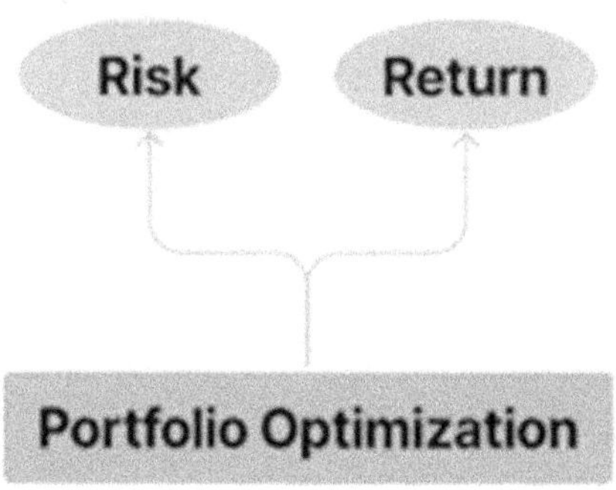

Case Study 2: Algorithmic Trading

In the world of high-frequency trading, algorithmic techniques supported by optimization algorithms execute trades at remarkable speeds while reducing market impact. Firms such as Renaissance Technologies have showcased immense financial success by employing complex trading algorithms that utilize intelligent optimization techniques.

5.2 Resource Allocation and Portfolio Optimization

A common challenge in project management is efficient resource allocation since there are limited resources that must be duly distributed across multiple projects to maximize the overall value. Intelligent optimization techniques assist project managers in determining the optimum allocation strategy, considering important factors such as constraints and objectives (Niu et al., 2021). By effectively allocating resources across multiple projects, businesses can finish projects more efficiently, reduce costs, and meet project deadlines. This is crucial for every industry, ranging from construction and manufacturing to IT project management.

Figure 7. Resource allocation in construction project management

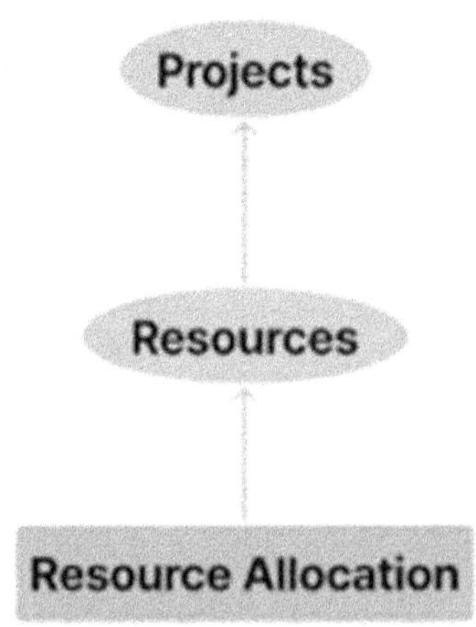

Case Study 3: Construction Project Management

Optimizing resource allocation is critical in the construction industry for completing projects on schedule and under budget. Turner Construction, for example, has used optimization models to efficiently manage labor, resources, and equipment across multiple construction projects. These models incorporate project deadlines, resource availability, and budget constraints.

5.3 Supply Chain Optimization

Optimization strategies are heavily used in supply chain management. These strategies are used by businesses to optimize inventory levels, distribution networks, and production schedules. They attempt to reduce shipping costs, shorten lead times, and ensure that items are available where and when they are needed. Supply chain optimization leads to cost reductions, improved customer service, and streamlined operations. This is particularly important in industries such as retail, manufacturing, and logistics.

Figure 8. Supply chain optimization in inventory management

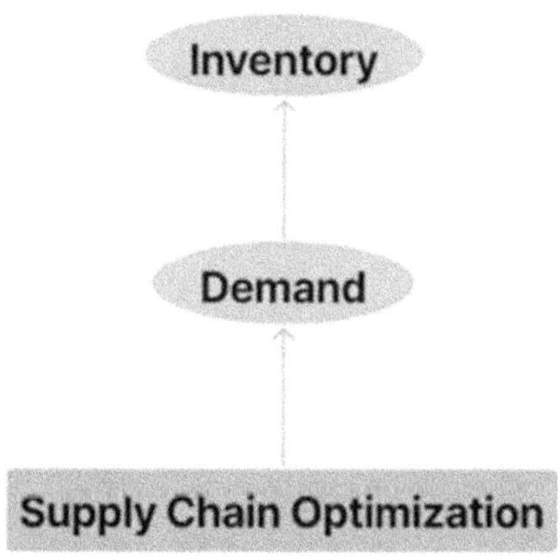

Case Study 4: Amazon's Fulfillment Centers

Amazon, a leader in e-commerce, leverages intelligent optimization techniques to optimize its vast network of fulfillment centers. These techniques assist in making data-driven decisions on inventory placement, routing, and order fulfillment. As a result, Amazon can offer fast and cost-effective delivery to its customers, ultimately contributing to its competitive advantage (Tang & Meng, 2020).

Case Study 5: Walmart's Inventory Management

Walmart employs optimization to manage its extensive inventory efficiently. By optimizing inventory levels and distribution, Walmart minimizes carrying costs and ensures that products are available to customers when needed. This strategic use of optimization aids in reducing costs while maintaining high service levels.

5.4 Predictive Modeling and Customer Segmentation

In marketing and e-commerce, predictive modeling and customer segmentation are essential. Intelligent optimization techniques help companies analyze vast datasets to identify customer segments, predict consumer behavior, and tailor marketing strategies to individual preferences. By effectively using predictive models and customer segmentation, businesses can boost their marketing ROI, improve customer satisfaction, and optimize product recommendations. This is applicable to e-commerce, digital advertising, and retail (Sangaiah et al., 2020).

Figure 9. Predictive modeling in customer segmentation

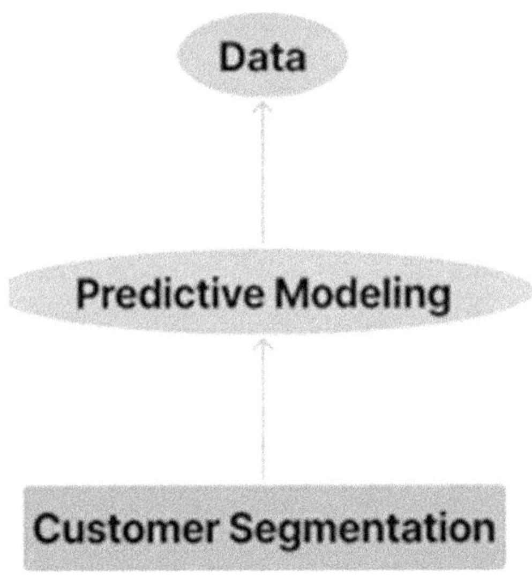

Case Study 6: Netflix Recommendation System

Netflix's recommendation system is a prime example of predictive modeling and customer segmentation in action. The streaming giant uses ML algorithms to analyze user data, predicting what users are likely to watch next. This has led to a substantial increase in user engagement and customer satisfaction.

Case Study 7: Amazon's Personalization

Amazon employs predictive modeling to personalize the shopping experience for its customers. By analyzing browsing and purchase history, Amazon recommends products that users are likely to be interested in, significantly increasing conversion rates and overall revenue. These applications exemplify the versatility of intelligent optimization techniques in business analytics. By harnessing the power of data-driven decision-making, these techniques empower organizations across diverse domains to make more informed choices, allocate resources efficiently, and stay competitive in an ever-changing market landscape (Sarker, 2021). In the following sections, we will examine how the integration of intelligent optimization with data analytics technologies enhances the potential of these applications even further (Sarker, 2021). These real-world case studies and examples demonstrate the tangible impact of intelligent optimization techniques in diverse business domains. They highlight how businesses can harness the power of data-driven decision-making to achieve efficiency, cost savings, and competitive advantages. The integration of these techniques with data analytics tools amplifies their impact, leading to more informed and optimized operations."

6. INTEGRATION WITH DATA ANALYTICS

The integration of intelligent optimization techniques and data analytics is a significant conjunction that amplifies the potential for more informed, accurate, and efficient decision-making. In this section, we will investigate the interplay between them and how these two disciplines together redefine the field of business analytics.

6.1 Synergy Between Intelligent Optimization and Data Analytics

Intelligent optimization and data analytics are intrinsically linked. While data analytics is a tool for extracting and collecting valuable insights from data, intelligent optimization techniques enable a business to use these insights. The synergy between the two disciplines lies in the fact that data analytics detects patterns and trends, while intelligent optimization techniques assist in determining the best course of action based on these insights.

Figure 10. Integration between intelligent optimization and data analytics

6.2 Enhancing Data-Driven Decision-Making

Intelligent optimization techniques improve data-driven decision-making by converting analytical findings and results into actionable and feasible solutions (Tang & Meng, 2020). Optimization techniques enable organizations to leverage data and its insights effectively, whether it is optimizing supply chain routes based on real-time demand data or tailoring marketing campaigns to reach a specific client demographic.

By integrating data analytics and optimization, businesses can:

a) **Leverage Predictive Insights:** Optimization models can incorporate predictive analytics to anticipate future scenarios, such as demand fluctuations or market trends, allowing businesses to proactively adjust their strategies.
b) **Real-Time Decision Support:** Data analytics tools provide real-time data, and optimization techniques can generate real-time solutions, ensuring that organizations can make timely and well-informed decisions.
c) **Resource Allocation:** Data analytics can identify underutilized resources, and optimization can suggest how to redeploy them efficiently, resulting in cost savings.

6.3 The Role of Advanced Analytics Tools and Technologies

Advanced analytical tools and technologies facilitate the easy integration of intelligent optimization with data analytics. ML platforms, big data frameworks, and cloud computing solutions are essential for enabling organizations to manage and process vast datasets, perform complex optimization calculations, and quickly adapt to changing data dynamics (Olaniyi et al., 2023).

After the development of powerful tools and technologies, organizations can unlock the full potential and all the capabilities of this integration. They can amplify their data analytics and optimization initiatives, making them more responsive to the ever-changing business landscape (Romero et al., 2021).

In the following sections, we will investigate the potential challenges and ethical dilemmas that emerge when utilizing intelligent optimization techniques in the context of business analytics, hence highlighting the importance of responsible AI usage (Andronie et al., 2021).

7. CHALLENGES AND ETHICAL CONSIDERATIONS

The integration of intelligent optimization techniques into business analytics comes with its own difficulties and ethical dilemmas. In this section, we will discuss the obstacles that organizations face while utilizing these strategies as well as the importance of ethical decision-making.

7.1 Challenges and Limitations

Although there are many advantages to using intelligent optimization techniques, there are also drawbacks and obstacles to consider. These include:

a) **Complexity:** Implementing these techniques can be complex and require specialized expertise. This complexity may pose challenges for organizations with limited resources or knowledge in the field.
b) **Data Quality:** The success of optimization is heavily reliant on data quality. Inaccurate or incomplete data can lead to suboptimal results and poor decision-making.
c) **Scalability:** Scaling optimization efforts to handle large datasets and complex scenarios can be technically demanding, potentially requiring significant computational resources.
d) **Interpretability:** Some optimization models, particularly those driven by ML, may lack interpretability, making it difficult to explain the reasoning behind specific decisions.

7.2 Ethical Considerations

Businesses continue to depend more and more on intelligent optimization techniques; therefore, it is necessary to consider ethical repercussions. Important ethical considerations are as follows:

a) **Data Privacy:** Organizations must ensure that data used in optimization is handled with care, respecting individual privacy and adhering to data protection regulations. Informed consent and data anonymization are critical.

b) **Bias and Fairness:** Optimization models can inadvertently perpetuate biases present in historical data. Mitigating bias and ensuring fairness in decision-making processes is essential to avoid discriminatory outcomes.

c) **Transparency:** Transparent decision-making is vital. Businesses should strive to make the rationale behind optimization decisions understandable to stakeholders and customers.

d) **Accountability:** Establishing clear lines of accountability for optimization outcomes is essential. Organizations should have mechanisms in place to address and rectify any adverse consequences of decisions made through optimization.

Figure 11. Ethical framework for implementing intelligent optimization in business analytics

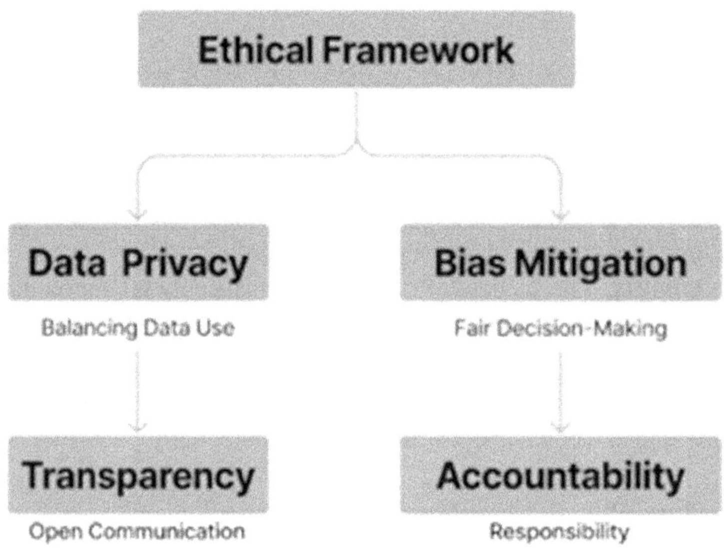

To harness the complete capabilities of intelligent optimization in business analytics, it is a must to tackle these challenges and ethical dilemmas effectively. By taking this action, businesses can guarantee that their optimization initiatives are not only effective and successful but also moral and aligned with societal values. In this section, we will understand the critical role of intelligent optimization in influencing business analytics while emphasizing the need for ethical and responsible use of AI.

8. FUTURE PERSPECTIVES

Intelligent optimization techniques will continue to play an increasingly crucial role as the field of business analytics continues to evolve. In this section, we will take a peek into the future of intelligent optimization, predicting emerging trends and technologies that will influence the landscape of business analytics in the years to come.

8.1 The Future of Intelligent Optimization

Intelligent optimization in business analytics has a bright future of sustained growth and innovation (Romero et al., 2021). Some key insights into what lies ahead include:

a) **Hybrid Approaches:** The integration of optimization with ML will become more seamless. Hybrid approaches will leverage the strengths of both optimization techniques and ML models to address complex problems effectively.

b) **Real-Time Optimization:** The demand for real-time decision-making will drive the development of optimization models that can adapt and optimize in near real-time, making them indispensable for dynamic industries like e-commerce and finance.

c) **Edge Computing:** Optimization at the edge will become more prevalent, allowing organizations to perform optimization calculations closer to data sources, reducing latency and enabling quicker responses.

Figure 12. Infographic: Future trends in intelligent optimization

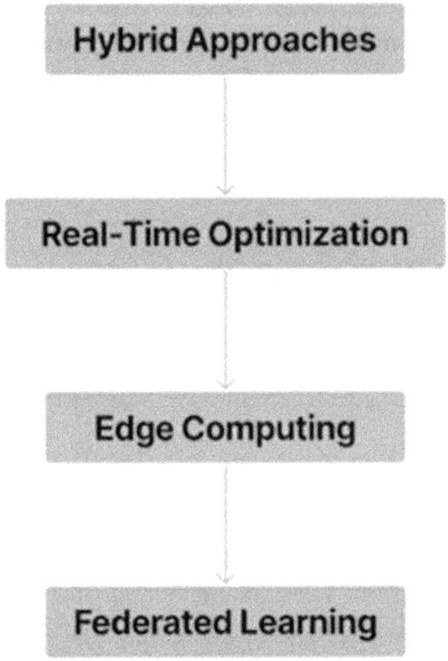

8.2 Emerging Trends and Technologies

Trends and technologies that will influence the future of intelligent optimization in business analytics are:

a) **Explainable AI:** The need for transparent, explainable AI solutions will lead to the development of optimization models that are easier to interpret and trust (Andronie et al., 2021).
b) **Quantum Computing:** With the rise of quantum computing, optimization problems that were once considered intractable may be solvable, opening new frontiers for optimization.
c) **AI Ethics and Governance:** Ethical considerations in AI and optimization will drive the development of governance frameworks and tools to ensure responsible AI usage.
d) **Federated Learning:** Optimization models that can leverage federated learning, allowing data to remain on the edge while contributing to global models, will become more prevalent.

8.3 Shaping the Business Landscape

Intelligent optimization techniques will have a huge impact on the business landscape:

a) **Competitive Advantage:** Businesses that embrace intelligent optimization will gain a competitive edge by making more efficient, data-driven decisions, and optimizing resource allocation (Olaniyi et al., 2023).
b) **Cost Reduction:** Optimization can lead to cost reductions in various operational aspects, providing financial benefits and strengthening business resilience.
c) **Innovation:** The use of intelligent optimization in emerging technologies and industries, such as autonomous vehicles and smart cities, will drive innovation and transform the way we live and work.
d) **Ethical Leadership:** Organizations that prioritize ethical AI usage and transparent optimization processes will build trust with customers and stakeholders, establishing themselves as ethical leaders in their industries.

The future of intelligent optimization in business analytics offers an environment that prioritizes data-driven decision-making, efficiency, and responsible use of AI (Andronie et al., 2021). Organizations that adopt new trends and technologies will improve and optimize their operations and help create a more sophisticated, data-informed, and morally-driven business environment.

9. CONCLUSION

Through this chapter, we took a deep dive into the ever-evolving field of business analytics-related intelligent optimization strategies. We have explored the fundamentals, evolution, applications, challenges, and ethical considerations related to these powerful tools. Let's analyze the key takeaways and emphasize the profound significance of intelligent optimization in the evolving landscape of modern business analytics (Romero et al., 2021).

Our journey began with an understanding of optimization as the science and art of searching for the best solution from a set of alternatives. We observed its importance in decision-making, resource allocation, and strategic planning across a wide range of business domains.

The evolution of optimization techniques uncovered how these methods have transformed from classical approaches to intelligent paradigms that utilize the strength of data, ML, and AI (Bharadiya, 2023). Based on case studies from the real world, we observed how these strategies have enabled businesses to improve consumer experiences, optimize their portfolios, and streamline their supply networks.

The integration of intelligent optimization with data analytics highlighted the interplay between these disciplines. The partnership of both disciplines enables organizations to translate analytical insights into actionable strategies, providing real-time decision support, predictive insights, and efficient resource allocation.

However, our journey did not avoid addressing the challenges and ethical dilemmas that are raised by these advancements. We acknowledged the complexity, scalability, and interpretability issues and emphasized the importance of data privacy and protection, fairness, and responsible AI usage (Bharadiya, 2023).

Intelligent optimization in business analytics is set to have an exciting and innovative future. Real-time optimization, edge computing, and hybrid techniques are on the horizon. This landscape will continue to evolve and shape as a result of trends like explainable AI, quantum computing, and federated learning, which will promote ethical leadership, creativity, and cost reduction.

To summarize, it is impossible to exaggerate the significance of intelligent optimization strategies in modern business analytics. These strategies give businesses the ability to deploy resources effectively, make data-driven decisions, and acquire a competitive edge in a market that is constantly changing. They are at the forefront of innovation, cost reduction, and responsible AI usage and are paving the way for a future where data-driven success is within reach for all. Let intelligent optimization serve as our guiding force as we continue to traverse the challenging landscape of business analytics, pointing the way towards effectiveness, innovation, and responsible leadership in the digital era.

REFERENCES

Akkara, S., & Selvakumar, I. (2023). Review on optimization techniques used for smart grid. *Measurement. Sensors*, *30*, 100918. doi:10.1016/j.measen.2023.100918

Albright, S. C., & Winston, W. L. (2020). *Business analytics : Data analysis and decision making*. Cengage Learning, Inc. https://thuvienso.hoasen.edu.vn/handle/123456789/11614

Andronie, M., Lăzăroiu, G., Iatagan, M., Uță, C., Ștefănescu, R., & Cocoșatu, M. (2021). Artificial Intelligence-Based Decision-Making Algorithms, Internet of Things Sensing Networks, and Deep Learning-Assisted Smart Process Management in Cyber-Physical Production Systems. *Electronics (Basel)*, *10*(20), 2497. doi:10.3390/electronics10202497

Barrere, M. (1997). *Simulated annealing to solve optimisation problems*. Internal Report, CardiV School of Engineering, Intelligent Systems Research Laboratory, University of Wales CardiV.

Bharadiya, J. P. (2023). A Comparative Study of Business Intelligence and Artificial Intelligence with Big Data Analytics. *American Journal of Artificial Intelligence.*, *7*(10), 24–30. doi:10.11648/j.ajai.20230701.14

Duan, Q., Fan, J., & Wang, L. (2020). A hybrid particle swarm optimization algorithm for portfolio optimization with transaction costs. *Applied Soft Computing*, *90*, 106126.

Eberhart, R. C., & Kennedy, J. (1995). A New optimizer using particle swarm theory. In *Proceedings of 6th Symposium on Micro Machine & Human Science*. IEEE Service Center. 10.1109/MHS.1995.494215

Kumar, D. N., & Reddy, M. J. (2007). Multipurpose reservoir operation using particle swarm optimization. *Journal of Water Resources Planning and Management*, *133*(3), 192–201. doi:10.1061/(ASCE)0733-9496(2007)133:3(192)

Li, C., Chen, Y., & Shang, Y. (2022). A review of industrial big data for decision making in intelligent manufacturing. *Engineering Science and Technology, an International Journal*, *29*, 101021. https://doi.org/ doi:10.1016/j.jestch.2021.06.001

Lu, J., Yan, Z., Han, J., & Zhang, G. (2019). Data-Driven Decision-Making (D3M): Framework, Methodology, and Directions. *IEEE Transactions on Emerging Topics in Computational Intelligence*, *3*(4), 286–296. doi:10.1109/TETCI.2019.2915813

Niu, Y., Ying, L., Yang, J., Bao, M., & Sivaparthipan, C. B. (2021). Organizational business intelligence and decision making using big data analytics. *Information Processing & Management*, *58*(6), 102725. doi:10.1016/j.ipm.2021.102725

OlaniyiO. O.OkunleyeO. J.OlabanjiS. O. (2023). Advancing Data-Driven Decision-Making in Smart Cities through Big Data Analytics: A Comprehensive Review of Existing Literature. *Current Journal of Applied Science and Technology*, *42*(25), 10-18. https://ssrn.com/abstract=4546193

Romero, C. A. T., Ortiz, J. H., Khalaf, O. I., & Prado, A. R. (2021). Business Intelligence: Business Evolution after Industry 4.0. *Sustainability (Basel)*, *13*(18), 10026. doi:10.3390/su131810026

Sangaiah, A. K., Goli, A., Tirkolaee, E. B., Ranjbar-Bourani, M., Pandey, H. M., & Zhang, W. (2020). Big Data-Driven Cognitive Computing System for Optimization of Social Media Analytics. *IEEE Access : Practical Innovations, Open Solutions*, *8*, 82215–82226. doi:10.1109/ACCESS.2020.2991394

Sarker, I. H. (2021). Data Science and Analytics: An Overview from Data-Driven Smart Computing, Decision-Making and Applications Perspective. *SN Computer Science*, *2*(5), 377. doi:10.1007/s42979-021-00765-8 PMID:34278328

Tang, L., & Meng, Y. (2020). Data analytics and optimization for smart industry. *Frontiers of Engineering Management.*, *8*(2), 157–171. doi:10.1007/s42524-020-0126-0

Chapter 2
Foundations of Machine Learning

Vishal Goar
Engineering College, Bikaner, India

Nagendra Singh Yadav
https://orcid.org/0000-0002-9591-4491
Engineering College, Bikaner, India

ABSTRACT

This chapter focuses on providing a complete grasp of the foundations of machine learning (ML). Machine learning is a rapidly evolving domain with wide-ranging applications, from natural language processing to autonomous vehicles. This chapter explores the basic ideas, techniques, and methodologies that underpin ML, laying the groundwork for a deeper dive into more advanced topics. Machine learning is a pivotal technology that has revolutionized numerous industries and continues to shape the future of artificial intelligence. Understanding its fundamental concepts is essential for anyone looking to explore the vast landscape of ML applications. This chapter will serve as a crucial reference point for readers embarking on their journey into the world of machine learning.

1. INTRODUCTION TO MACHINE LEARNING (ML)

Machine Learning (ML) is a revolutionary domain of artificial intelligence that delegates computers to grasp knowledge from data & enhance their capacity without explicit programming. In traditional programming, humans instruct computers on how to execute tasks by providing explicit instructions. However, in machine learning,

DOI: 10.4018/979-8-3693-1598-9.ch002

the computer grasps knowledge from patterns in data and makes projections without being explicitly programmed for each task (Carbonell et al., 1983).

Machine learning encompasses three primary categories i.e. supervised learning, unsupervised learning, & reinforcement learning. In supervised learning, algorithms undergo training using a dataset meticulously annotated with labels, where the input data is paired with corresponding output labels (Fradkov, 2020). Unsupervised learning includes algorithms grasping knowledge from patterns & structures from unlabeled data, and discovering inherent relationships within the information. Reinforcement learning aims at training algorithms to make decisions based on interactions with surroundings, receiving feedback in the form of rewards or penalties.

Historical Context and Evolution - The roots of machine learning trace back to the mid-20th century i.e. Alan Turing and his work on intelligent machines. However, the formalization of machine learning as a discipline began in the 1950s and 1960s. The word "machine learning" was invented by Arthur Samuel in 1959, who described it as the capacity of computers to learn from experience (Cohen, 2021).

In the following decades, machine learning witnessed periods of both advancement and stagnation. Limited computational power and data availability constrained progress until the late 20th century.

The 21st century has seen an explosive growth of machine learning applications across several domains, i.e. healthcare, and marketing. The evolution of machine learning algorithms, from traditional statistical methods to complex neural networks, has been a key driver of this transformative change.

Why Machine Learning Matters - The significance of machine learning exists in its capacity to uncover patterns & insights from huge volumes of data, enabling informed decision-making and predictions. Below are several compelling reasons highlighting the significance of machine learning -

Figure 1. Why machine learning?

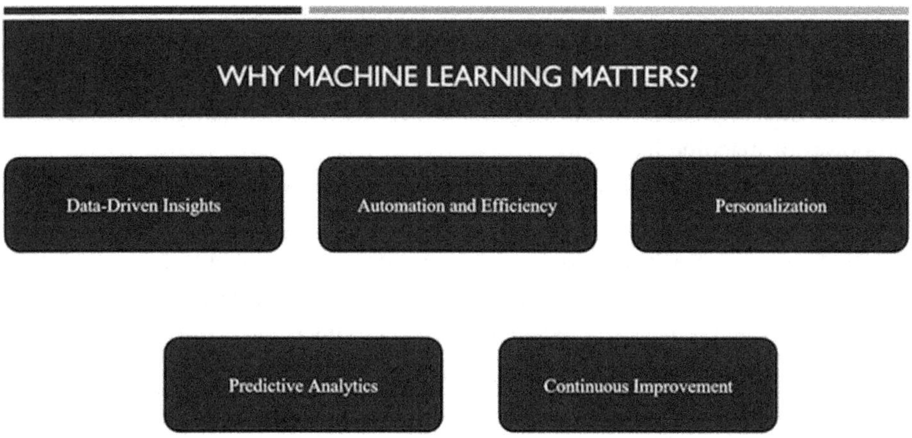

- **Data-Driven Insights** - Machine learning allows establishments to obtain precious insights from vast datasets that would be impossible to analyze manually. By identifying patterns and trends, businesses can make decisions based on data that lead to improved efficiency & competitive advantage (Mitchell, 1997).
- **Automation and Efficiency** - ML algorithms excel at automating repetitive tasks and learning from experience. This results in growing efficiency & capacity across several industries. i.e. In manufacturing, machine learning can fine-tune production procedures, reducing waste & improving quality (Hardt & Recht, 2021).
- **Personalization** - Personalized encounters on platforms i.e. social media, streaming services, and e-commerce are fueled by the capabilities of machine learning. By analyzing user behavior & preferences, these systems can tailor suggestions and content, enhancing user satisfaction.
- **Predictive Analytics** - Predictive analytics, an important part of machine learning, enables forecasting future trends and outcomes. This capability is invaluable in fields such as finance, where predicting market trends can inform investment strategies, or in healthcare, where predicting disease outcomes can guide treatment plans.
- **Continuous Improvement** - One of the most remarkable sides of machine learning is its capacity for continuous improvement. As models are exposed to new data, they can adapt and refine their predictions, ensuring that the system remains relevant and effective over time.

2. TYPES OF MACHINE LEARNING

In the vast landscape of machine learning, grasping the knowledge of diverse types of learning paradigms is essential for any aspiring data scientist, engineer, or enthusiast. Each type addresses unique challenges and scenarios, contributing to the versatility and power of machine learning.

2.1. Supervised Learning - Supervised learning is similar to having an educator guide the learning procedure. In this paradigm, the algorithm is instructed on a labeled dataset, where each input is coupled with the correct result (Nasteski, 2017). The objective is for the algorithm to master the plot between inputs & results, allowing it to make accurate projections on the latest, hidden data (Jiang et al., 2020). Common applications comprise image identification, speech identification, and regression problems.

2.2. Unsupervised Learning - Contrary to supervised learning, unsupervised learning includes employing unlabeled data. The algorithm discovers the inherent patterns & connections within the data without explicit guidance (Barlow, 1989). Clustering & dimensionality depletion are typical jobs in unsupervised learning. Clustering includes combining the same data points, while dimensionality depletion focuses on simplifying complex datasets by extracting essential features.

2.3. Semi-Supervised Learning - Semi-supervised learning rests at the intersection of supervised & unsupervised learning. It leverages both labeled & unlabeled data during training, capitalizing on the benefits of both paradigms (Chapelle et al., 2006). This approach is particularly practical when acquiring labeled data is costly. Semi-supervised learning is commonly applied in situations where capturing a fully labeled dataset is difficult.

2.4. Reinforcement Learning - Inspired by behavioral psychology, reinforcement learning models acquire knowledge by engaging with an environment (Sutton & Barto, 2005). The algorithm, known as the agent, takes actions within the environment, & depending on the consequences of those actions, it gets feedback in the form of rewards. The objective is for the agent to learn a strategy that increases rewards over time. Reinforcement learning proves invaluable across various domains i.e. autonomous systems (Sutton, 1992).

Other Specialized Types

- **Deep Learning -** Deep learning emerges as a specialized branch within the domain of machine learning, placing a spotlight on intricate neural networks characterized by multiple layers usually called deep neural networks. It has obtained immense popularity because of its capability to learn on its own about hierarchical representations from data. Deep learning shines in tasks i.e. image & speech identification, complex pattern identification.

- **Ensemble Learning -** Ensemble learning includes coupling the projections of many models to enhance overall performance. Methods like bagging and boosting create diverse models, and their combined output often outperforms individual models. Ensemble learning techniques i.e. Random Forests & Gradient Boosting, have gained widespread popularity in the domain of machine learning.
- **Transfer Learning -** Transfer learning enables a model trained on one task to be repurposed for a dissimilar but related task. This strategy is especially valuable when labeled data is scarce for the task of interest. Pre-trained models i.e. those trained on huge image datasets, can be enhanced for particular applications, saving time and resources.

3. DATA IN MACHINE LEARNING

Data serves as the foundation upon which machine learning algorithms build their understanding of patterns, relationships, and insights. In essence, the standard & quantity of data straightway affect the efficacy of the resulting models. Well-curated datasets enable machines to generalize from past experiences, making precise projections in the latest, hidden scenarios. The success of a machine learning project depends on the availability of relevant & representative data.

- **The significance of Data in Machine Learning -** Machine Learning (ML) is a discipline that empowers computers to acquire knowledge from data & enhance their performance over time without explicit programming (Jordan & Mitchell, 2015). At the heart of every successful machine learning model lies a robust and well-curated dataset. The significance of data in machine learning cannot be overstated; it is the raw material that fuels the learning process (Ge et al., 2017).
- **Data Preprocessing -** Before sending data into a machine learning model, it frequently needs preprocessing to enhance its quality and usability. Data preprocessing involves a series of steps i.e. cleaning, normalization, & managing lost values (Huang et al., 2015). Cleaning the data includes identifying and rectifying errors, outliers, and inconsistencies. Normalization ensures that different features are on a consistent scale, blocking some features from controlling the learning procedure because of their big magnitudes (Huang et al., 2015). Handling lost values is crucial to avert biases and inconsistencies in the model's projections.

- **Feature Engineering -** Feature engineering is an art within the realm of machine learning, involving the development of the latest features from existing ones to enhance model performance (Dong & Huan, 2018). Skillful feature engineering can significantly enhance a model's capability to capture meaningful patterns from the data. This process demands a deep grasp of the domain, as well as creativity to identify and construct relevant features that capture essential information (Data, 2020).
- **Data Sources and Collection -** The victory of a machine learning project begins with the selection of appropriate data sources and the grouping of high-quality data. Data can be gathered from various channels, i.e. databases, sensors, APIs, and more (Roh et al., 2021). Ensuring that the data is representative of the problem domain is critical for the model to generalize well. The collection process should be designed with careful consideration of potential biases, ethical implications, and privacy concerns (Torii et al., 2011). In an era where data privacy is a paramount concern, responsible and ethical data collection practices are essential.

4. LEARNING ALGORITHMS

In the vast landscape of machine learning, learning algorithms act as the foundation for the development of intelligent systems. These algorithms are the engines that drive the process of extracting patterns, making predictions, and enabling machines to learn from data.

Figure 2. Machine learning algorithms

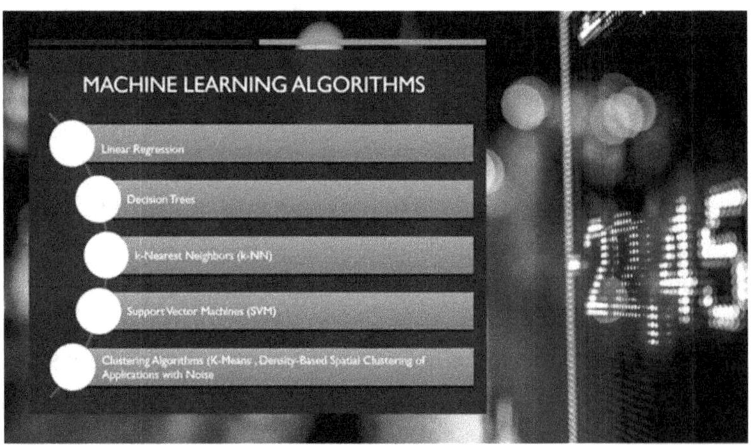

4.1. Linear Regression - Linear Regression is a cornerstone in the realm of supervised learning, particularly in regression tasks. The primary objective of this algorithm is to set up a linear relationship between the input features & the output variable (Maulud & Abdulazeez, 2020). In other words, it aims to fit a straight line that best represents the trend within the data.

Key Concepts -

- **Regression Line -** Linear Regression seeks to discover the finest-fitting line (regression line) that reduces the difference between the projected and actual values.
- **Coefficients -** The algorithm determines the coefficients (slope & intercept) of the regression line through a process known as gradient descent.
- **Mean Squared Error (MSE) -** The performance of the model is often evaluated based on the MSE, which quantifies the mean squared difference between projected & actual values.

4.2. Decision Trees - Decision Trees are flexible and intuitive algorithms that can be employed for both classification & regression tasks. These tree-kind structures include of nodes indicating decisions, branches indicating results, and leaves signifying the final prediction or classification (Dibike et al., 2001).

Key Concepts -

- **Nodes and Branches -** Decision Trees consist of decision nodes, which pose questions about the data, and branches, which lead to subsequent nodes or leaves.
- **Entropy and Information Gain -** Decision Trees leverage entropy and information gain to make decisions at each node, optimizing the tree for better predictions.
- **Pruning -** To prevent overfitting, pruning techniques are employed to remove unnecessary branches and nodes.

4.3. k-Nearest Neighbors (k-NN) - k-Nearest Neighbors is a straight & impactful algorithm used for classification & regression tasks (Zhang, 2016). It works on the fundamentals that the same data points are likely to have the same results, making projections based on the majority class or mean of the k-nearest neighbors.

Key Concepts -

- **Distance Metric -** The option of distance metric (e.g., Euclidean distance) ensures the proximity among data points.

- **Hyperparameter k -** The number of nearest neighbors (k) influences the algorithm's sensitivity to local variations.
- **Lazy Learning -** k-NN is a lazy learning algorithm, meaning it doesn't build a model during the training phase. Rather, it remembers the training data & makes predictions during the testing phase.

4.4. Support Vector Machines (SVM) - Support Vector Machines (SVM) represent a powerful class of machine learning algorithms that excel in both classification and regression tasks. Developed by Vladimir Vapnik and his colleagues in the 1990s, SVM has become a cornerstone in the field (Hearst et al., 1998). At its core, SVM seeks to discover the ideal hyperplane that best splits data points into distinct classes, increasing the margin among them. This approach not only provides robust classification but also increases generalization to new, unseen data. SVM's versatility extends to various kernel functions, allowing it to control complex, non-linear relationships effectively.

Clustering Algorithms

- **K-Means -** K-Means is a largely utilized clustering algorithm that divides a dataset into 'k' clusters depending on similarity. Developed by Stuart Lloyd in 1957, K-Means focuses on reducing the total of squared distances between data points & the centroid of their assigned cluster. This iterative process continues until convergence, resulting in well-defined clusters. K-Means is efficient and effective for several applications i.e. customer segmentation, image compression, & anomaly identification.
- **DBSCAN (Density-Based Spatial Clustering of Applications with Noise) -** DBSCAN, introduced by Martin Ester, Hans-Peter Kriegel, Jörg Sander, and Xiaowei Xu in 1996, is a density-based clustering algorithm. Unlike K-Means, DBSCAN doesn't need to define the number of clusters beforehand. It recognizes clusters based on dense regions of data points segregated by sparser areas. DBSCAN is particularly robust in handling noise and outliers, making it the best fit for datasets with irregular shapes & changing densities. Its ability to uncover clusters of arbitrary shapes contributes to its widespread use in spatial data analysis and anomaly detection.

5. TRAINING AND EVALUATIONS

Figure 3. Training and evaluations

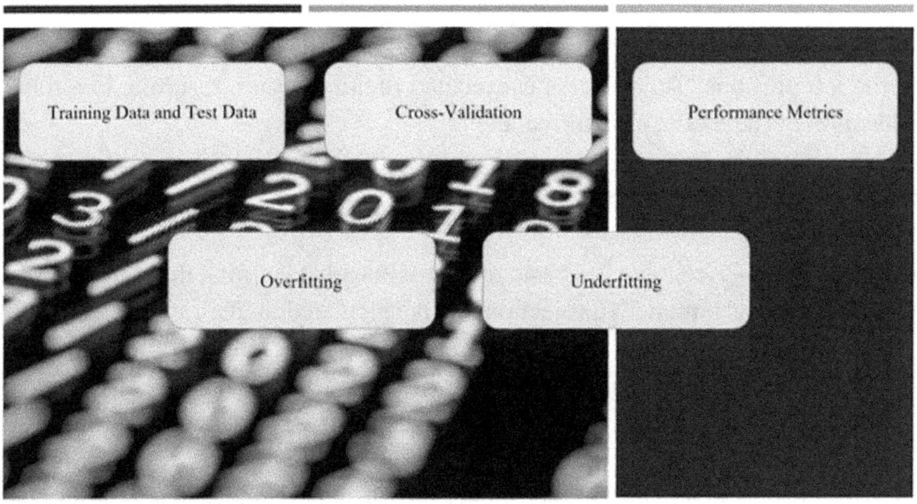

5.1. Training Data and Test Data

Machine learning (ML) is a dynamic field that leverages algorithms & statistical models to allow computers to perform tasks without explicit programming (Subaşı, 2020). In the journey of understanding machine learning, it's critical to delve into the fundamental concepts of training and evaluation.

- **Defining Training Data -** Training data forms the bedrock of machine learning models. It consists of examples that the algorithm uses to learn the patterns & relationships within the data. This learning process involves adjusting the model's parameters to reduce the difference between its projected results and the real outcomes in the training set.
- **Test Data: Assessing Generalization -** Once the model has been trained on the training data, it should be examined on an unrelated set of data that it has never seen before—the test data. This step is crucial to measure the model's capability to generalize to new, hidden instances. The success of a machine learning model is often determined by its performance on the test set.

5.2. Cross-Validation

A significant challenge in machine learning is ensuring that the model doesn't merely remember the training data but instead learns the underlying patterns. Cross-validation is a strategy employed to address this concern by partitioning the data into multiple subsets. The model is trained on a subset of the data & validated on the left portions. This process is executed multiple times, resulting in a robust evaluation of the model's performance.

5.3. Performance Metrics

- **Accuracy -** Accuracy is a basic metric in machine learning that calculates the accuracy of a model's projections. It is calculated as the ratio of accurately projected instances to the sum of instances (Erickson & Kitamura, 2021). Accuracy defines a general outline of a model's performance, it may be inadequate in instances with unbalanced datasets, where one class can outnumber the others.
- **Precision -** Precision is a metric that focuses on the relevance of the model's positive projections. It is the ratio of real positive predictions to the total of real positives & false positives. Precision is mostly helpful when the value of false positives is high, and precision helps in minimizing the false positive rate.
- **Recall –** Recall measures the model's ability to capture all positive situations. It is the ratio of true positives to the total of real positives & false negatives. The Recall is crucial in situations where absent positive instances are expensive.
- **F1-Score -** The F1-score is the harmonic mean of accuracy & recall, offering a balanced view of a model's performance. It is especially helpful when there is an irregular distribution between classes, providing a single metric that encapsulates both precision and recall.

5.4. Overfitting

Overfitting happens when a model learns the training data very well, identifying noise & variations instead of the underlying patterns. This phenomenon often results in a model that performs poorly on new, unseen data. Common signs of overfitting include a top precision on the training set but a lower precision on the validation or test set.

5.4.1. Addressing Overfitting

- **Regularization** - Introducing penalties for complexity in the model, discouraging it from fitting the impurities in the data.
- **Cross-validation** - segmenting the dataset into many subsets, training the model on several combinations, & measuring its performance. This aids in making sure that the model generalizes well to hidden data.

5.5. Underfitting

Underfitting, occurs when a model is way easier to obtain the underlying patterns in the data. It ends up in bad performance on the training & validation sets.

5.5.1 Addressing Underfitting

- **Model Complexity** - Growing the complexity of the model, such as adding more layers to a neural network or using a more sophisticated algorithm.
- **Feature Engineering** - Enhancing the quality of input features to provide the model with more information.

6. BIAS AND FAIRNESS IN MACHINE LEARNING

Machine Learning (ML) has rapidly evolved, becoming an integral part of various industries & applications. As ML systems play a critical part in decision-making procedures, it becomes crucial to address the ethical implications associated with their deployment. One of the key concerns in this realm is the issue of bias and fairness.

6.1. Bias in Data and Models - Data, the lifeblood of machine learning algorithms, is not immune to biases. Historical imbalances and prejudices present in training data can be perpetuated and amplified by ML models (Gianfrancesco et al., 2018). For example, if a hiring model is trained on historical data that reflects gender bias in hiring decisions, the model may inadvertently learn and perpetuate those biases, resulting in biased results for specific groups. Below are the Types of Bias -

- **Selection Bias** - Arises when the training data is not representative of the real-world population, resulting in skewed models.
- **Sampling Bias** - Occurs when specific groups are demeaned in the training data, resulting in models that may not generalize well for those groups.

- **Algorithmic Bias -** Emerges from the design and optimization choices made during the development of the ML algorithm, reinforcing existing biases in the data.

6.2. Fairness Considerations - Achieving fairness in machine learning involves conscious efforts to identify and rectify biases, ensuring that models are just and equitable across different demographic groups.

- **Fairness Metrics -** Quantitative measures such as different impact, equalized odds, & calibration are used to assess & enhance fairness in predictions across different groups (Pessach & Shmueli, 2022).
- **Fairness-aware Algorithms -** Developing algorithms that explicitly account for fairness considerations, attempting to mitigate biases during training and decision-making.
- **Explainability and Transparency -** Making ML models more interpretable and transparent can help in identifying and addressing biased decisions.

6.3. Ethical Implications - The ethical implications of biased machine learning models are far-reaching. They can lead to biased results in critical aspects i.e. finance, hiring, criminal justice, and healthcare, perpetuating & exacerbating existing social inequalities.

- **Reinforcing Discrimination -** Biased models can reinforce and perpetuate societal inequalities, amplifying historical injustices.
- **Lack of Accountability -** The blurriness of some ML models can hinder accountability, making it difficult to recognize & rectify biased outcomes.
- **Informed Decision-making -** Addressing unfairness & ensuring fairness is not only an ethical imperative but also critical for building confidence in machine learning systems.

7. FEATURE SELECTION AND DIMENSIONALITY REDUCTION

In the field of machine learning, the curse of dimensionality poses a significant challenge. As the count of features in a dataset rises, the complexity of the model also increases, often resulting in overfitting, increased computation time, and diminished model interpretability. To address these issues, practitioners turn to feature selection methods & dimensionality reduction strategies.

7.1. Curse of Dimensionality - This refers to the hurdles and problems that appear when encountering high-dimensional data. As the number of features rises, the volume of data essential to adequately represent the sample space grows exponentially. This results in sparse data & increases the fear of overfitting, making it difficult for machine learning models to generalize well to hidden data. Understanding the Curse of Dimensionality is crucial for developing an effective plan to reduce its impact.

7.2. Feature Selection Methods - Feature selection is the procedure of choosing a subset of applicable features from the primary set, aiming to enhance model performance & lower overfitting. Various methods exist for feature selection, including filter, wrapper & embedded methods. Filter methods assess the relevance of features independently of the chosen model, wrapper methods use the model's performance as a guide, & embedded methods incorporate feature selection as part of the model training procedure (Cai et al., 2018).

Commonly used feature selection techniques include:

- **Recursive Feature Elimination (RFE) -** RFE is a wrapper method that recursively eliminates the minimal crucial features depending on model performance until the desired number of features is achieved. It relies on the model's feedback to recognize the most applicable features.
- **Feature Importance from Tree-based Models -** Ensemble methods i.e. Random Forest & Gradient Boosting give feature significance scores. Features with top significance scores are viewed as more applicable & can be picked for model training.
- **Univariate Feature Selection -** Filter methods like chi-square tests or mutual information assess the statistical relationship between individual features & the target variable, selecting those with the highest scores.

7.3. Principal Component Analysis (PCA) - PCA is a dimensionality depletion technique that alters the primary features into a new set of uncorrelated variables known principal part. These parts obtain the highest difference in the data, allowing for a reduced representation while keeping as much information as possible.

Key steps in PCA:

- **Standardization -** Standardize the features to have zero average and unit variations.
- **Covariance Matrix Calculation -** Compute the covariance matrix of the standardized data.
- **Eigendecomposition -** Find the eigenvalues & eigenvectors of the covariance matrix.
- **Principal Components Selection -** Choose the top-k eigenvectors corresponding to the largest eigenvalues to form the principal parts.
- **Projection -** Project the original data onto the selected principal components.

7.4. Dimensionality Reduction - In addition to PCA, other dimensionality reduction techniques, i.e. t-Distributed Stochastic Neighbor Embedding, & Autoencoders, have gained popularity. These methods offer non-linear alternatives to PCA and are particularly effective when dealing with complex relationships within the data.

Understanding the Curse of Dimensionality, implementing effective feature selection methods, and leveraging dimensionality reduction techniques are crucial steps in improving the performance & interpretability of machine learning models, particularly in high-dimensional datasets.

8. HYPERPARAMETER TUNING

Machine learning models are powerful tools for making predictions and decisions depending on data. However, the performance of these models heavily depends on their configuration, known as hyperparameters. Hyperparameter tuning is a crucial step in the machine learning pipeline that includes discovering the best fit set of hyperparameter values for a corresponding model and dataset.

8.1. Understanding Hyperparameters - hyperparameters stand as external configuration settings distinct from the model's internal parameters, and they elude acquisition from the training data. They influence the learning process & directly impact the model's performance (Weerts et al., 2020). Examples of hyperparameters consist of learning rates, regularization strengths, & tree depths in decision trees.

Choosing the right values for these hyperparameters is a challenging task, as the optimal configuration often depends on the particular attributes of the dataset. Hyperparameter tuning focuses on discovering the most suitable combination of hyperparameter values to increase a model's performance.

8.2. Grid Search - Grid Search is a systematic strategy for hyperparameter tuning where an already defined set of hyperparameter values is specified, and the model is trained & inspected for each combination of these values. This method exhaustively searches through the entire hyperparameter space, making it a reliable but computationally expensive technique.

Consider a scenario where we are tuning two hyperparameters, A and B, each with three possible values. Grid Search would evaluate the model's performance for all nine combinations of A & B. While this approach promises to discover the best combination within the specified search space, it may become impractical for models with a large number of hyperparameters or when the hyperparameter space is vast.

8.3. Random Search -Random Search is a choice to Grid Search that introduces an element of randomness in the hyperparameter tuning process. Instead of exploring all probable combinations, Random Search randomly samples hyperparameter values from already defined distributions. This strategy can be more effective and useful than Grid Search, especially when the relevant hyperparameters are identified early in the search process.

Random Search is particularly advantageous when computational hardware is restricted, as it permits for a more focused discovery of the hyperparameter space. It also tends to perform well in situations where certain hyperparameters have a more notable impact on the model's performance than others.

8.4. Hyperparameter Optimization Tools -Several tools and libraries are available to streamline the hyperparameter tuning process. These tools often provide functionalities for both Grid Search and Random Search, along with advanced optimization techniques. Some popular hyperparameter optimization tools involve:

- **Scikit-learn** - Scikit-learn, a mostly utilized machine learning library, generates a simple and accessible interface for hyperparameter tuning. The `GridSearchCV` and `RandomizedSearchCV` classes allow users to perform Grid Search and Random Search easily. These tools seamlessly integrate with scikit-learn's models, making hyperparameter tuning a straightforward process.
- **Hyperopt** - Hyperopt is a powerful optimization library that uses a tree-structured Parzen estimator to model the objective function's performance. It supports both Grid Search and Random Search, as well as more advanced optimization algorithms. Hyperopt is specifically useful when addressing complex hyperparameter spaces & expensive objective functions.
- **Optuna** - Optuna is an open-source hyperparameter optimization framework that employs Bayesian optimization techniques. It provides a high-level API for explaining hyperparameter search spaces & offers various optimization algorithms. Optuna is well-suited for both small and large-scale hyperparameter tuning tasks and integrates seamlessly with popular machine learning frameworks.

9. MODEL DEPLOYMENT AND SCALING

9.1. Model Deployment Pipeline

The model deployment pipeline is a series of steps that transforms a trained machine learning model into a fully operational system capable of handling real-time requests or batch processing (Singh, 2021). A well-defined deployment pipeline ensures a smooth transition from development to production, minimizing disruptions and errors.

Steps in Model Deployment Pipeline

- **Model Serialization -** The first step involves serializing the trained model into a format that can be easily transported and loaded into a production environment. Common serialization formats include ONNX, TensorFlow's SavedModel, and Pickle for Python-based models.
- **Containerization -** Containerization using platforms like Docker enables the encapsulation of the model, its dependencies, & the inference code into a single container. This ensures consistency between development and production environments, making it easier to deploy across various infrastructure setups.
- **Orchestration -** Orchestration tools, such as Kubernetes, come into play to manage the deployment and scaling of containers. They provide a platform for automating the deployment, scaling, and operation of application containers.
- **Monitoring and Logging -** Developing reliable monitoring & logging mechanisms is critical for tracking the model's performance in real-time. This includes tracking input data distribution, model inference time, and resource utilization.
- **A/B Testing -** A/B testing is a valuable technique for measuring different versions of a model in a production setting. It helps in comparing the performance of models & making informed decisions about deploying new versions.

9.2. Scaling ML Models

9.2.1. Horizontal Scaling vs. Vertical Scaling

- **Horizontal Scaling -** Horizontal scaling includes the distribution of the workload across multiple instances. This approach enhances the system's capacity to handle increased traffic and provides fault tolerance. Cloud services like AWS Auto Scaling and Google Kubernetes Engine facilitate horizontal scaling.
- **Vertical Scaling -** Vertical scaling, on the other hand, involves increasing the power of a single machine by adding more resources, such as CPU, RAM, or GPU. While this can be a simpler solution, it may have limitations in terms of scalability.

9.2.2. Challenges in Scaling

Scaling machine learning models comes with challenges related to data consistency, model synchronization, and communication overhead. It needs cautious consideration of the architecture to make sure that scaling efforts lead to improved performance and efficiency.

9.3. Real-time vs. Batch Processing

- **Real-time Processing -** Real-time processing is characterized by low-latency requirements, allowing for immediate responses to incoming data. Deploying models in real-time scenarios is essential for applications like fraud detection, recommendation systems, and autonomous vehicles.
- **Batch Processing -** Batch processing, on the other hand, involves processing data in chunks or batches. It is suitable for scenarios where low-latency is not critical, such as training models on large datasets, generating reports, or performing periodic updates.
- **Hybrid Approaches -** In some cases, a hybrid approach that combines real-time and batch processing is the most effective. This allows for the benefits of both, catering to the diverse needs of different applications.

10. INTERPRETABLE MACHINE LEARNING

10.1. The Need for Interpretability

Machine learning algorithms have evolved rapidly in recent years, showcasing unprecedented accuracy and predictive power across various domains. However, as models become more complex, there is an increasing requirement for interpretability. Understanding the inner workings of these models is crucial for building trust, ensuring accountability, and making informed decisions (Du et al., 2019).

Interpretability is especially vital in fields where high-stakes decisions are made based on machine learning predictions, such as healthcare, finance, and criminal justice. Users of these systems need to comprehend why a model makes a specific prediction, which features are influential, and how confident they can be in the model's output. This demand for transparency has resulted in the development of techniques & tools that focus on making machine learning models more interpretable.

10.2. Model Interpretability Techniques

- **Feature Importance -** Identifying which features contribute mostly to a model's projections is fundamental for interpretability. Techniques like permutation importance, SHapley Additive exPlanations, & Local Interpretable Model-agnostic Explanations provide insights into the impact of each feature on the model's output. These methods help identify key factors influencing predictions, aiding users in grasping the rationale behind a model's decision (Du et al., 2019b).

- **Visualizations -** Visualizations offer an intuitive way to interpret complex models. Techniques i.e. partial dependence plots & individual conditional expectation plots give a graphical representation of how a model's output changes with variations in input features. Visualization tools help users identify patterns, trends, and potential biases, fostering a deep grasp of the model's conduct.
- **Rule-based Models -** Translating complex models into simpler, rule-based representations enhances interpretability. Decision trees, rule lists, and symbolic rule extraction methods create models with clear, human-readable rules. These models offer an adjustment between the complexity of the model & interpretability, making them suitable for scenarios where a comprehensible decision-making process is crucial.
- **Surrogate Models -** These models are simplified models trained to estimate the projections of a complex model. By training a more interpretable surrogate model alongside the original complex model, users can gain insights into the underlying decision logic. This approach facilitates model understanding without sacrificing the predictive power of the original model.

10.3. Model Explainability vs. Model Performance

Balancing model performance and explainability is an ongoing challenge. Highly interpretable models i.e. linear regression & decision trees, cannot often obtain complex relationships present in real-world data. Complex models i.e. deep neural networks may offer superior predictive performance but can be opted for "black boxes" because of their complicated architectures.

Striking the right balance involves considering the particular context and needs of the application. In situations where transparency and user trust are paramount, sacrificing a small amount of predictive performance for a more interpretable model may be justified. Alternatively, in applications where accuracy is of utmost importance, additional efforts may be directed towards post-hoc interpretability techniques to throw light on the decision-making procedures of the model.

11. FUTURE DIRECTIONS IN MACHINE LEARNING

Machine Learning (ML) has evolved rapidly over the past decade, pushing the boundaries of what was once thought possible. As we stand on the precipice of a new era, it is imperative to explore the future directions that machine learning is likely to take.

11.1. Current Trends in Machine Learning

- **AutoML: Empowering Non-Experts -** AutoML, or Automated Machine Learning, has emerged as a transformative trend, democratizing access to machine learning tools. It enables individuals without extensive ML expertise to develop models by automating the complex process of model selection, hyperparameter tuning, and feature engineering. As AutoML tools continue to evolve, they have the potential to make ML more accessible across various industries, fostering innovation and solving real-world problems more efficiently.
- **Federated Learning: Collaborative Intelligence -** Federated Learning is revolutionizing the way models are trained. Instead of centralizing data in one location, this approach allows models to be trained for several decentralized servers. This not only addresses privacy concerns by keeping sensitive data local but also enables collaborative model training without sharing raw data. Federated Learning has implications for sectors such as healthcare, where patient privacy is paramount, and IoT, where devices can collectively learn from each other.

11.2. Ethical and Societal Implications

- **Bias and Fairness: A Continuing Challenge -** The pressing ethical hurdle in machine learning is the perpetuation of bias. Models trained on partial datasets can unintentionally continue & even exacerbate current societal biases. Addressing this requires a concerted effort from the ML community to develop fair and unbiased algorithms. Ethical considerations should be the key priority of model development to make sure that AI systems treat all individuals fairly and equitably.
- **Accountability and Transparency -** As ML systems are becoming increasingly complicated, learning their decision-making procedures becomes a lot more difficult. The absence of transparency can result in losing public confidence. Future developments in machine learning must prioritize building transparent models and establishing accountability mechanisms. This involves providing clear explanations for model decisions and ensuring that systems are designed to be auditable and interpretable.

11.3. Challenges and Opportunities

- **Data Privacy and Security -** While federated learning addresses some privacy concerns, the broader issue of data privacy and security remains a significant challenge. As ML systems are trained on increasingly sensitive data, there is a growing need for robust privacy-preserving techniques. Innovations in homomorphic encryption & secure multi-party computation ensure safeguarding data while still allowing for meaningful analysis.
- **Explainability and Interpretability -** The "black box" nature of a few advanced ML models poses challenges for adoption, especially in critical applications like healthcare and finance. Future directions in machine learning must prioritize research into model explainability and interpretability. Ensuring that models can provide clear explanations for their decisions is crucial for gaining trust and acceptance in various domains.

12. CONCLUSION

It becomes abundantly clear that these foundational principles are the bedrock upon which the edifice of artificial intelligence stands. In this concluding chapter, we reflect upon the importance of mastering these fundamental concepts and the profound impact they have on shaping the landscape of technology and innovation.

Machine learning, often regarded as the linchpin of contemporary artificial intelligence, owes its transformative power to the depth and breadth of its fundamentals. The algorithms and models we've delved into form the building blocks of intelligent systems, enabling them to learn, adapt, and evolve with unprecedented efficiency. From the simplicity of linear regression to the complexity of neural networks, each fundamental concept acts as a pivotal part of the grand symphony of machine learning.

One of the paramount takeaways from our journey is the universality of these fundamentals. Whether you are an aspiring data scientist, a seasoned machine learning engineer, or a business leader navigating the realms of AI, a strong grasp of the basics is indispensable. These fundamentals provide a common language, fostering collaboration and communication across diverse domains. In a world where interdisciplinary collaboration is the key to solving complex problems, the ability to comprehend and apply machine learning fundamentals becomes a catalyst for innovation.

Business optimization using the application of machine learning techniques can make a big difference by adopting a data driven decision approach to push toward success. Organizations can use advanced algorithms, automation, and predictive analytics to gather valuable insights, design efficient procedures, and improve overall efficiency. The continuously changing business domain is evolving rapidly and machine learning acts as a substance for innovation by allowing organizations to adapt promptly based on dynamic market conditions.

Combining machine learning optimizes the workflow of operation and creates a tradition of continuous enhancements. This enables businesses to create informed strategic decisions, capture unidentified patterns, and unlock potential growth factors. Adopting machine learning offers a competitive edge to organizations to stay agile when it comes to uncertainties. The businesses are required to invest in resources required for learning, implementation, and refinement in machine learning applications. The collab among domain experts and data scientists is essential to deliver valuable insights by ensuring that the technology aligns with the goal of the organization.

Moreover, the ethical considerations embedded in the core of machine learning fundamentals cannot be overstated. As we entrust intelligent systems with decision-making powers, understanding the ethical implications of the algorithms we deploy is not just a responsibility but a necessity. By acknowledging the ethical dimensions of machine learning, we pave the way for a future where innovation is not only powerful but also responsible.

Machine learning is not a constant entity but a living discipline that evolves with the ebb and flow of technological advancements. A solid understanding of fundamentals equips us with the agility to adapt to new methodologies, frameworks, and paradigms that may emerge on the horizon.

In conclusion, the importance of machine learning fundamentals reverberates through the corridors of academia, industry, and society at large. They are the guiding lights that illuminate the path toward a future where artificial intelligence is not just intelligent but empathetic, ethical, and inclusive. As we continue to push the boundaries of what is possible, let us not forget the significance of the foundations upon which our AI-infused world is built. The journey may be complex, but with a solid understanding of machine learning fundamentals, the destination holds the promise of a brighter, more intelligent tomorrow.

REFERENCES

Barlow, H. B. (1989). Unsupervised learning. *Neural Computation, 1*(3), 295–311. doi:10.1162/neco.1989.1.3.295

Cai, J., Luo, J., Wang, S., & Yang, S. (2018). Feature selection in machine learning: A new perspective. *Neurocomputing, 300*, 70–79. doi:10.1016/j.neucom.2017.11.077

Carbonell, J. G., Michalski, R. S., & Mitchell, T. M. (1983). Machine Learning: A Historical and Methodological analysis. *AI Magazine*, *4*(3), 69. doi:10.1609/aimag.v4i3.406

Chapelle, O., Schlkopf, B., & Zien, A. (2006). Semi-Supervised Learning. In The MIT Press eBooks. doi:10.7551/mitpress/9780262033589.001.0001

Cohen, S. (2021). The evolution of machine learning: past, present, and future. In Elsevier eBooks (pp. 1–12). doi:10.1016/B978-0-323-67538-3.00001-4

Data. (2020). PDF download Feature Engineering for Machine Learning: Principles and Techniques for Data Scientists Full AudioBook. Zenodo *(CERN European Organization for Nuclear Research)*. doi:10.5281/zenodo.4192681

Dibike, Y., Velickov, S., Solomatine, D., & Abbott, M. B. (2001). Model Induction with Support Vector Machines: Introduction and Applications. *Journal of Computing in Civil Engineering, 15*(3), 208–216. https://doi.org/(208 doi:10.1061/(asce)0887-3801(2001)15:3

Dong, G., & Huan, L. (2018). Feature engineering for machine learning and data analytics. In CRC Press eBooks. doi:10.1201/9781315181080

Du, M., Liu, N., & Hu, X. (2019). Techniques for interpretable machine learning. *Communications of the ACM*, *63*(1), 68–77. doi:10.1145/3359786

Erickson, B. J., & Kitamura, F. (2021). Magician's corner: 9. Performance Metrics for Machine learning models. *Radiology*, *3*(3), e200126. doi:10.1148/ryai.2021200126 PMID:34136815

Fradkov, A. L. (2020). Early history of machine learning. *IFAC-PapersOnLine*, *53*(2), 1385–1390. doi:10.1016/j.ifacol.2020.12.1888

Ge, Z., Song, Z., Ding, S. X., & Huang, B. (2017). Data Mining and Analytics in the Process Industry: The role of Machine Learning. *IEEE Access : Practical Innovations, Open Solutions*, *5*, 20590–20616. doi:10.1109/ACCESS.2017.2756872

Gianfrancesco, M., Tamang, S., Yazdany, J., & Schmajuk, G. (2018). Potential biases in machine learning algorithms using electronic health record data. *JAMA Internal Medicine*, *178*(11), 1544. doi:10.1001/jamainternmed.2018.3763 PMID:30128552

Hardt, M., & Recht, B. (2021). Patterns, predictions, and actions: A story about machine learning. *arXiv (Cornell University)*. http://export.arxiv.org/pdf/2102.05242v1

Hearst, M. A., Dumais, S. T., Osman, E. M., Platt, J., & Schölkopf, B. (1998). Support vector machines. *IEEE Intelligent Systems & their Applications*, *13*(4), 18–28. doi:10.1109/5254.708428

Huang, J., Li, Y., & Xie, M. (2015). An empirical analysis of data preprocessing for machine learning-based software cost estimation. *Information and Software Technology*, *67*, 108–127. doi:10.1016/j.infsof.2015.07.004

Jiang, T., Gradus, J. L., & Rosellini, A. J. (2020). Supervised Machine Learning: A brief primer. *Behavior Therapy*, *51*(5), 675–687. doi:10.1016/j.beth.2020.05.002 PMID:32800297

Jordan, M. I., & Mitchell, T. M. (2015). Machine learning: Trends, perspectives, and prospects. *Science*, *349*(6245), 255–260. doi:10.1126/science.aaa8415 PMID:26185243

Maulud, D. H., & Abdulazeez, A. M. (2020). A review on Linear Regression comprehensive in Machine Learning. *Journal of Applied Science and Technology Trends*, *1*(4), 140–147. doi:10.38094/jastt1457

Mitchell, T. M. (1997). Does machine learning really work. *AI Magazine*, *18*(3), 11–20. doi:10.1609/aimag.v18i3.1303

Nasteski, V. (2017). An overview of the supervised machine learning methods. *Horizonti. Serija B. Prirodno-matematički, Tehničko-tehnološki, Biotehnički. Medicinski Nauki I Zdravstvo*, *4*, 51–62. doi:10.20544/HORIZONS.B.04.1.17.P05

Pessach, D., & Shmueli, E. (2022). A review on Fairness in Machine Learning. *ACM Computing Surveys*, *55*(3), 1–44. doi:10.1145/3494672

Roh, Y., Heo, G., & Whang, S. E. (2021). A survey on Data Collection for Machine Learning: A Big Data - AI Integration Perspective. *IEEE Transactions on Knowledge and Data Engineering*, *33*(4), 1328–1347. doi:10.1109/TKDE.2019.2946162

Singh, P. K. (2021). Deploy machine learning models to production. In Apress eBooks. doi:10.1007/978-1-4842-6546-8

Subaşı, A. (2020). Machine learning techniques. In Elsevier eBooks (pp. 91–202). doi:10.1016/B978-0-12-821379-7.00003-5

Sutton, R. S. (1992). Introduction: The challenge of reinforcement learning. *Machine Learning*, *8*(3–4), 225–227. doi:10.1007/BF00992695

Sutton, R. S., & Barto, A. G. (2005). Reinforcement Learning: An Introduction. *IEEE Transactions on Neural Networks*, *16*(1), 285–286. doi:10.1109/TNN.2004.842673

Torii, M., Wagholikar, K. B., & Liu, H. (2011). Using machine learning for concept extraction on clinical documents from multiple data sources. *Journal of the American Medical Informatics Association : JAMIA*, *18*(5), 580–587. doi:10.1136/amiajnl-2011-000155 PMID:21709161

Weerts, H., Mueller, A., & Vanschoren, J. (2020). Importance of tuning hyperparameters of machine learning algorithms. *arXiv (Cornell University)*. http://export.arxiv.org/pdf/2007.07588

Zhang, Z. (2016). Introduction to machine learning: K-nearest neighbors. *Annals of Translational Medicine*, *4*(11), 218. doi:10.21037/atm.2016.03.37 PMID:27386492

Chapter 3
Future Directions in the Application of Machine Learning and Intelligent Optimization in Business Analytics

Reeta Mishra
Delhi Technical Campus, Greater Noida, India

Padmesh Tripathi
https://orcid.org/0000-0001-9455-1652
Delhi Technical Campus, Greater Noida, India

Nitendra Kumar
https://orcid.org/0000-0001-7834-7926
Amity Business School, Amity University, Noida, India

ABSTRACT

This study envisions the future trajectory of intelligent optimization and machine learning (ML) in the realm of business analytics, introducing novel perspectives. It investigates the synergy between big data analytics and ML, underscoring the effectiveness of deep learning architectures in unravelling complex patterns. Emphasizing interpretability, the study explores the development of ML models tailored for business contexts and delves into decentralized model training and data privacy through edge computing and federated learning. In the optimization domain, it addresses the ascendancy of customized meta-heuristic algorithms and explores

DOI: 10.4018/979-8-3693-1598-9.ch003

the convergence of optimization and ML for heightened operational efficiency. This research contributes to a nuanced understanding, fostering innovative applications in the dynamic landscape of business analytics. It has been observed that machine learning and intelligent optimization techniques are very useful for business analytics.

1. INTRODUCTION

The applicability of emerging techniques like artificial intelligence (AI), machine learning (ML), deep learning (DL), etc. in different fields like healthcare (Tripathi, et. al 2024; Kumar, et al 2024), image processing (Rai, et. al 2023, Tyagi, et. al 2022), agriculture (Tripathi, et. al 2023, Tripathi, et al 2022) and many more has motivated the researchers to apply these techniques in business. According to *Bharadia (2023)*, business intelligence is the process of data collection from external as well as internal sources, turning it into insightful knowledge, and presenting it to decision-makers in a way that is clear and helpful using a variety of tools, technologies, and approaches. Business analytics now includes ML and adaptive optimization techniques as essential elements, providing previously unheard-of capabilities for data analysis, modelling predictions, and decision optimization. This study examines the state of intelligent optimization and machine learning within business analytics, emphasizing important techniques and applications. Also, explores new developments and potential paths, such as improvements in deep learning, reinforcement learning, and different types of meta-heuristic optimization, and how these may affect corporate decision-making procedures. This paper offers insights into the future terrain of ML and intelligent optimization in business analytics through a thorough study of opportunities and difficulties. One of machine learning's main advantages for businesses is its capacity to extract insightful knowledge from massive data sets, enabling them to make more accurate and effective decisions based on data. Machine learning gives organizations the ability to recognize patterns, trends, as well as anomalies that might not be seen using more conventional analysis techniques. It does this by utilizing advanced algorithms and predictive models. This enables businesses to acquire a competitive edge in quickly changing markets, manage processes, and enhance consumer experiences. Additionally, as new data becomes available, algorithms that use machine learning can adjust and learn from it, fostering innovation and constant improvement in a variety of business operations areas. Few of benefits of using machine learning in business sector as given below:

Figure 1. Incorporation of ML techniques in business sector

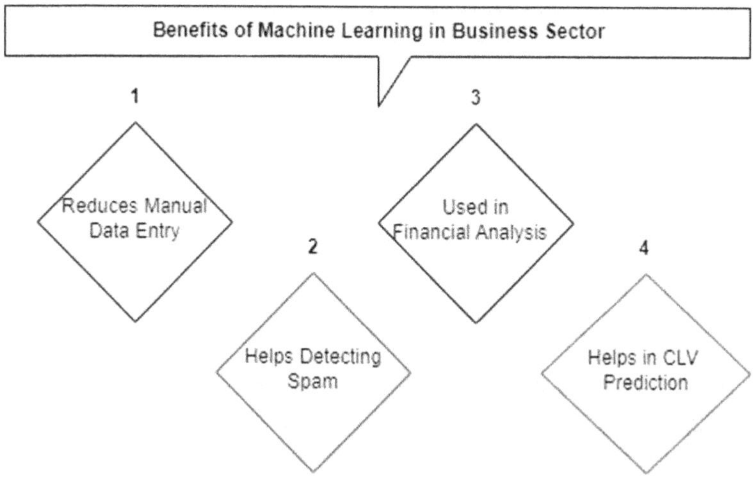

***Minimizing the need for human data entry*:** Incorrect and duplicate data are currently the most typical issues that firms deal with. Predictive modelling and machine learning algorithms both employ newly discovered data to prevent errors of this kind. Thus, by implementing machine learning, staff members can optimize their time more effectively.

***Identifying spam*:** By identifying spam, machine learning gives organizations additional value. Previously, email service providers used rule-based spam filtering techniques that were already in place. In order to identify spam and fraudulent messages, spam filters nowadays have developed new rules with the use of neural networks.

***Financial analysis*:** Financial analysis makes extensive use of large amounts of precise, quantitative historical data. In the financial industry, it's commonly utilized for loan underwriting, portfolio management, and algorithmic trading fraud detection. Additionally, chatbots, multiple sentiment analysis interfaces, and customer service will be among the upcoming uses of machine learning in finance.

***CLV prediction*:** The two most frequent issues that marketing experts deal with these days are client segmentation and CLV prediction. Since businesses can readily access large amounts of data, they may use it to gain useful business insights. Users' browsing and purchase history can be understood via ML and data mining, which can then be employed to present them with the greatest deals.

2. CURRENT STATE OF MACHINE LEARNING AND INTELLIGENT OPTIMIZATION IN BUSINESS ANALYTICS

2.1. Applications of Machine Learning in Business Analytics

As per *Mungoli et. al (2023)* that analysis of historical data and trend and pattern identification are done with machine learning algorithms. Machine learning (ML) has become an indispensable tool in business analytics due to its capability of analysis of large datasets, patterns identification and make predictions or recommendations. Businesses can now forecast future events with accuracy because to this.

"With a remarkable Compound Annual Growth Rate (CAGR) of 36.2%, the AI industry is expected to soar from USD 86.9 billion in 2022 to USD 407.0 billion by 2027 (Markets and Markets)."

Forecasting demand, maximizing inventory levels, and enhancing supply chain management (SCM) are a few of the ways predictive analytics helps businesses maximize their operations while reducing risks. Machine learning algorithms are extensively applied across diverse domains within business analytics:

2.1.1. Marketing Analytics

Customer Segmentation and Targeting: ML algorithms can investigate customer data to identify segments with similar characteristics or behaviours. Hierarchical clustering and k-means clustering are two popular clustering algorithms used commonly for grouping the customers based on different factors like purchase history, demographics, and preferences. Businesses can then tailor marketing campaigns, product recommendations, and pricing strategies to target specific customer segments more effectively. For identification of distinct segments based on demographics, behaviour and preferences, customer data is analyzed by ML algorithms.

Personalized marketing: ML models personalize marketing campaigns by predicting customer preferences and behaviour, leading to higher conversion rates and customer satisfaction.

***Sentiment Analysis and Customer Feedback*:** Sentiment analysis involves analyzing text data (e.g., customer reviews, social media posts, survey responses) to determine sentiment or opinion. Text can be classified as positive, negative, or neutral sentiment employing NLP (natural language processing) techniques and ML algorithms. Sentiment analysis aids businesses understand customer satisfaction, emerging trends identification, and address issues in a timely manner.

Image and Video Analysis: Machine learning techniques such as computer vision enable businesses to analyze images and videos for various applications. Object detection algorithms can identify objects, faces, or text within images and videos, while image classification algorithms can classify images into predefined categories. Businesses use image and video analysis for tasks such as product recognition, visual search, quality control, and security surveillance.

2.1.2. Financial Analytics

***Fraud Detection and Risk Management*:** ML algorithms can analyze transactional data to detect fraudulent activities and mitigate risks. Anomaly detection algorithms such as Isolation Forest and One-Class SVM can identify unusual patterns or behaviours that deviate from normal activity. Fraud detection systems help financial institutions, e-commerce platforms, and other organizations prevent financial losses and maintain trust with their customers. In short, ML algorithms detect anomalous patterns in financial transactions, flagging potentially fraudulent activities and reducing financial losses. In order to detect patterns, identify insider threats, detect malware in encrypted traffic, predict the locations of dangerous online neighbourhoods, keep users safe while browsing, or secure data in the cloud by spotting suspicious activity, machine learning has emerged as a critical cyber security technology. Clustering algorithms can be employed, for example, to detect policy violations, cyber-anomalies, etc. Machine learning classification models that consider the influence of security factors are helpful in detecting different kinds of cyber-attacks or intrusions coded by Sarker et. al. (2020). In short, cybersecurity experts can be more proactive in effectively averting dangers and cyber-attacks by utilizing the different learning strategies.

Credit scoring: ML models assess creditworthiness based on historical data, enabling financial institutions to make informed lending decisions while minimizing risks. Credit score models frequently take into account variables including duration of credit history, amount of outstanding debt, and payment history. Nevertheless, large-scale datasets can be analyzed by machine learning techniques like logistic regression, decision trees, and neural networks to find complex patterns and correlations that lead to more accurate credit evaluations. To augment standard credit bureau data, machine learning models can include non-traditional data sources such as social media activity, energy bill payments, and smart phone usage habits. This makes it possible for lenders to evaluate the credit risk of people who do not have a traditional banking relationship or who have a short credit history. Moreover, real-time data and trend adaptation are possible with machine learning algorithms, which improve the precision and responsiveness of credit scoring models. As a result, financial institutions are better equipped to manage risk and make more educated lending decisions, which may increase underprivileged people' access to credit.

Algorithmic trading: ML algorithms analyze market data and historical trends to identify trading opportunities and optimize investment strategies in financial markets. In the field of algorithmic trading, machine learning has become a disruptive force that is changing how financial markets function and how investment decisions are made. Machine learning techniques allow traders and investment firms to create and implement automated trading strategies with previously unheard-of levels of accuracy and efficiency by utilizing large datasets and complex algorithms. Regression and classification models are two examples of supervised learning algorithms that are frequently used for predictive modeling tasks. These algorithms help with asset price predictions, market trends, and volatility patterns. Unsupervised learning strategies, including clustering algorithms, are essential for market segmentation and anomaly identification because they help traders see connections and trading patterns that may not be immediately visible using more conventional analysis techniques. Reinforcement learning algorithms also enable traders to dynamically adjust their portfolio allocations and trading methods in response to feedback and real-time market conditions. By offering distinctive insights into market sentiment, supply chain dynamics, and commodity pricing trends, the integration of other data sources, such as social media sentiment analysis and satellite imagery, further improves trading techniques. Nevertheless, there are additional difficulties associated with market dynamics, liquidity provision, and regulatory compliance when implementing machine learning in algorithmic trading. Research on new trends including explainable AI, quantum computing, and ethical issues to protect the integrity and openness of ML-driven trading systems is being conducted in an effort to overcome these concerns as algorithmic trading develops. In summary, machine learning has the ability to completely transform algorithmic trading methods by providing new ways to manage risk, produce alpha, and quickly and accurately navigate intricate financial markets.

2.1.3. Operations Management

Predictive Analytics: In prediction of future outcome applying historical data, predictive analytics is used. ML algorithms like regression, random forests, decision trees, and neural networks may be employed to forecast sales, customer churn, inventory levels, and other business metrics. Predictive analytics helps businesses anticipate trends, optimize resource allocation, and make informed decisions. Predictive analytics relies on identifying and utilizing correlations between explanatory factors and anticipated variables from past occurrences to forecast an unknown result by Han et. al (2022). For example, detecting credit card fraud as it occurs or identifying suspects or an offender after a crime has been committed.

Another by Sarker et. al. (2019) use case is the improvement of inventory management, prevention of out-of-stock scenarios, and e-commerce logistics and warehousing through the use of machine learning algorithms by merchants. In the field, a variety of machine learning techniques are frequently employed, including decision trees, support vector machines, artificial neural networks, etc. Accurate forecasts can help businesses, industries, and nearly any organization make better decisions because they offer insight into the unknown.

Predictive maintenance: Machine Learning algorithms examine sensor data from machinery and equipment to predict potential failures and schedule maintenance activities proactively, reducing downtime and maintenance costs.

***Supply Chain Optimization*:** Machine learning algorithms can optimize various aspects of the supply chain, including inventory management, demand forecasting, logistics, and procurement. Demand forecasting models use historical sales data and external factors (e.g., seasonality, promotions, economic indicators) to predict future demand and optimize inventory levels. Optimization algorithms such as linear programming and genetic algorithms help businesses minimize costs, reduce lead times, and improve overall supply chain efficiency. Main motive of using these models to achieve minimize costs and improve operational efficiency.

Quality control: ML techniques analyze production data to defects and anomalies in manufactured products, ensuring adherence to quality standards and minimizing waste. With its ability to provide sophisticated methods for detecting, evaluating, and resolving problems at every stage of the production cycle, machine learning (ML) has become a game-changer in the field of industrial quality control. Defect identification and categorization are the cornerstones of machine learning-driven quality control. Convolutional neural networks (CNNs) and image recognition algorithms enable accurate defect diagnosis in real-time, enabling manufacturers to promptly resolve problems and reduce production disruptions. Another important use of machine learning is predictive maintenance, which uses previous data trends to forecast possible breakdowns and enable proactive equipment monitoring. Manufacturers can reduce costly downtime, maximize resource allocation, and extend equipment lifespan by foreseeing maintenance demands.

Additionally, by examining enormous datasets to find hidden patterns and connections, ML algorithms aid in process optimization. Manufacturers may optimize process parameters, reduce variability, and improve product consistency by using regression analysis and reinforcement learning. Beyond the manufacturing floor, machine learning plays a role in supply chain management. In this context, demand forecasting, inventory optimization, and logistical process streamlining are all achieved through predictive analytics models. Manufacturers may minimize lead times, lessen supply chain interruptions, and guarantee just-in-time delivery of high-quality goods by utilizing ML-driven insights.

ML allows thorough quality analytics and root cause analysis in addition to real-time monitoring and optimization. Manufacturers are able to discover the root causes of defects and inefficiencies and drive continuous improvement projects by closely examining historical data and detecting patterns, anomalies, and correlations. Actionable insights into quality performance measures are provided by ML-powered analytics solutions, enabling decision-makers to prioritize improvement initiatives and spend resources wisely based on data-driven evaluations.

All things considered, the use of ML in quality control procedures transforms manufacturing operations by raising output, productivity, and efficiency. Manufacturers stand to gain even more insights and efficiencies from machine learning (ML) technologies as they develop, which will help them compete more successfully and satisfy customers in the ever-changing global marketplace.

2.1.4. Customer Relationship Management (CRM)

Customer relationship management, or CRM, is the term for the set of procedures, approaches, and tools used by businesses to track and evaluate consumer information and interactions over the course of their customer relationships. Enhancing customer service interactions, helping with client retention, and promoting sales growth are the objectives. These systems gather client information from many channels and points of interaction between the client and the business. These may consist of the business's social media accounts, direct mail, live chat, website, phone number, and marketing materials. CRM systems can also provide customer-facing employees with comprehensive information about the personal details, past purchases, preferences, and concerns of their customers.

Customer churn prediction: ML models predict the likelihood of customer churn based on historical data and customer interactions, enabling businesses to implement targeted retention strategies. Predicting customer turnover has emerged as a crucial area of focus for companies looking to grow and keep their customers loyal in cutthroat industries. Effective churn mitigation and anticipation can be achieved by utilizing machine learning (ML) approaches. The first step in the process is gathering a wealth of data, including usage trends, interactions, transaction histories, and consumer profiles. Organizations get datasets ready for model training by performing data preparation techniques like cleaning, normalization, and feature engineering. Machine learning techniques, such as logistic regression, decision trees, and gradient boosting machines, examine past data to spot trends that can indicate customer attrition. In order to improve model accuracy and relevance, feature selection strategies further refine churn predictors.

Assessment criteria that determine the robustness and generalizability of a model include accuracy, precision, recall, and area under the receiver operating characteristic curve (AUC-ROC). Following validation, churn prediction models are put into use in real-world settings where they track customer behaviour constantly and make real-time predictions about the likelihood of turnover. By enabling automated, targeted retention campaigns and interventions, integration with customer relationship management (CRM) systems enables firms to effectively tailor their approach to at-risk clients. Churn prediction powered by machine learning not only helps lower churn rates but also improves client lifetime value, profitability, and overall customer experience.

Churn prediction analytics strategically guide decision-making in a range of company domains, such as customer experience initiatives, marketing strategies, and product and service advancements. Businesses may build enduring relationships with their customers, promote sustainable growth, and keep a competitive edge in ever-changing market environments by giving data-driven approaches to customer relationship management top priority. As machine learning (ML) technologies advance, companies need to stay flexible and adopt new tactics and tools to efficiently adjust to the shifting demands and preferences of their clientele. To sum up, ML-based churn prediction is an essential tool for companies looking to manage client relationships proactively and optimize value in today's increasingly digital and customer-focused market.

Cross-selling and up selling: ML algorithms analyze customer purchase history and behaviour to identify opportunities for cross-selling related products and upselling premium services. The field of up selling and cross-selling has seen a substantial transformation because to machine learning (ML), which has given companies new tools to tailor their products and services and increase revenue. Large-scale datasets like transaction histories, customer interactions, and browsing patterns are tapped into by ML algorithms to efficiently categorize customers. Companies are able to recognize discrete client segments and customize recommendations according to personal tastes and buying habits by using strategies such as collaborative filtering and clustering algorithms. Artificial intelligence (AI)-driven recommendation systems examine past data to find trends and connections, allowing companies to provide customized product recommendations based on the preferences and requirements of their target market. These recommendation engines increase the efficacy and relevance of cross-selling and upselling initiatives by utilizing hybrid techniques, content-based filtering, collaborative filtering, or both.

Additionally, predicting customer behaviour and lifetime value is a critical function of predictive analytics models. Through the application of machine learning algorithms, companies may predict future consumer behaviour and spot chances to promote further purchases or improvements. Utilizing a proactive strategy enables businesses to target consumers with the greatest potential for value creation when prioritizing their cross-selling and upselling efforts.

Aside from providing tailored suggestions and anticipatory knowledge, machine learning (ML) tactics enable companies to consistently enhance their upselling and cross-selling initiatives. Organizations can optimize the efficacy of their marketing endeavors by refining their tactics and rigorously testing A/B combinations, while closely monitoring crucial performance metrics like average order values and conversion rates.

But, companies must also handle privacy issues and ethical dilemmas as they adopt ML-driven cross-selling and upselling tactics. In order to preserve consumer trust and protect sensitive data, it is imperative that consent procedures, data usage transparency, and regulatory compliance be followed.

Customer lifetime value prediction: ML techniques estimate the lifetime value of customers based on their historical transactions and interactions, enabling businesses to prioritize customer acquisition and retention efforts. Take into consideration, for example, a customized skincare product subscription e-commerce platform. Through the use of machine learning algorithms, the platform is able to examine consumer information such as past purchases, frequency of transactions, average order value, and interactions with marketing campaigns.

The platform can create predictive models to estimate the CLV of specific clients over time using supervised learning approaches like gradient boosting machines (GBMs) and regression analysis. The potential revenue that each client is anticipated to create over the course of their relationship with the platform is estimated by these models, which take into account a number of variables including customer demographics, product preferences, and engagement habits.

The platform may also divide up its customer base according to expected CLV according to machine learning. VIP consumers, for instance, may be defined as high-value clients who consistently demonstrate strong levels of engagement and purchase activity. In order to encourage these consumers to keep using the platform and raise their lifetime value, it can then customize targeted marketing campaigns, special offers, and loyalty benefits.

The software can also maximize the use of resources and marketing expenditures thanks to ML-driven CLV prediction. The platform can direct resources toward customer acquisition campaigns that target comparable profiles by identifying customer categories with the most potential for long-term profitability. The platform may spend more money attracting users interested in this product category, for instance, if the ML model forecasts that consumers who buy skincare products to prevent aging will have a higher CLV. Additionally, the platform uses machine learning (ML) to continuously improve its CLV prediction models based on client input and real-time data. The platform's ability to adjust its tactics to changing market dynamics and client preferences, along with the incorporation of new data streams and ongoing monitoring of customer behaviour, guarantees that its CLV predictions will continue to be precise and applicable over time.

Recommendation Systems: Recommendation systems use machine learning algorithms to suggest products, services, or content to users based on their preferences and behaviour. Collaborative filtering, content-based filtering, and hybrid approaches are common techniques used in recommendation systems. Consider the suggestion system used by the world's largest online retailer, Amazon. Amazon creates customized suggestions by examining product features, purchase history, and user behaviour through machine learning algorithms. Amazon's recommendation system, which finds patterns and similarities between consumers based on their interactions with products, uses collaborative filtering as a fundamental machine learning technique. Through the examination of user-item interactions spanning millions of users, the system is able to forecast user preferences and recommend things that are pertinent to their interests. Moreover, content-based filtering techniques are frequently included in recommendation systems driven by ML. These algorithms compare product features, genres, and categories to user preferences by looking at these attributes. For example, if a person buys science fiction novels a lot, the algorithm can suggest related books based on shared features and content. Recommendation systems can also utilize ML to improve recommendations by utilizing contextual data and user input. When a user gives a movie a high rating, for example, the algorithm can take the user's tastes and comments into consideration when making future recommendations. The capacity of ML-driven recommendation systems to continuously learn from and adjust to changing user patterns and preferences is what makes them so beautiful. Over time, machine learning algorithms refine their models based on user feedback and system interactions, resulting in suggestions that are increasingly pertinent and accurate. Few more examples include personalized product recommendations on e-commerce websites, movie or music recommendations on streaming platforms, and content recommendations on social media platforms.

2.2. Intelligent Optimization Techniques in Business Analytics

Intelligent optimization techniques play a crucial role in business analytics, particularly from 2024 onwards, as businesses seek to streamline operations, maximize efficiency, and remain competitive in rapidly evolving markets. One prominent trend is the integration of optimization algorithms with advanced machine learning models to tackle complex optimization problems more effectively. Businesses are increasingly adopting metaheuristic methods such as genetic algorithms, simulated annealing, and particle swarm optimization to optimize resource allocation, supply chain logistics, and workforce scheduling. Moreover, the emergence of hybrid optimization approaches, combining mathematical programming with machine learning techniques, enables organizations to achieve superior results in dynamic and uncertain environments. As businesses continue to leverage intelligent optimization techniques, they can unlock new opportunities for innovation, cost savings, and sustainable growth in the era of data-driven decision-making. Intelligent optimization techniques are instrumental in solving complex optimization problems and improving decision-making processes across various domains. Mungoli et,al (2023) stated that it enabling firms to obtain a thorough grasp of their consumers, market trends, operations, and competitive landscape is the aim of business intelligence. Bots known as chat and virtual assistants with artificial intelligence (AI) capabilities use NLP (natural language methods to comprehend and analyze client inquiries and deliver precise answers. By using massive datasets for training, machine learning algorithms allow them to continuously enhance their comprehension and response rates. Zhaohao et. al (2019) shown that intelligent big data analytics for management offers a managerial framework of intelligent big data analytics as a science, technology, system, service, and management for enhancing business decision making. It does this by taking into consideration the four managerial functions of planning, organizing, leading, and controlling. Before deep drive into it, let's refer the optimization techniques used in business analytics as given below.

Figure 2. Optimization techniques can be used in business analytics

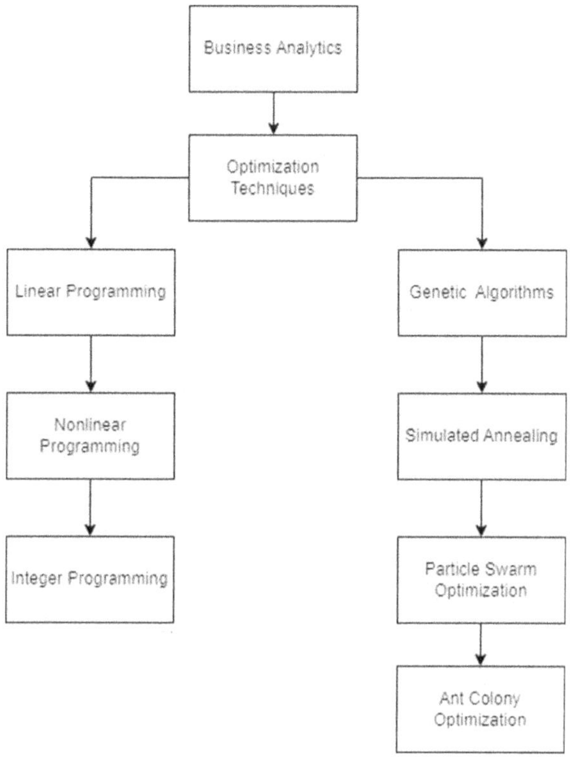

2.2.1. Supply Chain Management

Inventory optimization: Intelligent optimization algorithms determine optimal inventory levels, reorder points, and safety stock levels to minimize stockouts and excess inventory costs. In the inventory optimization space, machine learning (ML) has changed the game by giving businesses powerful tools to increase output, reduce costs, and simplify processes. Machine learning algorithms analyze supplier lead times, demand forecasts, historical sales data, and other relevant variables to optimize inventory levels and replenishment strategies. By considering past data, seasonal variations, and market dynamics, retailers, for example, might use machine learning (ML) algorithms to assess demand patterns and project future sales trends. By employing predictive analytics to forecast changes in demand and modify inventory levels appropriately, businesses may reduce stockouts and overstock issues.

Additionally, businesses can use ML algorithms to improve inventory replenishment strategies and order quantities. Demand forecasting, classification, and clustering are some of the approaches that businesses can use to identify the optimal lead times, reorder points, and safety stock levels to meet customer demand while lowering carrying costs and inventory obsolescence. Furthermore, because ML-driven inventory optimization allows businesses to adapt their inventory policies in real time to changing market conditions, supplier performance, and customer preferences.

Additionally, companies can incorporate external data, such as competitor activity, economic indicators, and weather trends, into their inventory optimization models using machine learning (ML). Companies that look at a range of data sources might gain deeper insights into demand drivers and market trends. This enables them to decide on inventory management in a more proactive and knowledgeable manner.

Route optimization: Optimization techniques optimize delivery routes, vehicle scheduling, and transportation logistics to minimize fuel consumption, transportation time, and operational costs. Route optimization is changing as a result of machine learning, which gives companies the ability to make data-driven choices and increase transportation efficiency. Take a delivery firm, for instance, that is in charge of a fleet of cars that are used to transport packages throughout a city. To determine the most cost-effective routes for every vehicle, machine learning algorithms can examine past traffic data, meteorological data, and delivery trends. These systems, which make use of predictive analytics, may foresee traffic jams or unfavourable weather patterns and reroute cars appropriately, reducing delays and guaranteeing on-time delivery.

Additionally, ML-driven models for route optimization can consider a range of goals and limitations, including driver schedules, vehicle capacity, and delivery windows. Businesses can create route plans that match consumer expectations while optimizing resource use by including these aspects into the optimization process. To maximize productivity and reduce fuel consumption, machine learning algorithms, for example, might assign delivery duties to trucks dynamically based on their capacity and proximity to the destination.

Furthermore, through iterative learning and adaptation, machine learning (ML) enables firms to continuously enhance their route optimization tactics. Businesses can improve their optimization models to more accurately represent evolving traffic patterns, delivery requirements, and company priorities by examining performance indicators and consumer feedback. Businesses may remain flexible and responsive to changing transportation needs thanks to this iterative process, which eventually improves operational effectiveness and customer satisfaction.

2.2.2. Production Planning and Scheduling

Production scheduling: Intelligent optimization algorithms schedule production activities, allocate resources, and sequence tasks to maximize production efficiency and minimize idle time.

Capacity planning: Optimization techniques optimize resource utilization and capacity allocation to meet production demands while minimizing costs and maximizing throughput.

2.2.3. Portfolio Management

Asset allocation: Intelligent optimization algorithms optimize investment portfolios by allocating assets across different asset classes, taking into account risk tolerance, return objectives, and investment constraints.

Portfolio rebalancing: Optimization techniques rebalance investment portfolios periodically to maintain desired asset allocations and mitigate portfolio drift.

2.2.4. Network Design and Layout Optimization

Facility location: Intelligent optimization algorithms determine optimal locations for facilities such as warehouses, distribution centres, and retail outlets to minimize transportation costs and maximize market coverage.

***Network design*:** Optimization techniques optimize the layout and configuration of transportation networks, supply chains, and distribution networks to streamline operations and enhance efficiency.

Table 1. Comparison between business analytics without ML, with ML, and intelligent optimization

S.No.	Keys	Without Machine Learning	With Machine Learning	Intelligent Optimization
1	Data Processing	Business analytics relies heavily on manual data processing and traditional statistical methods for analysis.	Machine learning automates data processing tasks, allowing for faster analysis of large and complex datasets.	Intelligent optimization techniques further enhance data processing by optimizing algorithms for efficiency and accuracy, reducing computational overhead.
2	Predictive Modeling	Predictive modeling in traditional business analytics often relies on simplistic models and historical trends.	These algorithms enable more accurate predictive modeling by identifying complex patterns and relationships within data.	It enhances predictive modeling by optimizing model parameters and hyperparameters, leading to better predictive accuracy and performance
3	Decision Making	In traditional business analytics are often based on static reports and human intuition.	This facilitates data-driven decision-making by providing insights and recommendations based on predictive analytics and pattern recognition.	This techniques optimize decision-making processes by considering multiple variables, constraints, and objectives simultaneously, leading to more informed and optimal decisions.
4	Scalability	Traditional business analytics methods may struggle to scale with increasing data volume and complexity.	Machine learning techniques are scalable and can handle large volumes of data, making them suitable for analyzing big data and real-time analytics.	Intelligent optimization algorithms are designed to scale efficiently, allowing businesses to solve complex optimization problems with large datasets and multiple variables.
5	Adaptability	Traditional business analytics approaches may lack adaptability to changing business environments and evolving data trends.	Machine learning models can adapt and learn from new data, allowing businesses to respond quickly to changing market conditions and customer preferences.	Intelligent optimization techniques are dynamic and adaptive, enabling businesses to optimize processes in real-time and adjust strategies based on evolving business objectives and constraints
6	Complexity Handling	Traditional business analytics methods may struggle to handle the complexity of modern data sources such as unstructured data and streaming data.	It can analyze and extract insights from complex and diverse data types, including text, images, and sensor data.	These can handle complex optimization problems with multiple constraints, variables, and objectives, enabling businesses to find optimal solutions in complex decision-making scenarios.
7	Resource Efficiency	Traditional business analytics methods may require significant human intervention and manual effort, leading to inefficiencies and errors.	It automates many data processing tasks, improving resource efficiency and reducing the need for manual intervention.	It optimizes resource allocation and utilization, helping businesses minimize costs and maximize efficiency across various operational processes.
8	Innovation	These methods may limit innovation by relying on established practices and conventional approaches.	It fosters innovation by enabling businesses to discover new insights, uncover hidden patterns, and develop innovative products and services.	It focused in drive innovation by optimizing complex processes, enabling businesses to explore new opportunities and improve existing workflows.
9	Competitive Advantage	• Businesses relying solely on traditional business analytics may struggle to maintain a competitive edge in fast-paced and data-driven industries.	• It empowers businesses to gain a competitive advantage by leveraging data insights to drive strategic decision-making, enhance customer experiences, and innovate products and services.	• These techniques help businesses optimize operations, reduce costs, and improve efficiency, positioning them for sustained success and competitive advantage in dynamic markets.
10	Interpretability	Traditional business analytics methods often produce results that are easy to interpret and understand.	Machine learning models, especially deep learning models, may lack interpretability, making it challenging to understand how decisions are made.	It typically provide transparent and interpretable results, allowing businesses to understand the rationale behind optimization decisions and recommendations.

3. EMERGING TRENDS AND FUTURE DIRECTIONS

Bharadiya, et.al (2023) & Rawat, et.al (2022) stated that predictive analytics employs ML techniques, statistical algorithms, and historical data to identify potential future events or patterns. Instead, by learning from data, machine learning helps systems to become more efficient. It does this by helping them identify patterns, correlations, and anomalies that would go undetected using traditional analytical methods. *Ali et. al. (2024)* demonstrated Big Data Analytics model to enhance electronic customer relationship management (e-CRM) and electronic word of mouth (e-WOM). Further research revealed that social media, e-WOM, and e-CRM all enhance market performance, which in turn increases competitive advantage. Expanding on the emerging trends and future directions in utilization of intelligent optimization and machine learning in business analytics, several key areas can be explored.

3.1. Advancements in Deep Learning

Business analytics has seen a significant transformation thanks to deep learning, a kind of machine learning based on artificial neural networks. Deep learning is shaking up decision-making procedures, spurring innovation, and opening up new perspectives for businesses in a variety of sectors because to its capacity to analyze enormous volumes of complex data and discern minute patterns. We go into the developments of deep learning in the context of business analytics in this exhaustive investigation, looking at its uses, advantages, drawbacks, and potential. The world of business analytics has changed as a result of deep learning techniques, which are defined by multi-layered neural networks that can learn representations of data. Text, picture, audio, and video analysis is one of the main domains in which deep learning performs exceptionally well. By extracting insights from textual data sources like customer reviews, social media posts, and support tickets, for instance, natural language processing (NLP) models driven by deep learning algorithms can help businesses better understand the attitudes, preferences, and feedback of their customers. On computer vision and image identification tasks, deep learning models have also shown impressive performance. Deep learning algorithms are running creative solutions that boost operational efficiency, increase safety, and drive automation across a variety of domains, from identifying objects and faces in photos to spotting irregularities in manufacturing processes or tracking traffic patterns through security cameras. Furthermore, with the ability to create more reliable and accurate forecasting and decision support models, deep learning is transforming predictive analytics within enterprises. In order to help organizations forecast customer behaviour, market trends, and business performance more accurately, deep neural networks are particularly good at identifying intricate patterns and relationships inside data. To provide traders and investors with important insights and competitive advantages in volatile markets, deep learning models are used, for example, in the financial sector to evaluate market data, anticipate stock prices, and optimize investment strategies.

Recommendation systems are another field in which deep learning is making notable advancements. Businesses may tailor suggestions for goods, services, and information based on the tastes, activities, and previous interactions of individual users by utilizing sophisticated neural networks. Across streaming services, digital content providers, and e-commerce platforms, deep learning-powered recommendation engines are increasing user engagement, generating sales, and improving customer happiness. Deep learning is also making rapid progress in conversational AI and natural language generation (NLG) possible for businesses. This means that they can create chatbots, virtual assistants, and voice-enabled interfaces that automate tasks and improve consumer experiences. In addition to automating repetitive operations and decreasing response times, these AI-powered systems can comprehend natural language inquiries, respond to them, and offer personalized recommendations. These capabilities boost productivity in customer service, sales, and support roles.

Deep learning offers particular difficulties and things to think about for businesses, even with its revolutionary potential. Significant computing power, knowledge, and infrastructure investments are needed to support deep neural network complexity and processing. Deploying deep learning solutions in real-world situations requires organizations to negotiate difficulties pertaining to data quality, model interpretability, and ethical considerations. The necessity of strong governance frameworks and openness in AI-driven decision-making processes is further highlighted by worries about data privacy, security, and regulatory compliance.

Deep learning in business analytics has a remarkably bright future ahead of it. The acceptance and scalability of deep learning solutions will be further accelerated by ongoing developments in hardware technology, such as graphics processing units (GPUs) and specialist AI circuits. Furthering the capabilities and usefulness of deep learning across a wide range of domains and application cases are scientific advances in fields such as reinforcement learning, self-supervised learning, and transfer learning. Working together, data scientists, domain experts, and business stakeholders will be crucial as companies continue to leverage deep learning to optimize the benefits and effects of AI-driven projects. Investing in training initiatives, interdisciplinary teamwork, and talent development will also be essential to fostering an innovative and data-driven decision-making culture in institutions.

Deep learning, a subset of machine learning that utilizes neural networks with multiple layers, has witnessed significant advancements and continues to drive innovation in various domains:

3.1.1. ***Unsupervised Learning*****:** Future research in deep learning will focus on advancing unsupervised learning techniques, such as autoencoders and generative adversarial networks (GANs), for tasks such as anomaly detection, data denoising, and feature learning without explicit labels.

3.1.2. ***Transfer Learning:*** Transfer learning, which involves transferring knowledge from one task to another, will be increasingly explored to address data scarcity and domain adaptation challenges in business analytics. Pre-trained deep learning models can be fine-tuned or adapted to specific business contexts, accelerating model development and deployment.

3.1.3. ***Explainable AI:*** Enhancing the interpretability and explainability of deep learning models will be a key focus area to promote trust and transparency in business applications. Future research will explore techniques for visualizing and interpreting deep learning models, enabling stakeholders to understand model predictions and decisions.

3.2. Reinforcement Learning for Decision Optimization

Because it can solve decision optimization issues in uncertain and dynamic situations, the machine learning subfield of reinforcement learning, or RL, has attracted a lot of attention. Artificial intelligence (RL) models acquire the ability to make sequential decisions through environmental interaction, feedback in the form of incentives or penalties, and action modification to optimize long-term goals. We examine the fundamentals, practical applications, difficulties, and potential future developments of applying RL to decision optimization in this thorough investigation. Interacting agents with their surroundings is the fundamental idea of reinforcement learning. In response, the environment changes to a new state and gives feedback in the form of incentives or penalties. The agent acts based on its present condition. Through time, the agent learns to maximize cumulative rewards by refining its decision-making technique through repeated encounters. In order to ensure that the agent learns efficiently while navigating the intricacies of the environment, the main difficulty in reinforcement learning (RL) is striking a balance between exploration, which involves trying out novel actions to find their consequences, and exploitation, which involves using knowing information to maximize rewards.

Robotics, banking, healthcare, gaming, and autonomous systems are just a few of the industries in which reinforcement learning has found widespread use. Robotics employs reinforcement learning (RL) techniques to teach agents how to carry out intricate tasks including precisely manipulating robotic arms, grabbing items, and navigating through surroundings. Financial decision-making in volatile and dynamic markets is made possible by the use of reinforcement learning (RL) models in portfolio management, algorithmic trading, and risk assessment. With the application of RL approaches, healthcare settings can optimize resource allocation and improve patient outcomes through individualized treatment planning, clinical decision support, and medication development. Robustness in handling sequential decision-making issues with delayed rewards is one of reinforcement learning's key characteristics. Artificial intelligence (AI) agents learn by making mistakes and getting feedback from their surroundings. This is in contrast to supervised learning, in which a model is trained on labeled data to generate predictions. Long-term planning and optimization problems are well-suited for RL agents because of their ability to acquire intricate decision-making rules that optimize cumulative rewards over prolonged time horizons thanks to this feedback mechanism. The trade-offs between exploration and exploitation, sampling efficiency, and generalization to new contexts are some of the major issues that RL presents. Real-world applications with limited data availability or high experimentation costs cannot use RL algorithms because they must frequently learn effective decision-making techniques from vast amounts of interaction data. Agents in reinforcement learning (RL) must strike a balance between exploring novel actions and utilizing established tactics in order to optimize rewards. This is a fundamental trade-off that is presented by the exploration-exploitation conundrum. To guarantee that RL agents pick up resilient and adaptable decision-making strategies, the ideal ratio between exploration and exploitation must be struck. Reinforcement learning (RL), a branch of machine learning focused on learning optimal decision-making policies through trial and error, holds immense potential for addressing complex optimization problems in business analytics:

3.2.1. ***Multi-Agent Systems:*** Future research in reinforcement learning will explore multi-agent systems, where multiple agents interact and learn within a shared environment, to model complex business ecosystems and dynamics. Applications include dynamic pricing strategies, supply chain coordination, and negotiation scenarios.

3.2.2. ***Safe Reinforcement Learning:*** Ensuring the safety and reliability of RL algorithms in real-world environments will be a priority for future research. Techniques for incorporating safety constraints, risk-aware exploration, and human-in-the-loop supervision will be developed to mitigate potential risks and ensure robust decision-making.

3.2.3. ***Transferable Policies:*** Developing transferable policies that generalize across different business domains and environments will enable more efficient and scalable deployment of reinforcement learning algorithms. Transfer learning techniques will be explored to leverage knowledge from related tasks and domains to accelerate learning and adaptation.

3.3. Integration of Meta Heuristic Optimization With Machine Learning

Akter et. al. (2024) stated that it is a novel approach to business analytics is the combination of machine learning (ML) and metaheuristic optimization techniques, which enables enterprises to solve intricate optimization issues, find hidden patterns, and derive useful insights from massive datasets. Metaheuristic optimization techniques, Aljehani et. al (2024) suggested that it is derived from biological and natural events, provide strong algorithms for resolving combinatorial optimization issues, including scheduling, resource allocation, portfolio optimization, and vehicle routing, among other issues.

Figure 3. Meta-heuristic algorithm for better and quick prediction

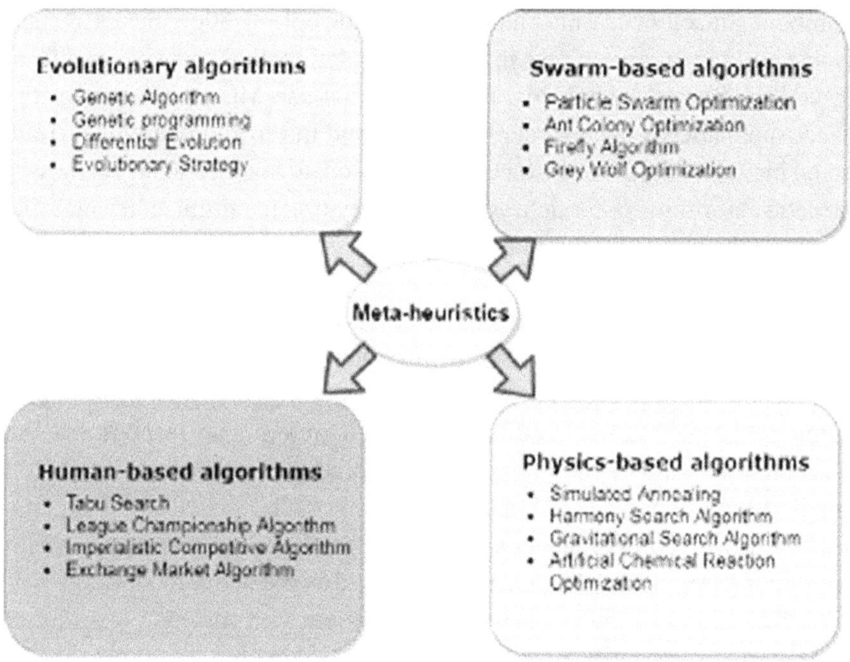

In terms of business above mention algorithms generate new chances for cost savings, efficiency increases, and strategic decision-making. In short by fusing the advantages of metaheuristic optimization with the adaptability and flexibility of machine learning algorithms leads to better decision making power. The idea of searching and using search spaces to obtain excellent answers to optimization issues is the foundation of metaheuristic optimization. Metaheuristic algorithms, which include ant colony optimization, particle swarm optimization, simulated annealing, and genetic algorithms, use iterative search processes to search through large solution spaces, assess potential solutions, and then refine their search according to predetermined goals or criteria. When faced with complicated optimization problems including huge solution spaces, non-linear constraints, and noisy or unpredictable environments, these algorithms do exceptionally well at locating close to optimal solutions.

In contrast, machine learning provides strong tools for predictive modeling, pattern identification, and data analysis. Organizations may extract insights from data, find underlying patterns and relationships, and make defensible decisions based on data-driven insights thanks to machine learning (ML) techniques, which include supervised learning, unsupervised learning, and reinforcement learning. Businesses may create prediction models, categorize data, group related entities, and improve processes based on historical data and real-time inputs by utilizing ML approaches. By combining machine learning and metaheuristic optimization, business analytics can solve optimization problems that are computationally expensive or difficult to solve with traditional techniques. Businesses can use ML techniques to forecast demand, spot patterns in customer behaviour, and improve procurement strategies based on historical data. For instance, in supply chain management, businesses can use genetic algorithms or particle swarm optimization to optimize inventory levels, production schedules, and distribution routes.

Similar to this, businesses can utilize metaheuristic algorithms in financial portfolio optimization to build diversified investment portfolios that balance risk and maximize returns by accounting for variables like investor preferences, market dynamics, and asset correlations. Businesses can optimize asset allocations, improve portfolio performance, and modify investment strategies in response to shifting market conditions and investor goals by incorporating machine learning (ML) tools for predictive modeling and risk analysis.

Furthermore, companies can optimize marketing campaigns, customer segmentation, and tailored recommendations based on predictive models and customer insights by integrating metaheuristic optimization with machine learning (ML). Organizations can identify high-value customer segments, customize marketing messages to individual preferences, and optimize marketing spend to maximize return on investment and customer engagement by combining ML algorithms for predictive modeling and clustering with genetic algorithms or simulated annealing.

But there are particular difficulties and things to think about for firms when integrating ML and metaheuristic optimization. The difficulty and computational burden involved in training and fine-tuning ML models and metaheuristic algorithms on massive datasets is one of the main obstacles. While ML models might have problems including over-fitting, a lack of data, and interpretability, metaheuristic optimization techniques frequently need substantial parameter modification and experimentation to get optimal performance. Moreover, algorithmic trade-offs, computational resources, and domain-specific limitations must all be carefully taken into account when integrating metaheuristic optimization with machine learning. Based on the nature of the issue, the data at hand, and the intended results, businesses must carefully choose the right optimization algorithms and machine learning approaches. Furthermore, to guarantee that the finished solutions are reliable, scalable, and in line with corporate goals, the integration of metaheuristic optimization with ML necessitates interdisciplinary cooperation between data scientists, domain experts, and business stakeholders.

Going forward, there is a great deal of promise and opportunity for combining ML and metaheuristic optimization in business analytics. The capabilities and use of ML algorithms and metaheuristic optimization approaches are being extended to a wider range of domains and use cases due to ongoing breakthroughs in algorithmic methodologies, computational resources, and real-world applications. Additionally, more effective, scalable, and adaptable solutions to challenging optimization issues in business analytics are being made possible by scientific advances in fields like hybrid optimization algorithms, multi-objective optimization, and parallel computing. Meta-heuristic optimization techniques, which mimic natural phenomena to search for optimal solutions, can be seamlessly integrated with machine learning models to address complex optimization challenges in business analytics:

3.3.1. ***Hybrid Approaches:*** Future research will focus on developing hybrid approaches that combine meta-heuristic optimization algorithms with machine learning techniques, such as genetic algorithms with neural networks or particle swarm optimization with deep reinforcement learning. These hybrid approaches leverage the strengths of both paradigms to achieve superior performance and scalability.

3.3.2. ***Large-Scale Optimization:*** Scaling metaheuristic optimization techniques to handle large-scale optimization problems will be a key research direction. Parallel and distributed optimization frameworks will be developed to harness the computational power of modern hardware architectures and cloud computing platforms.

3.3.3. ***Adaptive Meta heuristics:*** Developing adaptive meta heuristic optimization algorithms that can dynamically adjust their search strategies based on problem characteristics and environmental changes will enhance robustness and effectiveness in solving complex optimization problems. Adaptive mechanisms inspired by biological and social systems will be explored to enable self-adaptation and self-regulation.

4. CHALLENGES AND OPPORTUNITIES

4.1. Data Privacy and Ethical Considerations

As organizations collect and analyze large volumes of data, ensuring data privacy, security, and ethical use of data becomes increasingly important. Future research will focus on developing privacy-preserving machine learning techniques, enhancing transparency and accountability in algorithmic decision-making, and addressing biases and fairness issues in data-driven systems.

4.2. Interpretability and Explainability of ML Models

The interpretability and explainability of machine learning models are essential for building trust and understanding in business settings. Future research will focus on developing techniques for interpreting and explaining complex ML models, enabling stakeholders to understand model decisions, identify biases, and assess model reliability in critical decision-making processes.

As business analytics involves a huge amount of data, it is always advisable to de-noise the data before performing the analysis (Tripathi & Siddiqi 2016, 2017; Tripathi 2020).

5. CONCLUSION

The integration of machine learning and intelligent optimization techniques offers unprecedented opportunities for organizations to gain insights, optimize processes, and make informed decisions in an increasingly data-driven world. By embracing emerging trends and innovative methodologies, organizations can unlock new possibilities for leveraging data analytics to drive innovation, enhance competitiveness, and create value. However, realizing the full potential of ML and intelligent optimization in business analytics requires addressing challenges related to data privacy, interpretability, and ethical considerations. It also directs researchers and practitioners toward creative ideas and tactics for dealing with challenging business problems. Future research efforts should focus on developing robust and scalable solutions that empower organizations to harness the power of ML and intelligent optimization for sustainable growth and success.

REFERENCES

Adib, H., Ali, M. K., & Abuzaraida, M. A. (2024). Artificial Intelligence Trust, risk and security management (AI trism): Frameworks, applications, challenges and future research directions. *Expert Systems with Applications*, *240*, 122442. doi:10.1016/j.eswa.2023.122442

Akter, A., Ehsanul, I. Z., Dana, N. H., Joysoyal, R., Sarker, S. K., Li, L., Muyeen, S. M., Das, S. K., & Kamwa, I. (2024). A review on microgrid optimization with meta-heuristic techniques: Scopes, trends and recommendation. *Energy Strategy Reviews*, *51*, 101298. doi:10.1016/j.esr.2024.101298

Alaa, A., & Orji, R. (2024). Machine learning techniques for emotion detection and sentiment analysis: Current state, challenges, and future directions. *Behaviour & Information Technology*, *43*(1), 139–164. doi:10.1080/0144929X.2022.2156387

Aljehani, S. S., & Alotaibi, Y. A. (2024). Preserving Privacy in Association Rule Mining Using Metaheuristic-based Algorithms: A Systematic Literature Review. *IEEE Access : Practical Innovations, Open Solutions*, *12*, 21217–21236. doi:10.1109/ACCESS.2024.3362907

Alshawawreh, A. R. E., Liébana-Cabanillas, F., & Blanco-Encomienda, F. J. (2024). Impact of big data analytics on telecom companies, competitive advantage. *Technology in Society*, *76*, 102459. doi:10.1016/j.techsoc.2024.102459

Bharadia, J. P. (2023). The role of machine learning in transforming business intelligence. *International Journal of Computing and Artificial Intelligence*. . doi:10.33545/27076571.2023.v4.i1a.60

Bharadiya, J. P. (2023). Machine learning and AI in business intelligence: Trends and opportunities. [IJC]. *International Journal of Computer*, *48*(1), 123–134.

Farooque, M., Khan, M. A. I., & Rashid, M. A. A. (2022). Big Data Analytics for Dealing with COVID-19: An Innovative Trend in Business Intelligence. New Innovations in Economics. *Business and Management*, *8*, 50–55. doi:10.9734/bpi/niebm/v8/2050B

Feng, W., Joey, S. A. (2023). Enhancing Operational Efficiency: Integrating Machine Learning Predictive Capabilities in Business Intelligence for Informed Decision-Making. *Frontiers in Business, Economics and Management*. doi:10.54097/fbem.v9i1.8694

Han, J., Jian, P., & Hanghang, T. (2022). *Data mining: concepts and techniques*. Morgan kaufmann.

Kumar, N., Tripathi, P., Nanda, R. P., Tiwari, S., & Sharma, S. (2024). Machine Learning for Smart Health Services in the Framework of Industry 5.0. In M. Khan, R. Khan, P. Praveen, A. R. Verma, & M. K. Panda (Eds.), *Infrastructure Possibilities and Human-Centered Approaches With Industry 5.0* (pp. 215–230). IGI Global. doi:10.4018/979-8-3693-0782-3.ch013

Lemonakis, C., & Zopounidis, C. (2023). *The future of business: artificial intelligence, machine learning and deep learning*. doi:10.4337/9781839106750.00010

Luca, L., Brcic, M., & Cabitza, F. (2024). Explainable artificial intelligence (XAI) 2.0: A manifesto of open challenges and interdisciplinary research directions. *Information Fusion*, 102301.

Mishra, D. K., Johari, K., Ghildiyal, S., Upadhyay, A. K., & Sharma, S. (2022). A Novel Approach in Business Intelligence for Big Data Analytics Using an Unsupervised Technique. *ECS Transactions*, *107*(1), 12525–12533. doi:10.1149/10701.12525ecst

Mishra, R., & Chadhuary, N. (2023). A Comprehensive Study on Detection of Cyber-Attack using ML Techniques & Future Scope. *International Journal of Engineering Research in Computer Science and Engineering*, *10*(3), 47–59.

Mungoli, N. (2023). Deciphering the Blockchain: A Comprehensive Analysis of Bitcoin's Evolution, Adoption, and Future Implications. *arXiv preprint arXiv:2304.02655.* doi:10.4108/eai.18-11-2022.2327194

Rai, M., Tyagi, N., Tripathi, P., Kumar, N., & Kumari, P. (2023). Advancement in Agricultural Techniques With the Introduction of Artificial Intelligence and Image Processing. In M. Khan, B. Gupta, A. Verma, P. Praveen, & C. Peoples (Eds.), *Smart Village Infrastructure and Sustainable Rural Communities* (pp. 47–68). IGI Global. doi:10.4018/978-1-6684-6418-2.ch004

Rajagopalan, S., & Iyer, S. S. (2022). Advancing Industrial Analytics Using Machine Learning (ML) and Mathematical Optimization. *2022 American Control Conference (ACC)*, 1065-1065. 10.23919/ACC53348.2022.9867615

Sahija, D. (2021). *Critical review of machine learning integration with augmented reality for discrete manufacturing*. Independent Researcher and Enterprise Solution Manager in Leading Digital Transformation Agency.

Sarker, I. H., Abushark, Y. B., Alsolami, F., & Khan, A. (2020). Intrudtree: A machine learning based cyber security intrusion detection model. *Symmetry*, *12*(5), 754. doi:10.3390/sym12050754

Sarker, I. H., Watters, P., & Kayes, A. S. M. (2019). Effectiveness analysis of machine learning classification models for predicting personalized context-aware smartphone usage. *Journal of Big Data*, *6*(1), 1–28. doi:10.1186/s40537-019-0219-y

Singh, A., Dwivedi, A. (2023). *Integrating Machine Learning in Business Decision Making: Application and Future directions*. doi:10.1109/ICCIKE58312.2023.10131790

Singh, A., Dwivedi, A., & Dubey, S. (2023). Integrating Machine Learning in Business Decision Making: Application and Future directions. *2023 International Conference on Computational Intelligence and Knowledge Economy (ICCIKE)*, 397-401. 10.1109/ICCIKE58312.2023.10131790

Sundar, R. (2024). Future Directions of Artificial Intelligence Integration: Managing Strategies and Opportunities. *Journal of Intelligent & Fuzzy Systems*. Advance online publication. doi:10.3233/JIFS-238830

Tripathi, P. (2020). Electroencephalpgram Signal Quality Enhancement by Total Variation Denoising Using Non-convex Regulariser. *International Journal of Biomedical Engineering and Technology*, *33*(2), 134–145. doi:10.1504/IJBET.2020.107709

Tripathi, P., Kumar, N., Paroha, K. K., Rai, M., & Panda, M. K. (2024). Applications of Deep Learning in Healthcare in the Framework of Industry 5.0. In M. Khan, R. Khan, P. Praveen, A. R. Verma, & M. K. Panda (Eds.), *Infrastructure Possibilities and Human-Centered Approaches With Industry 5.0* (pp. 215–230). IGI Global. doi:10.4018/979-8-3693-0782-3.ch005

Tripathi, P., Kumar, N., Rai, M., & Khan, A. (2022). *Applications of Deep Learning in Agriculture. In Artificial Intelligence Applications in Agriculture and Food Quality Improvement*. IGI Global. doi:10.4018/978-1-6684-5141-0.ch002

Tripathi, P., Kumar, N., Rai, M., Shukla, P. K., & Verma, K. N. (2023). Applications of Machine Learning in Agriculture. In M. Khan, B. Gupta, A. Verma, P. Praveen, & C. Peoples (Eds.), *Smart Village Infrastructure and Sustainable Rural Communities* (pp. 99–118). IGI Global. doi:10.4018/978-1-6684-6418-2.ch006

Tripathi, P., & Siddiqi, A. H. (2016). Denoising Raman spectra using a non-Convex regularizer in Total Variation. *Indian Journal of Science and Technology*, *9*(48), 1–5. doi:10.17485/ijst/2016/v9i48/99920

Tripathi, S., & Siddiqi, A. H. (2016). Solution of Inverse Problem for de-noising Raman Spectral Data with Total variation using Majorization-Minimization Algorithm *Int. J. Computing Science and Mathematics*, *7*(3), 274–282. doi:10.1504/IJCSM.2016.077855

Tyagi, N., Rai, M., Sahw, P., Tripathi, P., & Kumar, N. (2022). *Methods for the Recognition of Human Emotions Based on Physiological Response: Facial Expressions in Smart Healthcare for Sustainable Urban Development*. IGI Global. doi:10.4018/978-1-6684-2508-4.ch013

Witten, I. H., & Frank, E. (2005). *Data Mining: Practical machine learning tools and techniques*. Morgan Kaufmann.

Zhaohao, S. (2019). Intelligent Big Data Analytics: A Managerial Perspective. In Managerial Perspectives on Intelligent Big Data Analytics (pp. 1-19). doi:10.4018/978-1-5225-7277-0.ch001

Chapter 4
Deciphering the Realities of Deep Learning in Business Analytics: A Bibliometric Analysis

Soumya Mukherjee
Techno India, Hooghly, India

Avik Chatterjee
https://orcid.org/0000-0003-2704-6941
Techno College, Hooghly, India

Sayantan Dass
https://orcid.org/0000-0002-5441-6170
Techno College, Hooghly, India

ABSTRACT

In the 21st century, business and data are tightly intertwined, and organizations are increasingly reliant on artificial intelligence (AI) and machine learning (ML) to fuel data-driven decision-making and maintain competitiveness. While deep learning (DL) offers significant potential for extracting valuable insights from data, its widespread adoption in business analytics is hindered by various challenges. This chapter delves into the complexities surrounding the integration of DL into business analytics, highlighting computational complexities, infrastructure limitations, skill shortages, and the inherent black-box nature of DL models as key barriers. Furthermore,

DOI: 10.4018/979-8-3693-1598-9.ch004

empirical evidence suggests that DL may not consistently outperform traditional ML models, particularly in scenarios involving structured datasets with fixed-length feature vectors. Through a biometric analysis of current research work, this chapter provides insights into navigating the complexities of integrating DL into business analytics and outlines a roadmap for future research in this rapidly evolving field.

1. INTRODUCTION

In today's fast-changing business world, using data smartly is super important for companies to stay competitive and keep growing (Davenport, 2018). Technology is everywhere in businesses, and being able to understand data helps make better decisions and keep moving forward (Schmitt, 2023). Deep learning is a special kind of technology that's part of machine learning (Canhoto & Clear, 2020), which is all about computers learning from data. It's like a new way of looking at data that can really change how businesses operate. This new approach has the potential to make companies more efficient, help them run better, and connect with customers in new ways. It's like opening up a whole new world of possibilities for businesses to thrive and succeed (Thakur, 2024).

As companies get excited about using deep learning for business analytics, they're finding that it's not as easy as they hoped. They had big hopes for how deep learning could change how they do things, but they're running into problems actually putting it into action (Kraus & Oztekin, 2020). They're realizing it's not just about the cool technology – they also need to make sure it fits with what they're trying to achieve as a company. Plus, there are technical issues to deal with, like handling huge amounts of data, and ethical questions to consider (Kushwaha, Kar& Dwivedi, 2021). All these challenges make it tricky for businesses to make the most of deep learning for analyzing data.

One of the primary challenges for businesses is making sure their deep learning plans match up with what they want to achieve (Schmitt, 2023). Even though deep learning can bring lots of advantages, it's important for organizations to connect their data analysis efforts with their main business objectives. For example, retail stores use deep learning tricks to figure out how customers behave, pick the best mix of products, and tailor marketing to suit different tastes. When businesses line up their deep learning strategies with the aim of making customers happy and boosting sales, they can make the most out of their data analysis investments.

Furthermore, dealing with technology limits is a big hurdle in using deep learning for analytics. To make deep learning work, you need strong computers and lots of data-processing power (Gupta & Farahat, 2020). This means spending a lot on fancy machines, software, and experts, which can be tough for many companies.

But, thanks to things like cloud computing and flexible analytics tools, businesses can tackle these problems and use deep learning to understand their data better.

In simple terms, as businesses use more advanced deep learning technology for making decisions, they also need to think about ethics (Kratsch et al., 2021). This means considering things like privacy, fairness, and how clear the algorithms are. For example, banks need to make sure they're following rules and being fair when using deep learning to decide who to lend money to. And in healthcare, it's important to protect patients' privacy when using deep learning to study their medical records. By being careful about these ethical issues and following good rules for handling data, businesses can use deep learning responsibly and earn trust from the people they serve.

Despite the obstacles, using deep learning brings exciting possibilities for pushing innovation and expanding in the digital age. By tapping into artificial intelligence and machine learning, companies can find new ways to improve, automate, and predict things. Take social media platforms, for instance. They use deep learning to study what users post, spot trends, and suggest things that users might like, boosting how much users interact and how much money the platform makes. In manufacturing, deep learning helps predict when machines might break down, so companies can keep them running smoothly and avoid costly downtime. It's all about finding smarter ways to work and save money.

Besides looking at the practical problems, a bibliometric analysis of current research in deep learning (DL) for business analytics helps us understand what's popular, who's making the biggest impact, and what new topics are coming up. This analysis helps us see where there are gaps in what we know and where different studies agree. It's like a roadmap for future research and helps share knowledge among researchers.

Here are the questions this study wants to answer:

- What are researchers currently focusing on when it comes to using deep learning in business analytics?
- Who are the most important authors, organizations and publishers contributing to this field?
- Which journals have the greatest influence, impact and dominance on the field of deep learning in business analytics?
- Which themes are most prevalent in this field of study?

2. RELATED WORKS

The literature surrounding the integration of DL into business analytics provides valuable insights into the challenges, opportunities, and current trends in this rapidly evolving business community. This section synthesizes key findings from existing research, focusing on computational complexities, infrastructure limitations, skill shortages, the black-box nature of DL models, empirical performance comparisons with traditional business analytics models including statistical and other conventional machine learning techniques, and the implications of ethical considerations.

In many literatures, authors talk about a big problem with DL algorithms. These algorithms are very complex to compute. DL models have lots of layers of neurons, which need a lot of computing power to train and use. Park & Song (2020) said training deep neural networks (DNNs) takes a lot of time and resources. It needs special equipment like GPUs or TPUs to work well. This makes it hard for small businesses to use DL for analyzing their data because they may not have enough money or resources.

Apart from the computational complexities, infrastructure limitations emerge as a significant barrier to the adoption of DL in business settings. Sengupta et al. (2020) emphasizes the importance of robust data infrastructure capable of handling large volumes of heterogeneous data for effective DL implementation. However, many organizations struggle with outdated or inadequate IT infrastructure, impeding their ability to leverage DL for data-driven decision-making. Furthermore, Ashawa et al. (2022) discuss the scalability of DL algorithms poses challenges for deployment in cloud-based environments, necessitating efficient resource allocation strategies and optimization techniques.

The shortage of skilled professionals proficient in DL techniques emerges as another critical impediment to the widespread adoption of DL in business analytics. According to Sarkar and Kedas(2023), the demand for data scientists and machine learning engineers with expertise in DL exceeds the available talent pool, leading to recruitment challenges for organizations seeking to harness the potential of DL. Moreover, the interdisciplinary nature of DL necessitates proficiency in mathematics, statistics, computer science, and domain-specific knowledge, further exacerbating skill shortages in the workforce.

The black-box nature of DL models presents additional challenges for businesses seeking to deploy DL solutions for decision-making. DL models, characterized by their complex architectures and high-dimensional feature representations, often lack interpretability, making it challenging to understand the underlying factors driving model predictions by Li et al. (2022). This lack of transparency raises concerns regarding accountability, fairness, and regulatory compliance, particularly in industries with stringent requirements for model interpretability such as finance and healthcare.

Empirical comparisons between DL and traditional ML models offer valuable insights into the relative performance of these techniques in business analytics contexts. While, Razavi (2021) describes DL has demonstrated remarkable success in domains such as image recognition and natural language processing, empirical evidence suggests that DL may not consistently outperform traditional ML algorithms in all scenarios. For instance, in situations involving structured datasets with fixed-length feature vectors, traditional ML models such as support vector machines (SVMs) or random forests may yield comparable or superior performance to DL models, highlighting the importance of selecting appropriate algorithms based on the specific characteristics of the data and problem domain.

Ethical considerations loom large in discussions surrounding the adoption of DL in business analytics, with implications for privacy, fairness, and algorithmic transparency. Chowdhury et al. (2023) highlights the ethical dilemmas arising from the use of DL algorithms in sensitive domains such as criminal justice and healthcare, where biases in training data or model outputs can perpetuate discrimination or exacerbate disparities. Ensuring ethical AI practices requires proactive measures such as bias mitigation techniques, algorithmic audits, and stakeholder engagement to promote transparency and accountability in DL-driven decision-making processes.

In summary, the literature review underscores the multifaceted challenges and opportunities associated with integrating DL into business analytics. Computational complexities, infrastructure limitations, skill shortages, the black-box nature of DL models, empirical performance comparisons, and ethical considerations all play crucial roles in shaping the landscape of DL adoption in business settings. Addressing these challenges requires a concerted effort from academia, industry, and policymakers to foster innovation, mitigate risks, and ensure responsible AI deployment for sustainable business growth and societal benefit.

3. EXPLORING DEEP LEARNING TECHNIQUES

Deep learning, a subset of machine learning, draws inspiration from brain neural networks organized into hierarchical information-processing stages, including input, hidden, and output layers (Kratsch et al., 2021). It plays a pivotal role in driving the digital revolution in business analytics (Schmitt, 2023), with prominent architectures such as Multi-Layer Perceptron (MLP), Convolutional Neural Networks (CNN), and Recurrent Neural Networks (RNN) offering unparalleled problem-solving capabilities (Sengupta et al., 2020).

3.1 Multi-Layer Perceptron (MLP)

MLP serves as a foundational architecture in deep learning, operating as a fully connected feedforward artificial neural network (ANN) with an input layer, hidden layers, and an output layer. It utilizes activation functions such as ReLU, Tanh, Sigmoid, and Softmax to determine outputs, while being trained using backpropagation. Optimization techniques like Stochastic Gradient Descent (SGD) and Adaptive Moment Estimation (Adam) are applied during training. Despite requiring tuning of hyperparameters like hidden layers and neurons, MLP offers the advantage of learning non-linear models in real-time or online through partial fit.

3.2 Convolutional Neural Network (CNN)

CNN stands out as a popular discriminative deep learning architecture that learns directly from input data, eliminating the need for human feature extraction. It enhances traditional ANN designs and incorporates techniques like dropout to address overfitting. CNNs excel in handling 2D spatial data and are widely employed in various domains such as visual recognition, medical image analysis, and natural language processing, owing to their ability to automatically discover essential features from input data.

3.3 Recurrent Neural Network (RNN)

RNN utilizes sequential or time-series data, feeding the output from the previous step as input to the current stage, leveraging memory to influence current input and output based on previous information. Unlike typical DNNs, RNNs rely on prior elements within the sequence. However, they face challenges like vanishing gradients for long data sequences. Several variants of RNNs have been developed to address these challenges and perform effectively in various real-world applications.

4. METHODS

To successfully address the research inquiries, an extensive methodology that makes use of online databases and VOSviewer—a tool of substantial academic significance (van Eck et al., 2010; van Eck & Waltman, 2010)—will be utilized in this investigation. In order to gather relevant data, this research will apply particular syntactic criteria to extract insights from the Dimensions Publication, an impactful data base (Thelwall, 2018). The final dataset will be skillfully shown using a variety of charts, effectively highlighting years of particular importance and precisely capturing publication trends. After processing this data, an integrated algorithm in the online database will provide yearly trends in the field of deep learning research focused on business analytics. This graphic representation is an invaluable reference tool for researchers and practitioners alike.

In addition, the analysis will make use of VOSviewer, a powerful program that is well-known for its effectiveness in grouping papers and evaluating results, in order to do an extensive bibliographic review, to assume current research status and development (Lyu, Liu & Yao, 2023). VOSviewer clusters academic texts using citation networks and works well in both solitary and group settings. In terms of research applications, the visualization capabilities of VOSviewer greatly improve the analysis of clustering results, illuminating the complex interrelationships between business analytics and deep learning. This tool will examine notable authors, connections, places of origin, documents, and sources with great care, giving a comprehensive picture of how deep learning and business analytics meet.

VOSviewer's capabilities go beyond just highlighting the most important components found in the visible literature (Lyu, Liu & Yao, 2023); it is a priceless tool for performing a comprehensive investigation of the field of business analytics in deep learning or neural networks.

5. RESULTS

5.1 The Correlating Relationship Between Deep Learning and Business Analytics in Terms of Chronology

With an emphasis on business analytics themes, this study explores recent literature that was taken from the Core Collection of Dimensions publishing on January 5, 2024. After a thorough search strategy using keywords like "Deep Learning," "Neural Network," "Machine learning," "Data Driven Decision Making," "Digital Transformation," "Digital Strategy," "Prediction Model," and "Business Analytics," 1100 relevant articles from 2014 to 2023 were found. This corpus, which covers a wide range of topics including information and computing sciences, commerce, management, tourism and services, data management, information systems, machine learning, distributed computing, artificial intelligence, human-centered computing, and cognitive psychology, was compiled by eminent authors connected to esteemed universities. This study highlights how business analytics research is interdisciplinary and important from a scholarly standpoint.

Table 1. Article inclusion and exclusion criteria

Selection Criteria	Exclude	Include
Database: "Dimension" Date of Search: "5th February 2024" Period of Publications: 2014-2023		
Search term: "Deep Learning" OR "Neural Network" OR "Machine learning" OR "Data Driven Decision Making" OR "Digital Transformation" OR "Digital Strategy" OR "Prediction Model" AND "Business Analytics"	-	5,683
Subject area: "Information and Computing Sciences, Commerce, Management, Tourism and Services, Data Management and Data Science, Information Systems, Machine Learning, Distributed Computing and Systems Software, Artificial Intelligence, Human-Centered Computing and Cognitive and Computational Psychology"	1,898	3,785
Publication type: "Article"	2,519	1,266
Journal List: "UGC Journal List Group II"	166	1,100
Language screening: "Include documents published in English only"	0	1,100

Although previous studies on the use of deep learning to business analytics have been published, our analysis, which was informed by the search parameters shown in Figure 1, indicates a significant change in the field's importance, especially after the epidemic began. There has been a noticeable increase in academic interest in this junction, with 2020 seeing the biggest increase in interest. This temporal pattern points to an increased awareness of the value and effectiveness of Deep Learning techniques in the context of Business Analytics, probably prompted by the pressures of the global health crisis and the need for paradigms of data-driven decision-making.

Figure 1. Visualization of the yearly publication on the topic of the influence of deep learning in business analytics

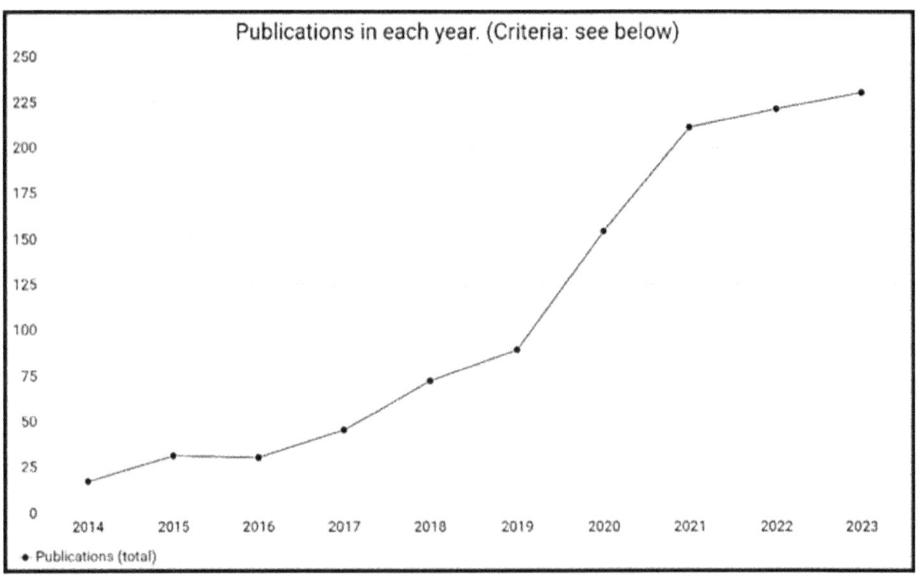

5.2 Assessing Author, Organization, and Country Contributions to Research on the Use of the Deep Learning in Respect to Business Analytics

When attempting to identify key players and organizations in the field of Deep Learning in relation to Business Analytics, citation counts become extremely important as they provide researchers with a direct path for future investigation. Using bibliographic data files and co-authorship analysis methods, researchers use VOS viewer to produce a detailed map and a list of the top ten authors, organizations, and countries based on full counting (see Table 2). The results shed light on a certain group of authors and organizations that have received a large number of citations, highlighting their important contributions to the discipline and drawing focus to particular areas of research.These results provide insightful information for academics and professionals in the industry who are interested in learning more about the relationship between Deep Learning and its implications for Business Analytics. This will enhance the conversation and help professionals make well-informed decisions in both the academic and professional domains.

Table 2. Most influential authors, organizations, and country

TC	Author	TP	TC	Organization	TP	TC	Country	TP
735	Delen, Dursun	21	860	University of Johannesburg	13	8842	United States	284
587	Duan, Lian	5	755	Vellore Institute of Technology University	9	4371	China	178
442	Oztekin, Asil	11	743	Oklahoma State University	22	3901	India	142
413	Feuerriegel, Stefan	8	591	Rutgers, The State University of New Jersey	9	3287	United Kingdom	99
342	Topuz, Kazim	9	540	University of Southampton	16	1885	Australia	51
340	Coussement, Kristof	11	514	Western Michigan University	5	1836	Germany	66
332	Tanwar, Sudeep	15	504	University of Massachusetts Lowell	13	1514	France	59
330	Lessmann, Stefan	7	485	Unsw Sydney	5	1238	Italy	24
325	Dag, Ali	10	471	Hofstra University	5	1225	South Korea	48
313	Bravo, Cristián	7	434	Humboldt-Universität Zu Berlin	11	1163	Spain	26

Within the current study, the list of top journals, as shown in Table 3, is a crucial tool for both practitioners and researchers, providing a priceless database of references to support their academic work. Through a careful examination of both instances and references, this research offers valuable perspectives on the leading publications in the domain, allowing interested parties to remain up to date on current research directions and critical questions. In addition, the list of prestigious journals provides a means of obtaining the most recent developments and ground-breaking works, providing a conclusive viewpoint on the topic.These carefully chosen resources promote informed discourse and serve as a catalyst for future research initiatives in the academic and professional domains. They also aid in the development of a nuanced understanding of the complexities inherent in the convergence of Deep Learning and Business Analytics.

Figure 2. Visualization of the publication by author on the influence of deep learning on business analytics

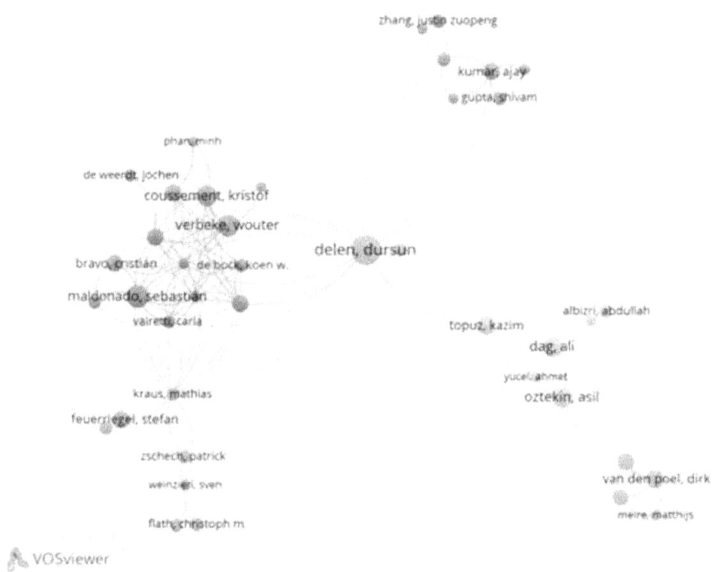

Figure 3. Visualization of the publication by country on the influence of deep learning on business analytics

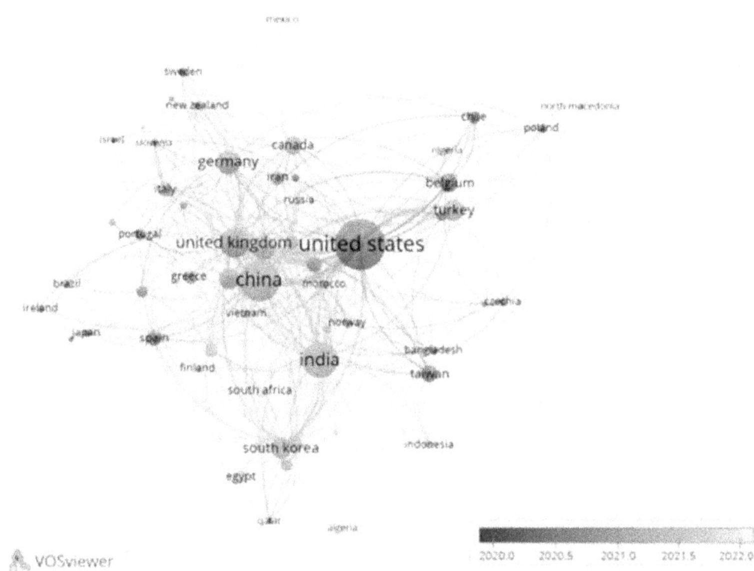

Figure 4. Visualization of the publication by organizations on the influence of deep learning on business analytics

5.3 The Most Influential Journals to Shed Light on the Application of Deep Learning in Business Analytics

The prestigious interdisciplinary journal "Decision Support Systems" focuses on the use of information technology to assist decision-making processes across a range of fields. The magazine publishes cutting-edge research on issues like artificial intelligence, data analytics, decision theory, and organizational decision-making, with a heavy focus on both theoretical developments and practical applications. Prominent for its stringent peer review procedure and contributions from top academics across the globe, "Decision Support Systems" functions as an essential forum for spreading cutting-edge research that molds the terrain of business analytics and decision support systems.

Published by the Institute of Electrical and Electronics Engineers (IEEE), "IEEE Access" is a highly acclaimed multidisciplinary open-access publication. Artificial intelligence, machine learning, data science, and information systems are just a few of the many topics it covers in the fields of engineering, technology, and computer science. "IEEE Access" offers a forum for researchers to share their discoveries worldwide and encourages interdisciplinary collaboration and innovation within the scientific community thanks to its quick publication process and large audience.

Table 3. Most influential journals for deep learning in respect to business analytics

TC	Journals	Name of the Publisher	TP
2741	Decision Support Systems	Elsevier	65
1506	IEEE Access	IEEE	73
1190	Knowledge-Based Systems	Elsevier	4
1160	Expert Systems With Applications	Elsevier	26
1043	Journal of Industrial Information Integration	Elsevier	6
778	Journal of Business Research	Elsevier	17
679	Journal of Big Data	Springer	8
590	European Journal of Operational Research	Elsevier	28
566	Enterprise Information Systems	Taylor & Francis	5
542	Technological Forecasting and Social Change	Elsevier	16

Figure 5. Visualization of the publication of Journals on the influence of deep learning on business analytics

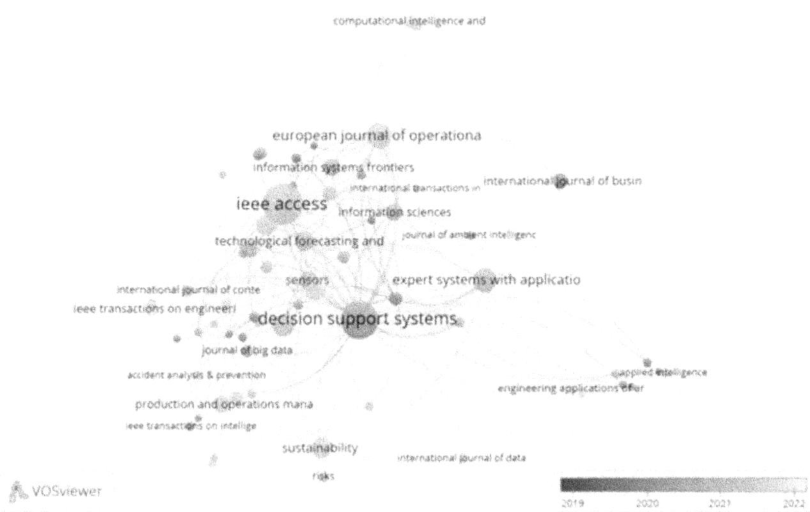

5.4 Understanding Thematic Cluster to Assess the Influence of Deep Learning in the Perspective of Business Analytics

Based on bibliographic coupling analysis, Table 4 presents a summary of subject clusters in the field of deep learning in business analytics. This analysis groups important subjects and associated concepts and provides a visual representation of them by clarifying shared references between academic papers. This table can be an invaluable tool for researchers and educators to identify recurrent themes and trends, which will help them, gain a deeper grasp of the changing dynamics between business analytics and deep learning in academic discourse.

Cluster 1 Big Data: Óskarsdóttir et al. (2019)investigates the use of Big Data in credit scoring by utilizing mobile phone data and social network analytics to improve financial inclusion. Batistič & Laken (2019) examines the historical development and future course of Big Data and analytics, highlighting their relationship to organizational performance.

Cluster 2 Future Trends of Big Data: The cluster on Big Data's future trends looks at new opportunities and inclinations across industries, providing practitioners with strategic insights. By means of methodical evaluations and analyses, academics predict how Big Data applications will develop, directing future investigation and creativity (Cui, Kara & Chan, 2020). This collection is an essential tool for interested parties trying to understand and profit from the ever-changing field of big data technologies.

Cluster 3 Artificial Intelligence: The Artificial Intelligence cluster showcases state-of-the-art studies and inventions that propel advances in cognitive computing and machine learning (Guo et al., 2020). Academics investigate innovative algorithms, uses, and moral issues, influencing the development of AI-enabled technology in the future. This cluster is an essential resource for comprehending artificial intelligence's transformational potential and societal ramifications.

Cluster 4 Big Data Application: The Big Data Application cluster presents cutting-edge studies and useful applications of data-driven solutions in a variety of fields (Chen et al., 2020). In order to fully utilize big data's potential for solving difficult problems and promoting organizational success, researchers are investigating innovative approaches and technological advancements.

Cluster 5 Big Data Analytics: The Big Data Analytics cluster explores cutting edge approaches and strategies to draw conclusions from large, intricate datasets (Khanra et al., 2020). Researchers look at novel methods of data analysis that can be used to make well-informed decisions and uncover important information in environments with vast amounts of data.

Cluster 6 Sentiment Analysis: The Sentiment Analysis cluster studies methods and programs for identifying and evaluating sentiment in textual data. Researchers investigate the use of machine learning and natural language processing to extract subjective opinions and sentiment polarity (Samuel et al., 2020), providing important insights into social trends, consumer sentiment, and public opinion.

Cluster 7 Sustainable Potential Frameworks: The cluster on Sustainable Potential Frameworks investigates frameworks and methods for evaluating and improving sustainability across a range of industries (Nguyen et al., 2018). Researchers look into cutting-edge methods for calculating the effects on the environment, society, and economy in order to support sustainable development projects and make educated decisions.

Cluster 8 Potential Application of Survey: The Potential Use of Survey cluster explores cutting-edge techniques and uses of survey research in a variety of sectors. Researchers investigate cutting-edge survey approaches and procedures to acquire information, guide decision-making (Queiroz et al., 2020), and tackle current issues in public policy, business, and academia.

Table 4. Thematic clusters of deep learning in business analytics through bibliographic coupling

Thematic Cluster	Authors	Title	TC
Big Data	Ascarza (2018)	Retention Futility: Targeting High-Risk Customers Might be Ineffective	168
	Batistič (2019)	History, Evolution and Future of Big Data and Analytics: A Bibliometric Analysis of Its Relationship to Performance in Organizations	118
	Coussement (2017)	A comparative analysis of data preparation algorithms for customer churn prediction: A case study in the telecommunication industry	129
	Delen (2018)	The analytics paradigm in business research	108
	Jabeur (2021)	CatBoost model and artificial intelligence techniques for corporate failure prediction	111
	Kitchens (2018)	Advanced Customer Analytics: Strategic Value Through Integration of Relationship-Oriented Big Data	151
	Loureiro (2018)	Exploring the use of deep neural networks for sales forecasting in fashion retail	138
	Miguéis (2018)	Early segmentation of students according to their academic performance: A predictive modelling approach	123
	Mohammadi (2015)	Extreme learning machine based prediction of daily dew point temperature	105
	Nti (2020)	A comprehensive evaluation of ensemble learning for stock-market prediction	120
	Óskarsdóttir (2019)	The value of big data for credit scoring: Enhancing financial inclusion using mobile phone data and social network analytics	131
	Pospieszny (2018)	An effective approach for software project effort and duration estimation with machine learning algorithms	136
	Speiser (2019)	A comparison of random forest variable selection methods for classification prediction modeling	604

Continued on following page

Table 4. Continued

Thematic Cluster	Authors	Title	TC
FutureTrends of Big data	Bilal (2016)	Big Data in the construction industry: A review of present status, opportunities, and future trends	425
	Bolón-Canedo (2019)	Ensembles for feature selection: A review and future trends	322
	Chen (2017)	LRSSLMDA: Laplacian Regularized Sparse Subspace Learning for MiRNA-Disease Association prediction	220
	Cui (2020)	Manufacturing big data ecosystem: A systematic literature review	188
	Duan (2015)	Big data analytics and business analytics	131
	Gill (2022)	AI for next generation computing: Emerging trends and future directions	210
	Qolomany (2019)	Leveraging Machine Learning and Big Data for Smart Buildings: A Comprehensive Survey	128
	Shashi (2019)	Managing supply chain resilience to pursue business and environmental strategies	102
	Thibaud (2018)	Internet of Things (IoT) in high-risk Environment, Health and Safety (EHS) industries: A comprehensive review	179
	Zhong (2017)	Food supply chain management: systems, implementations, and future research	136
Artificial Intelligence	Di Vaio (2020)	Artificial intelligence and business models in the sustainable development goals perspective: A systematic literature review	344
	Ghofrani (2018)	Recent applications of big data analytics in railway transportation systems: A survey	212
	Guo (2020)	Optimized Graph Convolution Recurrent Neural Network for Traffic Prediction	195
	Kaffash (2021)	Big data algorithms and applications in intelligent transportation system: A review and bibliometric analysis	180
	Long (2019)	Deep learning-based feature engineering for stock price movement prediction	275
	Loureiro (2021)	Artificial intelligence in business: State of the art and future research agenda	162
	Nallaperuma (2019)	Online Incremental Machine Learning Platform for Big Data-Driven Smart Traffic Management	157
	Wu (2020)	Adaptive stock trading strategies with deep reinforcement learning methods	113
	Zhang (2021)	Study on artificial intelligence: The state of the art and future prospects	340

Continued on following page

Table 4. Continued

Thematic Cluster	Authors	Title	TC
DataMining Application	Amani (2017)	Data mining applications in accounting: A review of the literature and organizing framework	111
	Appelbaum (2017)	Impact of business analytics and enterprise systems on managerial accounting	248
	Chen (2020)	Selecting critical features for data classification based on machine learning methods	349
	Gepp (2018)	Big data techniques in auditing research and practice: Current trends and future opportunities	197
	Li (2018)	Effective tourist volume forecasting supported by PCA and improved BPNN using Baidu index	183
	Mariani (2018)	Business intelligence and big data in hospitality and tourism: a systematic literature review	264
	Schmitt (2020)	Predictive model-based quality inspection using Machine Learning and Edge Cloud Computing	105
	Tantalaki (2019)	Data-Driven Decision Making in Precision Agriculture: The Rise of Big Data in Agricultural Systems	106
	Tomasevic (2020)	An overview and comparison of supervised data mining techniques for student exam performance prediction	209
Big Data Analytic	Galetsi (2020)	Big data analytics in health sector: Theoretical framework, techniques and prospects	123
	Kashani (2021)	A systematic review of IoT in healthcare: Applications, techniques, and trends	212
	Khanra (2020)	Big data analytics in healthcare: a systematic literature review	138
	Metzger (2014)	Comparing and Combining Predictive Business Process Monitoring Techniques	113
	Mrquez-Chamorro (2017)	Predictive Monitoring of Business Processes: A Survey	155
Sentiment Analysis	Kratzwald (2018)	Deep learning for affective computing: Text-based emotion recognition in decision support	214
	Ravi (2015)	A survey on opinion mining and sentiment analysis: Tasks, approaches and applications	900
	Samuel (2020)	COVID-19 Public Sentiment Insights and Machine Learning for Tweets Classification	267
	Shayaa (2018)	Sentiment Analysis of Big Data: Methods, Applications, and Open Challenges	118

Continued on following page

Table 4. Continued

Thematic Cluster	Authors	Title	TC
Sustainable Analytical Frameworks	Kumar (2018)	A big data driven sustainable manufacturing framework for condition-based maintenance prediction	126
	Nguyen (2018)	Big data analytics in supply chain management: A state-of-the-art literature review	369
	Ryman-Tubb (2018)	How Artificial Intelligence and machine learning research impacts payment card fraud detection: A survey and industry benchmark	103
	Seyedan (2020)	Predictive big data analytics for supply chain demand forecasting: methods, applications, and research opportunities	138
Potential Application of Survey	Chang (2014)	The effects of hedonic/utilitarian expectations and social influence on continuance intention to play online games	157
	Da Xu (2018)	Big data for cyber physical systems in industry 4.0: a survey	403
	Maddikunta (2022)	Industry 5.0: A survey on enabling technologies and potential applications	611
	Queiroz (2020)	Blockchain adoption in operations and supply chain management: empirical evidence from an emerging economy	162

Figure 6. Visualization of the thematic cluster on the influence of deep learning on business analytics

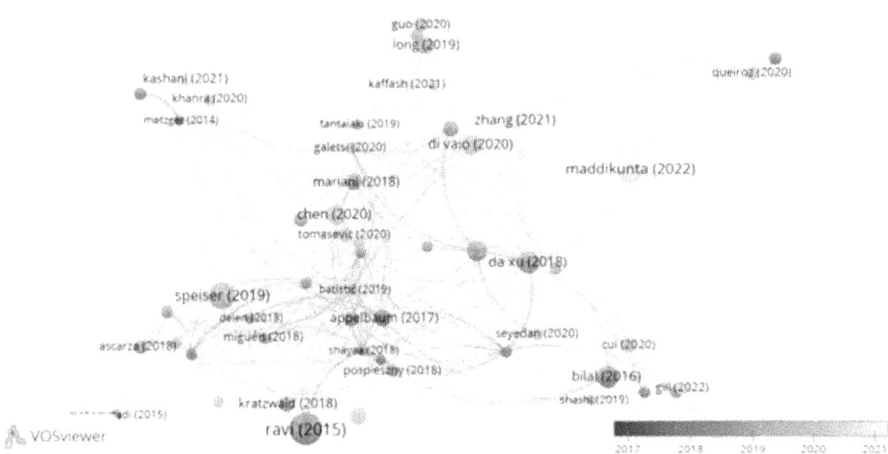

6. DISCUSSIONS

The examination of current literature highlights the expanding significance of deep learning in business analytics, which was made more clear by the spike in scholarly interest that followed the start of the worldwide epidemic. The interdisciplinary nature of current research is shown by citation counts and topic grouping, which identify important trends and authors in this field. The discovery of significant writers, institutions, and publications provides insightful information for further investigation and cooperation, influencing the direction of business analytics and deep learning research. This comprehensive understanding serves as a compass, guiding future endeavors and collaborations aimed at advancing the frontiers of knowledge in business analytics through the lens of deep learning.

7. CONCLUSION

7.1 Major Findings

To sum up, this research highlights how deep learning may revolutionize data-driven decision-making in a variety of industries. Researchers may traverse the changing field of business analytics, promoting innovation in both academia and industry and achieving positive societal effect, by embracing innovative approaches and using interdisciplinary viewpoints. In order to further our understanding and use of deep learning in the field of business analytics, collaboration and ongoing scholarly research will be essential.

7.2 Limitations

The restricted focus on articles from the Core Collection of Dimensions publication and the study's dependence on keyword search keywords, which may have left out pertinent research, are two of its shortcomings. Furthermore, the most recent advancements might not be captured within the temporal frame.

7.3 Future Implication

It is recommended that future research contemplate broadening the scope of the study to encompass a wider array of databases and sources, in addition to integrating qualitative analysis and longitudinal studies. These initiatives have the potential to follow deep learning's changing trends over time and offer deeper insights into the real-world implementations of the technology in business analytics.

REFERENCES

Amani, F. A., & Fadlalla, A. M. (2017). Data mining applications in accounting: A review of the literature and organizing framework. *International Journal of Accounting Information Systems*, *24*, 32–58. doi:10.1016/j.accinf.2016.12.004

Appelbaum, D., Kogan, A., Vasarhelyi, M., & Yan, Z. (2017). Impact of business analytics and enterprise systems on managerial accounting. *International Journal of Accounting Information Systems*, *25*, 29–44. doi:10.1016/j.accinf.2017.03.003

Ascarza, E. (2018). Retention futility: Targeting high-risk customers might be ineffective. *JMR, Journal of Marketing Research*, *55*(1), 80–98. doi:10.1509/jmr.16.0163

Ashawa, M., Douglas, O., Osamor, J., & Jackie, R. (2022). Improving cloud efficiency through optimized resource allocation technique for load balancing using LSTM machine learning algorithm. *Journal of Cloud Computing (Heidelberg, Germany)*, *11*(1), 87. doi:10.1186/s13677-022-00362-x

Batistič, S., & van der Laken, P. (2019). History, evolution and future of big data and analytics: A bibliometric analysis of its relationship to performance in organizations. *British Journal of Management*, *30*(2), 229–251. doi:10.1111/1467-8551.12340

Batistič, S., & van der Laken, P. (2019). History, evolution and future of big data and analytics: A bibliometric analysis of its relationship to performance in organizations. *British Journal of Management*, *30*(2), 229–251. doi:10.1111/1467-8551.12340

Bilal, M., Oyedele, L. O., Qadir, J., Munir, K., Ajayi, S. O., Akinade, O. O., Owolabi, H. A., Alaka, H. A., & Pasha, M. (2016). Big Data in the construction industry: A review of present status, opportunities, and future trends. *Advanced Engineering Informatics*, *30*(3), 500–521. doi:10.1016/j.aei.2016.07.001

Bolón-Canedo, V., & Alonso-Betanzos, A. (2019). Ensembles for feature selection: A review and future trends. *Information Fusion*, *52*, 1–12. doi:10.1016/j.inffus.2018.11.008

Canhoto, A. I., & Clear, F. (2020). Artificial intelligence and machine learning as business tools: A framework for diagnosing value destruction potential. *Business Horizons*, *63*(2), 183–193. doi:10.1016/j.bushor.2019.11.003

Chang, I. C., Liu, C. C., & Chen, K. (2014). The effects of hedonic/utilitarian expectations and social influence on continuance intention to play online games. *Internet Research*, *24*(1), 21–45. doi:10.1108/IntR-02-2012-0025

Chen, R. C., Dewi, C., Huang, S. W., & Caraka, R. E. (2020). Selecting critical features for data classification based on machine learning methods. *Journal of Big Data*, *7*(1), 52. doi:10.1186/s40537-020-00327-4

Chen, X., & Huang, L. (2017). LRSSLMDA: Laplacian regularized sparse subspace learning for MiRNA-disease association prediction. *PLoS Computational Biology*, *13*(12), e1005912. doi:10.1371/journal.pcbi.1005912 PMID:29253885

Chowdhury, S., Joel-Edgar, S., Dey, P. K., Bhattacharya, S., & Kharlamov, A. (2023). Embedding transparency in artificial intelligence machine learning models: Managerial implications on predicting and explaining employee turnover. *International Journal of Human Resource Management*, *34*(14), 2732–2764. doi:10.1080/09585192.2022.2066981

Coussement, K., Lessmann, S., & Verstraeten, G. (2017). A comparative analysis of data preparation algorithms for customer churn prediction: A case study in the telecommunication industry. *Decision Support Systems*, *95*, 27–36. doi:10.1016/j.dss.2016.11.007

Cui, Y., Kara, S., & Chan, K. C. (2020). Manufacturing big data ecosystem: A systematic literature review. *Robotics and Computer-integrated Manufacturing*, *62*, 101861. doi:10.1016/j.rcim.2019.101861

Davenport, T. H. (2018). From analytics to artificial intelligence. *Journal of Business Analytics*, *1*(2), 73–80. doi:10.1080/2573234X.2018.1543535

Delen, D., & Zolbanin, H. M. (2018). The analytics paradigm in business research. *Journal of Business Research*, *90*, 186–195. doi:10.1016/j.jbusres.2018.05.013

Di Vaio, A., Palladino, R., Hassan, R., & Escobar, O. (2020). Artificial intelligence and business models in the sustainable development goals perspective: A systematic literature review. *Journal of Business Research*, *121*, 283–314. doi:10.1016/j.jbusres.2020.08.019

Duan, L., & Xiong, Y. (2015). Big data analytics and business analytics. *Journal of Management Analytics*, *2*(1), 1–21. doi:10.1080/23270012.2015.1020891

Galetsi, P., Katsaliaki, K., & Kumar, S. (2020). Big data analytics in health sector: Theoretical framework, techniques and prospects. *International Journal of Information Management*, *50*, 206–216. doi:10.1016/j.ijinfomgt.2019.05.003

Gepp, A., Linnenluecke, M. K., O'Neill, T. J., & Smith, T. (2018). Big data techniques in auditing research and practice: Current trends and future opportunities. *Journal of Accounting Literature*, *40*(1), 102–115. doi:10.1016/j.acclit.2017.05.003

Ghofrani, F., He, Q., Goverde, R. M., & Liu, X. (2018). Recent applications of big data analytics in railway transportation systems: A survey. *Transportation Research Part C, Emerging Technologies*, *90*, 226–246. doi:10.1016/j.trc.2018.03.010

Gill, S. S., Xu, M., Ottaviani, C., Patros, P., Bahsoon, R., Shaghaghi, A., Golec, M., Stankovski, V., Wu, H., Abraham, A., Singh, M., Mehta, H., Ghosh, S. K., Baker, T., Parlikad, A. K., Lutfiyya, H., Kanhere, S. S., Sakellariou, R., Dustdar, S., ... Uhlig, S. (2022). AI for next generation computing: Emerging trends and future directions. *Internet of Things : Engineering Cyber Physical Human Systems*, *19*, 100514. doi:10.1016/j.iot.2022.100514

Guo, K., Hu, Y., Qian, Z., Liu, H., Zhang, K., Sun, Y., Gao, J., & Yin, B. (2020). Optimized graph convolution recurrent neural network for traffic prediction. *IEEE Transactions on Intelligent Transportation Systems*, *22*(2), 1138–1149. doi:10.1109/TITS.2019.2963722

Guo, K., Hu, Y., Qian, Z., Liu, H., Zhang, K., Sun, Y., Gao, J., & Yin, B. (2020). Optimized graph convolution recurrent neural network for traffic prediction. *IEEE Transactions on Intelligent Transportation Systems*, *22*(2), 1138–1149. doi:10.1109/TITS.2019.2963722

Gupta, C., & Farahat, A. (2020, August). Deep learning for industrial AI: Challenges, new methods and best practices. In *Proceedings of the 26th ACM SIGKDD International Conference on Knowledge Discovery & Data Mining* (pp. 3571-3572). 10.1145/3394486.3406482

Jabeur, S. B., Gharib, C., Mefteh-Wali, S., & Arfi, W. B. (2021). CatBoost model and artificial intelligence techniques for corporate failure prediction. *Technological Forecasting and Social Change*, *166*, 120658. doi:10.1016/j.techfore.2021.120658

Kaffash, S., Nguyen, A. T., & Zhu, J. (2021). Big data algorithms and applications in intelligent transportation system: A review and bibliometric analysis. *International Journal of Production Economics*, *231*, 107868. doi:10.1016/j.ijpe.2020.107868

Kashani, M. H., Madanipour, M., Nikravan, M., Asghari, P., & Mahdipour, E. (2021). A systematic review of IoT in healthcare: Applications, techniques, and trends. *Journal of Network and Computer Applications*, *192*, 103164. doi:10.1016/j.jnca.2021.103164

Khanra, S., Dhir, A., Islam, A. N., & Mäntymäki, M. (2020). Big data analytics in healthcare: A systematic literature review. *Enterprise Information Systems*, *14*(7), 878–912. doi:10.1080/17517575.2020.1812005

Kitchens, B., Dobolyi, D., Li, J., & Abbasi, A. (2018). Advanced customer analytics: Strategic value through integration of relationship-oriented big data. *Journal of Management Information Systems, 35*(2), 540–574. doi:10.1080/07421222.2018.1451957

Kratsch, W., Manderscheid, J., Röglinger, M., & Seyfried, J. (2021). Machine learning in business process monitoring: A comparison of deep learning and classical approaches used for outcome prediction. *Business & Information Systems Engineering, 63*(3), 261–276. doi:10.1007/s12599-020-00645-0

Kratzwald, B., Ilić, S., Kraus, M., Feuerriegel, S., & Prendinger, H. (2018). Deep learning for affective computing: Text-based emotion recognition in decision support. *Decision Support Systems, 115*, 24–35. doi:10.1016/j.dss.2018.09.002

Kraus, M., Feuerriegel, S., & Oztekin, A. (2020). Deep learning in business analytics and operations research: Models, applications and managerial implications. *European Journal of Operational Research, 281*(3), 628–641. doi:10.1016/j.ejor.2019.09.018

Kumar, A., Shankar, R., & Thakur, L. S. (2018). A big data driven sustainable manufacturing framework for condition-based maintenance prediction. *Journal of Computational Science, 27*, 428–439. doi:10.1016/j.jocs.2017.06.006

Kushwaha, A. K., Kar, A. K., & Dwivedi, Y. K. (2021). Applications of big data in emerging management disciplines: A literature review using text mining. *International Journal of Information Management Data Insights, 1*(2), 100017. doi:10.1016/j.jjimei.2021.100017

Li, S., Chen, T., Wang, L., & Ming, C. (2018). Effective tourist volume forecasting supported by PCA and improved BPNN using Baidu index. *Tourism Management, 68*, 116–126. doi:10.1016/j.tourman.2018.03.006

Li, X., Xiong, H., Li, X., Wu, X., Zhang, X., Liu, J., Bian, J., & Dou, D. (2022). Interpretable deep learning: Interpretation, interpretability, trustworthiness, and beyond. *Knowledge and Information Systems, 64*(12), 3197–3234. doi:10.1007/s10115-022-01756-8

Long, W., Lu, Z., & Cui, L. (2019). Deep learning-based feature engineering for stock price movement prediction. *Knowledge-Based Systems, 164*, 163–173. doi:10.1016/j.knosys.2018.10.034

Loureiro, A. L., Miguéis, V. L., & Da Silva, L. F. (2018). Exploring the use of deep neural networks for sales forecasting in fashion retail. *Decision Support Systems, 114*, 81–93. doi:10.1016/j.dss.2018.08.010

Loureiro, S. M. C., Guerreiro, J., & Tussyadiah, I. (2021). Artificial intelligence in business: State of the art and future research agenda. *Journal of Business Research*, *129*, 911–926. doi:10.1016/j.jbusres.2020.11.001

Lyu, P., Liu, X., & Yao, T. (2023). A bibliometric analysis of literature on bibliometrics in recent half-century. *Journal of Information Science*. doi:10.1177/01655515231191233

Maddikunta, P. K. R., Pham, Q. V., Prabadevi, B., Deepa, N., Dev, K., Gadekallu, T. R., ... Liyanage, M. (2022). Industry 5.0: A survey on enabling technologies and potential applications. *Journal of Industrial Information Integration*, *26*, 100257. doi:10.1016/j.jii.2021.100257

Mariani, M., Baggio, R., Fuchs, M., & Höepken, W. (2018). Business intelligence and big data in hospitality and tourism: A systematic literature review. *International Journal of Contemporary Hospitality Management*, *30*(12), 3514–3554. doi:10.1108/IJCHM-07-2017-0461

Márquez-Chamorro, A. E., Resinas, M., & Ruiz-Cortés, A. (2017). Predictive monitoring of business processes: A survey. *IEEE Transactions on Services Computing*, *11*(6), 962–977. doi:10.1109/TSC.2017.2772256

Metzger, A., Leitner, P., Ivanović, D., Schmieders, E., Franklin, R., Carro, M., Dustdar, S., & Pohl, K. (2014). Comparing and combining predictive business process monitoring techniques. *IEEE Transactions on Systems, Man, and Cybernetics. Systems*, *45*(2), 276–290. doi:10.1109/TSMC.2014.2347265

Miguéis, V. L., Freitas, A., Garcia, P. J., & Silva, A. (2018). Early segmentation of students according to their academic performance: A predictive modelling approach. *Decision Support Systems*, *115*, 36–51. doi:10.1016/j.dss.2018.09.001

Mohammadi, K., Shamshirband, S., Motamedi, S., Petković, D., Hashim, R., & Gocic, M. (2015). Extreme learning machine based prediction of daily dew point temperature. *Computers and Electronics in Agriculture*, *117*, 214–225. doi:10.1016/j.compag.2015.08.008

Nallaperuma, D., Nawaratne, R., Bandaragoda, T., Adikari, A., Nguyen, S., Kempitiya, T., De Silva, D., Alahakoon, D., & Pothuhera, D. (2019). Online incremental machine learning platform for big data-driven smart traffic management. *IEEE Transactions on Intelligent Transportation Systems*, *20*(12), 4679–4690. doi:10.1109/TITS.2019.2924883

Nguyen, T., Li, Z. H. O. U., Spiegler, V., Ieromonachou, P., & Lin, Y. (2018). Big data analytics in supply chain management: A state-of-the-art literature review. *Computers & Operations Research*, *98*, 254–264. doi:10.1016/j.cor.2017.07.004

Nti, I. K., Adekoya, A. F., & Weyori, B. A. (2020). A comprehensive evaluation of ensemble learning for stock-market prediction. *Journal of Big Data*, *7*(1), 20. doi:10.1186/s40537-020-00299-5

Óskarsdóttir, M., Bravo, C., Sarraute, C., Vanthienen, J., & Baesens, B. (2019). The value of big data for credit scoring: Enhancing financial inclusion using mobile phone data and social network analytics. *Applied Soft Computing*, *74*, 26–39. doi:10.1016/j.asoc.2018.10.004

Park, G., & Song, M. (2020). Predicting performances in business processes using deep neural networks. *Decision Support Systems*, *129*, 113191. doi:10.1016/j.dss.2019.113191

Pospieszny, P., Czarnacka-Chrobot, B., & Kobylinski, A. (2018). An effective approach for software project effort and duration estimation with machine learning algorithms. *Journal of Systems and Software*, *137*, 184–196. doi:10.1016/j.jss.2017.11.066

Qolomany, B., Al-Fuqaha, A., Gupta, A., Benhaddou, D., Alwajidi, S., Qadir, J., & Fong, A. C. (2019). Leveraging machine learning and big data for smart buildings: A comprehensive survey. *IEEE Access : Practical Innovations, Open Solutions*, *7*, 90316–90356. doi:10.1109/ACCESS.2019.2926642

Queiroz, M. M., Fosso Wamba, S., De Bourmont, M., & Telles, R. (2021). Blockchain adoption in operations and supply chain management: Empirical evidence from an emerging economy. *International Journal of Production Research*, *59*(20), 6087–6103. doi:10.1080/00207543.2020.1803511

Ravi, K., & Ravi, V. (2015). A survey on opinion mining and sentiment analysis: Tasks, approaches and applications. *Knowledge-Based Systems*, *89*, 14–46. doi:10.1016/j.knosys.2015.06.015

Razavi, S. (2021). Deep learning, explained: Fundamentals, explainability, and bridgeability to process-based modelling. *Environmental Modelling & Software*, *144*, 105159. doi:10.1016/j.envsoft.2021.105159

Ryman-Tubb, N. F., Krause, P., & Garn, W. (2018). How Artificial Intelligence and machine learning research impacts payment card fraud detection: A survey and industry benchmark. *Engineering Applications of Artificial Intelligence*, *76*, 130–157. doi:10.1016/j.engappai.2018.07.008

Samuel, J., Ali, G. M. N., Rahman, M. M., Esawi, E., & Samuel, Y. (2020). Covid-19 public sentiment insights and machine learning for tweets classification. *Information (Basel), 11*(6), 314. doi:10.3390/info11060314

Samuel, J., Ali, G. M. N., Rahman, M. M., Esawi, E., & Samuel, Y. (2020). Covid-19 public sentiment insights and machine learning for tweets classification. *Information (Basel), 11*(6), 314. doi:10.3390/info11060314

Sarkar, S., & Kedas, S. (2023). Globally distributed talent communities: A typology of innovation problems and talent characteristics. *Thunderbird International Business Review, 65*(1), 89–102. doi:10.1002/tie.22272

Schmitt, J., Bönig, J., Borggräfe, T., Beitinger, G., & Deuse, J. (2020). Predictive model-based quality inspection using Machine Learning and Edge Cloud Computing. *Advanced Engineering Informatics, 45*, 101101. doi:10.1016/j.aei.2020.101101

Schmitt, M. (2023). Automated machine learning: AI-driven decision making in business analytics. *Intelligent Systems with Applications, 18*, 200188. doi:10.1016/j.iswa.2023.200188

Schmitt, M. (2023). Deep learning in business analytics: A clash of expectations and reality. *International Journal of Information Management Data Insights, 3*(1), 100146. doi:10.1016/j.jjimei.2022.100146

Sengupta, S., Basak, S., Saikia, P., Paul, S., Tsalavoutis, V., Atiah, F., Ravi, V., & Peters, A. (2020). A review of deep learning with special emphasis on architectures, applications and recent trends. *Knowledge-Based Systems, 194*, 105596. doi:10.1016/j.knosys.2020.105596

Seyedan, M., & Mafakheri, F. (2020). Predictive big data analytics for supply chain demand forecasting: Methods, applications, and research opportunities. *Journal of Big Data, 7*(1), 53. doi:10.1186/s40537-020-00329-2

Shashi, C., Centobelli, P., Cerchione, R., & Ertz, M. (2020). Managing supply chain resilience to pursue business and environmental strategies. *Business Strategy and the Environment, 29*(3), 1215–1246. doi:10.1002/bse.2428

Shayaa, S., Jaafar, N. I., Bahri, S., Sulaiman, A., Wai, P. S., Chung, Y. W., ... Al-Garadi, M. A. (2018). Sentiment analysis of big data: Methods, applications, and open challenges. *IEEE Access : Practical Innovations, Open Solutions, 6*, 37807–37827. doi:10.1109/ACCESS.2018.2851311

Speiser, J. L., Miller, M. E., Tooze, J., & Ip, E. (2019). A comparison of random forest variable selection methods for classification prediction modeling. *Expert Systems with Applications, 134*, 93–101. doi:10.1016/j.eswa.2019.05.028 PMID:32968335

Tantalaki, N., Souravlas, S., & Roumeliotis, M. (2019). Data-driven decision making in precision agriculture: The rise of big data in agricultural systems. *Journal of Agricultural & Food Information*, *20*(4), 344–380. doi:10.1080/10496505.2019.1638264

Thakur, R. (2024). Introduction to artificial intelligence and its importance in modern business management. In *Leveraging AI and emotional intelligence in contemporary business organizations* (pp. 133–165). IGI Global.

Thelwall, M. (2018). Dimensions: A competitor to Scopus and the Web of Science? *Journal of Informetrics*, *12*(2), 430–435. doi:10.1016/j.joi.2018.03.006

Thibaud, M., Chi, H., Zhou, W., & Piramuthu, S. (2018). Internet of Things (IoT) in high-risk Environment, Health and Safety (EHS) industries: A comprehensive review. *Decision Support Systems*, *108*, 79–95. doi:10.1016/j.dss.2018.02.005

Tomasevic, N., Gvozdenovic, N., & Vranes, S. (2020). An overview and comparison of supervised data mining techniques for student exam performance prediction. *Computers & Education*, *143*, 103676. doi:10.1016/j.compedu.2019.103676

van Eck, N. J., & Waltman, L. (2010). Software survey: VOSviewer, a computer program for bibliometric mapping. *Scientometrics*, *84*(2), 523–538. doi:10.1007/s11192-009-0146-3 PMID:20585380

van Eck, N. J., Waltman, L., Dekker, R., & van den Berg, J. (2010). A comparison of two techniques for bibliometric mapping: Multidimensional scaling and VOS. *Journal of the American Society for Information Science and Technology*, *61*(12), 2405–2416. doi:10.1002/asi.21421

Wu, X., Chen, H., Wang, J., Troiano, L., Loia, V., & Fujita, H. (2020). Adaptive stock trading strategies with deep reinforcement learning methods. *Information Sciences*, *538*, 142–158. doi:10.1016/j.ins.2020.05.066

Xu, L. D., & Duan, L. (2019). Big data for cyber physical systems in industry 4.0: A survey. *Enterprise Information Systems*, *13*(2), 148–169. doi:10.1080/17517575.2018.1442934

Zhang, C., & Lu, Y. (2021). Study on artificial intelligence: The state of the art and future prospects. *Journal of Industrial Information Integration*, *23*, 100224. doi:10.1016/j.jii.2021.100224

Zhong, R., Xu, X., & Wang, L. (2017). Food supply chain management: Systems, implementations, and future research. *Industrial Management & Data Systems*, *117*(9), 2085–2114. doi:10.1108/IMDS-09-2016-0391

Chapter 5
Exploring the Impact of Deep Learning and Neural Networks on Business Analytics

Yogesh Chandra
Government P.G. College, Bazpur, Kumaun University Nainital, India

Manjuleshwar Panda
Independent Researcher, India

ABSTRACT

This chapter explores the substantial uses of deep learning and neural networks in scientific business analytics, as well as how they are transforming the field. The story walks readers through the incorporation of data science into scientific business analytics, starting with an overview of the fundamental ideas and technological history of these tools. An in-depth examination of neural network topologies is necessary before delving into their use in various commercial contexts. The story ends with a prospective examination of upcoming developments and trends, pondering the future of scientific business analytics in the era of developing deep learning technologies and the growing significance of artificial intelligence. This chapter, in its whole, offers readers a thorough exploration of the complex world of deep learning and neural networks, providing them with an understanding of the significant influence these technologies have on scientific business analytics, ranging from fundamental ideas to real-world applications and implications for the future.

DOI: 10.4018/979-8-3693-1598-9.ch005

1. INTRODUCTION TO DEEP LEARNING AND NEURAL NETWORKS

1.1 Defining Deep Learning

Deep Learning (DL) is a branch of machine learning that uses artificial neural networks to simulate the composition and operation of the human brain to model and solve complicated issues. Deep learning, in contrast to typical machine learning techniques, makes use of multi-layered neural networks, which enable it to automatically learn complex data representations. Deep learning models perform exceptionally well in a variety of tasks, including speech recognition, image recognition, and natural language processing, because of this hierarchical feature extraction (Goodfellow, Bengio, Courville, & Bengio, 2016; LeCun et al., 2015; Schmidhuber, 2015).

Figure 1. ML and deep learning

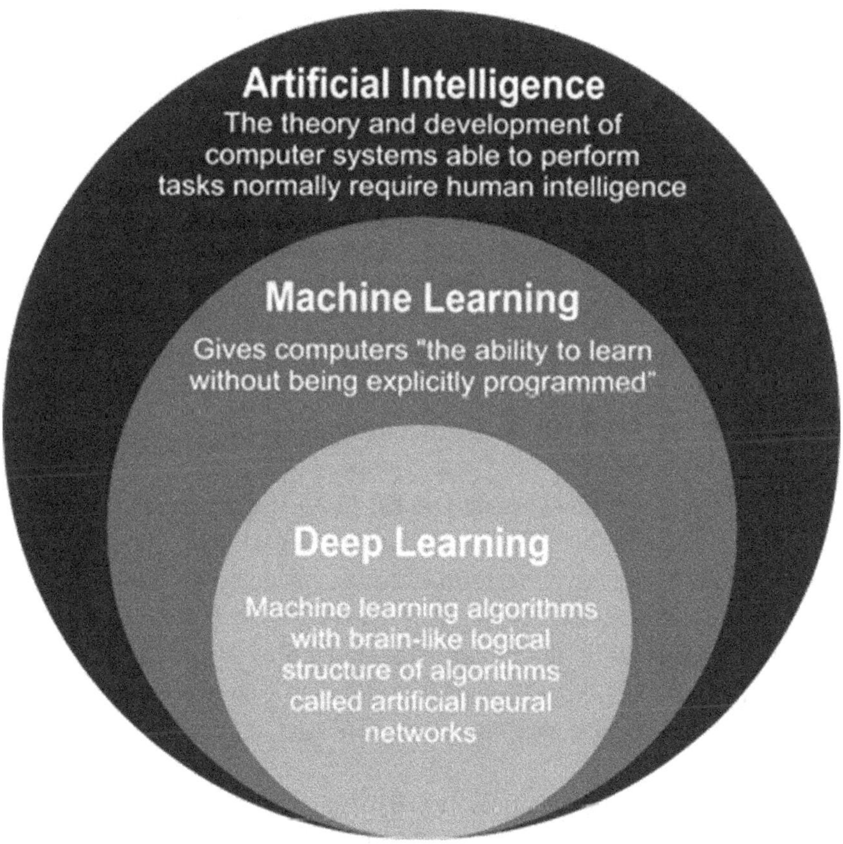

1.1.1 Key Components of Deep Learning

(I) **Neural Networks:** Neural networks, which are made up of layers of connected nodes or neurons, are the foundation of deep learning (Goodfellow, Bengio, Courville, & Bengio, 2016). The number of layers in a network indicates its depth, and each layer handles information. An input layer, one or more hidden layers, and an output layer make up neural.

(II) **Activation Functions:** By adding non-linearity to the network, activation functions enable the network to recognize and approximate intricate correlations seen in the data. Sigmoid, hyperbolic tangent (tanh), and rectified linear unit (ReLU) are examples of common activation functions (Nair & Hinton, 2010; Nielsen, 2015).

(III) **Weights and Biases:** The neural network's weights and biases are parameters that are changed throughout training. These variables control the activation function shift and the strength of connections between neurons, respectively (Nielsen, 2015).

(IV) **Training and Optimization:** During the training phase, deep learning models pick up knowledge from data. The model modifies its parameters during training to reduce the discrepancy between expected and actual results. Gradient descent and other optimization algorithms are used to fine-tune the weights and biases (Rumelhart et al., 1986).

1.1.2 Applications of Deep Learning

(I) **Computer Vision:** Tasks including picture categorization, object detection, and facial recognition have been transformed by deep learning. Convolutional Neural Networks (CNNs) do exceptionally well when processing visual data (Krizhevsky et al., 2017).

(II) **Natural Language Processing (NLP):** In NLP, deep learning models such as Transformer topologies and Recurrent Neural Networks (RNNs) have demonstrated impressive performance in tasks including sentiment analysis, language synthesis, and machine translation (McCulloch & Pitts, 1943).

(III) **Speech Recognition:** With models like Long Short-Term Memory networks (LSTMs) and Deep Speech networks attaining state-of-the-art results, deep learning is commonly used in speech detection applications (Krizhevsky et al., 2017).

(IV) **Autonomous Systems:** With models like Long Short-Term Memory networks (LSTMs) and Deep Speech networks attaining state-of-the-art results, deep learning is commonly used in speech detection applications. Because deep learning allows machines to sense and react to their surroundings, it is essential to autonomous systems, such as robotics and self-driving cars (Rosenblatt, 1957).

Figure 2. Deep learning applications

In conclusion, deep learning is a potent machine learning paradigm that provides the capacity to automatically extract intricate patterns and representations from data. Its growing range of applications are propelling advances in artificial intelligence and technology.

1.2 Evolution of Neural Networks

Over the course of several decades, there have been many notable advances, failures, and turning points in the development of neural networks. Recent years have witnessed a resurgence in interest in and success with neural networks, which are inspired by the structure and operation of the human brain. This is partly due to advancements in computing power, data availability, and algorithmic improvements. An outline of the major stages in the development of neural networks is provided below:

(I) **Early Concepts (1940s–1950s):** With the help of scientists like Warren McCulloch and Walter Pitts, who put out a mathematical model of artificial neurons, the conceptual groundwork for neural networks was established in the 1940s and 1950s. Frank Rosenblatt first presented the perceptron, one of the early neural network architectures that could perform binary classification, in 1957 (Cortes & Vapnik, 1995; Krizhevsky et al., 2012). However, because of their linearity, perceptrons were not very good at handling complicated issues.

(II) **AI Winter (1970s–1980s):** In the 1970s and 1980s, the lack of sufficient data, computing power constraints, and difficulties in training deep networks caused interest in neural networks to decline. The discipline went through a phase called the "AI Winter" during which interest in and financing for artificial intelligence—including neural networks—dropped (Krizhevsky et al., 2012).

(III) **Backpropagation Algorithm (1986):** Geoffrey Hinton, David Rumelhart, and Ronald Williams made a huge breakthrough with the creation of the backpropagation algorithm in 1986. Deeper designs may be trained because neural networks could effectively modify their weights during training thanks to backpropagation. This development established the foundation for contemporary neural network training (Krizhevsky et al., 2012).

(IV) **The 1990s saw the rise of support vector machines:** Neural networks were eclipsed by support vector machines (SVMs) as the most widely used machine learning technique in the 1990s. Because of their easier training and superior generalization, SVMs were thought to be more useful for a wide range of applications (Hochreiter & Schmidhuber, 1997).

(V) **Deep Learning Resurgence (2000s Onward):** Thanks to developments in training methods, huge datasets, hardware, neural networks had a resurgence in popularity in the 2000s. Deep learning models started to outperform conventional machine learning techniques in a variety of tasks, especially deep neural networks with several layers.

(VI) **The 2012 ImageNet Competition:** When a deep convolutional neural network named AlexNet defeated competing techniques to win the ImageNet Large Scale Visual Recognition Challenge in 2012, it was the turning point for deep learning. The widespread use of deep learning in computer vision was sparked by this occasion (Vaswani, Shazeer, Parmar, Uszkoreit, Jones, Gomez, & Polosukhin, 2017).

(VII) **Diverse Architectures (From the 2010s onward):** Deep learning is now applicable to a wider range of tasks, such as sequential data analysis and natural language processing, thanks to the introduction of diverse architectures such as recurrent neural networks (RNNs), long short-term memory networks (LSTMs), and attention mechanisms in later years (Howard et al., 2017; Vaswani, Shazeer, Parmar, Uszkoreit, Jones, Gomez, & Polosukhin, 2017).

(VIII) **From the 2010s onward, Transfer Learning and Pre-Trained Models:** Deep learning has been used in real-world applications more quickly thanks to pre-trained models and transfer learning, which is the adaptation of models trained on one job to new ones. With this method, knowledge from robust models and massive datasets may be applied to new, specialized jobs that require less data. Neural network evolution emphasizes how dynamic and iterative science is. Neural networks are a key component in the development of artificial intelligence since research on them keeps addressing issues, improving model capabilities, and exploring new ground (Box & Muller, 1958).

2. FOUNDATIONS OF SCIENTIFIC BUSINESS ANALYTICS

2.1 Historical Overview of Business Analytics

Over time, the area of business analytics has changed, moving from simple statistical analysis to becoming a crucial part of organizational decision-making. Here is a timeline showing how business analytics have evolved throughout time:

(I) **1950s–1960s:** The Development of Fundamental Statistical Analysis Businesses used to mostly rely on simple statistical methods for analysis in the early days. This required organizing and interpreting data using straightforward techniques, with an emphasis on descriptive statistics to provide an overview of the data. Retrospective analysis and historical data were the primary foci (Power, 2007).

(II) **The advent of Decision Support Systems (DSS) in the 1970s and 1980s:** In the 1970s, Decision Support Systems (DSS) became available with the introduction of computers. To facilitate managerial decision-making, these systems incorporated data, analytical models, and user interfaces. The emphasis moved to interactive systems that gave executives the means to examine and represent data to make strategic decisions (Inmon, 1992).

(III) **Online analytical processing (OLAP) and data warehousing gained popularity in the 1990s and 2000s:** Data warehousing became a foundational idea in corporate analytics during the 1990s. Businesses began combining data from disparate sources into centralized repositories so that it could be analyzed (Turban et al., 2011). With the advent of Online Analytical Processing

(OLAP) tools, business data could be explored more dynamically and in several dimensions.

(IV) **Performance management and business intelligence (BI) in the 2000s:** Business Intelligence (BI) solutions, which aimed to give executives and decision-makers easily assimilated insights from data, became increasingly popular in the 2000s (Kimball et al., 1996). With an emphasis on key performance indicators (KPIs) and dashboards to track and improve organizational performance, performance management systems have become widely used.

(V) **Late 2000s–2010s:** Big Data and Predictive Analytics Emerge: Predictive analytics gained traction as digital data proliferated and processing capacity grew. Companies started using machine learning algorithms and statistical models to predict future trends and take preventative action. Furthermore, the emergence of Big Data technology enabled enterprises to handle and examine enormous volumes of data at previously unheard-of levels (Davenport, Harris, & Shapiro, 2010).

(VI) **2010s to Present:** AI and Advanced Analytics Integration: Artificial intelligence (AI) and machine learning are two examples of advanced analytics approaches that have been included into business analytics over the last ten years. These technologies are used by businesses to streamline operations, automate decision-making procedures and obtain deeper insights (Davenport, Harris, & Shapiro, 2010). The use of predictive and Prescriptive analytics has become crucial for businesses looking to gain a competitive advantage.

(VII) **Present Trends:** Real-Time and Cloud-Based Analytics: Cloud-based analytics solutions have been more popular in recent years since they offer scalability and accessibility to companies of all sizes. Another important component that has emerged is real-time analytics, which enables businesses to make decisions instantly based on the most recent data (Provost & Fawcett, 2013).

(VIII) **Prospects:** Ethical Analytics and Explainable AI Explainable AI is becoming more and more important as corporate analytics develops, guaranteeing that machine learning models can deliver clear and intelligible findings (Provost & Fawcett, 2013). Organizations are emphasizing the appropriate and objective application of analytics to build stakeholder trust, which highlights the growing significance of ethical considerations.

In summary, the development of business analytics across time may be seen as a progression from simple statistical analysis to the incorporation of cutting-edge technologies such as artificial intelligence. The subject is expected to develop further as companies use data to make strategic decisions, emphasizing ethical behavior, real-time insights, and cutting-edge analytics solutions.

2.2 Integration of Scientific Methods in Business Decision-Making

The application of scientific methodologies is essential for improving decision-making in today's data-driven, dynamic corporate world. Scientific techniques offer an organized and fact-based approach to comprehending challenging business problems. These techniques comprise methodical observation, experimentation, and analysis. Here is a brief explanation of how the application of scientific methodology enhances the quality and efficacy of business decision-making:

(I) **Data-Driven Decision Making:** Data collection and analysis are key components of scientific methodologies. This translates into a move towards data-driven methods in business decision-making. To glean valuable insights from massive datasets, organizations use machine learning, data analytics, and statistical techniques (Provost & Fawcett, 2013). Businesses can make more objective and well-informed decisions if they base their decisions on empirical evidence rather than just gut feeling. For data-driven decision-making in scientific corporate decision-making, consider the following succinct mathematical expression:

Data-Driven Decision Making = Data + Analysis→Informed Decisions
Within this phrase:

- **Data:** Represents the data gathered from multiple sources.
- **Analysis:** refers to the procedure used to analyze and understand the data in order to derive important insights.
- **Informed Decisions:** The ultimate goal of data-driven decision-making is to empower decision-makers with insights derived from data analysis, enabling them to make informed and optimal decisions in a scientific business context.

(II) **Testing and Experimentation of Hypotheses:** Two key components of scientific methodology are the development of hypotheses and the execution of experiments to test them. This translates into A/B testing and controlled experiments in a business setting (Clemen & Reilly, 2001). Businesses can determine what works best and base choices on empirical facts rather than conjecture by methodically testing various methods or product changes.

Predictive Analytics: Predictive analytics is another area where scientific approaches are integrated. Models that anticipate future trends and outcomes are constructed using previous data (Clemen & Reilly, 2001). Predictive analytics gives businesses the ability to foresee consumer behavior, industry trends, and possible hazards, which forms the foundation for proactive decision-making.

Predictive Analytics→Data + Models→Informed Decisions

In this expression:

- **Data:** Represents the unprocessed data that has been gathered from multiple sources.
- **Models:** Refers to machine learning and statistical models that are used to examine data and forecast future results.
- **Informed Decisions:** Predictive analytics' ultimate objective is to provide decision makers with the knowledge gained from data analysis so they may decide as best they can in a scientific business setting.

Simulation and Optimization: Businesses may make judgments in complicated, uncertain settings and optimize operations by using scientific methodologies (Clemen & Reilly, 2001). While simulation enables the investigation of various scenarios, optimization techniques aid in the discovery of the optimal solutions. This is especially helpful for strategy planning, resource allocation, and supply chain management.

Simulation + Optimization→Maximize (Profit, Efficiency, Performance)

Where:

- **Simulation:** Refers to the method of employing mathematical models to simulate real-world situations.
- **Optimization:** Involves selecting the optimal course of action from a range of possibilities, frequently by maximizing performance, efficiency, or profit.
- **Maximize:** Indicates the intention to employ the simulation and optimization approaches in tandem to get the greatest potential outcome for the business, be it maximizing profit, efficiency, or performance.

(V) Quantitative Risk Assessment: Businesses can discover and assess possible hazards objectively by using scientific methodologies to facilitate quantitative risk assessment. Organizations can prioritize and minimize risks through the application of statistical models and risk analysis tools, resulting in decision-making processes that are more resilient (Montgomery & Runger, 2014). This is a succinct mathematical phrase for scientific business decision-making that involves quantitative risk assessment:

$$\text{Risk} = \text{Probability} \times \text{Impact}$$

In this phrase:

- **Probability:** Expresses the probability that a specific risk event will occur.
- **Impact:** Refers to the extent of the effects or repercussions in the event that the risk event materializes.
- **Risk:** Evaluates the probability and impact of prospective hazards to determine the total amount of risk connected with a given choice or situation.

(VI) Culture of Continuous Learning and progress: The scientific method promotes a culture of ongoing learning and progress. This entails routinely evaluating and revising strategies in a business setting considering continuous analysis and input. Organizations can adjust to shifting market conditions and improve their decision-making process over time with this iterative method (Davenport, Harris, & Shapiro, 2010).

(VII) Interdisciplinary Collaboration: Data science, statistics, and domain-specific knowledge are just a few of the fields that frequently need to work together to integrate scientific methodologies (Wheelan, 2013). Interdisciplinary teams that contribute a variety of views and skill sets to the data analysis and interpretation processes are beneficial for business decision-making.

(VIII) Ethical Decision-Making: By encouraging accountability, transparency, and reproducibility, scientific approaches also support ethical decision-making (Taleb, 2007). Businesses can make sure that their decisions are ethically sound and based on sound processes by doing thorough analysis and documentation.

To sum up, the incorporation of scientific methodologies into commercial decision-making improves the decision-making process's objectivity and rigor. Organizations may manage complexity, reduce risks, and maximize results by utilizing data, experimentation, and analytical tools. This eventually promotes an evidence-based decision-making culture in the business sector.

3. THE RISE OF DATA SCIENCE IN SCIENTIFIC BUSINESS

3.1 Emergence of Data Science in Business Practices

The application of data science to business processes has revolutionized how companies' function, make choices, and extract value from their data. Businesses may extract useful insights from large and complicated information by using data science, an interdisciplinary area that integrates statistics, computer science, and domain experience. An outline of the main causes behind the growth of data science in the corporate world is provided below:

(I) Data Proliferation: Businesses have been producing exponentially more data in terms of volume, velocity, and variety in the last few decades. A data explosion has been caused by the introduction of the internet, social media, IoT devices, and other technologies. The methods and resources needed to use this abundance of data for strategic decision-making are provided by data science (O'Reilly, 2019).

(II) Technological Developments: The expansion of data science has been greatly aided by the development of processing power and storage capacities (O'Reilly, 2019). Organizations can efficiently process and analyze large datasets thanks to distributed computing frameworks, cloud infrastructure, and high-performing computing. Real-time insights can now be derived from complex challenges because of technological advancements.

(III) Access to Open-Source Tools: Advanced analytics are now more widely available thanks to the open-source nature of many data science tools and frameworks, including R and Python. These technologies can be used by businesses of any size to do activities such as exploratory analysis, data cleaning, and machine learning model creation without requiring large software investments (Laudon & Laudon, 2016). Here are several open-source tools with a brief introduction for data science in scientific business:

- **Python -** Python is a flexible programming language that comes with a large number of libraries for statistical analysis (NumPy, SciPy), machine learning (scikit-learn), data management (Pandas, for example), and visualization (Matplotlib, Seaborn). Python is an effective tool for a variety of data science activities because of its libraries, which enable mathematical operations, data processing, and statistical analysis.
- **R -** R is a popular statistical programming language used for data analysis, statistical modeling, and visualization in both academia and business. R is a good choice for rigorous quantitative analysis in scientific corporate decision-making because it offers a large range of statistical analysis packages, such as time series analysis, regression analysis, and hypothesis testing.

- **Jupyter Notebooks -** Users can create and share documents with live code, equations, visualizations, and narrative text using the open-source web application Jupyter Notebooks. Jupyter Notebooks facilitate the use of many programming languages, such as Python and R, allowing users to run experiments, analyze data, and record findings in an interactive and collaborative setting.
- **Apache Spark -** An open-source distributed computing platform called Apache Spark is made for handling and analyzing large amounts of data. With the help of distributed computing techniques, Apache Spark offers a single framework for large-scale data processing, machine learning, and graph analysis. This allows scientific commercial applications to manage big datasets effectively.
- **Tensor Flow -** Google created the open-source Tensor Flow machine learning framework to create and implement deep learning models. Tensor Flow is a computational graph-based neural network building and training tool that enables users to express intricate mathematical operations and optimize models for a range of scientific business applications, including time series forecasting, image recognition, and natural language processing.

These technologies give organizations access to a whole range of data science capabilities for scientific business, allowing them to use data-driven insights for creative and well-informed decision-making.

(IV) Machine Learning and Predictive Analytics: Building predictive models and automating decision-making processes is made possible for businesses by the intimate relationship between data science, machine learning, and predictive analytics (Laudon & Laudon, 2016). This holds special significance in domains such as demand forecasting, fraud detection, and consumer segmentation.

Figure 3. Fundamental series on building analytics

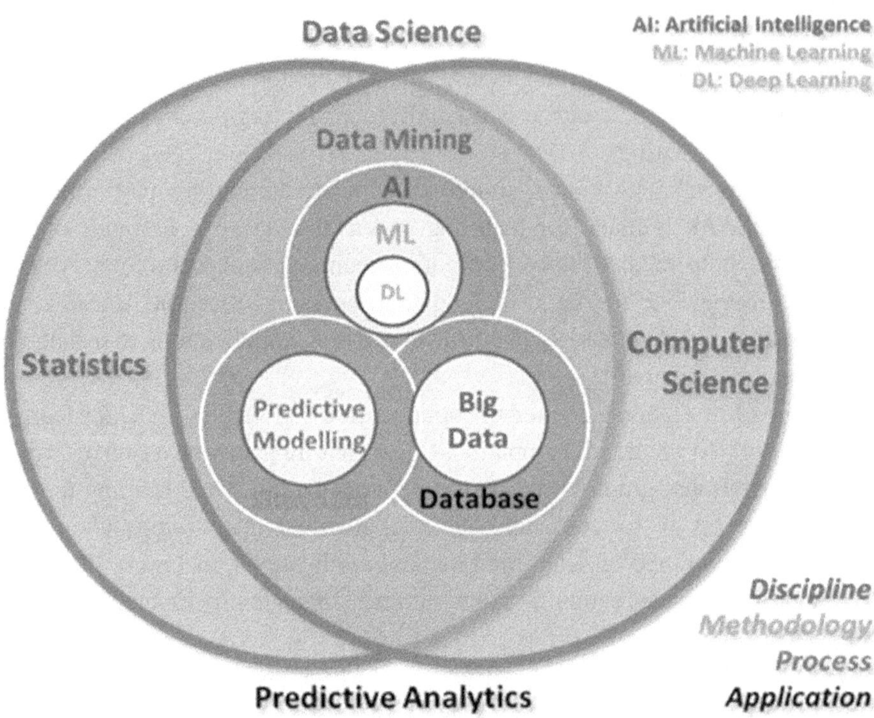

(V) Business Intelligence and Reporting: Tools for data science aid in the creation of reliable reporting and business intelligence systems. Data-driven decision-making and fast insight acquisition are made possible for stakeholders by interactive reports, dashboards, and visualizations. Organizational agility is improved by this information's accessibility (McKinsey Global Institute, 2011).

(VI) Personalization and Customer Experience: When it comes to tailoring goods and services to each unique customer's tastes and habits, data science is essential. Recommendation systems which are driven by machine learning algorithms improve user experience by offering personalized information and recommendations (McKinsey Global Institute, 2011).

(VII) Optimization and Efficiency: Companies use data science to increase operational efficiency and optimize procedures. Organizations can utilize data-driven insights to find areas for improvement, streamline processes, and cut costs in a variety of areas, including supply chain management and resource allocation (Provost & Fawcett, 2013).

Optimization $\Rightarrow$ Efficiency

(VIII) Risk Management: By offering instruments for quantitative risk assessment and modeling, data science supports efficient risk management (McKinney, 2018). By identifying possible risks, evaluating their effects, and putting mitigation plans in place, businesses can increase their overall resilience.

(IX) Cross-Functional Collaboration: The collaborative aspect of data science fosters relationships among domain experts, business stakeholders, and data scientists (McKinney, 2018). This partnership guarantees that data science solutions are pertinent to industry concerns and in line with corporate objectives.

(X) Strategic Decision-Making: The use of data science in strategic decision-making processes has grown in importance. Businesses can create strategies that stimulate development, innovation, and competitive advantage by evaluating past data, seeing patterns, and forecasting the future (James, Witten, Hastie, & Tibshirani, 2013).

For Example - Predictive modeling is a tool used by businesses to estimate product demand. It carefully modifies its production plans and inventory levels in accordance with the forecasts in order to reduce holding costs and guarantee adequate stock availability. This results in the inventory turnover rate being optimized, which is represented mathematically as follows:

Inventory Turnover Rate = Cost of Goods sold / Average Inventory

Through proactive inventory turnover management, the organization optimizes profitability and improves operational efficiency.

To sum up, the introduction of data science into business processes signifies a paradigm change in the way companies use data to inform decisions. Data science is predicted to play a more significant role in influencing the future of numerous industries as companies continue to see the potential of data as a strategic asset.

3.2 The Interplay Between Data Science and Scientific Business Analytics

The combination of data science and scientific business analytics creates a potent synergy that improves an organization's ability to extract meaningful insights from data (Hastie, Tibshirani, & Friedman, 2009). Advanced statistical approaches, machine learning algorithms, and computational methodologies are utilized in data science to extract patterns and predictions from complicated and large-scale datasets. Contrarily, scientific business analytics places a strong emphasis on using experimentation and thorough analysis to understand business difficulties in a methodical and evidence-based manner. A comprehensive approach to decision-making is made possible by the combination of various disciplines (Hastie, Tibshirani, & Friedman, 2009). Extensive data processing and analysis can be facilitated by data science, and scientific business analytics guarantees a systematic approach, hypothesis testing, and experimental validation. When combined, they allow organizations to find hidden patterns and trends and validate hypotheses through empirical testing, resulting in a more rigorous and trustworthy decision-making process that is in line with scientific principles and data-driven insights. This cooperative interaction makes tackling difficult business difficulties more knowledgeable, effective, and resilient. The foundation of deep learning is neural networks, which are computer architectures modeled after the structure of the human brain (Chollet, 2017). Think of them as layers of networked nodes, or neurons. An input layer, one or more hidden layers, and an output layer make up a simple feedforward neural network. Every node has a bias, represented as b, and every connection between nodes has a weight, represented as W. Activation functions, usually represented as g, work their magic by giving the system non-linearity. The activation function transforms the weighted sum of a neuron's inputs and biases, z=Input, a=g(z), to calculate each neuron's activation.

Until the desired result is obtained, this process is repeated through the layers. Visualization is helpful. Imagine nodes with weights at each layer, connected by lines, making a network. Weights and biases are adjusted during training to reduce the discrepancy between expected and actual outputs. Neural networks can handle challenging tasks like image identification and natural language processing because of this iterative learning process that uses methods like backpropagation (Davenport & Harris, 2007).

4. UNDERSTANDING NEURAL NETWORK ARCHITECTURES

4.1 Types of Neural Network Architectures

There are several varieties of neural network architectures, each intended to handle data structures and problem categories (Goodfellow, Bengio, Courville, & Bengio, 2016). Here is a detailed look at a few well-known types:

(I) Feedforward Neural Networks (FNN):

Description - Information goes from input to output through layers of nodes in the simplest architecture known as a feedforward neural network (FNN). No cycles or feedback loops exist.

Figure 4. Feedforward neural networks (FNN)

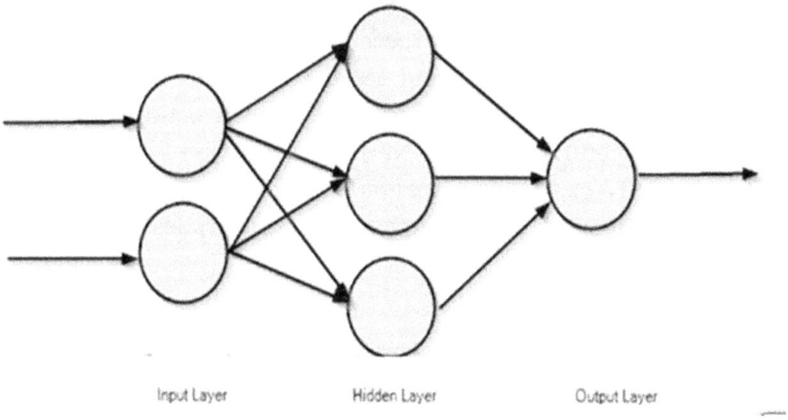

Applications - Frequently utilized for basic tasks such as classification and regression.

(II) Radial Basis Function Networks (RBFN):

Description - The input, hidden, and output layers make up RBFNs. The hidden layer can express complicated relationships since it uses radial basis functions as activation functions. Useful for applications involving pattern recognition and function approximation.

Figure 5. Radial basis function networks (RBFN)

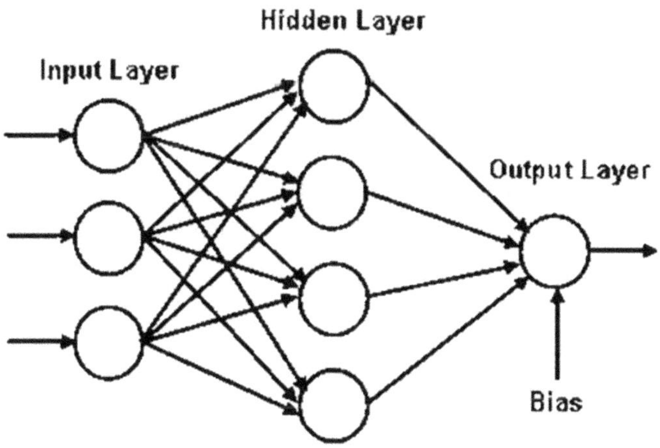

Applications - Because of its versatility, RBFNs are used in time series prediction in engineering, finance, and meteorology. They perform exceptionally well in jobs involving pattern recognition, such as speech and picture recognition; they support control systems in the identification and adaptive control of systems; and they find anomalies in data streams for cybersecurity and fraud detection.

(III) Recurrent Neural Networks (RNN):

Description: RNNs can store information and display temporal dynamics because, in contrast to FNNs, they feature connections that create cycles. appropriate for data that is consecutive.

Figure 6. Recurrent neural networks (RNN)

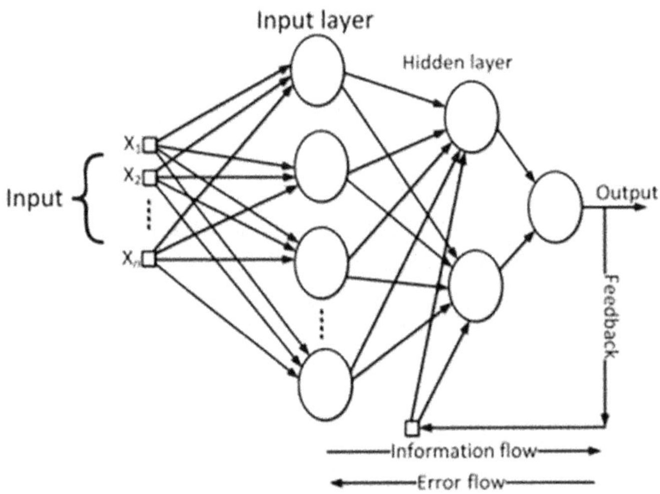

Applications - Superior for time-series analysis, speech recognition, and natural language processing.

(IV) Long Short-Term Memory Networks (LSTM):

Description: LSTMs are a specific kind of RNN that solves the vanishing gradient issue, enabling them to recognize and retain long-term dependencies in sequential data.

Figure 7. Long short-term memory networks (LSTM)

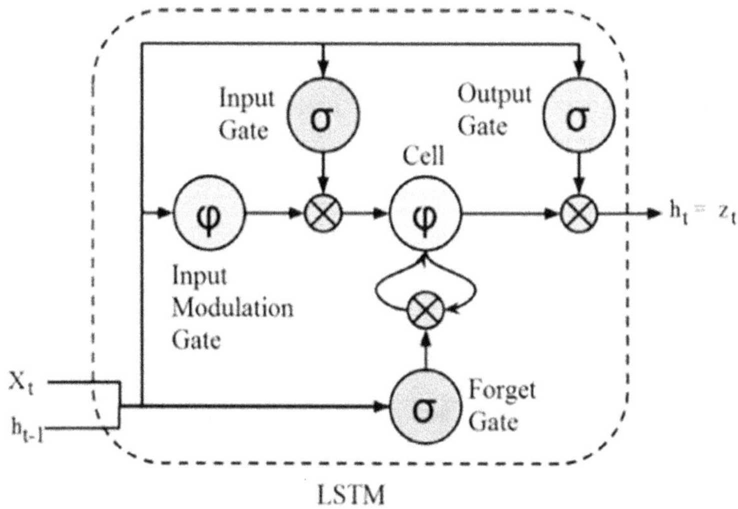

Uses: utilized extensively in context- and memory-sensitive applications like speech recognition and language modeling.

(V) Convolutional Neural Networks (CNN):

Description - CNNs use convolutional layers to find patterns in structured grid data, such as photographs. Convolutional, pooling, and fully linked layers are usually included.

Figure 8. Convolutional neural networks (CNN)

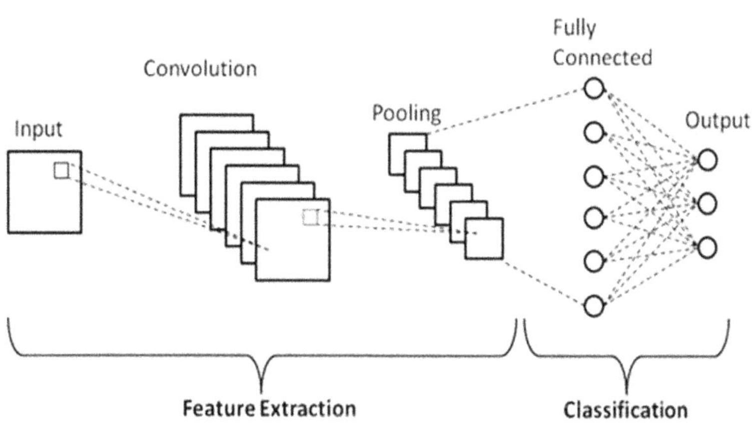

Applications: Cutting edge facial recognition, object identification, and image and video processing.

(VI) Generative Adversarial Networks (GAN):

Description - GANs are made up of two networks that are competing to learn: a discriminator and a generator. Realistic synthetic data is produced by the generator to trick the discriminator.

Figure 9. Generative adversarial networks (GAN)

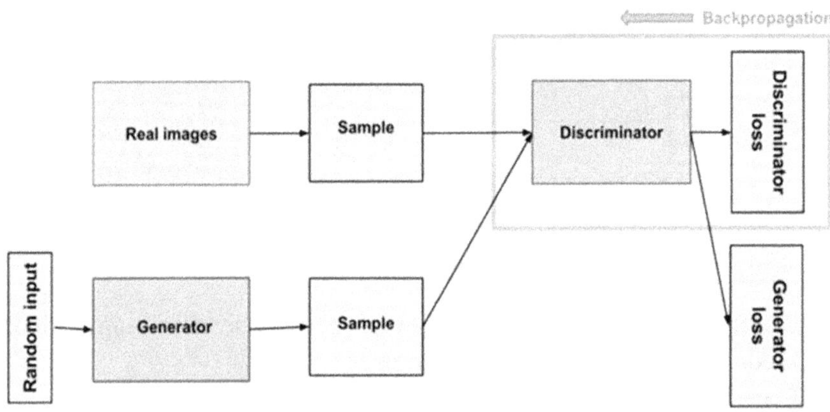

Uses: Data augmentation, style transfer, and image production.

(VII) Auto encoders:

Description - Auto encoders, which consist of an encoder and a decoder, are employed in unsupervised learning. Their goal is to recover the input data while acquiring effective representations.

Figure 10. Everything about auto encoders

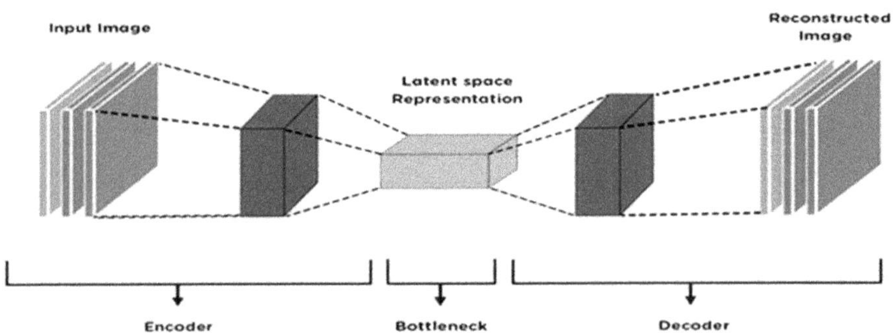

Uses - feature learning, anomaly detection, and dimensionality reduction.

(VIII) Self-Organizing Maps (SOM):

Description - SOMs are unsupervised learning networks that project high-dimensional data onto a lower-dimensional grid. Neurons in the grid compete for data representation.

Figure 11. Self-organizing maps (SOM)

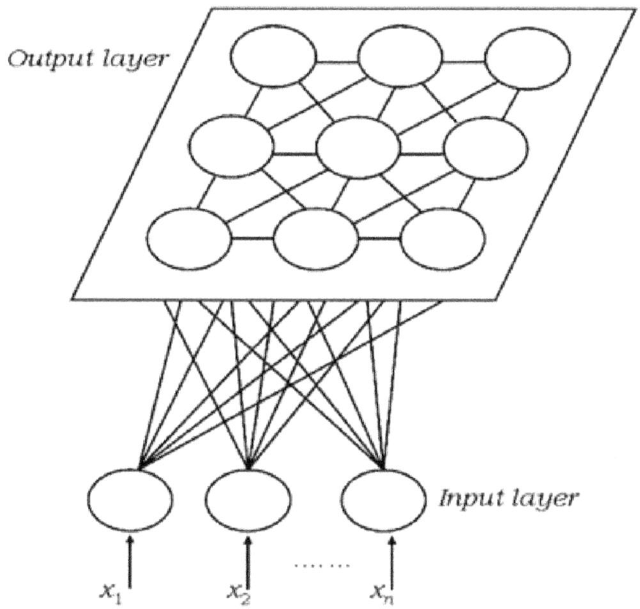

Applications - Clustering, data visualization, and exploratory data analysis.

(IX) Hopfield Networks:

Description - Hopfield networks are employed in associative memory to store and recover patterns in response to noisy or incomplete input. A completely connected network is formed by all the nodes.

Figure 12. Hopfield networks

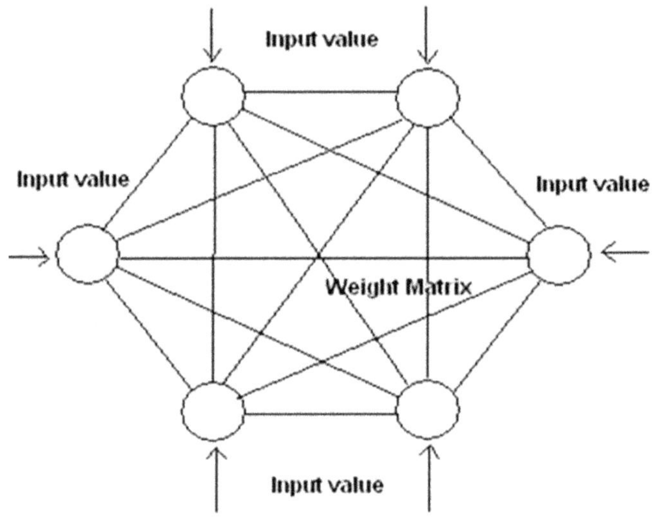

Uses - Pattern recognition, optimization issues, and content-addressable memory.

(X) Transformers:

Description - Transformers were first introduced for sequence-to-sequence tasks. They model context and relationships effectively by using self-attention processes to weigh different elements of the input sequence differently.

Figure 13. Transformers

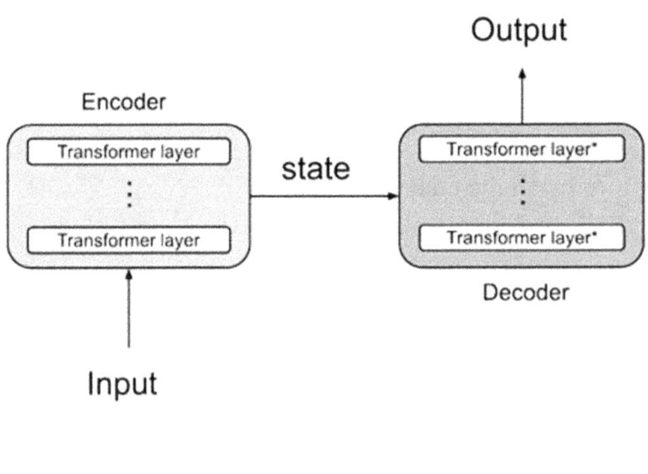

Applications - Prominent in tasks related to natural language processing, such as sentiment analysis, text summarization, and language translation. The variety and adaptability of neural networks to different data kinds and problem areas are reflected in these architectures. Hybrid architectures and innovative network topologies are constantly appearing as the discipline develops, greatly enhancing neural networks and further capacity to solve challenging problems.

5. DEEP LEARNING TECHNIQUES FOR SCIENTIFIC BUSINESS ANALYTICS

5.1 Supervised Learning in Business Applications

A key machine learning paradigm known as supervised learning has emerged as a vital tool for a wide range of corporate applications (Goodfellow, Bengio, Courville, & Bengio, 2016). This method involves teaching algorithms on labeled training data so they can predict or make judgments based on input features and the labels that correspond to those features in the output. Supervised learning has a wide-ranging and significant impact on business. It facilitates demand forecasting, individualized marketing campaigns, and consumer segmentation in sales and marketing, optimizing tactics for higher levels of customer involvement. Supervised learning-powered categorization models in customer service improve overall productivity by classifying and prioritizing requests, hence streamlining support operations. Credit scoring models, fraud detection algorithms, and investment forecasts are useful tools in finance that support risk management and well- informed decision-making. Supervised learning aids in talent recruiting, employee performance forecasting, retention tactics, and workforce management optimization in human resources. Supervised learning is used in healthcare to diagnose diseases, evaluate patient risks, and plan treatments, all of which lead to more individualized and efficient healthcare solutions. Forecasting models help supply chain management by lowering expenses, increasing inventory levels, and optimizing them. Notwithstanding its effectiveness, obstacles including overfitting and the requirement for large amounts of labeled data must be overcome (Cao, 2019). But as technology develops, supervised learning in the workplace appears to have a bright future. Deep learning and ensemble approaches, for example, promise to provide even more precise and adaptable answers to challenging problems (Cao, 2019).

A brief mathematical representation of supervised learning in science-related commercial applications is as follows:

$$\text{Model}(X) = f(X; \Theta)$$

In this expression:

- Based on input features X, the trained model's prediction or output is represented by the variable Model(X).
- $f(X; \Theta)$ denotes the function learned by the model, parameterized by Θ, which captures the relationship between input features and target variables.

5.2 Unsupervised Learning for Scientific Insights

A key component of machine learning, unsupervised learning has become a valuable tool for scientists by enabling them to draw conclusions from large, unlabeled datasets and draw conclusions that are useful (Montgomery et al., 2008). This paradigm offers a flexible method for revealing hidden knowledge by using algorithms to search through and find patterns, structures, and relationships within data. Clustering algorithms are a popular way that unsupervised learning is applied. Similar data points are grouped together via algorithms like K-Means or hierarchical clustering, which uncover underlying structures in datasets (Goodfellow, Bengio, Courville, & Bengio, 2016). This method, for example, helps uncover unique gene expression patterns in genomics, providing insight into putative functional links. Simplifying complex datasets is a critical function of dimensionality reduction techniques like Principal Component Analysis (PCA) and t-Distributed Stochastic Neighbor Embedding (t-SNE) (James, Witten, Hastie, & Tibshirani, 2013). Researchers can see intricate linkages by using these strategies to convert high-dimensional data into more comprehensible forms. For example, dimensionality reduction in neuroscience makes complex neural datasets easier to comprehend and provide insights into patterns of brain activity. Another aspect of unsupervised learning that is very useful in science is anomaly detection. Finding outliers in datasets can reveal new phenomena or indicate mistakes. Anomaly detection aids in the identification of anomalies in sensor data for environmental monitoring, which may point to anomalous environmental phenomena (Hastie, Tibshirani, & Friedman, 2009). Topic modeling in the context of textual data is aided by unsupervised learning methods such as Latent Dirichlet Allocation (LDA). This makes it possible for academics to identify recurring themes in large collections of scientific material. LDA helps in the field of bioinformatics to classify and comprehend the diverse range of study subjects that are commonly found in scholarly articles. Self-Organizing Maps (SOMs) offer an original method for displaying intricate data (Hastie, Tibshirani, & Friedman, 2009). SOMs provide a visually intuitive way to analyze complex datasets by arranging data into a low-dimensional grid while maintaining topological linkages. SOMs are used by scientists studying climate science to comprehend the spatial distribution of climate variables, which helps them identify patterns and anomalies in the climate

(Hastie, Tibshirani, & Friedman, 2009). Scientific insights are greatly enhanced by image analysis and pattern identification, which are fueled by unsupervised learning techniques like auto encoders or K-Means clustering. For example, in medical imaging, these methods support the diagnosis and planning of treatments by assisting in the identification and classification of structures within diagnostic pictures. Association rule mining is a technique used to find patterns and hidden relationships in datasets. This method aids in the identification of co-occurring species or environmental elements in ecological investigations, offering insights into intricate ecological interactions. When unsupervised and reinforcement learning are combined, adaptive systems with constant feedback-based behavior optimization are produced. This combination directs autonomous systems in modifying experimental parameters in materials research, speeding up the search for new materials with desired characteristics.

For scientific insights, consider the following brief mathematical expression of unsupervised learning:

$$\text{Cluster}(X) = \text{f}(X)$$

In this expression:

- The gathering or clustering of data items X into meaningful clusters is represented by the function Cluster(X).
- The function that recognizes the underlying structure or patterns in the data without the need for target variables to be labeled is represented by the symbol f(X).

To sum up, unsupervised learning is essential to the search for new scientific understandings. Because of its wide range of applications in several fields, researchers may more easily explore the complexities of large, complicated datasets, revealing links and patterns that deepen our understanding of the natural world. Unsupervised learning is expected to play a bigger part in scientific inquiry as technology develops, opening new fields for investigation and learning.

5.3 Reinforcement Learning for Decision Optimization

A dynamic subset of machine learning called reinforcement learning allows systems to interact with their surroundings to learn optimal behaviors, which provides a strong foundation for decision optimization (Bishop, 2006). The way people learn by making mistakes and getting feedback in the form of incentives or punishments served as the model for this paradigm. Reinforcement learning becomes a transformative tool in decision optimization, enabling algorithms to adjust and improve their tactics over time. The agent-environment interaction is the core idea of reinforcement learning. The agent acts in a way that produces results by making decisions within a predetermined context. The environment directs the agent toward maximizing cumulative benefits over an extended period by providing feedback in the form of rewards or punishments based on the agent's activities. Reinforcement learning is particularly useful in decision optimization when it is difficult to collect labeled data or explicit instructions. Rather, the algorithm gains knowledge by experimenting with different actions and evaluating the results, then modifying its decision-making processes in response to the input it receives. This flexibility is especially useful in situations where decisions are complicated and dynamic. Real-time navigation and decision-making by agents in autonomous systems is a well-known use of reinforcement learning in decision optimization. For example, self-driving cars optimize decision-making for safe and efficient travel by utilizing reinforcement learning to adjust their driving behavior depending on continuously changing traffic conditions. Reinforcement learning is used in business applications to optimize pricing, marketing, and resource allocation techniques. By continuously modifying their tactics in response to feedback from the changing business environment, algorithms are trained to make judgments that result in increased returns on investment, customer satisfaction, or operational efficiency. The following is a brief mathematical representation of decision optimization using reinforcement learning:

$$\text{Maximize (Reward)} = \text{f}\,(S, A)$$

In this expression:

- To maximize the cumulative reward over time, use the function Maximize(Reward).
- f (S, A) denotes the function that maps states (S) and actions (A) to the expected cumulative reward.

Furthermore, reinforcement learning supports individualized treatment regimens in the medical field. Patient reactions are used to optimize treatment plans and adaptive medication dosages, which results in more efficient and patient-centered healthcare decisions. Notwithstanding its effectiveness, there are drawbacks to reinforcement learning, including the exploration-exploitation trade-off and the requirement for effective incentive systems. Scientists are always improving algorithms to find a way to combine discovering new possibilities with utilizing tried and true winning tactics. Reinforcement learning is a potential method for maximizing choices in a range of domains, particularly as decision-making grows more complex in our linked world. The ability of reinforcement learning to learn from experience and modify techniques places it as a vital actor in the pursuit of intelligent decision optimization, whether in the fields of robotics, finance, or healthcare (Bishop, 2006).

6. DATA PREPROCESSING AND FEATURE ENGINEERING IN SCIENTIFIC BUSINESS ANALYTICS

6.1 Importance of Quality Data in Scientific Business

It is impossible to exaggerate the significance of high-quality data in scientific business, since it provides the foundation for sound judgment, creativity, and long-term expansion (Sutton & Barto, 2018). The validity of research findings and strategic objectives are directly impacted by the dependability and quality of data in the field of scientific business, where precision and accuracy are crucial. A decision-making process that is based on reliable analyses and insights is enhanced using high-quality data. Strong data quality lowers the possibility of errors, improves operational efficiency, and encourages the creation of precise predictive models. Furthermore, in scientific research and development, the validity of experiments, the reproducibility of results, and the general growth of knowledge are all directly impacted by the quality of data. The integrity and quality of the underlying data are fundamental factors that determine the success and credibility of the firm in an era where data-driven insights direct the path of scientific business efforts (Sutton & Barto, 2018).

6.2 Feature Engineering for Enhanced Predictive Modeling

To improve the performance of predictive models, feature engineering—a critical stage in the machine learning pipeline—involves creating and selecting pertinent features from raw data (Wang & Strong, 1996). The process of converting input variables into a format that better captures the underlying patterns and complies with the needs of the selected model is a fine art. Creating new features, scaling, normalizing, and handling missing values are all part of effective feature engineering, which extends beyond simple data processing. Feature engineering helps to create prediction models that are more reliable, accurate, and understandable by choosing or developing features that include the most relevant information for the task at hand. Using methods like one-hot encoding or label encoding to convert categorical data into numerical representations is a standard practice in feature engineering. This guarantees that categorical data may be interpreted and utilized by machine learning algorithms in an efficient manner. Furthermore, models can learn more intricate patterns by capturing complex interactions between variables through the creation of interaction terms or polynomial features. To ensure that all variables contribute equally to the model and prevent features with bigger scales from dominating, features might be normalized or scaled to a specified range. Another crucial component is managing missing data using imputation techniques, which ensures the stability of the model and prevents the loss of important information. Adding complexity is just one aspect of feature engineering; another is dimensionality reduction. By locating and keeping the most informative characteristics, methods like Principal Component Analysis (PCA) or feature selection algorithms aid in simplifying the model without sacrificing its predictive ability.

For Example: By designing features that capture the physical characteristics of amino acids, higher-order sequence patterns like motifs or domains, and evolutionary information from different sequence alignments, we can improve the predictive modeling of protein activities in bioinformatics. These cutting-edge characteristics improve the model's prediction ability, facilitating precise classification and offering insightful knowledge about protein biology for use in scientific studies and applications.

Essentially, feature engineering acts as a link between the effectiveness of a prediction model and the raw data. By utilizing a carefully designed set of features, one may unleash the data's latent potential and empower machine learning models to derive significant insights and produce precise predictions. Feature engineering is an iterative and creative process that allows data scientists and machine learning practitioners to improve their predictive models, which in turn leads to more significant and successful data-driven decision-making (Wang & Strong, 1996).

7. CASE STUDIES: APPLICATIONS OF DEEP LEARNING IN SCIENTIFIC BUSINESS

7.1 Predictive Modeling for Scientific Business Forecasting

A key component of scientific business forecasting, predictive modeling provides a potent process for gleaning important insights from data to guide strategic choices (Guyon & Elisseeff, 2003). Predictive modeling uses statistical and machine learning approaches to examine historical data, find patterns, and project future trends in the field of scientific business, where accuracy is critical. Predictive models help organizations generate data-driven forecasts, optimize workflows, and allocate resources efficiently by utilizing the richness of knowledge buried in historical data. Predictive modeling is essential to scientific research and development because it helps to anticipate experimental results, optimize research protocols, and direct decision-making in fields including bioinformatics, materials science, and drug discovery. Predicting how complicated systems will behave or if an experiment will be successful improves efficiency, lowers costs, and quickens the rate of scientific advancement. Predictive modeling helps with illness risk assessment, therapy optimization, and patient outcome prediction in the healthcare industry. Predictive models support customized medicine by assessing patient data, such as demographics, medical histories, and results of diagnostic tests. This allows medical personnel to customize interventions based on unique patient features. Predictive modeling aids in business forecasting in the financial sector by identifying investment risks, projecting market trends and streamlining portfolio management. Algorithms can help firms make informed decisions in a dynamic and constantly changing market environment by analyzing previous financial data to find patterns and signals. Predictive modeling also helps with demand forecasting, inventory optimization, and production planning in manufacturing and supply chain management. Organizations can forecast future demand, optimize production procedures and reduce waste by examining past sales data and market patterns. Here's a mathematical expression with a short description about predictive modeling for scientific business forecasting:

In scientific business forecasting, the following is a basic expression for predictive modeling:

Predicted Outcome = Predictive Model (Input Features)

This term describes the process of estimating future outcomes from input features using a predictive model. The model helps with forecasting and decision-making in scientific business situations by using patterns in the features and previous data to generate predictions. The quality of the data, the selection of features, and the selection of suitable algorithms are critical to the effectiveness of predictive modeling in scientific business forecasting. Predictive modeling's iterative process enables constant improvement, guaranteeing that models adjust to shifting scientific paradigms and changing business realities.

To sum up, predictive modeling is essential to scientific business forecasting since it provides a methodical, data-driven way to predict future trends and results (Guyon & Elisseeff, 2003). Predictive modeling is set to become increasingly prevalent in scientific business as data becomes more readily available and technology progresses. This will enable decision-makers to be more informed and flexible as they pursue both commercial and scientific innovation.

7.2 Customer Segmentation Using Neural Networks

Neural network-based consumer segmentation is an advanced strategy that uses artificial intelligence to classify customers according to shared traits and behaviors (James, Witten, Hastie, & Tibshirani, 2013). Neural networks are a useful tool for identifying tiny differences between various customer profiles because of their capacity to capture intricate patterns and relationships in data. Neural networks automatically recognize different client segments by analyzing a wide range of input parameters, including demographic data, purchase history, and online behavior. Segmentation makes it easier to implement customized client experiences, personalized recommendations, and targeted marketing campaigns. Neural networks' adaptive nature guarantees the dynamic evolution of client segments, allowing firms to react to shifting consumer trends and preferences. To put it simply, using neural networks to segment customers improves the accuracy and effectiveness of marketing campaigns, strengthening client relationships and propelling corporate success (James, Witten, Hastie, & Tibshirani, 2013). Here is a brief explanation of consumer segmentation using neural networks along with a mathematical expression:

$$\text{Cluster}\ (X) = \arg\max_j\ (\sigma(\mathrm{w}_j \cdot \mathrm{x} + b_j))$$

A neural network architecture for consumer segmentation is represented by this equation, where, Cluster (X) denotes the predicted cluster for input features X. The neural network consists of neurons corresponding to different clusters, each with its own weights (w_j) and bias (b_j). The activation function σ introduces non-linearity, and the arg $\max_j$ operator selects the cluster with the highest activation as the predicted segment for the input data X.

7.3 Anomaly Detection in Scientific Data

Finding occurrences or trends in scientific data that drastically depart from the norm is known as anomaly detection, and it is a crucial component of data analysis (Bishop, 1995). Identifying anomalies is essential for maintaining the integrity of experimental results and spotting potential inconsistencies in intricate datasets in scientific research, where precision and accuracy are critical. Anomaly detection is accomplished using a variety of approaches, from sophisticated machine learning algorithms to statistical procedures. Anomalies in scientific studies might be a sign of unanticipated events, equipment faults, or measurement errors that need more research. Data distributions and patterns are examined by anomaly detection techniques to pinpoint data points that substantially depart from the predicted behavior. This procedure is especially important in science domains like physics, chemistry, and biology, where anomalies can reveal experimental setup problems or lead to novel findings. An expanding number of machine learning algorithms are being used for anomaly identification in scientific data, such as density-based techniques, classification, and clustering. These algorithms identify trends in past data and highlight instances of anomalous behavior. Anomalous patterns in sensor data, for instance, might be found using anomaly detection algorithms in environmental monitoring, suggesting possible equipment problems or disturbances in the environment.

Anomaly detection is also essential for quality control procedures, guaranteeing that produced goods fulfill strict requirements. Anomalies in material qualities or production processes can have far-reaching effects in domains such as materials science and engineering. Maintaining the quality and dependability of the final product depends on identifying and correcting these irregularities early in the process. The significance of anomaly identification increases with the amount and complexity of scientific datasets. Researchers and scientists can preserve the validity of their findings, improve experimental designs, and guarantee the accuracy of scientific results by identifying outliers and anomalies (Bishop, 1995). Additionally, it advances the more general objective of data-driven decision-making in scientific pursuits by promoting a more precise and thorough comprehension of the natural world.

Figure 14. Anomaly detection in data science

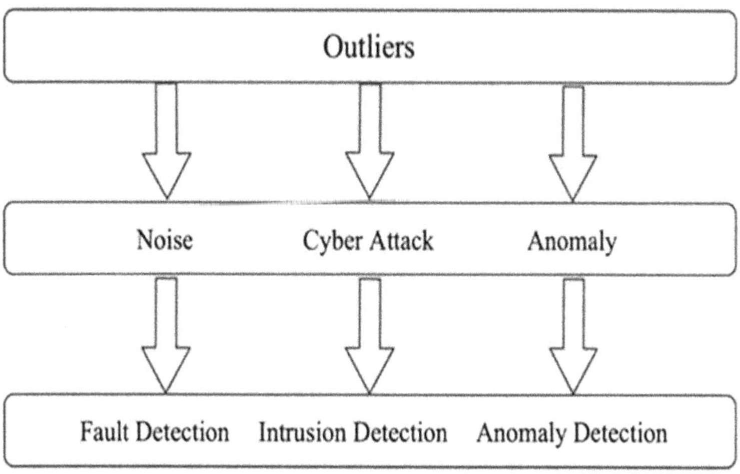

8. CHALLENGES AND SOLUTIONS IN IMPLEMENTING NEURAL NETWORKS IN SCIENTIFIC BUSINESS

8.1 Overcoming Data Challenges

In the current era, where organizations and researchers increasingly rely on data-driven insights, overcoming data difficulties is an important undertaking (Chandola et al., 2009). The main obstacles are the sheer amount and variety of data, quality control, and guaranteeing data security and privacy. Organizations invest in cutting-edge data management systems, use effective preprocessing and cleaning methods and put data governance frameworks in place to address these issues. Utilizing artificial intelligence and machine learning algorithms, significant patterns can be extracted from massive information, transforming data difficulties into chances for well-informed decision-making (Chandola et al., 2009). Establishing a data-centric culture in companies also raises awareness of the value of high-quality data and fosters cross-team cooperation to tackle data-related problems. The process of overcoming data difficulties is a continuous and revolutionary one, as new technologies such as edge computing and federated learning emerge and further revolutionize how we handle and get value from data.

8.2 Ethical Considerations in Scientific Business Analytics

The responsible and transparent use of data for decision-making in scientific business analytics is contingent upon ethical issues (Manyika et al., 2011). Organizations are using advanced analytics tools more and more, which raises ethical questions about permission, privacy, prejudice, and the exploitation of sensitive data. It's critical to strike a balance between protecting individual rights and using statistics to draw conclusions. To safeguard individual identities, it entails putting strong data governance frameworks into place, getting informed consent for data gathering, and making sure data anonymization is maintained. Furthermore, it's critical to overcome biases in algorithms and models to prevent the perpetuation of inequality. To promote trust and responsible innovation in the data-driven business landscape, ethical considerations in scientific business analytics necessitate constant awareness, adherence to regulatory standards, and a commitment to upholding the principles of fairness, accountability, and transparency (Manyika et al., 2011).

9. INTEGRATION OF DEEP LEARNING IN SCIENTIFIC RESEARCH AND DEVELOPMENT

9.1 Collaborations Between Research and Business

Research and business collaborations are a mutually beneficial connection that promotes creativity, propels technological progress, and expedites the conversion of research outcomes into practical applications (Floridi & Taddeo, 2016). These collaborations create a dynamic ecosystem that is advantageous to both domains by fusing the theoretical rigor of academic research with the real-world requirements and resources of enterprises. Working together with businesses gives scientists access to financing opportunities, industry knowledge, and real-world data when conducting scientific research. This enhances the study procedure and guarantees that scholarly inquiries are based on real-world implementations and industry significance. Conversely, companies can access state-of-the-art information, innovative technologies, and a workforce of highly qualified researchers, which helps them to become leaders in innovation. Joint research endeavors, technology transfer initiatives, and shared facilities are common manifestations of collaborative activities. These initiatives facilitate the free exchange of concepts, knowledge, and resources, creating an atmosphere in which theoretical discoveries are used in real-world situations. Research-business cooperation, for example, has been essential to developments in a wide range of sectors, including information technology, materials science, and healthcare. Collaborations also act as a link for the commercialization of research findings. Enterprises could utilize scholarly findings to create novel goods, offerings, or remedies that fulfill consumer needs. Researchers simultaneously have the chance to witness firsthand how their work affects society, fostering both social advancement and economic expansion. But productive partnerships require clear communication, a common aim, and an awareness of each other's limitations and objectives. It is essential to have explicit agreements on publication rights, data sharing, and intellectual property to create a framework that works for everyone. Through funding initiatives and partnership-building programs, government organizations, business associations, and academic institutions frequently play a facilitating role in creating such relationships (Floridi & Taddeo, 2016).

In summary, partnerships between industry and research produce a potent synergy that spurs innovation and advances society. Through the establishment of links between scholarly research and practical implementations, these collaborations foster an active and mutually advantageous sharing of resources, knowledge, and skills.

9.2 Accelerating Innovation Through Deep Learning

Deep learning's ability to accelerate innovation is a revolutionary step forward for artificial intelligence, changing how researchers and companies tackle challenging issues. Neural networks with numerous layers that can automatically learn complex characteristics from data are the hallmark of deep learning, a type of machine learning that makes it possible to extract high-level representations and patterns (Etzkowitz & Leydesdorff, 1997). This technology has demonstrated its ability to stimulate innovation in a multitude of fields. One significant area of application is image and speech recognition, where deep learning models have produced previously unheard-of levels of accuracy. This has opened doors for systems like voice-activated assistants, driverless cars, and facial identification. Deep learning helps with disease diagnosis, drug discovery, and medical image analysis in the healthcare industry. This quickens research and enhances patient outcomes. Deep learning is very good in business analytics at supply chain optimization, marketing strategy personalization, and customer behavior prediction. Organizations may obtain meaningful insights thanks to their capacity to manage enormous volumes of data and identify complex patterns. This promotes innovation in consumer interaction and product creation as well as improved decision-making processes (Etzkowitz & Leydesdorff, 1997). This is how Accelerating Innovation through Deep Learning might be expressed mathematically:

Innovation = $f(DL)$

In this expression:

- Innovation is a measure of the degree or pace of innovation attained.
- The function or influence of deep learning (DL) approaches on speeding up innovation is shown by the symbol f(DL).

This statement demonstrates how deep learning methods and innovation acceleration are related. Because deep learning techniques enable enhanced capabilities in domains like computer vision, natural language processing, and autonomous systems, they have the potential to transform a number of sectors. The way that the adoption and implementation of deep learning approaches enhance innovation in research, product development, and problem-solving across several disciplines is captured by the function f(DL).

Deep learning has transformed the field of natural language processing (NLP), resulting in advances in sentiment analysis, language translation, and chatbot interactions. This has significant ramifications for international communication, removing linguistic obstacles and expediting the sharing of information. Furthermore, deep learning has been essential to scientific study since it has made it possible to analyze complicated datasets, simulations, and experiments (Silver et al., 2017). Its uses accelerate advances across a wide range of scientific fields, from material property prediction to biological system dynamics understanding. Deep learning's effectiveness is contingent upon the availability of substantial labeled datasets and computational resources, and ethical issues pertaining to bias and transparency continue to be major problems. To overcome these obstacles and fully realize deep learning's promise for innovation promotion, further research and cooperation between academic institutions, business partners, and policymakers are needed. To put it simply, deep learning is accelerating innovation at a rate that is altering industries, advancing technology, and ushering in a time where artificial intelligence is being integrated into more and more facets of our lives with more impact (Etzkowitz & Leydesdorff, 1997). Deep learning's ability to provide fresh answers to challenging issues is still a major factor pushing advancement in the area.

10. FUTURE TRENDS AND INNOVATIONS IN SCIENTIFIC BUSINESS ANALYTICS

10.1 Advances in Deep Learning Technologies

Deep learning's ability to accelerate innovation is a revolutionary step forward for artificial intelligence, changing how researchers and companies tackle challenging issues. Neural networks with numerous layers that can automatically learn complex characteristics from data are the hallmark of deep learning, a type of machine learning that makes it possible to extract high-level representations and patterns (Silver et al., 2016). This technology has demonstrated its ability to stimulate innovation in a multitude of fields. One significant area of application is image and speech recognition, where deep learning models have produced previously unheard-of levels of accuracy. This has opened doors for systems like voice-activated assistants, driverless cars, and facial identification. Deep learning helps with disease diagnosis, drug discovery, and medical image analysis in the healthcare industry. This quickens research and enhances patient outcomes. Deep learning is very good in business analytics at supply chain optimization, marketing strategy personalization, and customer behavior prediction. Organizations may obtain meaningful insights thanks to its capacity to manage enormous volumes of data and identify complex patterns. This promotes innovation in consumer interaction and product creation as well as improved decision-making processes.

- Computer vision has undergone a revolution thanks to deep learning methods, which have made it possible to do amazing feats like object detection, picture recognition, and facial recognition with previously unheard-of accuracy and speed.
- Deep learning techniques have made major strides in natural language processing, enabling more human-like interactions with computers and improving cross-cultural communication in areas like machine translation, sentiment analysis, and language synthesis.

Deep learning has transformed the field of natural language processing (NLP), resulting in advances in sentiment analysis, language translation, and chatbot interactions. This has significant ramifications for international communication, removing linguistic obstacles and expediting the sharing of information. Furthermore, deep learning has been essential to scientific study since it has made it possible to analyze complicated datasets, simulations, and experiments. Its uses accelerate advances across a wide range of scientific fields, from material property prediction to biological system dynamics understanding. Deep learning's effectiveness is contingent upon the availability of substantial labeled datasets and computational resources, and ethical issues pertaining to bias and transparency continue to be major problems. To overcome these obstacles and fully realize deep learning's promise for innovation promotion, further research and cooperation between academic institutions, business partners, and policymakers are needed (Silver et al., 2016). To put it simply, deep learning is accelerating innovation at a rate that is altering industries, advancing technology, and ushering in a time where artificial intelligence is being integrated into more and more facets of our lives with more impact. Deep learning's ability to provide fresh answers to challenging issues is still a major factor pushing advancement in the area.

10.2 The Role of Artificial Intelligence in Shaping the Future of Scientific Business

Artificial intelligence (AI) is going to play a revolutionary role in the future of scientific business, bringing in a new era of efficiency, creativity, and data-driven decision-making. Artificial intelligence (AI) technologies, in machine learning and deep learning, have the potential to completely transform several scientific commercial operations and research projects (Chen et al., 2014).

(I) **Research and Development is Accelerated:** AI analyzes large datasets, finds patterns, and forecasts results to speed up research and development. Artificial intelligence (AI) speeds up drug development, material design, and genomic research in industries including biotechnology, materials science, and pharmaceuticals. This results in speedier innovation and discoveries (Rajkomar et al., 2019).

(II) **Data-Driven Decision Making:** By gleaning insightful information from intricate datasets, artificial intelligence (AI) enables organizations to make well-informed judgments. AI algorithms can find trends, correlations, and prediction patterns in scientific business analytics, which helps with resource efficiency, market analysis, and consumer segmentation (O'Leary, 2013).

(III) **Personalized Medicine and Healthcare:** Artificial Intelligence is essential in customizing healthcare regimens for each patient. Machine learning-driven diagnostic tools and genomic data-driven individualized treatment plans are just two examples of how artificial intelligence (AI) is advancing precision medicine, improving patient outcomes, and enhancing medical decision-making (Vaswani, Shazeer, Parmar, Uszkoreit, Jones, Gomez, & Polosukhin, 2017).

(IV) **Predictive Maintenance and Operations:** AI-driven predictive maintenance guarantees optimal machinery performance and minimizes downtime in sectors like manufacturing and logistics. Businesses can take proactive measures to address problems before they get worse by using machine learning algorithms to evaluate sensor data and predict equipment breakdowns (O'Leary, 2013).

(V) **Supply Chain Optimization:** AI forecasts demand, maximizes inventory, and streamlines logistics to improve supply chain operations. Enhanced automation and predictive analytics make supply chains more responsive and nimbler by increasing productivity, cutting expenses, and guaranteeing product delivery on time.

(VI) **Using Natural Language Processing (NLP) for Communication:** Chatbots and virtual assistants are examples of NLP applications that simplify consumer interactions and communication. AI driven language processing can help businesses in scientific research and services by answering questions, supplying data and promoting cooperation.

(VII) **Robots and Automation:** AI-driven automation systems and robots simplify repetitive processes, improve precision, and boost productivity in manufacturing and laboratory settings. This lowers labor expenses while freeing up experienced workers to concentrate on more intricate and imaginative areas of their work.

(VIII) **Ethical and Responsible Innovation:** AI also demands that ethical issues, responsible data use, bias correction, and transparency be prioritized. Ensuring that technical breakthroughs are in line with society norms and fostering trust are two important reasons to incorporate ethical considerations into AI applications. AI's influence on scientific business will grow as it develops, providing fresh approaches to challenging problems and spurring ongoing innovation. To navigate the ethical, legal, and societal ramifications of AI and make sure that these technologies contribute to a sustainable and equitable future for scientific enterprises, collaboration between scientists, corporations, and legislators is essential.

11. CONCLUSION: THE TRANSFORMATIVE IMPACT OF DEEP LEARNING IN SCIENTIFIC BUSINESS ANALYTICS

11.1 Summarizing Key Findings

In summary, a new era of data-driven innovation and decision-making is being ushered in by the paradigm-shifting influence of deep learning in scientific business analytics, which goes beyond conventional methods. Important discoveries highlight deep learning's amazing powers, especially its aptitude for managing intricate, unstructured information and identifying subtle patterns that were previously difficult to identify (Vaswani, Shazeer, Parmar, Uszkoreit, Jones, Gomez, & Polosukhin, 2017). Convolutional Neural Networks (CNNs) and Transformers are two examples of neural network architectures that have enabled deep learning to drive advancements in a variety of fields, from retail personalization and supply chain optimization to pharmaceutical drug development and drug discovery (Rajkomar et al., 2019).

The applicability of deep learning models in a variety of applications, from audio and picture recognition to natural language processing (NLP), is one important finding. Deep learning adaptability guarantees its significance in several scientific enterprise domains, permitting establishments to take advantage of its potential for sophisticated problem-solving, sentiment analysis, and predictive modeling. Furthermore, the efficiency of pre-trained models and transfer learning has shown to be a game- changer, enabling companies to take advantage of information that has already been obtained and minimizing the requirement for large, labeled datasets. The integration of deep learning into scientific business analytics has been further accelerated by the democratization of deep learning through user- friendly frameworks and cloud computing services, opening this game-changing technology to a wider audience.

But it's important to recognize that deep learning raises ethical questions about bias, interpretability, and privacy, among other things. It is critical to address these issues in order to promote the fair and responsible application of deep learning technology in scientific business analytics (Jordan & Mitchell, 2015). Essentially, deep learning has a disruptive effect that goes beyond simple technology progress; it signifies a change in the fundamental structure of how scientific business operations use data. There is a lot of potential for innovation, discovery, and the realization of previously unheard-of efficiencies in scientific business analytics in the future as long as firms keep improving and growing their deep learning programs.

11.2 Looking Ahead to Continued Innovations and Discoveries

In terms of the future, the revolutionary influence of deep learning on scientific business analytics is expected to bring in a new era of ongoing advancements and discoveries (O'Leary, 2013). When businesses and researchers continue to investigate the unrealized potential of deep learning applications, the landscape is set for revolutionary breakthroughs (Vaswani, Shazeer, Parmar, Uszkoreit, Jones, Gomez, & Polosukhin, 2017). Future developments in hardware capabilities and algorithmic efficiency, along with the growth of neural network topologies, point to even greater power and versatility for deep learning models (Jordan & Mitchell, 2015). It is anticipated that interdisciplinary partnerships will be essential in promoting synergy between data scientists and domain experts. Tailored solutions are expected to become more prevalent in industries like healthcare, manufacturing, and finance as deep learning models grow more specialized, interpretable, and able to handle difficult real-world problems. Explainable AI integration will take care of ethical issues and provide accountability and openness in decision-making procedures. Furthermore, a wider audience will be empowered by the democratization of deep learning tools and platforms, opening the door for companies of all sizes to take use of this technology's revolutionary potential. Deep learning will be used responsibly and fairly to shape the future of scientific business analytics if research and development expenditures are sustained, and ethical issues are taken seriously. Opportunities for invention, discovery, and constructive transformation abound on the horizon, indicating a dynamic and exciting trip to come.

REFERENCES

Bishop, C. M. (1995). *Neural Networks for Pattern Recognition*. Oxford University Press. doi:10.1093/oso/9780198538493.001.0001

Bishop, C. M. (2006). *Pattern Recognition and Machine Learning*. Springer.

Box, G. E. P., & Muller, M. E. (1958). A note on the generation of random normal deviates. *Annals of Mathematical Statistics*, *29*(2), 610–611. doi:10.1214/aoms/1177706645

Cao, L. (2019). *Data Science*. Springer.

Chandola, V., Banerjee, A., & Kumar, V. (2009). Anomaly detection: A survey. *ACM Computing Surveys*, *41*(3), 1–58. doi:10.1145/1541880.1541882

Chen, M., Mao, S., & Liu, Y. (2014). Big data: A survey. *Mobile Networks and Applications*, *19*(2), 171–209. doi:10.1007/s11036-013-0489-0

Chollet, F. (2017). *Deep Learning with Python*. Manning Publications.

Clemen, R. T., & Reilly, T. (2001). *Making Hard Decisions with Decision Tools*. Duxbury Press.

Cortes, C., & Vapnik, V. (1995). Support-vector networks. *Machine Learning*, *20*(3), 273–297. doi:10.1007/BF00994018

Davenport, T. H., & Harris, J. (2007). *Competing on Analytics: The New Science of Winning*. Harvard Business Review Press.

Davenport, T. H., Harris, J., & Shapiro, J. (2010). Competing on talent analytics. *Harvard Business Review*, *88*(10), 52–58. PMID:20929194

Davenport, T. H., Harris, J., & Shapiro, J. (2010). Competing on talent analytics. *Harvard Business Review*, *88*(10), 52–58. PMID:20929194

Etzkowitz, H., & Leydesdorff, L. (1997). Universities in the Global Economy: Culture, Technology and Innovation. *The Journal of Technology Transfer*, *22*(2), 2–3.

Floridi, L., & Taddeo, M. (2016). What is data ethics? *Philosophical Transactions. Series A, Mathematical, Physical, and Engineering Sciences*, *374*(2083), 20160360. doi:10.1098/rsta.2016.0360 PMID:28336805

Goodfellow, I., Bengio, Y., Courville, A., & Bengio, Y. (2016). *Deep learning* (Vol. 1). MIT Press.

Guyon, I., & Elisseeff, A. (2003). An introduction to variable and feature selection. *Journal of Machine Learning Research*, *3*, 1157–1182.

Hastie, T., Tibshirani, R., & Friedman, J. (2009). *The Elements of Statistical Learning: Data Mining, Inference, and Prediction*. Springer. doi:10.1007/978-0-387-84858-7

Hastie, T., Tibshirani, R., & Friedman, J. (2009). *The Elements of Statistical Learning*. Springer. doi:10.1007/978-0-387-84858-7

Hochreiter, S., & Schmidhuber, J. (1997). Long short-term memory. *Neural Computation*, *9*(8), 1735–1780. doi:10.1162/neco.1997.9.8.1735 PMID:9377276

Howard, A. G., Zhu, M., Chen, B., Kalenichenko, D., Wang, W., Weyand, T., . . . Adam, H. (2017). MobileNets: Efficient Convolutional Neural Networks for Mobile Vision Applications. *arXiv preprint arXiv:1704.04861*.

Inmon, W. H. (1992). *Building the Data Warehouse*. Wiley.

James, G., Witten, D., Hastie, T., & Tibshirani, R. (2013). *An Introduction to Statistical Learning: with Applications in R*. Springer. doi:10.1007/978-1-4614-7138-7

Jordan, M. I., & Mitchell, T. M. (2015). Machine learning: Trends, perspectives, and prospects. *Science*, *349*(6245), 255–260. doi:10.1126/science.aaa8415 PMID:26185243

Kimball, R., Ross, M., Thornthwaite, W., Mundy, J., & Becker, B. (1996). *The Data Warehouse Lifecycle Toolkit*. Wiley.

Krizhevsky, A., Sutskever, I., & Hinton, G. E. (2012). ImageNet Classification with Deep Convolutional Neural Networks. In Advances in neural information processing systems (pp. 1097-1105). Academic Press.

Krizhevsky, A., Sutskever, I., & Hinton, G. E. (2017). ImageNet Classification with Deep Convolutional Neural Networks. *Communications of the ACM*, *60*(6), 84–90. doi:10.1145/3065386

Laudon, K. C., & Laudon, J. P. (2016). *Management Information Systems: Managing the Digital Firm*. Pearson.

LeCun, Y., Bengio, Y., & Hinton, G. (2015). Deep learning. *Nature*, *521*(7553), 436–444. doi:10.1038/nature14539 PMID:26017442

Manyika, J., Chui, M., Brown, B., Bughin, J., Dobbs, R., Roxburgh, C., & Byers, A. H. (2011). *Big data: The next frontier for innovation, competition, and productivity*. McKinsey Global Institute.

McCulloch, W., & Pitts, W. (1943). A logical calculus of the ideas immanent in nervous activity. *The Bulletin of Mathematical Biophysics*, *5*(4), 115–133. doi:10.1007/BF02478259

McKinney, W. (2018). *Python for Data Analysis: Data Wrangling with Pandas, NumPy, and IPython*. O'Reilly Media.

McKinsey Global Institute. (2011). *Big data: The next frontier for innovation, competition, and productivity*. Author.

Montgomery, D. C., Jennings, C. L., & Kulahci, M. (2008). *Introduction to Time Series Analysis and Forecasting*. John Wiley & Sons.

Montgomery, D. C., & Runger, G. C. (2014). *Applied Statistics and Probability for Engineers*. John Wiley & Sons.

Nair, V., & Hinton, G. E. (2010). Rectified Linear Units Improve Restricted Boltzmann Machines. *Proceedings of the 27th International Conference on Machine Learning (ICML-10),* 807-814.

Nielsen, M. A. (2015). *Neural Networks and Deep Learning*. Determination Press.

O'Leary, D. E. (2013). Artificial intelligence and big data. *IEEE Intelligent Systems, 28*(2), 96–99. doi:10.1109/MIS.2013.39

O'Reilly, T. (2019). *What is Data Science?* O'Reilly Media.

Power, D. J. (2007). *A brief history of decision support systems. DSSResources*. COM.

Provost, F., & Fawcett, T. (2013). *Data Science for Business: What You Need to Know about Data Mining and Data-Analytic Thinking*. O'Reilly Media.

Rajkomar, A., Dean, J., & Kohane, I. (2019). Machine learning in medicine. *The New England Journal of Medicine*, *380*(14), 1347–1358. doi:10.1056/NEJMra1814259 PMID:30943338

Rosenblatt, F. (1957). *The perceptron, a perceiving and recognizing automaton. Project Para*. Cornell University.

Rumelhart, D. E., Hinton, G. E., & Williams, R. J. (1986). Learning representations by back-propagating errors. *Nature*, *323*(6088), 533–536. doi:10.1038/323533a0

Schmidhuber, J. (2015). Deep learning in neural networks: An overview. *Neural Networks*, *61*, 85–117. doi:10.1016/j.neunet.2014.09.003 PMID:25462637

Silver, D., Huang, A., Maddison, C. J., Guez, A., Sifre, L., Van Den Driessche, G., . . . Hassabis, D. (2016). Mastering Chess and Shogi by Self-Play with a General Reinforcement Learning Algorithm. *arXiv preprint arXiv:1712.01815*.

Sutton, R. S., & Barto, A. G. (2018). *Reinforcement Learning: An Introduction*. MIT Press.

Taleb, N. N. (2007). *The Black Swan: The Impact of the Highly Improbable*. Random House.

Turban, E., Sharda, R., Delen, D., & Aronson, J. E. (2011). *Decision Support and Business Intelligence Systems*. Prentice Hall.

Vaswani, A., Shazeer, N., Parmar, N., Uszkoreit, J., Jones, L., Gomez, A. N., . . . Polosukhin, I. (2017). Attention is all you need. In Advances in neural information processing systems (pp. 5998-6008). Academic Press.

Wang, R. Y., & Strong, D. M. (1996). Beyond accuracy: What data quality means to data consumers. *Journal of Management Information Systems*, *12*(4), 5–33. doi :10.1080/07421222.1996.11518099

Wheelan, C. (2013). *Naked Statistics: Stripping the Dread from the Data*. W. W. Norton & Company.

Chapter 6
AI-Driven Financial Forecasting:
The Power of Soft Computing

Nitendra Kumar
https://orcid.org/0000-0001-7834-7926
Amity Business School, Amity University, Noida, India

Priyanka Agarwal
Amity Business School, Amity University, Noida, India

Gauri Gupta
Amity Business School, Amity University, Noida, India

Sadhana Tiwari
Sharda University, India

Padmesh Tripathi
https://orcid.org/0000-0001-9455-1652
Delhi Technical Campus, Greater Noida, India

ABSTRACT

In today's dynamic and complex financial landscape, accurate and reliable financial forecasting is crucial for businesses to make informed decisions, manage risks, and achieve long-term success. Artificial intelligence (AI) has emerged as a transformative force in the financial industry, offering a powerful set of tools and techniques for enhancing financial forecasting capabilities. This chapter delves into the realm of AI-driven financial forecasting, exploring the role of soft computing techniques in harnessing the power of AI for data-driven financial insights. Soft computing, a branch of computational intelligence, encompasses a suite of methodologies that mimic human reasoning and learning processes to handle complex and uncertain

DOI: 10.4018/979-8-3693-1598-9.ch006

data. A comprehensive overview of AI-driven financial forecasting, highlighting the strengths and applications of soft computing techniques in this domain, has been envisaged beginning by introducing the fundamental concepts of AI in financial forecasting, including data pre-processing, feature selection, and model evaluation. It then delves into the specific applications of soft computing techniques in financial forecasting, exploring their use in various forecasting tasks, such as stock price prediction, exchange rate forecasting, and credit risk assessment. The transformative potential of AI-driven financial forecasting, empowered by the power of soft computing techniques, have also been underscored. The effectiveness of soft computing techniques has been shown through real-world examples and case studies, demonstrating their ability to outperform traditional forecasting methods in various financial scenarios. It also discusses the challenges and limitations of using AI in financial forecasting, emphasizing the importance of data quality, model interpretability, and ethical considerations.

1. INTRODUCTION

1.1 AI-Driven Financial Forecasting

The financial landscape is evolving at breakneck speed, characterized by vast data volumes, unpredictable volatility, and an ever-growing demand for personalized investment strategies. Traditional forecasting methods, often reliant on historical trends and limited data analysis, struggle to keep pace with this dynamic environment. This is where AI-driven forecasting emerges as a game-changer, poised to disrupt the industry and unlock new levels of accuracy, efficiency, and personalization (Singh et al., 2023).

1.1.1 Limitations of Traditional Approaches: Imagine wading through a sea of financial data, searching for hidden patterns and insights. Traditional forecasting tools are like outdated boats, ill- equipped to navigate this vast ocean. They typically suffer from:

- Data Overload: The sheer volume and velocity of financial data overwhelm these models, hindering their ability to capture the intricate relationships that drive market movements.
- Volatility Blindness: Historical trend-based models falter in the face of unexpected shifts and black swan events, leaving investors and institutions vulnerable to unforeseen risks.

- Limited Personalization: One-size-fits-all forecasts fail to cater to the diverse needs and risk profiles of individual investors, stunting the potential for customized investment strategies.

1.1.2 AI to the Rescue: AI, a powerful engine capable of analysing vast datasets, uncovering hidden patterns, and adapting to changing dynamics. AI-powered forecasting models offer a paradigm shift in financial prediction, with the potential to address these limitations and unlock new possibilities:

- Advanced Analytics: AI algorithms can sift through mountains of data, including unstructured sources like news and social media, to identify hidden relationships and generate insights that traditional models miss.
- Adaptive and Dynamic: Unlike static historical models, AI can continuously learn and adapt to evolving market conditions, providing more accurate forecasts even in turbulent environments.
- Personalized Precision: AI can tailor forecasts to individual risk profiles and investment goals, enabling investors and institutions to make informed decisions aligned with their specific needs.

1.1.3 Benefits beyond Accuracy: The advantages of AI-driven forecasting extend far beyond simply predicting market trends. This transformative technology offers a multitude of benefits, including:

- Enhanced Efficiency: AI automates data analysis and forecasting processes, freeing up human resources for strategic decision-making and value-added activities.
- Cost Optimization: By streamlining workflows and minimizing errors, AI can lead to significant cost savings for financial institutions.
- Democratization of Finance: AI can make sophisticated forecasting tools accessible to a wider range of investors, promoting financial inclusion and levelling the playing field.

1.1.4 Challenges and the Road Ahead: While AI holds immense potential, navigating this uncharted territory requires caution and responsible development. Key challenges to address include:

- Data Quality and Bias: AI models are only as good as the data they are trained on. Ensuring data quality and mitigating biases is crucial for reliable and unbiased forecasts.

- Explain ability and Transparency: Understanding how AI models arrive at their predictions is essential for building trust and ensuring responsible use of this powerful technology.
- Regulation and Ethics: The development and deployment of AI in finance must be guided by ethical frameworks and robust regulatory oversight to ensure fairness and consumer protection.

By addressing these challenges and embracing the transformative power of AI, the financial industry can unlock a new era of precise insights, efficient operations, and personalized investment strategies. This journey towards a future powered by AI-driven forecasting holds the promise of a more informed, inclusive, and dynamic financial landscape for all.

1.2 The Need for Advanced Forecasting

In today's financial landscape, traditional forecasting methods are like outdated maps trying to navigate an ever-shifting labyrinth. The complexity of modern markets, characterized by constant fluctuations and intricate interdependencies, renders historical trend analysis and rigid models woefully inadequate. To truly excel in this dynamic environment, financial institutions and investors require advanced forecasting powered by Artificial Intelligence (AI).

1.2.1 Limitations of Traditional Methods: Imagine staring at a bewildering array of charts, each line twisting and turning like a cryptic path in a hidden garden. Traditional forecasting approaches grapple with this data deluge, often falling prey to:

- Data Blindness: They struggle to capture the intricate relationships between internal and external factors, from economic indicators and consumer sentiment to geopolitical events and technological disruptions. These hidden patterns, invisible to traditional models, hold the key to accurate predictions.
- Volatility Blindness: Historical trends alone offer little guidance in the face of sudden market swings and black swan events. Traditional models, anchored in the past, are blindsided by unexpected shifts, leading to disastrous consequences for unprepared investors.
- Personalization Pitfalls: One-size-fits-all forecasts fail to cater to the diverse needs and risk profiles of individual investors and institutions. This rigid approach hinders optimal decision-making and leaves potential opportunities untapped.

1.2.2 Challenges of Dynamic Financial Markets: The Dawn of AI-Driven Forecasting: A powerful beacon cutting through the fog of financial uncertainty. Unlike its traditional counterparts, AI can:

- Unravel the Data Tapestry: AI algorithms weave through vast datasets, meticulously analysing every thread and connection. They uncover hidden relationships, predict with greater accuracy, and anticipate volatile shifts before they materialize.
- Embrace Change with Open Arms: Unlike static historical models, AI models are constantly learning and adapting. They evolve alongside the market, providing up-to-date insights even in the face of unexpected turbulence.
- Craft Personalized Roadmaps: AI can tailor forecasts to individual needs and risk profiles. This personalized approach empowers investors and institutions to make informed decisions aligned with their specific goals and objectives.

By addressing the limitations of traditional methods and embracing the dynamic nature of financial markets, AI-driven forecasting offers a crucial edge in navigating the complexities of modern finance.

1.3 Leveraging Soft Computing Techniques

Soft computing is a branch of computer science that deals with methodologies tolerant to imprecision and uncertainty. Unlike traditional computing methods, which rely on precise algorithms and data, soft computing techniques embrace the inherent fuzziness and ambiguity of real-world problems. This makes them ideal for tackling complex optimization and decision-making tasks in dynamic environments like cloud computing.

Neural Networks is inspired by the human brain, neural networks are interconnected nodes that process information and learn from experience.

Figure 1. Neural network architecture

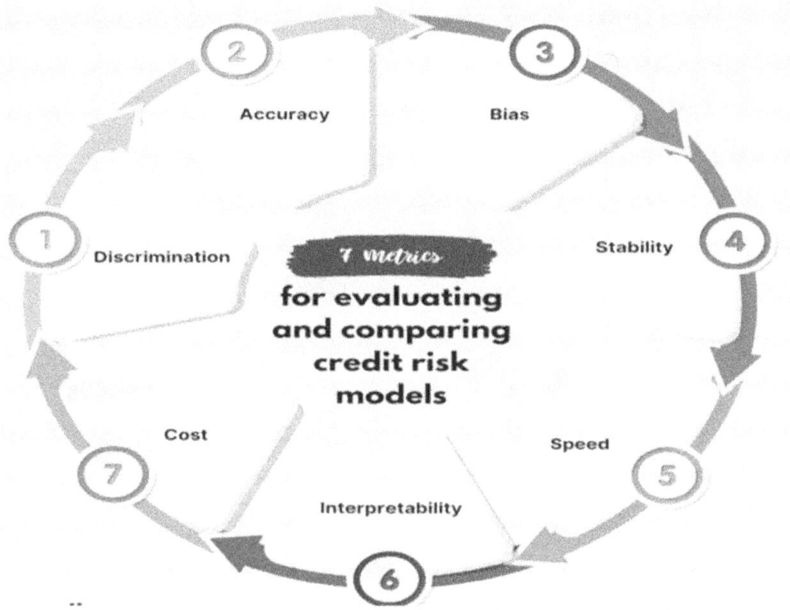

Fuzzy Logic: Fuzzy logic allows for representing and reasoning with partial truths and degrees of uncertainty. This is particularly useful in cloud environments where workloads can be dynamic and resource availability can fluctuate. Fuzzy logic can help make decisions under such conditions by considering the trade-offs between different options and prioritizing tasks based on their urgency and resource requirements.

Figure 2. Input membership function of fuzzy logic

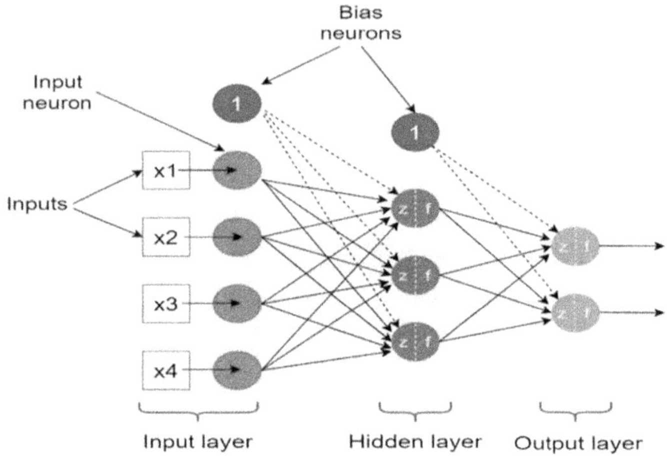

Evolutionary Algorithms: These algorithms mimic the process of natural selection, iteratively improving solutions through generations. They can be used to optimize scheduling algorithms for cloud resources, finding the best way to distribute tasks among available virtual machines while minimizing costs and response times.

Figure 3. Flowchart of standard genetic algorithm

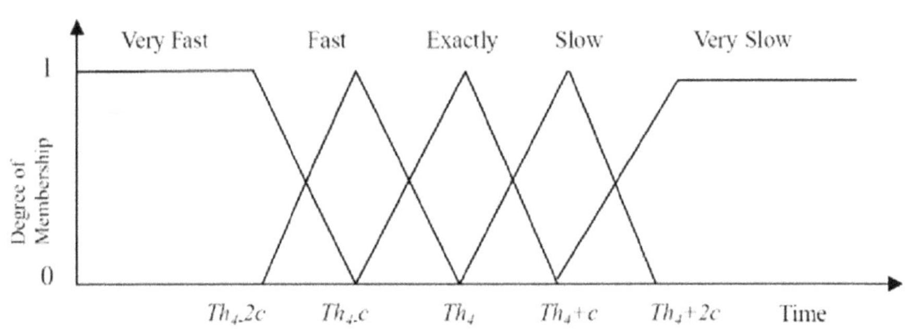

1.4 Benefits and Soft Computing Applications in Cloud Computing

- Adaptability: Soft computing techniques can adapt to changing workloads and resource availability in real-time, making them ideal for the dynamic nature of cloud computing.
- Efficiency: By optimizing resource allocation and scheduling, soft computing can reduce costs and improve resource utilization in cloud environments.
- Accuracy: Predictive capabilities of neural networks and fuzzy logic can help anticipate future resource demands and prevent bottlenecks.
- Decision-making: Soft computing can provide insights and recommendations for resource allocation, workload scheduling, and cost optimization, supporting informed decision-making.
- Dynamic resource provisioning: Soft computing algorithms can predict resource needs and automatically scale up or down cloud resources based on demand.
- Workload scheduling: AI-powered scheduling optimizes task allocation across virtual machines, minimizing completion times and resource utilization.
- Cost optimization: Soft computing techniques can analyse resource usage patterns and identify opportunities to reduce cloud-computing costs.
- Fault tolerance: AI can be used to predict and prevent system failures, ensuring high availability and reliability of cloud services.

By leveraging the adaptability and intelligence of soft computing techniques, cloud service providers (CSPs) can achieve efficient resource management, optimize costs, and improve service quality.

2. UNVEILING THE POWERHOUSE TECHNIQUES

2.1 Neural Networks

Within the burgeoning field of AI-driven financial forecasting, neural networks take centre stage, acting as adept navigators of the labyrinthine realm of market data. Unlike traditional methods, often limited by rigid assumptions and linear models, neural networks embrace the inherent dynamism and non-linearity of financial landscapes. This section delves into the captivating capabilities of these intelligent models, highlighting their ability to learn from historical data and model complex non-linear relationships, ultimately unlocking the key to predicting future market movements with remarkable accuracy.

Figure 4. Neural network diagram with financial data inputs and forecasting outputs

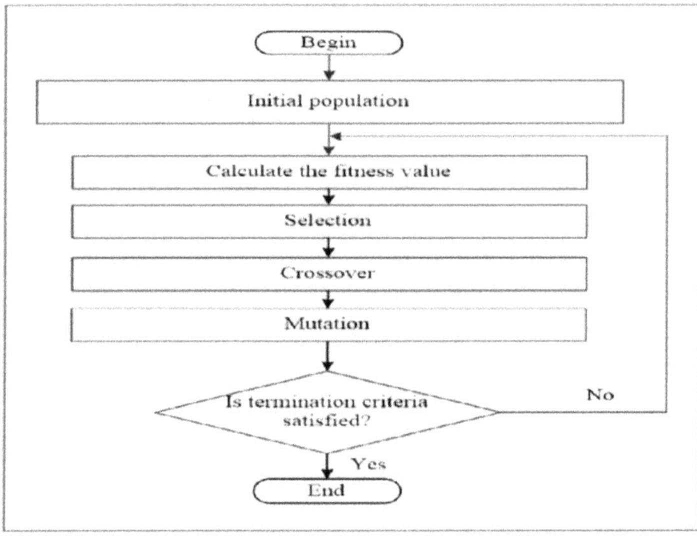

Neural networks, akin to digital scholars, meticulously pore over these tomes, gleaning patterns and weaving them into an intricate tapestry of market understanding. They discern subtle correlations amongst seemingly disparate data points, building an internal map of the causal relationships that drive financial movements.

Financial landscapes rarely abide by the rigidity of straight lines. Stock prices pirouette and plunge like unpredictable ballerinas, economic indicators twist and turn like vines in a whirlwind. Yet, neural networks fear not these complexities. Their strength lies in modelling these non-linear relationships, capturing the intricate web of forces that influence market movements. Through hidden layers of interconnected nodes, they translate past data into future whispers, predicting trends with an uncanny accuracy that surpasses mere linear models.

The key capabilities of neural networks:

- Learning from historical data: Neural networks analyse vast amounts of historical data, identifying subtle patterns and relationships that traditional methods might miss.
- Modelling non-linear relationships: Unlike linear models, neural networks can capture the intricate and often non-linear dynamics of financial markets, leading to more accurate predictions.

- Making future predictions: By decoding the market's intricate language, neural networks can provide rich and comprehensive insights into future trends, empowering informed decision-making.

This serves as a strong foundation for delving deeper into the specific intricacies of neural networks and their applications in financial forecasting.

2.2 Fuzzy Logic

Innovation, the elusive engine of economic success, often thrives in the murky waters of uncertainty and subjectivity. While traditional measurement tools struggle to grapple with these nuances, fuzzy logic emerges as a beacon of clarity, illuminating the path towards reliable and insightful innovation evaluation. This section delves into the unique capabilities of fuzzy logic, highlighting its ability to handle uncertainty and vagueness and effectively model subjective factors within the context of innovation management.

Figure 5. Fuzzy logic membership functions applied to financial variables

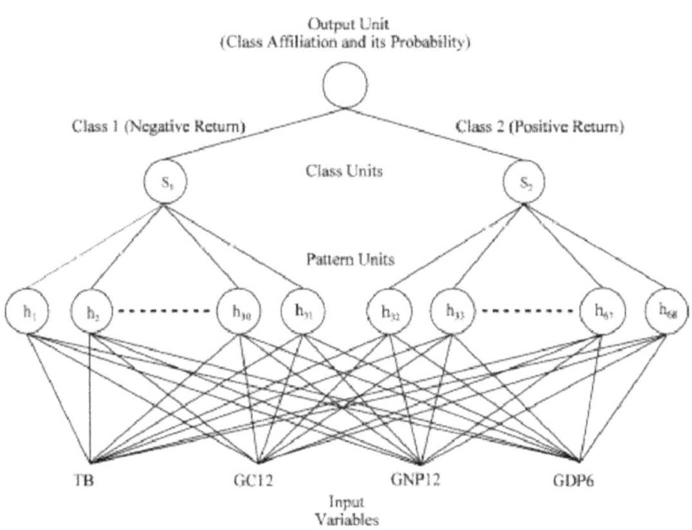

Traditional logic operates within a realm either of binary choices— an asset is either undervalued or overvalued, a company is financially stable or at risk. However, fuzzy logic challenges this rigid dichotomy, recognizing that financial reality often exists within a spectrum of possibilities. It introduces the concept of membership functions, which assign degrees of truth to data points, allowing them to belong to multiple categories simultaneously. Imagine a stock's price hovering near a critical threshold—it can be simultaneously considered "somewhat undervalued" and "somewhat overvalued" within fuzzy logic, capturing the nuances of its uncertain position.

Financial decision-making often involves subjective assessments—expert opinions on market sentiment, creditworthiness evaluations, or risk tolerance assessments. Fuzzy logic provides a language to quantify and integrate these subjective factors into forecasting models. It translates linguistic variables like "high risk" or "strong growth potential" into mathematical representations, bridging the gap between human judgment and numerical analysis.

2.3 Evolutionary Algorithms

Within the ever-evolving landscape of financial forecasting, finding the optimal model configuration often resembles a quest for the Holy Grail. Traditional optimization methods, while valiant, can falter in the face of the market's inherent complexity and non-linear dynamics. However, fear not, for a potent armamentarium stands ready in the form of evolutionary algorithms (EAs). Inspired by the relentless ingenuity of natural selection, EAs offer a powerful approach to optimizing forecasting models and identifying the elusive goldmine of accurate parameters.

EA lies in a captivating ballet of algorithms, mimicking the core tenets of evolution. A diverse population of candidate models, each representing a unique set of parameters, undergoes rigorous evaluation against historical data. The fittest, demonstrably superior in their forecasting prowess, are then granted the privilege of "procreation." Through crossover and mutation operators, they share their parameter values with the next generation, creating variations. This iterative cycle of selection, variation, and inheritance perpetuates over generations, relentlessly honing the population's predictive accuracy.

Unlike their rigid counterparts, EAs excel at navigating the financial market's noise, mis-information, and local optima pose no significant threat. The inherent diversity of the population ensures exploration of vast swathes of the parameter space, significantly increasing the chances of stumbling upon the global optimum – the pinnacle of forecasting accuracy. This freedom from being stuck in local maxima empowers EAs to consistently deliver superior results compared to traditional methods.

The journey of EAs in financial forecasting is far from over. With ongoing research into novel crossover and mutation operators, adaptive fitness functions, and hybrid approaches combining EAs with other optimization techniques, the future promises even more potent tools for navigating the market's intricate dance. As we continue to refine and unleash the power of EAs, they stand poised to revolutionize the art of financial forecasting, guiding us towards a future where the Holy Grail of accurate parameters no longer remains a myth, but a tangible reality within reach.

Figure 6. Evolutionary algorithm flowchart for financial model optimization

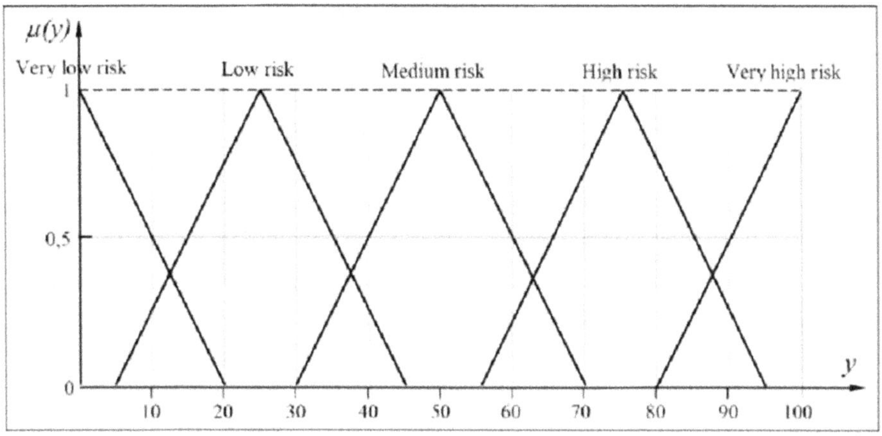

3. REAL-WORLD APPLICATIONS

3.1 Stock Market Prediction

The alluring promise of outsmarting the market has long captivated investors, drawing them towards the siren song of stock market prediction. While the elusive nature of market movements often leads to pronouncements of its inherent randomness, advancements in machine learning (ML) techniques are illuminating new pathways for navigating this turbulent landscape. By harnessing the power of algorithms, investors can now wield predictive models as their compass, steering their decisions towards lucrative trading opportunities and potentially mitigating investment risks.

Predicting stock price movements remains a complex riddle, with myriad factors, both tangible and intangible, influencing the intricate dance of supply and demand. However, advancements in ML, particularly deep learning architectures like recurrent neural networks (RNNs), offer potent tools for unravelling these complexities. RNNs excel at processing sequential data, making them adept at capturing the temporal dependencies inherent in historical price movements. By ingesting vast amounts of historical data, including price fluctuations, trading volume, and economic indicators, these models can identify hidden patterns and relationships, paving the way for more accurate predictions of future price trends.

The narrative surrounding a company, industry, or broader economic landscape can exert a significant influence on market sentiment. Text mining techniques enable us to tap into this rich vein of information, analysing news articles, social media chatter, and even corporate filings to gauge investor sentiment and predict potential market reactions. By analysing, the emotional tenor of online discourse or identifying key phrases and topics associated with positive or negative market sentiment, these techniques offer valuable insights that can complement and refine quantitative models based solely on numeric data.

In the quest for the most robust prediction models, ensemble techniques offer a powerful strategy. By leveraging the complementary perspectives of diverse algorithms, ensemble methods often yield more accurate and reliable predictions, empowering investors with a clearer picture of potential market movements.

The integration of ML-powered forecasting tools into the investment landscape represents a significant shift from intuition-driven decisions to data-driven insights. By providing investors with objective, statistically grounded predictions, these models can help reduce the influence of emotional biases and impulsive decisions, leading to more informed and potentially profitable trades. Additionally, the ability to identify potentially lucrative trading opportunities, such as short-term price fluctuations or undervalued stocks, further enhances the potential returns for investors utilizing these cutting-edge tools.

Figure 7. Stock market prediction dashboard powered by AI

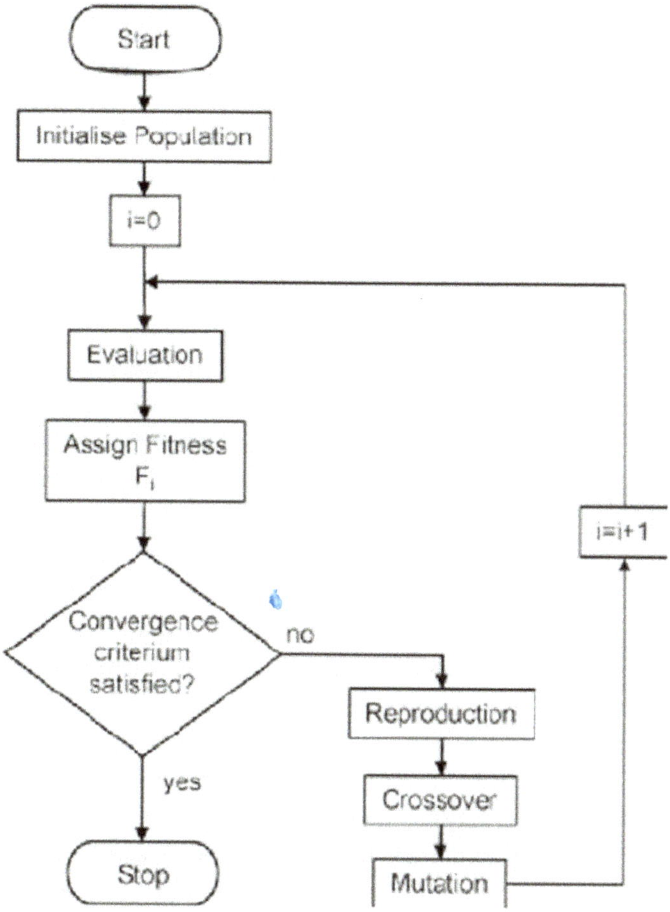

This section merges the concepts of real-world applications with stock market prediction, focusing on two key sub-topics:

- Predicting stock price movements: The section highlights how ML techniques like RNNs can learn from historical data and identify patterns to forecast future price trends.
- Identifying trading opportunities: It emphasizes the potential of text mining and ensemble techniques to provide valuable insights for capitalizing on lucrative market fluctuations and undervalued stocks.

3.2 Credit Risk Assessment

In the labyrinthine world of finance, one of the most crucial decisions banks face is assessing creditworthiness. Predicting whether a borrower will default on a loan is like navigating a treacherous path, fraught with uncertainty and potential losses. Fortunately, machine learning (ML) has emerged as a powerful tool, illuminating the path and enabling banks to make informed decisions with greater accuracy and confidence.

Traditionally, credit risk assessment relied on static factors like income, credit history, and employment. However, this approach often fails to capture the dynamic complexities of individual circumstances and the ever-evolving economic landscape. ML algorithms, like support vector machines and random forests, can delve deeper into the data, uncovering hidden patterns and relationships that traditional methods miss. By analysing a wider range of variables, including past loan behaviours, spending habits, and even social media activity, these algorithms can paint a more nuanced picture of a borrower's financial health and risk profile.

The ability to predict loan defaults lies at the heart of effective credit risk management. By employing ML models trained on historical data, banks can anticipate potential defaults with greater accuracy. This allows them to make informed decisions about loan approvals, interest rates, and even offer personalized financial products tailored to individual risk profiles. Early detection of potential defaults not only mitigates financial losses but also empowers banks to take proactive measures to support struggling borrowers, potentially preventing defaults altogether.

While quantitative data plays a crucial role in credit risk assessment, the human element remains an important factor. ML models can be combined with expert judgment through techniques like goal programming. This approach allows banks to incorporate the subjective insights of experienced professionals into the decision-making process, ensuring a more holistic and nuanced assessment of creditworthiness. By leveraging both quantitative and qualitative data, banks can create robust prediction models that capture the full spectrum of factors influencing loan repayment behaviour.

The integration of ML into credit risk assessment is not just a technological advancement; it is a transformative leap forward. By empowering banks to make more informed decisions, ML can lead to reduced loan defaults, improved risk management, and ultimately, a more stable and vibrant financial ecosystem. Moreover, the ability to offer personalized financial products based on individual risk profiles can foster financial inclusion and empower individuals to access credit opportunities previously unavailable to them.

Figure 8. Credit risk assessment system

This revised section merges the concepts of real-world applications with credit risk assessment, focusing on two key sub-topics:

- Assessing creditworthiness: The section highlights how ML algorithms can analyse a wider range of variables to create a more nuanced picture of a borrower's financial health and risk profile.
- Predicting loan defaults: It emphasizes the ability of ML models to anticipate potential defaults with greater accuracy, allowing banks to make informed decisions and take proactive measures.

3.3 Fraud Detection

The digital tapestry of the financial world, while woven with convenience and accessibility, also bears the scars of a persistent threat – fraud. From credit card frauds to insurance swindles, these malicious activities can inflict significant financial losses on both individuals and institutions. Fortunately, the realm of machine learning (ML) offers a potent shield, enabling banks and other financial players to identify fraudulent transactions and protect their financial fortresses.

Traditional fraud detection methods, often reliant on static rules and manual review, struggle to keep pace with the ever-evolving tactics of fraudsters. ML algorithms, however, possess the uncanny ability to learn from vast amounts of data, uncovering hidden patterns and anomalies that hint at fraudulent activity. By analysing transaction history, customer behaviour, and other relevant data points, these algorithms can identify subtle yet telltale signs of deception, even when they deviate from established fraud typologies.

The realm of fraud is not static; it is a constant arms race between perpetrators and protectors. ML algorithms, however, can adapt and evolve in real-time. By employing predictive analytics and continuously learning from new data, these models can stay ahead of the curve, identifying emerging fraud patterns and updating their defences accordingly. This real-time protection is particularly crucial in the age of online transactions, where fraudulent activity can occur within seconds and cause immediate damage.

Figure 9. Fraud detection system flagging suspicious transactions

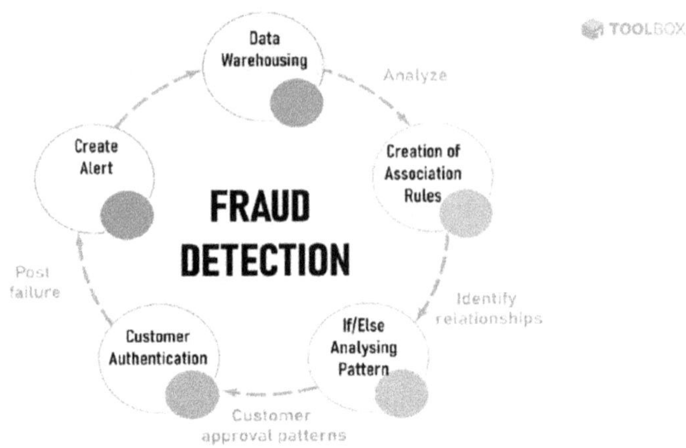

The integration of ML into the realm of fraud detection is not just a technological advancement; it is a significant step towards building a more secure and resilient financial ecosystem. By empowering financial institutions with the ability to identify and thwart fraudulent activities with greater accuracy and speed, ML can help protect individuals and businesses from financial losses, fostering trust and confidence in the digital financial world. As ML algorithms continue to evolve and become even more sophisticated, the future holds the promise of a financial landscape where fraudsters find it increasingly difficult to breach the defences, paving the way for a safer and more secure financial future for all.

4. CHALLENGES AND FUTURE DIRECTIONS

4.1 Interpretability and Explainability

One of the most significant challenges facing the widespread adoption of federated learning (FL) in real-world applications lies in its inherent lack of interpretability and explainability. Unlike traditional machine, learning models, where the relationships between inputs and outputs are readily apparent, and the distributed nature of FL makes it difficult to understand how and why the model arrives at its predictions. This opacity poses several key challenges:

Without clear insights into the reasoning behind FL model predictions, stakeholders can struggle to trust their accuracy and reliability. This is particularly critical in high-stakes situations, such as healthcare or financial decision-making, where misinterpretations can have dire consequences. Lack of understanding can also hinder debugging and identifying potential biases within the model, further amplifying trust concerns.

In sectors like healthcare or finance, regulations often mandate explainability for decisions made by artificial intelligence systems. With opaque FL models, complying with such regulations becomes a major hurdle. Additionally, building trust with users and ensuring transparent compliance with data privacy regulations is crucial for gaining widespread adoption of FL technology.

The field of soft computing offers a promising avenue for addressing the interpretability and explainability challenges of FL. By integrating techniques like fuzzy logic, evolutionary algorithms, and neuro-fuzzy systems, researchers are developing innovative approaches to shed light on the inner workings of FL models.

Here are some promising avenues:

1. Local Explanations: Instead of attempting to explain the entire global model, these techniques focus on providing localized explanations for individual predictions. This can be achieved by identifying the specific data points or features that had the most significant influence on a particular prediction within the federated model.
2. Counterfactual Explanations: These techniques explore "what-if" scenarios by simulating how the model's output would change if certain input features were altered. This provides valuable insights into the reasoning behind the model's predictions and can help identify potential biases or unfairness within the model.
3. Feature Importance Ranking: By leveraging soft computing algorithms, researchers can rank the importance of different features in influencing the

model's predictions. This allows users to prioritize and focus on the most relevant information. Singh et al. (2023).

4.2 Data Quality and Availability

In the ever-evolving landscape of big data and machine learning, data quality and availability are akin to the high-octane fuel that powers these sophisticated engines. Just as a sputtering engine cannot deliver optimal performance, unreliable or inaccurate data can cripple the effectiveness of even the most advanced machine learning models. Therefore, ensuring high quality, readily accessible data is a fundamental prerequisite for harnessing the full potential of this revolutionary technology.

In the world of algorithms, garbage in truly means garbage out. High-quality data refers to data that is accurate, complete, consistent, and relevant to the target task. Noise, inconsistencies, and missing values can introduce biases and distort patterns, leading to unreliable and misleading model outputs. Therefore, robust data cleaning and pre-processing techniques are crucial to ensure the integrity and usability of the data before it is fed into the machine-learning pipeline Manimala et al. (2011)

The power of machine learning lies not just in its analytical prowess, but also in its ability to learn and adapt. This, however, hinges on continuous access to a steady stream of data. Limited availability can hinder model training and refinement, restricting its ability to evolve and adapt to changing patterns and contexts. Therefore, adopting innovative data acquisition and integration trends becomes critical, enabling us to tap into diverse and dynamic data sources, enriching the learning process and maximizing the potential of machine learning models.

Recognizing the crucial role of high quality, readily available data, researchers are actively exploring novel trends to address these challenges.

Here are some promising avenues:

- Federated Learning: This distributed learning paradigm allows us to train models on multiple devices or servers without centralizing the data, offering a privacy-preserving approach to data integration.
- Active Learning: By strategically querying users or selecting informative data points, this technique optimizes data acquisition, focusing on gathering the most relevant information for model training.
- Data Augmentation: By artificially manipulating existing data, this technique creates synthetic samples, effectively increasing the available data volume and addressing issues like data scarcity.
- Real-time Data Integration: Streamlining the process of ingesting and analysing real-time data streams facilitates dynamic model updating and enables them to adapt to rapidly evolving situations (Devillers, 2023).

4.3 Ethical Considerations

As artificial intelligence (AI) permeates every facet of our lives, the need for ethical considerations becomes paramount. From the intricate algorithms shaping our online experiences to the robots automating physical tasks, understanding and addressing the ethical implications of these technologies is crucial to ensure responsible AI practices.

4.3.1 Algorithmic bias: One of the primary ethical concerns surrounding AI is the potential for algorithmic bias. These biases, often embedded in the data used to train the algorithms, can lead to discriminatory outcomes, exacerbating social inequalities and perpetuating injustices. For example, biased facial recognition algorithms can misidentify individuals based on race or gender, while biased loan approval algorithms can unfairly restrict access to credit demographics. Recognizing and mitigating algorithmic bias is critical to ensure equitable and fair outcomes for all individuals (Devillers, L., & Cowie, R.2023).

4.3.2 Data privacy: Another key ethical concern lies in the realm of data privacy. AI systems rely on vast amounts of personal data to learn and function effectively. However, collecting and utilizing this data raises concerns about individual privacy and control over personal information. Data breaches, unauthorized access, and the potential for misuse of personal data for profiling and manipulation are all valid concerns that need to be addressed through robust data privacy regulations and ethical protocols (Demiris, 2009)

4.3.3 Responsible AI practices: Implementing ethical considerations in AI goes beyond simply identifying potential pitfalls. Building responsible AI practices requires a holistic approach that encompasses several key principles:

- Transparency and Explainability: Understanding how AI systems arrive at their decisions is crucial for building trust and ensuring accountability. Transparent and explainable models allow stakeholders to evaluate the fairness and reliability of AI outputs, preventing discriminatory or harmful outcomes.
- Human Oversight and Control: While AI can automate many tasks, human oversight remains essential to ensure ethical decision-making and adherence to human values. AI systems should complement human intelligence, not replace it, with mechanisms in place for human intervention and control when necessary.
- Accountability and Responsibility: Identifying and assigning responsibility for the actions of AI systems is crucial. This includes addressing issues of liability in situations where AI-driven algorithms cause harm or contribute to discriminatory outcomes. Transparent processes for identifying and

addressing the responsible parties are essential for ensuring accountability and justice (Carlisle, 1999).

5. CONCLUSION

As we stand at the crossroads of technology and humanity, the realm of artificial intelligence (AI) beckons with both immense promise and potent challenges. From the intricate algorithms shaping our online interactions to the autonomous robots automating physical tasks, AI is rapidly transforming the very fabric of our lives. In this intricate tapestry, machine learning emerges as a powerful thread, weaving together data, algorithms, and insights to empower intelligent machines to learn, adapt, and ultimately, surpass human capabilities in specific domains.

However, this transformative power must be wielded with wisdom and responsibility. As we delve deeper into the world of AI, ethical considerations become paramount. From ensuring transparent and explainable algorithms to safeguarding data privacy and promoting responsible AI practices, we must prioritize principles of fairness, accountability, and human well-being. Only then can we truly harness the power of AI for good, building a future where intelligent machines augment and empower humanity, not replace or exploit it.

The future of AI stretches before us, brimming with breath-taking possibilities. Machine learning algorithms will continue to evolve, becoming increasingly sophisticated and capable of tackling challenges that are even more complex.

Here are some exciting avenues of future advancements:

- Democratizing AI: Machine-learning tools will become more accessible and user-friendly, empowering individuals and organizations beyond tech giants to leverage the power of AI for innovation and problem solving.
- Human-AI collaboration: The future lies not in competition but in collaboration. Humans and AI will work together, pooling their unique strengths to achieve optimal results. AI will augment human decision-making, providing invaluable insights and automating routine tasks, allowing humans to focus on creativity, critical thinking, and ethical considerations.
- Personalized AI: Machine learning will become increasingly adept at tailoring experiences and solutions to individual needs and preferences. Whether it's personalized healthcare or dynamic educational interventions, AI will usher in an era of customized solutions that cater to the unique complexities of each individual.
- Explainable AI: As AI models become more complex, the need for transparency and explainability will become even more crucial. Future

advancements will focus on developing algorithms that are not only powerful but also understandable, fostering trust and acceptance of AI within society.

The path forward for AI is not without its challenges. Issues like algorithmic bias, data privacy, and the potential for job displacement need to be addressed proactively through ethical frameworks, responsible development practices, and continuous dialogue between researchers, policymakers, and the public. By navigating these challenges with wisdom and foresight, we can unlock the boundless potential of AI, shaping a future where intelligent machines work alongside us, augmenting our capabilities and contributing to a more just, equitable, and prosperous world.

REFERENCES

Abdallah, A., Maarof, M. A., & Zainal, A. (2016). Fraud detection system: A survey. *Journal of Network and Computer Applications*, *68*, 90–113. doi:10.1016/j.jnca.2016.04.007

Adedugbe, O., Benkhelifa, E., Campion, R., Al-Obeidat, F., Bani Hani, A., & Jayawickrama, U. (2020). Leveraging cloud computing for the semantic web: Review and trends. *Soft Computing*, *24*(8), 5999–6014. doi:10.1007/s00500-019-04559-2

Alfaro García, V. G., Gil-Lafuente, A. M., & Alfaro Calderon, G. (2015). A fuzzy logic approach towards innovation measurement. *Global Journal of Business Research*, *9*(3), 53–71.

Bartz-Beielstein, T., Branke, J., Mehnen, J., & Mersmann, O. (2014). Evolutionary algorithms. *Wiley Interdisciplinary Reviews. Data Mining and Knowledge Discovery*, *4*(3), 178–195. doi:10.1002/widm.1124

Bennouna, G., & Tkiouat, M. (2018). Fuzzy logic approach applied to credit scoring for microfinance in Morocco. *Procedia Computer Science*, *127*, 274–283. doi:10.1016/j.procs.2018.01.123

Bughin, J., Hazan, E., Sree Ramaswamy, P., DC, W., & Chu, M. (2017). Artificial intelligence the next digital frontier. Academic Press.

Bustos, O., & Pomares-Quimbaya, A. (2020). Stock market movement forecast: A systematic review. *Expert Systems with Applications*, *156*, 113464. doi:10.1016/j.eswa.2020.113464

Carlisle, J. P. (1999). Ethical considerations of the software-dependent organization. *Journal of Systems and Software, 44*(3), 251–255. doi:10.1016/S0164-1212(98)10061-4

Chen, A. S., Leung, M. T., & Daouk, H. (2003). Application of neural networks to an emerging financial market: Forecasting and trading the Taiwan Stock Index. *Computers & Operations Research, 30*(6), 901–923. doi:10.1016/S0305-0548(02)00037-0

Cocianu, C. L., & Grigoryan, H. (2015). An artificial neural network for data forecasting purposes. *Informações Econômicas, 19*(2), 34–45. doi:10.12948/issn14531305/19.2.2015.04

Covas, J., & Gaspar-Cunha, A. (2009). Extrusion Scale-up: An Optimization-based Methodology. *International Polymer Processing, 24*, 67-82. . doi:10.3139/217.2200

Demiris, G., Doorenbos, A. Z., & Towle, C. (2009). Ethical considerations regarding the use of technology for older adults: The case of telehealth. *Research in Gerontological Nursing, 2*(2), 128–136. doi:10.3928/19404921-20090401-02 PMID:20077974

Devillers, L., & Cowie, R. (2023). Ethical Considerations on Affective Computing: An Overview. *Proceedings of the IEEE.* 10.1109/JPROC.2023.3315217

García, F., Giménez, V., & Guijarro, F. (2013). Credit risk management: A multicriteria approach to assess creditworthiness. *Mathematical and Computer Modelling, 57*(7-8), 2009–2015. doi:10.1016/j.mcm.2012.03.005

How, M. L., Cheah, S. M., Khor, A. C., & Chan, Y. J. (2020). Artificial intelligence-enhanced predictive insights for advancing financial inclusion: A human-centric ai-thinking approach. *Big Data and Cognitive Computing, 4*(2), 8. doi:10.3390/bdcc4020008

John, S. N., Anele, C., Kennedy, O. O., Olajide, F., & Kennedy, C. G. (2016, December). Realtime fraud detection in the banking sector using data mining techniques/algorithm. In 2016 international conference on computational science and computational intelligence (CSCI) (pp. 1186-1191). IEEE.

Manimala, K., Selvi, K., & Ahila, R. (2011). Hybrid soft computing techniques for feature selection and parameter optimization in power quality data mining. *Applied Soft Computing, 11*(8), 5485–5497. doi:10.1016/j.asoc.2011.05.010

Martin-del-Brio, B., & Serrano-Cinca, C. (1993). Self-organizing neural networks for the analysis and representation of data: Some financial cases. *Neural Computing & Applications*, *1*(3), 193–206. doi:10.1007/BF01414948

Patel, J., Shah, S., Thakkar, P., & Kotecha, K. (2015). Predicting stock and stock price index movement using trend deterministic data preparation and machine learning techniques. *Expert Systems with Applications*, *42*(1), 259–268. doi:10.1016/j.eswa.2014.07.040

Pitchai, R., Babu, S., Supraja, P., & Anjanayya, S. (2019). Prediction of availability and integrity of cloud data using soft computing technique. *Soft Computing*, *23*(18), 8555–8562. doi:10.1007/s00500-019-04008-0

Shah, D., Isah, H., & Zulkernine, F. (2019). Stock market analysis: A review and taxonomy of prediction techniques. *International Journal of Financial Studies*, *7*(2), 26. doi:10.3390/ijfs7020026

Singh, R. K., Verma, V. K., Kumar, N., Agarwal, P., & Tiwari, S. (2023). Time series forecasting of stock price of AirAsia Berhad using ARIMA model during COVID- 19. *Journal of Statistics and Management Systems*, *26*(6), 1421–1429. doi:10.47974/JSMS-1189

Singh, S., Singh, S., Koohang, A., Sharma, A., & Dhir, S. (2023). Soft computing in business: Exploring current research and outlining future research directions. *Industrial Management & Data Systems*, *123*(8), 2079–2127. doi:10.1108/IMDS-02-2023-0126

Supriya, Y., & Gadekallu, T. R. (2023). A Survey on Soft Computing Techniques for Federated Learning-Applications, Challenges and Future Directions. *ACM Journal of Data and Information Quality*, *15*(2), 1–28. doi:10.1145/3575810

Thennakoon, A., Bhagyani, C., Premadasa, S., Mihiranga, S., & Kuruwitaarachchi, N. (2019, January). Real-time credit card fraud detection using machine learning. In *2019 9th International Conference on Cloud Computing, Data Science & Engineering (Confluence)* (pp. 488-493). IEEE. 10.1109/CONFLUENCE.2019.8776942

Turkson, R. E., Baagyere, E. Y., & Wenya, G. E. (2016, September). A machine learning approach for predicting bank credit worthiness. In *2016 Third International Conference on Artificial Intelligence and Pattern Recognition (AIPR)* (pp. 1-7). IEEE. 10.1109/ICAIPR.2016.7585216

Veerendra, P., & Rao, T. (2021). Optimized scheduling techniques focused on powerful heuristics leveraging cloud services soft computing. *International Journal of Pervasive Computing and Communications*, *18*(1), 5–17.

Vikhar, P. A. (2016, December). Evolutionary algorithms: A critical review and its future prospects. In *2016 International conference on global trends in signal processing, information computing and communication (ICGTSPICC)* (pp. 261-265). IEEE. 10.1109/ICGTSPICC.2016.7955308

Whitley, D., Rana, S., Dzubera, J., & Mathias, K. E. (1996). Evaluating evolutionary algorithms. *Artificial Intelligence*, *85*(1-2), 245–276. doi:10.1016/0004-3702(95)00124-7

Chapter 7
An Analysis of Stock Price Prediction Techniques

Surya Pal
https://orcid.org/0000-0001-8701-2095
Sharda University, India

Prem Shankar Jha
Patna University, India

Rita Roy
GITAM University, India

Maheshwar Pathak
Sharda University, India

Arun Kumar
Sharda University, India

Hari Shankar Shyam
Sharda University, India

ABSTRACT

As the stock market is an intricate, complex activity influenced by hundreds of factors, predicting such prices with accuracy or absolute conviction is quite difficult. This chapter focuses on the potential use of support vector machines (SVM), decision tree algorithm, and ARIMA model for predicting stock market prices using specific data obtained from Yahoo Finance. The authors train the model using daily price data derived from Yahoo Finance and make great efforts to estimate how well the model predicts market prices. The chapter adds value to the existing knowledge by showing that algorithms tend to work in this field. Insights from the study will help investors and traders take a better course of action in the market.

DOI: 10.4018/979-8-3693-1598-9.ch007

1. INTRODUCTION

Since the market value is volatile and of a mercurial nature, it is very hard to predict. However, today, with the help of machine learning (ML) algorithms, newer possibilities for doing so have cropped up (Wolff & Echterling, 2024). This research paper discusses ML algorithms in market value prediction. This research will develop an effective forecasting model to predict future prices with relative accuracy using previous market history. Yahoo Finance is, therefore, very important in achieving this goal. Being one of the most used and trusted sources of financial information, the prospects of getting the necessary data from Yahoo Finance are so important. The data obtained includes daily price information for publicly traded companies. After that, powerful predictive models capturing complex patterns and other key patterns are derived from business data through ML algorithms. Therefore, Machine-learning techniques are competent in carrying out this since they work under the model's linear and non-linear relations. These are utilized in the model training to capture the underlying patterns or relationships with price movements. Perfectly fitted models can provide good predictions associated with the future data point, more so regarding product price prediction. The findings of this study could contribute to important implications for investment strategy and portfolio management and offer a new type of data-driven approach to business model predictions. As emphasized above, conventional time series methods have always been very challenging to model because of the innate dynamism associated with stock trading.

An exchange market receives several other economic, political, and social factors. Hence, it becomes very difficult to model how a product's performance relates to the operating costs. It is a very tough task since the prices of the stocks are very easy to change. Less inevitable events such as natural disasters or political conflicts may disastrously affect prices and constitute an entirely unpredictable element; that part always lies in the next move. Some products may be scarce in their historical data, thus making it very hard to train machine-learning models with rich data. This happens when a ML model learns too much from the input training data and performs poorly on the new unseen instances. Hundreds of ML models are available for predicting stock prices. It becomes tedious as it is predominantly trial and error to pinpoint some to implement for a particular problem precisely. These issues reflect the need to design suitable methods to forecast product prices, considering the peculiarity of market sales and the insufficiency of available information when tested.

Used to capture all reliable and comprehensive financial history information (Majidi et al., 2024). It is a package that helps do fast arithmetical and array operations while processing data. Used for a process to run on huge numbers of datasets, with its primary focus being on the pre-processing and transformation of the data. It is applied for visually plotting data; it creates charts, graphs, and other informative reports to describe and represent results. The tools of ML include SVM, benchmarks, and the use of pre-processing data. It is why a combination of both EvalML and feature tools is advantageous, as it becomes easy to evaluate the performance and enable the potential of a ML model.

2. LITERATURE SURVEY

A selected list related to some studies regarding learning algorithms for predicting market prices is as follows: (Hur et al., 2006) reviewed financial and physical assets and international trade development through cross-country analysis. The research findings insist a positive relationship exists between the development of financial and physical assets on one side and international trade on the other, highlighting the pivotal role of finance in promoting cross-border trade. In this regard, he has found a strong relationship between the two since economic activity leads to large support for the growth of any economy. That gives the importance of efficiency in supporting economic growth (2). This artificial neural network (ANN) paper examines its application to market value forecasting. It has been evidenced that artificial neural networks can predict market value with great accuracy and provide the best performance compared to statistical methods (Nabipour et al., 2020). The article provides further research on improving the performance of ANN stock exchange market prediction. After he had done some research concerning pricing products for five firms, he concluded the fact that ANN can predict more accurately the prices for products compared to RF (Vijh et al., 2020).

In their research, (Subasi et al., 2021) used seven categories: Random Forest, Bagging, Island Boost, Decision Tree, SVM, K-NN, and ANN for stock market prediction. It yielded a conclusion that the NYSE model of SVM was high in predicting the accuracy for Nasdaq, and the same had provided excellent accuracy for Nikkei and FTSE, among others. The accuracy of the FTSE random forest is among the highest.

In this line, (Singh et al., 2019) developed a two-stage model for stock price prediction with the main aim of leveraging ensemble ML techniques toward improving the accuracy of predictions, which is fundamental to informed investment decisions within financial markets. Different groups of complex advanced ML models are slated to forecast data in such a way that each capture one part of the different dynamics in the data. 1. "Integrating highly advanced statistical methodologies with predictive modeling approaches, the framework provides a comprehensive toolset in navigating the intricacies of financial markets, offering invaluable insights to investors and analysts". (Mehtab et al., 2020) implemented an integrated approach by adding financial factors to the previous feature space to forecast the stock market price.

The authors applied various methodologies in statistics and ML to evaluate the ability of prediction by sentiment obtained from Twitter in forecasting the movements of stock markets. Through the unity of these different sources of information, the study tries to increase the precision and robustness of the prediction ability of stock markets. Their research supported such a line of thinking when they concluded that using social media data jointly with macroeconomic indicators for predictive analytics regarding financial markets offers valuable insights into the rapid change in dimensions of stock market prediction (Mehtab & Sen, 2020). The study aimed to investigate and push the boundaries of the application level of advanced deep learning models in stock market predictions. Concerned about financial market problems, they researched how well such ML techniques work for stock price forecasts. Similar studies were also conducted to make better and more precise predictions and capture the dynamics of stock market trends by experimenting with past market details through algorithms like ANNs, SVMs, and LSTMs (Mehtab & Sen, 2022).

(Ferreira, 2021) provided a comprehensive glance at how Artificial Intelligence is used in stock trading by explaining the historical perspectives of research development from the 1990s. They emphasized: "Particularly, this field has placed a lot of focus and publicity on how the epoch of fast take-off of technology and personal computer democratization has finally arrived—thirty years later" (sec. 1). In this paper, after analysing 2326 papers retrieved from the Scopus database on the stock markets published during the period between 1995 and 2019, the authors categorize it into four primary domains of review: stock market prediction using AI, portfolio optimization, financial sentiment analysis, and their combinations. The review has shown a very high, ever-glowing interest in the appraisal of AI through the stock market investment strategies and observed a trend towards growing precision and depth of the research, thus reflecting advancement in method sophistication of that topic (Sarode et al., 2019). (Nabipour et al., 2020) have converted a personalized recommendation system for stock investment into a recommendation system using ML to develop a holistic framework for stock recommendation investments. In their paper, the authors recommend an advanced recommendation engine platform with ML algorithms and distributed computing for large-volume financial data processing (Mehtab et al., 2021).

(Murkute & Sarode, 2015) elaborated on the relevance of ML and artificial intelligence methods in the prediction of behaviours in stock markets because the future is vague. The major contribution of their work is the in-depth analysis of predictive analytics tools and how they are supposed to be applied in deciphering stock market dynamics. This paper will introduce the reader to the strengths and weaknesses of ML techniques concerning predicting stock markets and provide insight into financial engineering. Their research also supports the influence of advanced technologies on financial analysis as part of a new trend in the latest market predictions. (Masoud, 2013) addressed one of the well-known questions concerning the stock market: forecasting returns, accounting for its strong dynamism and non-linearity. In their analysis of these models based on standard strategic indicators, parameters for model accuracy led to low values that would suggest efficiency in predicting stock closing prices.

However, with all its technological advancements and ML, stock price prediction remains a dreary job. Financial markets are complex and unpredictable due to many factors, such as economic indicators, geopolitical events, and investor sentiments, to name a few, which make any reliable pattern hardly decipherable. These relationships are too complicated and non-linear to be caught by traditional models dealing with datasets for stocks (Hur et al., 2006).

Heavy financial losses for wrong forecasting of stock prices may occur as a result, and they may interfere with effective decision-making processes. Therefore, exact prediction is very important for optimal trading, which investors or traders usually do in large numbers. Integration of web technologies with statistical methods for predicting the stock price requires consideration of data integrity, processing speed, and user interface design, endowing it with real-time data processing capability and interactive visualization tools. However, this requires real software development skills with data management and user experience designs while implementing these methods into real web applications. The fast speed in financial markets, combined with the volume of data in play, tends to work against accurate real-time prediction. Evolving market dynamics are monitored and improved upon with time such that it is essential to run statistical models frequently on a follow-up. The system will be a web-based platform that uses real-time data feeds, interactive visualization tools, and advanced analytics to empower users to make informed decisions and optimize trading in changing market conditions.

3. IMPLEMENTATION

This study aims to develop a learning-based model for forecasting items. The formula will be used here: The predictive model based on the study will be evaluated in two ways: with regard to the performance compared with traditional time-based models and the performance of the neural network models from which its results are derived. The following stages will realize the work: Develop a ML model using historical data capable of forecasting the future condition of the market. The implementation will include collecting and pre-processing historical data about quotations and shares, along with other financial metrics, which ML algorithms will later leverage for training.

The data to be used in this project was to scrape off the Yahoo Finance website. Some other features of forecasting models can also include financial journals and opinion polls. Mean square error, root mean square error, and R^2 (coefficient of determination) are some evaluation indicators for the performance of ML models. A comparison will be made with other commercial applications dealing in market price forecasting; thus, the project encompasses the ML model, which should accurately predict the market prices for which it offers information for investors and traders. The outcome to be stated will inform the broader area of conducting financial data analysis and business forecasting. This will research the suitability of these algorithms in predicting movement in stock markets and derive a working model for profitable investment decision-making. The findings of this project will be applied to the financial analysis process in the financial sector with paramount importance. The research would thus be useful for the following reasons:

The process includes how data from Yahoo Finance is sourced, collected, and organized to support training and testing ML models. This information includes historical market prices, stocks, and other financial metrics. If necessary, cleaning, transformation, and modelling will be identified for the data to meet the criteria usable in ML modelling. This will be followed by the model selection of the best ML algorithm to predict the stock market. An attempt will be made to check the performance of all the algorithms, say, SVMs, decision trees and ARIMA models. Model Training: The selected ML model will be trained on pre-processed data. This may include adjusting the hyper-parameters of the algorithm to enhance its performance and avoid overfitting.

The ML models trained will be tested over a different product purchase from the shelf, which stakeholders will do. This software must be put to its best use in the last leg. This is where the model built should be integrated into a website or mobile application so that an investor or trader could reach a more informed decision point about investment. It will be a project that results in various models to predict stock prices accurately based on historical data. The program's system will be expanded into financial data analysis and business forecasting to give insight to investors and traders.

Figure 1. SVM predicted and actual frequency

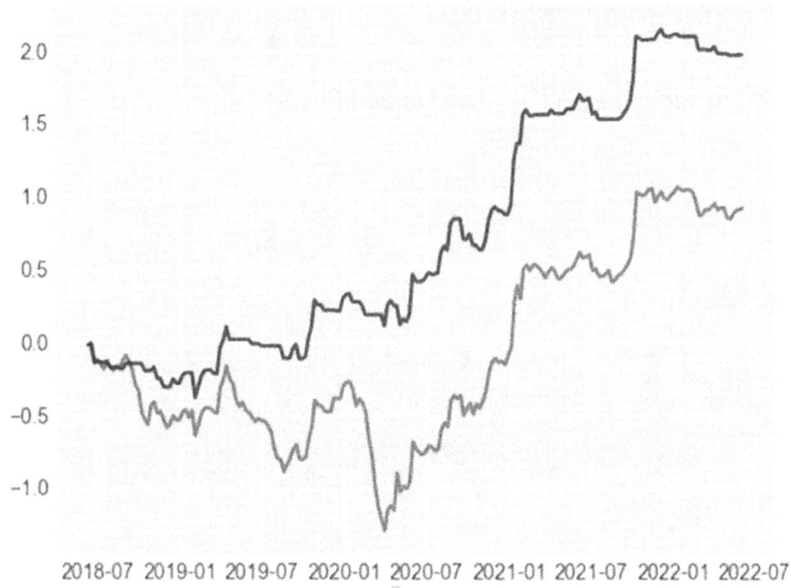

SVM is a kind of artificial algorithm. It expects and reproduces the reality you manage for SVM to foresee class events, where "expectation and actual replication" are used here. Naming one case in comparison, the files with subscripts are often used in classification problems. Based on this information, the SVM algorithm will be trained to learn a line of separation of classes. After training, the SVM can be used to make predictions about new and never shown to its data. The "predicted frequency" is how many cases the SVM algorithm puts into a certain class, and the "actual frequency" is how the events are distributed across the class. Here are the following terms defined: TP (True Probability): A true condition correctly predicted by the SVM. FP (False Positives): Those events that the SVM indicates to be positive are false positives. A truly negative condition is indicated as a negative prediction by the SVM. Those true samples are wrongly assumed to be negatives by the SVM.

We can derive some metrics from the above. Accuracy: The expected quality received concerning the expected quality (accuracy = TP / (TP + FP)). Feedback (removed): Positive feedback rate of each perception removed from the actual category (attributes = TP / (TP + FN)). Accuracy: Percentage accuracy for understanding to be possible (accuracy = (TP + TN) / (TP + TN + FP + FN)). The F1 score combines recall and precision (F1 score = 2 / (precision + recall)). All help in surveying the exhibition of the SVM with a display regarding its capacity to arrange instances into various classes appropriately. Such measurements could be visualized using instruments such as confusion grids.

Figure 2. Decision tree predicted and actual frequency

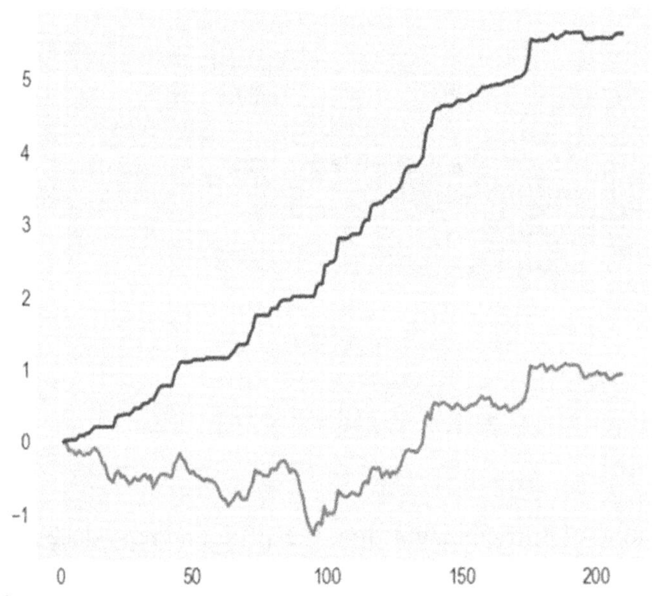

One such is a SVM, an artificial intelligence algorithm often used for science and economics analysis. With this method, the representation of your model is rather tested by comparing the demands and requirements of the result in each of your two groups in managing a selected tree in a workgroup. One can measure the performance of your SVM with parameters like positive (TP), negative (FP), negative (TN), and negative (FN). TP (True Positive) = A true condition predicted true as a feature by the chosen tree. FP (False Positive) = In this case, events are not true positives, but the trees selected are mistakenly considered real. TN (True Negative) = A truly negative condition where the selected tree is predicted to be in poor condition. False Negatives (FN): This consists of data classified wrongly by the tree. Different metrics can be derived using these attributes: Accuracy: It measures the proportion of correctly predicted cases to the total cases available for building and testing the model (Accuracy = TP / (TP + FP)). Recommendation (Default): The relative amount of predicted recommendation over each actual positive to the body of all positives in a person-wise fashion (Recommendation = TP / (TP + FN)). TRUE. Responding to the behaviour that causes and indicates the numbers of real strengths, weaknesses, failures and negatives. Based on these measurements, with the help of assessing the performance of the selected tree model, a possibility can be made to understand a tree's ability to identify events falling into different categories. They are very important tools concerning measurements and evaluations of cognitive structure.

Figure 3. ARIMA tree predicted and actual frequency

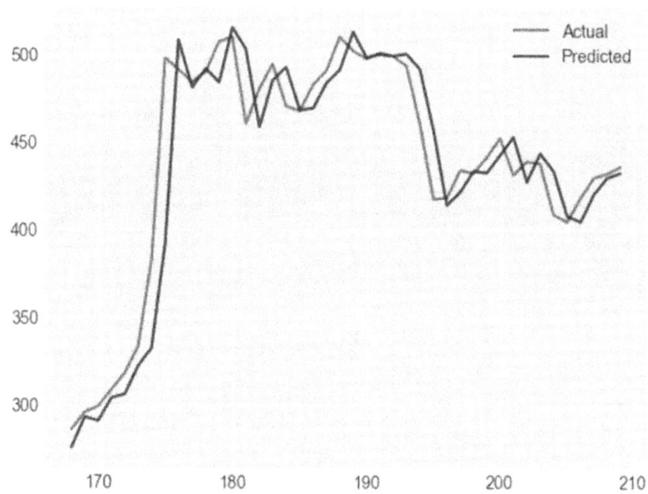

The general method adopted in collecting data from the Yahoo Finance API is as outlined below: generally, for interfacing with the Yahoo Finance API and processing the financial data obtained. The libraries will include the requests library for sending HTTP requests to the Yahoo Finance API endpoints and the JSON library for parsing the responses received in the JSON format. It is implemented using the requests library to interact with the Yahoo Finance API, which has real-time financial data such as stock prices and information on the concerned companies.

One would have to employ some of Python's data manipulation libraries, such as Pandas, for handling and managing the financial data acquired during subsequent analysis and processing. Emphasis will be on using a solid error-handling mechanism to manage exceptions and other unexpected error situations that one may face in processing the obtained data to ensure that each application works.

ARIMA is one of the time series forecasting techniques that refers to the integrated autoregressive moving average model and is used for predicting future values on historical time series data. In the broadest sense, it captures a whole variety of patterns in data, from trends in seasonality to random fluctuations. For instance, if it has been applied in stock price analysis, one can establish the movement of prices of stocks over some stated duration just by knowing the behaviour in the past.

Figure 4. ARIMA model integrated visualization

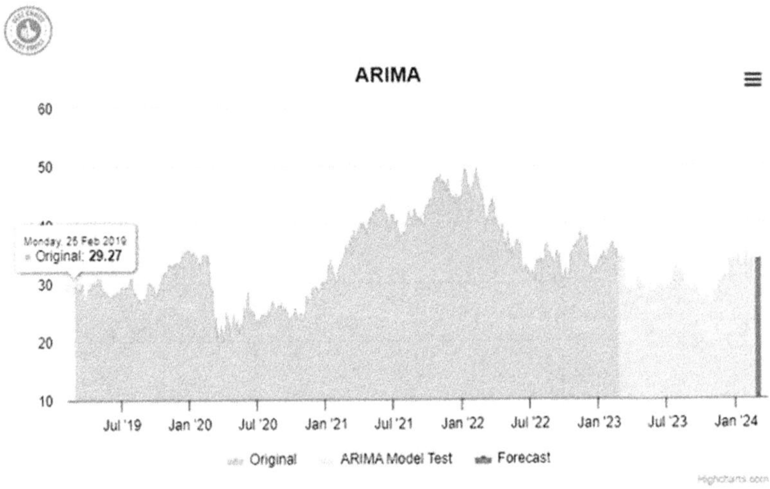

It is a supervised ML algorithm applied to regression problems. In predicting stock prices, SVR would analyse historical data to reveal underlying patterns and relationships. Identification of such patterns supports SVMs in predicting future moves in prices, in turn helping investors and analysts make better decisions.

Regression

It is a statistical method of building models between a dependent variable (in this case, stock prices) and more independent variables (e.g., market indices), helping determine the influence of independent variables on the dependent variable, hence providing salient inputs about how an outcome is being affected by independent variables.

Figure 5. Regression integrated visualization

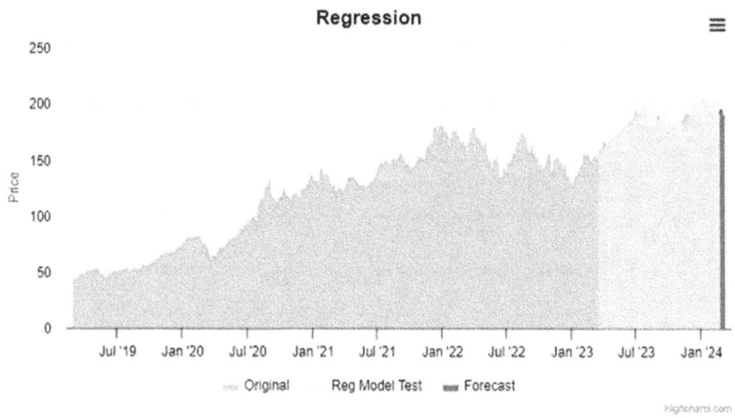

R-squared is a statistical measure that ascertains the proportional variability in the dependent variables to the dependent variable variations. Its value is between 0 and 1, where closer values of R-squared being near 1 exhibit a good fit of the model vis-à-vis the dataset. This is generally explained by the percentage of changes in the independent variable that quantifies the change in the dependent variable. Root Mean Squared Error (RMSE) is an error parameter that measures the average error between estimated and observed values in a model. It carries valuable information about the performance of a particular prediction, where a smaller RMSE means a better ability to predict. This has made the RMSE very useful for assessing the models' forecasting ability, and in general terms, stock price prediction ability, because it quantifies the degree of the errors of the predictions made by the model.

Correlation assesses the degree to which two variables move concerning each other, particularly in the stock market, where it shows how well the returns of two different stocks co-vary. Values range from 1 to -1, with 1 showing a perfect positive correlation and -1 for a perfect negative correlation. A correlation enables an investor to predict the direction in which two stocks will move concerning each other. It is very often used in the context of constructing a portfolio to satisfy diversification objectives.

Figure 6. Correlation table

Alike Stock		Neutral Stock		Unlike Stock	
ADBE	0.89	FNMA	-0.24	PAA	-0.61
ADSK	0.88	GAS	-0.2	ACOR	-0.44
AKAM	0.86	WBA	-0.18	AAL	-0.37
EA	0.81	AIV	-0.17	T	-0.36
ABT	0.77	MO	-0.15	BUD	-0.34

Beta quantifies the fluctuation of a stock's returns in response to changes in the larger market, capturing its systematic risk or volatility. In actuality, it is a number that helps illustrate the magnitude by which a stock can be expected to move in conjunction with a movement in the market indices. A beta greater than 1 represents a more volatile stock than the market. In contrast, a beta below one signals one of less volatility, and a beta of exactly 1 implies synch volatility with the market. Beta is derived statistically by analysing how the returns on a stock move over time about a market index—usually lined up against better benchmarks, such as the S&P 500—and graded in terms of volatility, where the slope of the straight-line regression equals beta. A high beta has been coined as a riskier stock but possibly returning more, while a low beta represents that the stock is less risky but can give lower returns.

Figure 7. Beta analysis

Beta Analysis/ Volatility	Beta: 2.18	Indicates that the stock is more volatile than the market

4. RESULTS AND DISCUSSION

The topic "Technical Analysis for Stock Price Prediction" is quite critical and, at the same time, very pertinent in the financial world today. It might be said that with ever greater possibilities to collect data and massive advances made in artificial intelligence, the promise of an exact prediction for stock prices is more and more realizable. The market offers stock price prediction with the help of machine-learning algorithm machines to enable an analysis using huge data sets with algorithms like decision trees, ARIMA, and support vectors. The method works through pattern recognition of relationships between an assorted set of factors that guide or determine the equity markets, including market indicators and earnings data, while considering the trends.

One key advantage of using ML in estimating business value is that it does away with needing manual analysis. It also saves a lot of time and reduces the chances of human errors occurring, too. In addition, machine-learning algorithms process large data sets in seconds. Hence, predictions are much faster compared to traditional methods. Applying ML in stock market prediction has serious implications for the entire financial market. Nonetheless, good data are still necessary, and it is also important to know the limitations of a ML algorithm. More research is necessary to improve these algorithms and to adapt them for retail usage.

5. FUTURE SCOPE AND FURTHER ENHANCEMENT

Generally, "Stock Price Prediction Techniques" is a good future project ripe for further development. After applying SVM, decision trees, and ARIMA models to the data, there are several ways to move next. One growth area includes extending this exercise to other algorithms, such as random forests, decision trees, or neural networks. Combining these models and assessing their value for better predictive performance by comparing their accuracy with other models is necessary. Another area of consideration for future development is parameter tuning. Various configurations such as feature selection, time delay and inclusion of other financial parameters may further help in data configuration that could be tested. This can heighten predictive performance if there is tuning and optimization of said parameters. A comparative analysis of different learning patterns would give better insights as to strengths and weaknesses; here, this would help in deciding which model gives the best performance with the right metrics for predicting the business model.

REFERENCES

Ferreira, A. (2021). Regulating smart contracts: Legal revolution or simply evolution? *Telecommunications Policy*, *45*(2), 102081. doi:10.1016/j.telpol.2020.102081

Hur, J., Raj, M., & Riyanto, Y. E. (2006). Finance and trade: A cross-country empirical analysis on the impact of financial development and asset tangibility on international trade. *World Development*, *34*(10), 1728–1741. doi:10.1016/j.worlddev.2006.02.003

Majidi, N., Shamsi, M., & Marvasti, F. (2024). Algorithmic trading using continuous action space deep reinforcement learning. *Expert Systems with Applications*, *235*, 121245. doi:10.1016/j.eswa.2023.121245

Masoud, N. M. H. (2013). The Impact of Stock Market Performance upon Economic Growth. *International Journal of Economics and Financial Issues*, *3*(4), 788–798. https://dergipark.org.tr/en/pub/ijefi/issue/31960/351956

Mehtab, S., & Sen, J. (2020). Stock Price Prediction Using CNN and LSTM-Based Deep Learning Models. *2020 International Conference on Decision Aid Sciences and Application, DASA 2020*, 447–453. 10.1109/DASA51403.2020.9317207

Mehtab, S., & Sen, J. (2022). Analysis and Forecasting of Financial Time Series Using CNN and LSTM-Based Deep Learning Models. *Lecture Notes in Networks and Systems*, *302*, 405–423. doi:10.1007/978-981-16-4807-6_39

Mehtab, S., Sen, J., & Dasgupta, S. (2020). Robust Analysis of Stock Price Time Series Using CNN and LSTM-Based Deep Learning Models. *Proceedings of the 4th International Conference on Electronics, Communication and Aerospace Technology, ICECA 2020*, 1481–1486. 10.1109/ICECA49313.2020.9297652

Mehtab, S., Sen, J., & Dutta, A. (2021). Stock Price Prediction Using Machine Learning and LSTM-Based Deep Learning Models. *Communications in Computer and Information Science*, *1366*, 88–106. doi:10.1007/978-981-16-0419-5_8

Murkute, A., & Sarode, T. (2015). Forecasting Market Price of Stock using Artificial Neural Network. *International Journal of Computer Applications*, *124*(12), 11–15. doi:10.5120/ijca2015905681

Nabipour, M., Nayyeri, P., Jabani, H., Shahab, S., & Mosavi, A. (2020). Predicting Stock Market Trends Using Machine Learning and Deep Learning Algorithms Via Continuous and Binary Data; A Comparative Analysis. *IEEE Access : Practical Innovations, Open Solutions*, *8*, 150199–150212. doi:10.1109/ACCESS.2020.3015966

Sarode, S., Tolani, H. G., Kak, P., & Lifna, C. S. (2019). Stock price prediction using machine learning techniques. *Proceedings of the International Conference on Intelligent Sustainable Systems, ICISS 2019*, 177–181. 10.1109/ISS1.2019.8907958

Singh, S., Madan, T. K., Kumar, J., & Singh, A. K. (2019). Stock Market Forecasting using Machine Learning: Today and Tomorrow. *2019 2nd International Conference on Intelligent Computing, Instrumentation and Control Technologies, ICICICT 2019*, 738–745. 10.1109/ICICICT46008.2019.8993160

Subasi, A., Amir, F., Bagedo, K., Shams, A., & Sarirete, A. (2021). Stock Market Prediction Using Machine Learning. *Procedia Computer Science*, *194*, 173–179. doi:10.1016/j.procs.2021.10.071

Vijh, M., Chandola, D., Tikkiwal, V. A., & Kumar, A. (2020). Stock Closing Price Prediction using Machine Learning Techniques. *Procedia Computer Science*, *167*, 599–606. doi:10.1016/j.procs.2020.03.326

Wolff, D., & Echterling, F. (2024). Stock picking with machine learning. *Journal of Forecasting*, *43*(1), 81–102. doi:10.1002/for.3021

Chapter 8
Credit Card Fraud Detection and Analysis With the Blend of Machine Learning and Blockchain

N. S. Kavitha
https://orcid.org/0000-0002-8876-1415
Dr. N.G.P. Institute of Technology, India

G. Revathy
https://orcid.org/0000-0002-0691-1687
Sastra University, India

S. Raja
St. Joseph's College of Engineering and Technology, India

P. Muruga Priya
Surya Engineering College, India

ABSTRACT

Credit card frauds are drastically increasing in number as compared to earlier days. Criminals are using fake identities and make use of various technologies to trap the users and get the money out from them. Therefore, it is essential to find a solution to these types of frauds. In the chapter, a model is planned to perceive the fraud in the credit card transactions. The model provides most of the important features required to detect illegal and illicit transactions.

DOI: 10.4018/979-8-3693-1598-9.ch008

I. INTRODUCTION

Machine learning is an important component of the current period since it allows systems to learn on their own and develop based on their experiences without being programmed externally. The Machine Learning algorithm, or source code, is incorporated into a computer and allows the machine to detect data and make predictions based on that data. The quantity of data used to develop a better model that predicts the output more correctly determines the accuracy of the projected output values (Gupta & Johari, 2011). With the use of statistical methods, an algorithm is trained to make classifications or predictions, and is used to uncover key insights in data mining areas. These insights subsequently drive decision making within the applications and as well as for the business, ideally impacting key growth metrics. As the Big Data contains greater variety, arriving in increasing volumes, the market demand for the data scientists will also increase. They will be required to help to identify the most relevant business questions and the data to answer them. Machine learning has created significant advancements for industries and set the pace for a future built on artificial intelligence (AI) technology. Understanding Machine learning security risks is one of the current technological aspects in undertaking because the consequences are extremely high, especially for industries and healthcare where lives are on the line (Gmbh & Co, 2016).

Most corporations aren't aware of the statistics they've and a way to leverage, analyze and recognize it, that can bring about the lack of a big amount of potentially beneficial information by normalizing fraud and other criminal sports in their tactics and make them hard to prevent and detect. Fraud detection thru large records analysis, information mining and machine mastering fashions uses traits, patterns and behaviors to stumble on and save you suspicious sports in shopping processes, credit sports, debts or transactions, inner and outside techniques, among others (Bolton & David, 2001). This makes possible to routinely detect fraud and allow agencies to consolidate, map and normalize huge amounts of facts that can be correctly analyzed to layout strategies that stumble on and set up connections among anomalous traits, observe a cybernetic attack or mark a security breach.

Online transactions entail the transfer and storage of delicate data and the ill-usage of this data leads to a host of frauds, credit card scam being one of the main threats. Online Shopping is a fast-growing trend. Mode of payments involving Credit Card, Debit Card and Net Banking is prone to frauds. Credit Card Fraud occurs Online as well as Offline. Hackers don't leave a chance to steal information and breach security.

Figure 1.

When a person uses another person's credit card for personal gain while the owner and card issuing authorities are unaware, this is referred to as credit card fraud. Credit card fraud is a simple but significant issue (Seyedhossein & Hashemi, 2011). E-commerce and many other online sites have increased the number of payment options available online, by raising the risk of online fraud. Due to rise in fraud rates, researchers try to employ various machine learning approaches to detect and analyze online transaction fraud. Credit card fraud is a common occurrence. Without pose any risks, a large sum of money withdrawn in a short period of time without the owner's knowledge. Fraudsters attempt to make each fraudulent transaction appear felony, making fraud detection a hard and time-ingesting task. Credit Card Fraud is described as while someone makes use of some other character's credit score card for non-public gain at the same time as the owner and card issuing authorities are uninformed. Due to the upward push and acceleration of E-commerce, there has been a huge growth inside the use of praise play cards for on-line buying, ensuing in a high amount of credit card frauds. The need to discover credit score card frauds has emerge as an increasing number of important in the digital age. Fraud detection includes monitoring and analysing the behaviour of a variety of customers with a view to discover or keep away from fraudulent hobby (Srivastava et al., 2008). Need to understand the numerous technology, algorithms, and types concerned in identifying credit card frauds so as to correctly locate credit score card frauds. An set of rules can inform whether or not a transaction is fraudulent or no longer. The categorization of all transactions after analysing the dataset.

Machine learning can analyze vast volumes of facts and detect outlines that whitethorn not be apparent using traditional rule-based systems.

One of the key advantages of machine learning in fraud detection is its ability to adapt to new and evolving fraud patterns. The algorithms can learn from past fraud cases and adapt to new patterns as they emerge, making them more effective in detecting and preventing fraudulent activities. By continually learning and improving, machine learning can stay ahead of fraudsters and detect new fraud patterns before they cause significant financial losses (Drummond & Holte, 2003).

Machine learning can also reduce false positives in fraud detection. Traditional rule-based systems often generate false positives, flagging legitimate transactions as potential fraudulent activities. This can be time-consuming for banks and frustrating for customers. Machine learning can reduce false positives by analyzing individual customer behavior and identifying patterns that are indicative of fraud while taking into account the individual behavior of each customer (Quah & Sriganesh, 2008).

Another advantage of machine learning in fraud detection is its skill to analyze huge volumes of data quickly. Machine learning algorithms can analyze vast amounts of transactional data in real-time, detecting potential fraudulent activities and flagging them for further investigation. This can help banks prevent financial losses and maintain customer trust by detecting and preventing fraudulent activities in real-time (Kundu et al., 2009).

In the current years, Supervised system learning strategies e.g. Okay-nearest neighbours, Bayes' theorem, decision tree, help vector gadget, random forest, neural community, convolutional neural network, recurrent neural network, lengthy short-term memory community, gated recurrent unit community, Unsupervised machine getting to know strategies e.g. Association regulations, ok-method, density-based totally spatial clustering of programs with noise, hierarchical clustering, deep notion networks, deep Boltzmann device, car-encoder, de-noising car-encoder, and so on. Reinforcement methods e.g. Generative adverse community, deep Q community, agree with region policy optimization, and so forth, and federated learning techniques had been carried out to security and verbal exchange networks. For instance, gadget mastering methods were used to research the behaviours of the information circulate in networks and extract the patterns of malicious sports such as packet dropping, malicious program propagation, jammer assaults, and so forth. for generating guidelines in intrusion detection systems. Furthermore, time-collection methods e.g. Neighborhood outlier element, cumulative sum, adaptive online thresholding, and many others. had been proposed to retrieve the time-collection capabilities of anomalous behaviours for stopping cyber-assaults and malfunctions (Shi et al., 2010).

Machine learning models can recognize unusual credit card transactions and fraud. The first and foremost step involves collecting and sorting raw facts, which is then castoff to train the model to predict the probability of fraud (Duman & Ozcelik, 2011). The solutions offered by machine learning for credit card fraudulent detection involve:

1. Identifying if credit card transactions are legitimate or fraudulent by applying techniques including logistic regression, random forests, support vector machines (SVMs), deep neural networks, autoencoders, long short-term memory (LSTM) networks, and convolutional neural networks (CNNs)
2. Predicting whether it is the cardholders or the fraudsters using the credit cards through credit card profiling
3. Using outlier detection methods to identify considerably different transactions (or 'outliers') from regular credit cards transactions to detect credit card fraud.

To detect fraud, a machine learning model first needs to collect data. The model analyzes all the data gathered, segments, and extracts the required features from it. Next, the machine learning model receives training sets that teach it to predict the probability of fraud. Finally, it creates fraud detection machine learning models (Bhattacharyya et al., 2011).

The first step, data input, differs for ML and humans. Whereas humans struggle to comprehend massive amounts of data, such a task is a piece of cake for ML. The more data an ML model receives, the better it can learn and polish its fraud detection skills.

Feature extraction is the next step. At this point, features describing good customer behavior and fraudulent behavior are added. These features usually include (but are not limited to) the customer's location, identity, orders, network, and chosen payment process. Founded on the complexity of the fraud detection scheme, the list of investigated features can differ.

Next, a training algorithm is launched. In a nutshell, this algorithm is a set of rules that an ML model has to follow when deciding whether an operation is legitimate or fraudulent. The more data a business can provide for a training set, the better the ML model will be.

Finally, when the training is over, the company receives a fraud detection machine learning model suitable for their business. This model can detect fraud in next to no time with high accuracy. To be effective in credit card fraud detection, a machine learning model needs to be constantly improved and updated. Payment fraud detection can be eliminated for a while using ML. But sooner or later, fraudsters will come up with new tricks to game the system unless you keep it updated.

Although being a rapidly growing area of scientific study, there are still a number of unresolved research issues that need to be explored and investigated in the field of machine learning approaches for security and communication networks. For instance, using machine learning techniques for malicious activity detection, attack detection, mobile endpoint analysis, repetitive security task automation, zero-day vulnerability prevention, and other security applications, as well as optimizing them, are crucial issues in computing and communications.

One of the key troubles with applying ML approaches to the praise score card scam detection trouble is that most of the posted paintings are not possible to reproduce. Since credit card transactions are surprisingly personal. Therefore, the datasets which might be used to expand ML fashions for credit card fraud detection include anonymized attributes. Moreover, credit score card fraud detection is a difficult undertaking because of the constantly changing nature and styles of the fraudulent transactions.

Machine learning models are processer applications which are castoff to apprehend style facts or variety forecasts. Device mastering models comprised of machine mastering algorithms, which might be skilled the usage of either labeled, unlabeled, or combined statistics. Distinct machine studying algorithms are perfect to unique desires, consisting of type or estimate model, so statistics scientists' usage distinct procedures as the premise for exceptional replicas (Sahin & Duman, 2011). As records is added to a selected set of rules, it is modified to higher control a specific mission and becomes a machine studying version. For instance, a choice tree is a commonplace set of rules used for each class and prediction modeling. A records scientist seeking to create a machine studying model that identifies specific animal species might teach a decision tree algorithm with diverse animal snap shots. Through the years, the set of rules might grow to be modified by using the facts and grow to be an increasing number of higher at classifying animal photos. In turn, this will sooner or later end up a system studying model.

Before a researcher trains a device studying algorithm, they must first set the hyperparameters for the algorithm, which act as external publications that direct how the set of rules will examine. As an example, the number of branches on a decision tree, the gaining knowledge of fee, and the variety of clusters in a clustering set of rules are all examples of hyperparameters (Mota et al., 2014).

As the algorithm is trained and directed through the hyperparameters, parameters begin to shape in response to the schooling facts. Those parameters consist of the weights and biases fashioned by way of the algorithm as it's miles being skilled. The final parameters for a gadget mastering version are called the version parameters, which preferably fit a statistics set without going over or underneath.

A file trained to recognize particular patterns is referred to as a machine learning model. By giving a model an algorithm to use to analyze and learn from a set of data, you may train it to perform calculations on those data. After the model has been trained, make predictions based on the given data. Take the case of creating a program that can identify a user's emotions based on their expressions on their face (Behdad et al., 2012). Train a model by providing it with images of faces that are each tagged with a certain emotion, and then you can use that model in an application that can recognize any user's emotion.

Figure 2.

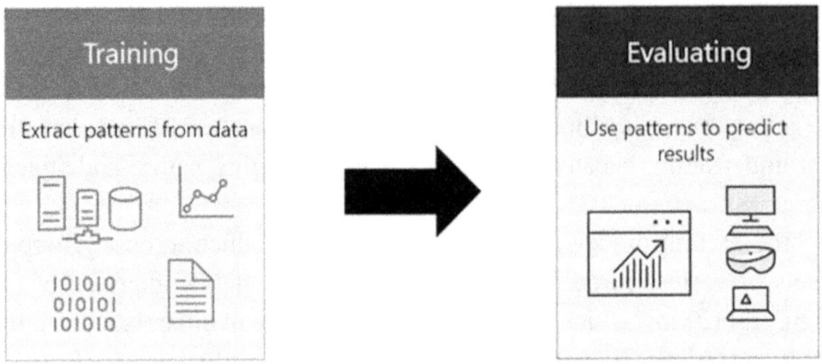

Records safety is the method of shielding records and touchy information from safety dangers. Facts protection in the cyber physical structures is furnished on the premise of CIA Triad, which comprises strategies like confidentiality, integrity, and availability. Confidentiality (or privacy) includes restricting access to the data. Its usage is a lot wished to be able to guard statistics from being accessed or changed with the resource of malicious entities. This will be completed by means of manner of utilizing encryption strategies, which include public-key cryptography and safety tokens (Ju & Vardi, 2001). Furthermore, integrity (or statistics integrity) consists of maintaining the trustworthiness and dependability of the records. It is practiced to hold the usability of information and achieve success it to be usable for extraordinary tasks. Furthermore, availability is the exercise of accessibility of records for retrieval and utilization by way of authorized entities. It's miles required to keep the data always through the maintaining systems which hold them.

In the field of data analytics, every algorithm has a price. But if we consider the overall scenario, then a maximum of the business problem has a classification task. It becomes quite difficult to intuitively know what to adopt considering the nature of the data. Random Forests have various applications across domains such as finance, healthcare, marketing, and more. They are widely used for tasks like fraud detection, customer churn prediction, image classification, and stock market forecasting.

The word 'Forest' in the term suggests that it will contain a lot of trees. The algorithm contains a bundle of decision trees to brand a cataloguing and it is also considered a saving technique when it comes to overfitting of a decision tree model. A decision tree model has tall alteration and little partiality which can give us pretty unstable output unlike the commonly adopted logistic regression, which has high bias and low variance (Ashfaq et al., 2022). That is the only point when Random

Forest comes to the rescue. But before discussing Random Forest in detail, let's take a quick look at the tree concept.

FUSION OF BLOCKCHAIN

The blockchain is connected to the machine learning model. The machine learning model is implemented and utilized to foretell the type of new incoming transactions in a smart contract that is written on the blockchain.

In addition to blockchain technology, other AI techniques can also be used to combat financial fraud. These techniques can analyze vast volumes of data in real-time and identify shapes and anomalies that may indicate fraudulent activity. Furthermore, NLP can be used to analyze text-based data such as emails and chat messages to detect fraudulent behavior .Overall, the financial sector faces significant challenges in combating cybercrime and fraud. However, with the use of advanced technologies such as blockchain, AI, and NLP, it is possible to develop more robust and secure systems to prevent and detect fraudulent activity. Ongoing research and development in these areas will continue to improve the refuge and pliability of financial systems in the aspect of embryonic cyber threats (Diro et al., 2021).

There are two important aspects of security handled by blockchain such as It ensures that the secure transactions completed by a participant cannot be tampered with; neither en route while being added to the chain nor after being added and it also ensures that every transaction allowed to be written conforms to the rules predefined by blockchain that are either programmed into the platform or added as smart contracts. Rely on the security of blockchain for the above reasons. But there is another aspect of security that is also important i.e., reducing the possibility of fraudulent transactions occurring by enhancing its fraud detection (Harris & Waggoner, 2019).

Technological advancements have led to the modernization of various industries, including the financial sector, where outmoded notes are being replaced by cardinal currencies. However, these transactions are defenseless to digital attacks, and detecting fraud and anomalies in digital transactions is critical for maintaining the integrity of the financial system. Anomaly detection techniques are used to detect illegal and fraudulent activities in financial transactions, but existing methods are designed for centralized systems. Blockchain technology offers a decentralized and immutable ledger that can address security issues in centralized systems. Blockchain-based systems have the potential to provide secure and transparent financial transactions while maintaining privacy (Ma et al., 2021). However, malicious actors can still exploit vulnerabilities in the blockchain network, and detecting fraudulent transactions in the blockchain is a challenging task. The application of machine learning techniques, such as XGBoost and random forest, to blockchain data has the potential to improve the detection of fraudulent transactions. In this proposed system, machine learning models are directly linked to the blockchain, and a blockchain-based smart contract is deployed to classify incoming transactions as fraudulent or legitimate.

Building fraud detection systems using machine learning offerings some tasks that need to be lectured to ensure their effectiveness. The first challenge is data quality. Machine learning requires huge sums of good data to learn and make accurate predictions. In fraud detection, the quality of data is essential to detect and prevent fraudulent activities effectively. However, data quality can be challenging to maintain in the banking industry due to the great bulk of data and the complexity of the data sources. Poor data quality can lead to inaccurate predictions and increased false positives, which can undermine the efficacy of the fraud detection system (Chen et al., n.d.).

Another challenge is the dynamic nature of fraud patterns. Fraudsters are continually evolving their tactics, and new fraud patterns emerge regularly. Building a fraud detection system that can adapt to these new patterns is critical to ensuring its effectiveness. However, this presents a significant challenge as it requires continuous monitoring of data and machine learning models, updating the models, and retraining them to detect new patterns. Failure to adapt to new patterns can lead to increased financial losses and damage to customer trust (Niranjanamurthy et al., 2019).

Fraud is an ever-present threat, causing financial losses and damages to a company's assets and reputation. But every problem has a solution, and here the solution lies in the adoption of blockchain.

Blockchain is a revolutionary technology that helps detect and prevent fraud by providing a transparent, immutable, and decentralized ledger that can't be altered, deleted, or manipulated. By leveraging the features of blockchain, such as smart contracts, authentication, and audit trail, businesses can build robust fraud prevention systems that trigger real-time alerts to prevent fraudulent activities..

This paper suggests a method by which e-commerce businesses might cooperate to develop reliable machine learning algorithms gradually while preserving business plans and minimizing privacy concerns. Authentic data from the actual market is necessary to provide existing solutions strength. This work makes use of cutting-edge blockchain technology to create a platform for training fraud detection ML models progressively and cooperatively while safeguarding the privacy of contributing businesses. In this study, smart contracts have been employed to completely and stably automate the procedure throughout the system. This creates complete trust among enterprises to share their data safely because no system functionality can be changed by anyone. To motivate companies by offering just incentives, an adaptive incentive system has been created.

As blockchain use cases continue to evolve across industries and gain wider adoption, we can expect to see more innovative approaches to secure the digital landscape. Thereby, it is imperative for businesses to embrace blockchain infrastructure as a service to protect themselves and their customers.

Moreover, existing ML models for credit card fraud detection be afflicted by a low detection accuracy and aren't capable of solve the extraordinarily skewed nature of credit score card fraud datasets. Consequently, it is critical to develop ML fashions which can carry out optimally and that could locate credit score card fraud with a high accuracy rating.Fraud detection is monitoring the behaviors of huge agencies of humans a good way to expect, detect, or minimize unacceptable interest which include fraud, intrusion, or defaulting. To analyze all authorized transactions and report suspect ones, gadget mastering techniques like Logistics Regression are used. Specialists evaluate these reports and contact cardholders to establish whether the transaction changed into legitimate or fraudulent. The investigators submit remarks to the automatic system, that's utilized to train and inform the algorithm over time to be able to recover fraud detection effectiveness.

RELATED WORKS

Credit card fraud rises significantly as credit card usage and trade volume increase. The main focus of bank risk management is on how to improve the detection and prevention of credit card fraud. An experiment-based model for identifying credit card fraud is proposed in the paper, and the results demonstrate that the methodology is both workable and effective. As electronic commerce continues to improve, fraud is becoming more and more prevalent globally and costing huge sums of money. In current scenario, major cause of financial losses is credit card fraud. It not only affects trades person but also individual clients. D Genetic algorithm, Meta learning strategy, neural network, HMM are the presented methods used to detect credit card frauds. In contemplate system for fraudulent detection, artificial intelligence concept of RFA random forest algorithm & decision tree is being used to solve the problem. Thus by implementation of the hybrid approach, financial losses can be reduced to greater extend.

The proposed RFA(Random forest algorithm)-based methodology is covered with numerous kernel involvement and also contains various fields of consumer profile in addition to spending profile, as opposed to just spending profile. The simulation results indicate a rise in the TP (true positive), TN (true negative), and FN (false negative) rates as well as a decline in the FP (falsc positive) & FP (false negative) rates. In the study, classification models based on decision trees and RFA are created and applied to issues of detecting credit card fraud. The study is one of the first to evaluate the effectiveness of RFA and decision tree approaches for detecting credit card fraud using actual data.

Using a real-world credit card data set, a novel cost-sensitive decision tree technique that lowers the sum of misclassification costs while choosing the splitting attribute at each non-terminal node is tested against the well-known traditional classification models. The master card application in fraud detection is fully integrated into the analysis. Several strategies, with a focus on neural networks, data mining, and distributed data mining, have been suggested for detecting credit card fraud. This area of research has attracted a lot of attention. Many books have been published and made available to the public, either as fraudulent or proven to be fraudulent to identify credit card fraud. Although these methods and algorithms have achieved unexpected success in some areas, have not provided reliable and consistent fraud detection solutions. The method has proven effective in reducing false positives and improving fraud detection performance. The author studies various methods of finding external objects. Credit card fraud can be addressed through external methods. These methods are useful for finding fraudulent jobs. To test these examples, 70% of the area is used for training and 30% is used,which makes it easy to prevent fraudulent activity and credit card fraud, and error checking is also simple and easy to find .An increase in Internet activity is directly related to an increase in the level of fraud. Fraud acts as an illicit fraud or a crime intended to the result of financial or personal gain. That is a deliberate act it is against the law, law or policy for the purpose of achieving it unauthorized financial gain. Many books on mysterious discovery or fraud on the domain have been published and are available public use. Extensive research by Clifton Phua and collaborators have revealed that the strategy leases on the domain include data mining applications, automatic fraud detection, enemy detection.

In Suman, student studies, GJUS & T at Hisar HCE introduce strategies together with Supervised and Unattended getting to know to locate credit card fraud. Although these methods and algorithms have performed surprising achievement in some places, it have failed to provide permanent and steady fraud detection answer. The identical research website became evolved via Wen- Fang YU and Na Wang, each perform the Outlier mines, the Outlier discover mines and Distance sum algorithms for correct accuracy expect fraudulent interest inside the simulation take a look at of credit score card set facts for specific trades the financial institution. Outlier mining is a discipline of information mining it is essentially utilized in monetary boards and the net. It's approximately to attain items extracted from the principle system i.e., false positives. The attributes purchaser behaviour and primarily based on their fee the attributes it is calculated that distance among the condo price of that attribute and its pre-determined value. Unusual techniques First, found database at Kaggle, a data analysis website that provides data sets. Within the database, there are 31 columns of which 28 are named v1-v28 to protect sensitive data. Some columns represent Time, Value and such as mixed data mining / complex network division algorithm is possible see illegal occurrences on real card data set, based on a network algorithm that allows to create deviations of single model deviations from the reference group appears to be operating normally in the middle limited online transactions. There have also been efforts to improve from the ground up a new feature. Efforts have been made to improve alert feedback interaction in the event of fraudulent activity. In the event of a fraudulent activity,an authorized system will do so be notified and a response to further denial will be sent transaction. Artificial Genetic Algorithm, one of the most widely used methods new light on the domain, fighting fraud from another guidance.

In Fraudulent Detection in Credit Card System Using SVM & Decision Tree (Vijayshree B. Nipane, Poonam S. Kalinge, Dipali Vidhate, Kunal War, Bhagyashree P. Deshpande), With growing advancement in the electronic commerce field, fraud is spreading all over the world, causing major financial losses. In the current scenario, Major cause of financial losses is credit card fraud; it not only affects tradesperson but also individual clients. Decision tree, Genetic algorithm, Metalearning strategy, neural network, HMM are the presented methods used to detect credit card frauds. In contemplating system for fraudulent detection, artificial intelligence concept of Support Vector Machine (SVM) & decision tree is being used to solve the problem. Thus by the implementation of the hybrid approach, financial losses can be reduced to greater extent.

In gadget gaining knowledge of based totally method to financial Fraud Detection process in cellular payment system (Dahee Choi and Kyungho Lee), cell fee fraud is the unauthorized use of mobile transaction thru identification theft or credit score card stealing to fraudulently achieve money. Cell payment fraud is a quick- growing difficulty via the emergence of smartphone and online transition offerings. Inside the real global, a particularly correct procedure in cellular fee fraud detection is wanted on account that economic fraud causes economic loss. Therefore, the technique proposed the general process of detecting mobile price fraud based totally on device studying, supervised and unsupervised technique to hit upon fraud and manner massive amounts of financial statistics.

Moreover, the approach performed sampling process and feature selection process for fast processing with large volumes of transaction data and to achieve high accuracy in mobile payment detection. F-measure and ROC curve are used to validate the proposed model. Supervised algorithms were presented. Deep learning. Logistic Regression, Nave Bayesian, Support Vector Machine (SVM), Neural Network, Artificial Immune System, K Nearest Neighbour, Data Mining. Decision Tree, Fuzzy logic based System, and Genetic Algorithm are some of the techniques used. Comparison of machine-learning algorithms results in prediction, clustering, and outlier detection. For fraud detection, different algorithms like Anomaly Detection Algorithm, K-Nearest Neighbour, Random Forest, K-Means and Decision Tree were used. Based on a given scenario, presented several techniques and predicted the best algorithm to detect deceitful transactions. To predict the fraud result, the system used various rules and algorithms to generate the Fraud score for that certain transaction.

PROPOSED WORK

RFA and DT are employed in the suggested device for the classification and regression of the dataset. Get the data from credit cards first, then evaluate it. Dataset cleaning is necessary after dataset analysis. Any dataset may frequently have numerous duplicate and null entries, hence cleaning is necessary to remove all of these values. The dataset was then divided into two classes—the trained dataset and the testing dataset—for comparison and reading. The RFA and DT are applied after the dataset has been divided. The dataset can be classified into 4 categories with the help of the RFA and DT in order to receive it as a bewilderment matrix. On comparison the Random forest model works higher than selection trees. So, RFA is applied, where the set of rules will provide the higher accuracy approximately the credit card fraud transactions. But statement of dataset suffers a extreme trouble of class imbalance. The magnificence imbalance trouble can be solved by numerous strategies. Oversampling is considered one of them. After solving imbalance issues the model plays better. In the end, within the evaluation the correctness of credit card fraud transactions can be received in an effort to be in the end represented inside the shape of graphical representation.

Decision Tree

Continually dividing the data based on a specific parameter, decision trees are a type of supervised machine learning. Decision nodes and leaves, which make up the tree, can both be understood. Decisions or outcomes are represented by the leaves. Furthermore, the data is divided at the decision nodes.

Decision tree technique is statistical data mining technique in which independent and dependent properties are logically expressed in a edifice in the form of a tree. The categorization rules derived from the decision tree are if then expressions, and to generate each rule, all tests must pass. Decision trees usually split a complex problem into many simple ones, and use iteration to solve sub - problems. The tree is a predictive decision support tool that creates mappings of possible outcomes from different observations. There are numerous prominent classifiers for generating class models from decision trees. A supervised machine learning technique called a decision tree is used to classify or forecast data based on how a priori questions were answered. Because the model is supervised learning, it is trained and tested using data sets that contain the required categorization.

The decision tree's foundation, or root node.

A node can be split into several sub-nodes by the splitting procedure.

A decision node is used when a sub-node is further divided into several sub-nodes.

When a sub-node does not further divide into sub-nodes, it becomes a leaf node, which indicates potential outcomes.

Pruning: The act of removing decision tree nodes from a tree.

Branch: An area of the decision tree that has several nodes.

Working process of Decision Tree based on credit card fraud detection, the decision tree has two stages.

1) The initial step is to build a decision tree using the training data provided, and
2) The later step is to use decision rules to classify incoming transactions.

Implementation of Decision Tree

Decision trees usually split a complex problem into many simple ones, and use iteration to solve sub- problems. The tree is a predictive decision support tool that creates mappings of possible outcomes from different observations. There are numerous prominent classifiers for generating class models from decision trees. To improve precision and avoid overfitting, during the pruning step, such classifiers create a decision tree and afterwards clean up subtrees from the decision tree. The tree can be created by applying machine learning algorithms to the credit card database, such as ID3, C4.5, and multi-layer pruned classifier (MLPC). The aim of the Decision Tree model is to build a small decision tree with high precision. Based on credit card scam detection, the decision tree has two stages. The initial step is to build a decision tree using the training data provided, and the later step is to use decision rules to classify incoming transactions. The decision tree's input data is labelled with class labels, such as legitimate or fraudulent. The system monitors each account individually using appropriate descriptors to identify transactions and flags as legitimate or legitimate.

Figure 3.

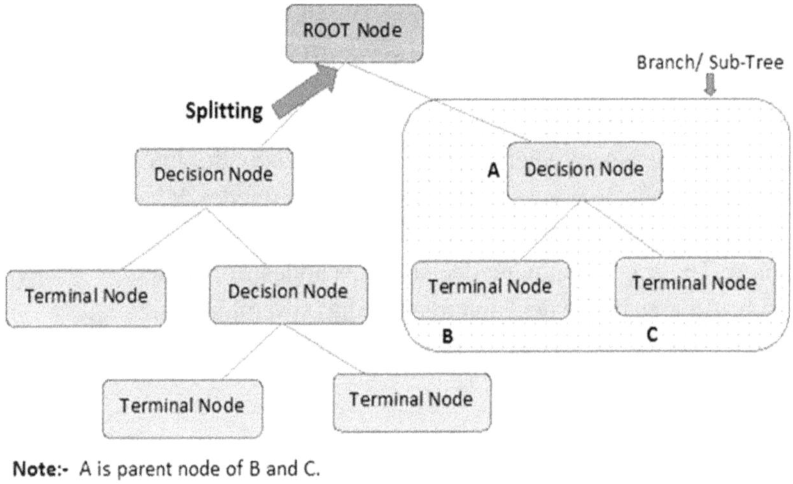

In the course of Decision Tree,all training examples start with one node representing the tree data set at the root node. Each node is split into child nodes in a method-specific binary or multipartition fashion. The decision rules are read one by one from the decision table for each transaction that classify as Match the transaction fields to each decision rule. It first finds an exact match and indicates the matched rule and transaction class of that class. If no match is found, the highest risk among matching rules is selected and the transaction class is populated with the matched rules of that class. It indicates if a new transaction is a fraud of the same form, The node has been renamed the leaf and is flagged as fraudulent.

The model is both quick and adaptable. The MLPC approach is utilized as pre-pruning, which stops the tree's growth at the pruning level specified before construction. It consists of a tree-top-down recursive partitioning and conquest method. Initially all training examples are maintained on the route. The sample is then recursively split based on the chosen attributes. the entropy metric, choose the split attribute.

Repeat the necessary stages until any of the four conditions is met:

1. All samples from a given node pertain to the same class.
2. There are also no other properties for partitioning.
3. There are no remaining sample.
4. Prune level is achieved as set.

Figure 4. Representation of decision tree

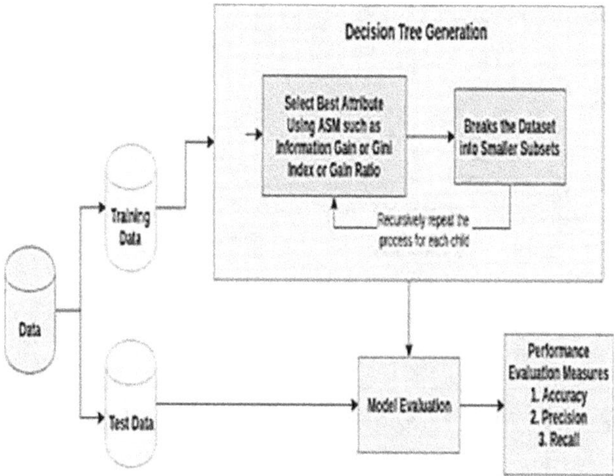

FLOW DIAGRAM FOR DECISION TREE

RFA Implementation in Credit Card Fraud Detection

The RFA provides higher accuracy in outcomes for credit card fraud detection. The dataset may first all be gathered and examined. The dataset will be cleaned up by the analysis system by removing all reproduction values and null values. The dataset can now be pre-processed based on the amount and transaction time to find the accuracy of the resulting dataset. Following the pre-processing of the dataset into amount and transaction time, the dataset may now be categorised. The dataset is divided into categories such as expert knowledge and test dataset. Use of a program called “Scikit-study” is made here for the dataset category.

Scikit-learn is a free tool for Python’s machine learning library that includes features like classification, regression, clustering techniques, and many other Python-compatible methods. Applying the RFA follows the dataset’s pre-processing. A confusion matrix could be obtained by doing a second analysis of the pre-processed dataset using RFA. The dataset can be divided into four blocks in the confusion matrix: real wonderful (TP), true negative (TN), false fantastic (FP), and false awful (FN). Now, until all of the data has been validated, the dataset will continually be partitioned. Various types of information can be assessed, and in the end, they will be displayed as different graphs.

These distinct graphs will only give slightly less accurate information about the resulting dataset. In order to improve accuracy, one can use RFA, which uses all the graph values to provide the best essential values with a higher level of precision than any other methods.

Figure 5.

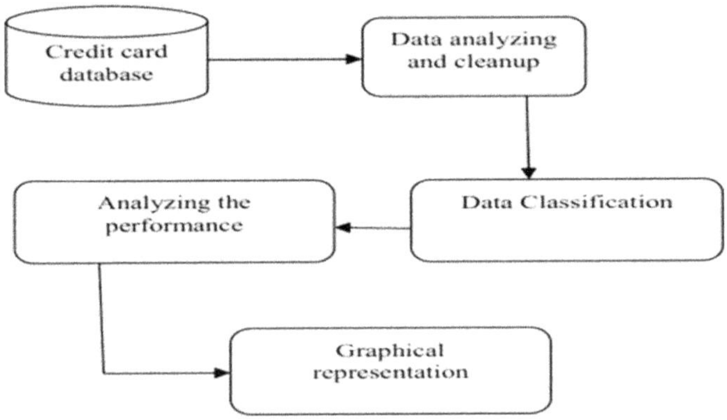

Have a credit card dataset in the architecture that contains all the credit card information first. For analysis and preprocessing of the dataset, however, simply consider the amount and transaction time. The process of data cleaning is the following phase, in which the dataset is evaluated and all duplicate and null values are removed from the original dataset.

The data partition is the following stage, in which the credit card dataset will be split into two parts as a trained dataset and a tested dataset. A confusion matrix will then be created after applying RFA. On the resulting confusion matrix, a performance analysis will now be conducted. According to performance study, the credit card fraud detection system has an accuracy rate of roughly 90%.

Working process of Random Forest

The following are the fundamental steps in using the random forest algorithm:

1. Choose N randomly selected records from the dataset.
2. Construct a decision tree using these N records.
3. Repeat Steps 1 and 2 after selecting the algorithm's number of trees.
4. For a classification issue, every tree in the forest may forecast which category the new record belongs in. The category that receives the most votes ultimately receives the new record.

Figure 6. Implementation of random forest algorithm

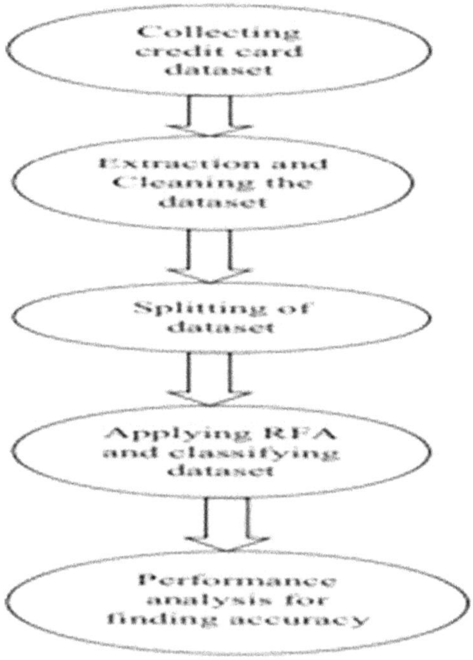

Training and Evaluating Models on the Dataset

Train and Evaluate the models on the Dataset. Training and evaluating the newly created models on the dataset and pick the best one. Train the decision tree and random forest models on the dataset using the fit() function. Record the predictions made by the models using the predict() function and evaluate. A confusion matrix is finally produced after using RFA AND DT. The generated data, which was previously collected as a confusion matrix, may now be assessed using a graphical representation, which provides more accuracy.

Address the Class-Imbalance Issue

The Random Forest model works better than Decision Trees. But, the observation on the dataset results in a serious problem of class imbalance. The genuine (not fraud) transactions are more than 99% with the credit card fraud transactions constituting 0.17%. With such a distribution, if the model trained without taking care of the imbalance issues, it predicts the label with higher importance given to genuine transactions (as there is more data about them) and hence obtains more accuracy. The elegance imbalance hassle can be solved via various techniques. Oversampling is considered one of them. Oversample the minority elegance is one of the tactics to address the imbalanced datasets. The very best solution includes doubling examples in the minority elegance, even though those examples make contributions no new facts to the version. As a substitute, new examples can be generated by way of replicating existing ones. The synthetic Minority Oversampling approach or SMOTE for short, is a way of statistics augmentation for the minority magnificence. The above SMOTE is gift inside the imblearn package deal.

CONCLUSION

From the analysis, the accuracy of Random wooded area is simply proper. The look at carried out an more desirable random woodland set of rules the usage of hyperparameters to discover the first-rate values to run the classifier and profits the very best viable accuracy. Overall performance of the SMOTE oversampling technique to overcome the imbalanced dataset issue. The end result showed that the classifier become capable of expect fraudulent transactions. Hence, acquired the result of an accurate value of credit card fraud detection i.e. 0.99989 using a random forest algorithm with new enhancements. In comparison to existing modules, the proposed module is applicable for the larger dataset and provides more accurate results. The Random forest algorithm will provide better performance with many training data, but speed during testing and application will still suffer. Usage of more pre- processing techniques would also assist. Future work will try to represent a software application and provide a solution for credit card fraud using the new technologies like Machine Learning, Artificial Intelligence. With the evaluation of effects, the use of specific metrics such as recall, precision, F1 rating, with a high accuracy stage was found. Consequences confirmed that the model, due to its rather trustworthy utility, is properly-proper to addressing the venture of imbalanced statistics in fraud detection.

FUTURE SCOPE

Although it have not been able to attain the goal of a hundred percentage accuracy with fraud detection, sooner or later developing a machine that could, with enough time and facts, get very near that purpose. The nature of the venture permits for plenty algorithms integration modules and their effects can be blended to increase the accuracy of the final result. The version can be further more desirable algorithms in it. However, the effect of those algorithms it wishes to be in the equal layout like the others. Precisely that the scenario is exceptional, the modules are clean to feature as it's far accomplished in them code. It offers a superb diploma of modularity as nicely project range. Additional development space can be found in the database. It can be done by making the system safer for merchants and customers to use certifications and new checks can be added to understand fraudulent trading patterns and alert respective card holders and bankers when fraudulent activity is detected. The dataset available in routine processing may be outdated; Having updated data is essential for effective fraud behaviour identification. Frauds use different techniques that are growing rapidly with new technology. The nature of the entry pattern can vary from one geographic location to another, which can be to pseudo positive detection. In such a case, future scope may be based on multiple models with different models focusing on improving effectiveness. In addition to blockchain technology, other AI techniques such as machine learning and natural language processing (NLP) can also be used to combat financial fraud.

These techniques can analyze vast amounts of data in real-time and identify patterns and anomalies that may indicate fraudulent activity. Furthermore, NLP can be used to analyze text-based data such as emails and chat messages to detect fraudulent behavior .Overall, the financial sector faces significant challenges in combating cybercrime and fraud. However, with the use of advanced technologies such as blockchain, AI, and NLP, it is possible to develop more robust and secure systems to prevent and detect fraudulent activity. Ongoing research and development in these areas will continue to improve the security and resilience of financial systems in the face of evolving cyber threats.

REFERENCES

Ashfaq, T., Khalid, M. I., Ali, G., Affendi, M. E., Iqbal, J., Hussain, S., Ullah, S. S., Yahaya, A. S., Khalid, R., & Mateen, A. (2022, September 25). An Efficient and Secure Energy Trading Approach with Machine Learning Technique and Consortium Blockchain. *Sensors (Basel)*, *22*(19), 7263. doi:10.3390/s22197263 PMID:36236363

Behdad, M., Barone, L., Bennamoun, M., & French, T. (2012). Natureinspired techniques in the context of fraud detection. *IEEE Transactions on Systems, Man, and Cybernetics. Part C, Applications and Reviews*, *42*(6), 1273–1290. doi:10.1109/TSMCC.2012.2215851

Bhattacharyya, S., Jha, S., Tharakunnel, K., & Westland, J. C. (2011). Data mining for credit card fraud: A comparative study. *Decision Support Systems*, *50*(3), 602–613. doi:10.1016/j.dss.2010.08.008

Bolton, R. J., & David, J. H. (2001). Unsupervised Profiling Methods for Fraud Detection. *Proc Credit Scoring and Credit Control, 7*, 5–7.

Chen, F., Wan, H., Cai, H., & Cheng, G. (n.d.). Machine learning in/for blockchain: Future and challenges. *The Canadian Journal of Statistics, 49*(4), 1364–1382.

Diro, A., Chilamkurti, N., Nguyen, V. D., & Heyne, W. (2021, December 13). A Comprehensive Study of Anomaly Detection Schemes in IoT Networks Using Machine Learning Algorithms". *Sensors (Basel), 21*(24), 8320. doi:10.3390/s21248320 PMID:34960414

Drummond, C., & Holte, R. C. (2003). C4.5, class imbalance, and cost sensitivity:why under sampling beats oversampling. *Proc of the Icml Workshop on Learning from Imbalanced Datasets II*, 1–8.

Duman, E., & Ozcelik, M. H. (2011). Detecting credit card fraud by genetic algorithm and scatter search. *Expert Systems with Applications, 38*(10), 13057–13063. doi:10.1016/j.eswa.2011.04.110

Gmbh & Co. (2016). *Global online payment methods: Full year 2016*. Tech. Rep.

Gupta, S., & Johari, R. (2011). A New Framework for Credit Card Transactions Involving Mutual Authentication between Cardholder and Merchant. *International Conference on Communication Systems and Network Technologies IEEE*, 22-26. 10.1109/CSNT.2011.12

Harris, J. D., & Waggoner, B. (2019). Decentralized and collaborative AI on blockchain. *Proc. IEEE Int. Conf. Blockchain (Blockchain),* 368–375.

Ju, W. H., & Vardi, Y. (2001). A hybrid high-order markov chain model for computer intrusion detection. *Journal of Computational and Graphical Statistics, 10*(2), 277–295. doi:10.1198/10618600152628068

Kundu, A., Panigrahi, S., Sural, S., & Majumdar, A. K. (2009). Blastssaha hybridization for credit card fraud detection. *IEEE Transactions on Dependable and Secure Computing, 6*(4), 309-315.

Ma, C., Kong, X., Lan, Q., & Zhou, Z. (2021, December). The privacy protection mechanism of hyperledger fabric and its application in supply chain finance. *Cybersecurity, 2*(1), 1–9.

Mota, G., Fernandes, J., & Belo, O. (2014). Usage signatures analysis an alternative method for preventing fraud in E-Commerce applications. *International Conference on Data Science and Advanced Analytics* (pp.203-208). IEEE. 10.1109/DSAA.2014.7058074

Niranjanamurthy, M., Nithya, B. N., & Jagannatha, S. (2019, November). Analysis of blockchain technology: Pros, cons and SWOT. *Cluster Computing*, *22*(S6), 14743–14757. doi:10.1007/s10586-018-2387-5

Quah, J. T. S., & Sriganesh, M. (2008). Real-time credit card fraud detection using computational intelligence. *Expert Systems with Applications*, *35*(4), 1721–1732. doi:10.1016/j.eswa.2007.08.093

Sahin, Y., & Duman, E. (2011). Detecting credit card fraud by decision trees and support vector machines. *Lecture Notes in Engineering and Computer Science, 2188*(1).

Seyedhossein, L., & Hashemi, M. R. (2011). Mining information from credit card time series for timelier fraud detection. *International Symposium on Telecommunications IEEE*, 619-624.

Shi, E., Niu, Y., Jakobsson, M., & Chow, R. (2010). Implicit Authentication through Learning User Behavior. *International Conference on Information Security* (Vol.6531, pp.99-113). Springer Verlag. 10.1007/978-3-642-18178-8_9

Srivastava, A., Kundu, A., Sural, S., & Majumdar, A. (2008). Credit card fraud detection using hidden markov model. *IEEE Transactions on Dependable and Secure Computing*, *5*(1), 37–48. doi:10.1109/TDSC.2007.70228

Chapter 9
Genetic Crossover Operator in Local Search of the Assembly Line Balancing Problem

Gustavo Erick Anaya-Fuentes
https://orcid.org/0000-0002-3708-6763
Autonomous University of Hidalgo, Mexico

Hector Rivera-Gómez
https://orcid.org/0000-0002-2903-2909
Autonomous University of Hidalgo, Mexico

Norberto Hernández-Romero
Autonomous University of Hidalgo, Mexico

Juan Carlos Seck Tuoh-Mora
https://orcid.org/0000-0003-3678-1120
Autonomous University of Hidalgo, Mexico

ABSTRACT

One of the biggest challenges facing the industry today lies in the assignment of robots to the workstations of production processes in order to perform tasks collaboratively between robots and human labor; this is known as Cobots. This document proposes to minimize the number of workstations by assigning robots, to reduce production costs. Additionally, it seeks to minimize the number of workers by assigning Cobots to a percentage of workstations. Due to the above, in this research, the Assembly Line Balancing Problem Type I (SALBP-1) is adapted with a Cobot assignment problem. This problem is considered NP-hard, so the use of a hybrid heuristic is proposed in the search to minimize the number of workers and the number of workstations. The hybrid consists of a modified genetic algorithm applying a local search within the genetic selection operator. The results demonstrate a decrease in the assignment of workstations, as well as a decrease in assignment of workers when using Cobots in some workstations using the proposed algorithm for the benefit of organizations.

DOI: 10.4018/979-8-3693-1598-9.ch009

1. INTRODUCTION

To analyze assembly lines, it is necessary to recognize the beginnings of manufacturing using assembly lines. It was Henry Ford who began this production model in the manufacture of the automobile known as the Model T. The layout of an assembly line is made up of a certain number of workstations connected sequentially by material transport devices. The assignment of tasks to workstations is carried out considering possible precedence restrictions and the completion time of activities in each workstation, this time must be the same in all workstations; It is known as cycle time (Grzechca, 2015). When the time used at a workstation is less than the predetermined cycle time, idle time is generated (Erel & Sarin, 1998). So it becomes necessary to find a sequencing of tasks and assignment of these to the workstations considering the cycle time and the restrictions that arise due to the nature of the process. This is called balance of production lines or set.

The balancing of assembly lines allows the process activities to be distributed across the workstations with the intention of avoiding bottlenecks, waiting times and waste. Its objective is to find an adequate distribution of capacity, to ensure a continuous and uniform flow of products through the different processes within the production plant, under conditions of quantity, balance and continuity (Peña-Orozco, Neira-García, & Ruiz-Grisales, 2016). Furthermore, the proper balance of production lines is capable of increasing productivity (Budi Rochayata & Widodasih, 2023).

In general, Assembly Line Balancing Problems (ALB) seek to balance assembly tasks with respect to some objective function (Kamarudin & Rashid, 2018). Balancing assembly lines is a priority in the mass production of a product. This problem is classified into: Simple Assembly Line Balancing Problem (SALBP) and General Assembly Line Balancing Problem (GALBP). The latter are divided into: Muti-trunkcd Line Balancing Problem (MALBP) and the U-shaped Line Balancing Problem (UALB) (Jirasirilerd, et al., 2020).

There are generalized limiting assumptions for the Assembly Line Balancing Problem, among which the following stand out:

1. Mass production without flexibility in the product.
2. There is a default way to process tasks.
3. The cycle time is fixed and according to the pace of demand.
4. There are precedence restrictions.
5. Task times are deterministic.
6. It is not possible to divide tasks.
7. All workstations have the same technology.

In practical cases, it is possible to adapt the previous conditions according to the needs and context. This is one of the purposes of the present investigation. In the following sections, the background information regarding the assembly line problem, the Type I Assembly Line Balancing Problem, Local Search, Genetic Algorithms and Cobots will be reviewed. Section 2 presents some key definitions, Section 3 details the problem statement, Section 4 presents the applied methodology, Section 5 presents several experimentations and results, Finally, Section 6 concludes the study.

1.1 Background

a) The Assembly Line Problem (ALB)

Balancing an assembly line emerged as an idea in a thesis work (Bryton, 1954) with a mathematical representation, later it was represented through the formulation in linear programming (Salveson, 1955). Formally, the assembly line balancing, ALB problem was posed by Helgeson and Birnie (Helgeson & Birnie, Assembly line balancing using the ranked positional weighting technique, 1961). However, it was shown that the problem is classified as NP-Hard (Gutjahr & Neumhauser, 1964) because the number of tasks can be thousands in a real system, generating computational complexity as it cannot be solved in polynomial time, this represented a problem when we try to use exact or linear programming methods in the search for solutions.

Therefore, to solve the ALB problem, a computational procedure was presented (Jackson, 1956) based on the iteration of the search for feasible sequences. Despite not comparing the results with others in the literature, the main contribution consists of a new mathematical definition of the problem and the method for assigning tasks to the workstations in a feasible way. However, the optimization problem continued due to computational complexity.

In the search to find more efficient methods using fewer resources, a technique was developed that does not use a computer (Kilbridge & Wester, 1961); It is based on the assignment of tasks in two columns. In the first column, jobs with the same number of feasible elements are assigned, while in the second column, jobs that will be feasible once those in the first column are executed are assigned. The results of these studies were not the most efficient, but the benefit was that fewer resources were used to find feasible solutions. In the efforts to find new techniques, the Helgeson technique was shown (Helgeson & Birnie, Assembly Line Balancing Using the Ranked Positional Weight Technique, 1961) establishing an allocation algorithm according to the sum of the work times and all the following elements so that the elements with the longest times are assigned first.

It was a matter of time before the need arose to compare the results achieved by different techniques, so the methods of Helgeson, Hoffman, Arcus, Held and Lexico Order were compared (Mastor, 1970). The latter turned out to be the best, those that follow respectively are Helgeson, Hoffman, Arcus and finally Held about the efficiency of the algorithms to solve the ALB problem. Some variation in the ALB problem appeared by modifying the restrictions of having parallel assembly lines (Pinto, Dannenbring, & Khumawala, 1975). By implementing them, the aim is to improve the production rate using linear programming mathematical tools. Later, researchers began to address the problem using integer programming algorithms more frequently, taking precedence activities and the predetermined cycle time as constraints; based on a systematic evaluation procedure (Talbot & Patterson, 1984).

b) The Simple Assembly Line Balancing (SALB) Problem

Subsequently, the ALB is published in its simple classification as SALBP Simple Assembly Line Balancing Problem. The term simple is because mixed models, assembly lines, or other restrictions are not considered. Furthermore, they presented alternative programming formulations and a general integer programming formulation (Baybars, 1986). The SALBP was bifurcated according to different objectives into SALBP-1 and SALBP-2 in the quest to improve the production rate or some equivalent parameter (Scholl & Vob, Simple Assembly Line Balancing-Heuristic Approaches, 1996). So new classifications for the SALB appeared, defining the following: The Simple Assembly Line Balancing Problem type 1, named SALBP-1, aims to minimize the number of workstations starting from a predetermined cycle time. The simple assembly line balancing problem type 2, named as SALBP-2, aims to minimize the cycle time given a fixed number of workstations. This occurs when the production plant does not have growth options or there is a high cost of incorporating new workstations. The SALBP-E simple assembly line efficiency trade-off problem seeks efficiency between workstations and cycle time, neither of these is fixed. The simple and feasible assembly line balancing problem SALBP-F aims to find feasible solutions in a process with fixed workstations and cycle times (Kamarudin & Rashid, 2018). The problem took different approaches such as the case of the U-shaped assembly line balancing problem, called UALBP (Miltenburg & Wijngaard, 1994) using SALBP types 1, 2 and E.

c) The Simple Type I Assembly Line Balancing Problem (SALB-1)

Among the first methods used to solve SALBP-1, the so-called 10-SP was used, in which the best solution from a group of 10 is selected. The ARCUS method is a multistep method and an iterative backtracking method called MALB (Dar-el, 1975).

Additionally, the problem was addressed using dynamic programming, achieving feasible sequences in assigning jobs to stations (Held, Karp, & Sharesian, 1963). In this instance of small size about the number of tasks, enumerated subsets were classified according to feasible subsets. They are considered feasible when the tasks in a subset meet the precedence constraints. A similar algorithm called Hoffman's technique (Hoffman, 1963) in which it seeks to combine the assignment of feasible tasks, that is, with precedence activities carried out to exactly reaching the limit time of the workstation known as work time. This involves minimizing ideal time. Different calculations are allowed within the algorithm such as removing tasks from the assignment list, including new ones and modifying the sequence. One of the main limitations of this method is due to the need to have a small number of tasks to perform a complete enumeration of the stations. Additionally, the need to evaluate additional parameters to those that had been considered until now was generated: number of workstations and production rates. Therefore, the parameter of early delivery in the processes was evaluated, considered as a difficulty, and was called the deterioration task. This is intended to be avoided because it occurs in a production process when the task begins before the planned time without reducing the cycle time (Noushabadi, Bahalke, Dolatkhahi, Dolatkhahi, & Makui, 2011).

Later the approaches to solve the SALBP-1 focused on the proposals of linear programming models (Scholl, Fliedner, & Boysen, Balancing assembly lines with assignment restrictions, 2008) and heuristic models (Glover, 1989) in the search for new algorithms that provide better results in efficiency parameters by minimizing workstations, number of employees and considering computational times. For this reason, heuristics such as the so-called Beam-ACO approach (Blum, 2008) were used, which is a hybrid between Ant Colony Optimization and Beam Search, improving results in 97% of the comparison instances in the literature. This is evidence of an efficient algorithm despite not reaching optimal values. Improvements to the models proposed were also presented as in the case of (Ritt & Costa, 2015) through a relaxation of the integer programming model on a SALBP-U (Simple Assembly Line Balancing Problem type U) with SALBP format. Another method used to address this problem is known as the Hybrid Swarm Intelligence Approach (Kalia, Dewedi, & Sharma, 2019) in which the support of robotic technology was additionally considered to balance the activities of the assembly line. In addition, other variants of the SALBP-1 emerged, such as the so-called MAL Multi-manned assembly line (Sepahi & Jalali, 2014) considering task times dependent on the concentration of workers at the workstation; The problem solution is relatively good considering that heuristic algorithms were used.

Among the new heuristic algorithms to solve the SALBP-1 is the Ranked Position Weighted RPW method (Tomar & Manoria, 2016), which consists of determining the position weight of each task, ordered in descending order and first selecting the higher weight tasks to generate a feasible task sequence. In addition to the COMSOAL method, the latter consists of first selecting tasks that do not have precedence to create a feasible sequence with them as far as possible and updating the precedence matrix as new activities are assigned. It is an iterative process with a stopping method called convergence. Hybrid algorithms became a trend in the search for efficient techniques that satisfy solutions to the SALPB-1 in feasible computational times, so the use of AG Genetic Algorithms was combined with the technique called Zoning Constraints (Belassiria, Mazouzi, ELfezazi, Cherrafi, & ELMaskaoui, 2017) with which the additional intention was to solve a problem with two objective functions to maximize the efficiency of the assembly line and minimize idle time. The two-objective problem was also implemented for the optimization of SALBP-1 with the intention of minimizing the mean of the total direction changes and at the same time minimizing the mean of the total tool changes (Ab Rashid, Tiwari, & Hutabarat, 2019). Additionally, new solution techniques were proposed such as the so-called Improved Immunological Algorithm (Han-ye, 2017), which introduces immunological adjustments, vaccine extraction, vaccination, and immunological selection. Finally, the immunological algorithm is obtained from the degradation of the population. The result concludes that the improved algorithm is efficient when compared with the results of similar instances in the literature.

Algorithms such as the one proposed by (Blum, 2008) were used to be modified to improve, in the case of the one proposed by (Huo, Wang, Chan, Lee, & Strandhagen, 2018), the results showed an efficiency of 95.54%, which represents a better percentage than the 97% achieved by the first in 2008 when compared with results from the literature.

Some time later, the efficiency of different exact methods was analyzed again, such as Branching and bounding, search direction, method of achieving upper and lower limits, dominance rules and search strategies (Li, Kucukkoc, & Tang, 2019); The results demonstrate that the use of high-performance structural parameters allows the performance of exact methods to be improved significantly. However, computational time is still a factor to consider in high-volume instances. In the search to find more efficient algorithms, hybrid chain algorithms have been proposed, such as the three-phase optimization method to solve the SALBP-I (Yin & Luo, 2020) based on the Dantzing-Wolf decomposition using branching and bounding to speed up search processes in the branches of the tree. The results show that the mentioned article has better efficiency in terms of the quality of solutions and computational time compared to the classic Branch-and-price method. Simulators have also been used to perform a random search for solutions from the literature and using the PLANT SIMULATION software (Sharma & Sharma, 2017). This tool is useful only for checking the results because it does not have a defined technique or heuristic to solve the problem.

Finally, the multi-manned assembly line balancing problem was combined with the U-Shaped problem considering stochastic times through the formulation of a linear programming model considering the cycle time and predetermined restrictions, optimizing the algorithm parameter through experimental design (Zakaraia, Zaher, & Ragaa, Solving Stochastic Multi-Manned U-Shaped Assembly Line Balancing Problem using differential evolution algorithm, 2021). The importance of solving this problem lies in the benefits of its applications, such as the Balancing of assembly lines in a case study of a power transformer in the electrical industry, reducing the number of workstations from 19 to 16 by modifying the layout of the workstations. the assembly line and increasing efficiency using evolutionary algorithms (Bakar, Ramli, Zakaria, Sin, & Masran, 2020). It has been used with a focus on the manufacturing industry using different heuristics (Abdullah, Faisae, Razali, & Perumal, 2017). The SALBP-1 approach was also used in the automotive industry through the use of GA with results that demonstrate an increase in the efficiency of the assembly line and a decrease in the variation in operating times (Didden, Lefeber, Adan, & Panhuijzen, 2023).

As we have seen in the previous lines, the SALBP-1 optimization models follow a trend towards adopting the real contexts of the problem; For this reason, the present research focuses on the search for optimization of the problem of minimization of workstations and workers considering conditions of technology collaboration, that is, with the support of robots. This topic is known as Cobots and below we will analyze the background to take the reader towards the amalgamation of SALBP-1 with the support of Cobots.

d) Human-Robot Collaborative Work (Cobots) in the Simple Type I Assembly Line Balancing Problem (SALB-1)

Cobots have been used in a wide variety of sectors specifically designed to work together with humans in a common workspace (Sultanov, Sulaiman, Li, Meshcheryakov, & Magid, 2022). It is important to note that the use of Cobots does not imply the substitution of labor, but rather these devices are designed to support human activities in the hope of being more efficient and effective in their processes and products. However, it has been pointed out that there is a risk that robots improve their skills during collaboration with workers, the risk is that the promise of not replacing workers with robots is not fulfilled due to the improvement of the robots' skills affecting human jobs (Sorell, 2022). The use of Cobots began to be studied with works similar to their use in the production of automobiles through assembly lines (Akella, et al., 1999) considering the study of Cobots as a sub-area of Intelligent Assistance Devices IADs and through the implementation of software called virtual guiding surfaces. Additionally, the aforementioned article emphasizes the importance of maintaining labor in production processes instead of replacing them with technology and also demonstrates the benefits of collaboration with robots. In addition, another article (Peshkin & Colgate, 1999) was responsible for explaining the study approach of Cobots as a tool for manipulating IAD devices and their applications in different areas such as medicine, design, and the industrial sector. An approach to SALBP-1 was carried out with its respective precedence restrictions considering the use of Cobots (Weckenborg, Kieckhafer, Müller, Grunewald, & Spengler, 2019). To solve the proposed instances, a GA was used as a solution technique; however, it was not compared with a literature benchmark.

In general, differences were identified between traditional industrial robots and collaborative industrial robots, highlighting that traditional ones have fixed installations with repetitive tasks that do not change frequently; and interact with the human factor only during programming. Benefits are only observable when production lot sizes are medium or large. Meanwhile, collaborative industrial robots have the flexibility to relocate; frequently change tasks; they interact frequently and safely with the worker; benefits can be observed even in a single production batch (Knudsen & Kaivo-Oja, 2020). The study of Cobots has had different approaches, such as the study of the synergy between human workers and managerial tasks through artificial intelligence (Sowa, Przegalinska, & Ciechanowski, 2021), proving that the use of Cobots allows for increasing the productivity of organizations. Another study focuses on the relationship and trends of Cobots with the fourth industrial revolution also known as Industry 4.0 (Kakade, 2023). In the study, important conditions were established to consider for the coexistence between human beings and robots, such as a robot cannot injure or injure a worker; the robot must obey orders except when the first point is not met; a robot must protect its existence as long as it is not in conflict with point one.

In the literature we find research articles from 2020 with trends toward including variables and restrictions present in the real scope of production; with models that consider the abilities of the robots, tools, and configuration times (Maruf, 2022). Therefore, the research carried out in this article proposes general but real conditions that occur in production processes. These will be explained in the Problem Statement section and in the method development, using a SALBP-1 approach.

e) Local Search Heuristic in SALBP-1

The Local Search Algorithm that we will henceforth call LS has been used to solve a wide variety of problems related to optimization, considering restrictions that must be satisfied (Tounsi & David, 2002). However, the number of works carried out with this heuristic to optimize the ALB, SALB-1 and SALB-2 is small. Thus, in the literature, we find that the Iterated Local Search heuristic has been modified in reference to the original algorithm with the objective of optimizing the SALBP-1 (Bautista, Suárez, Mateo, & Companys, 2000). More recent work than the one mentioned above combines the Multi-Manned and U-Shaped Assembly Line Balancing Problem with a SALBP-1 approach; the problem is addressed by LS. The results obtained are competitive with those presented in the literature (Zakaraia, Zaher, & Ragaa, Stochastic Local Search for Solving Chance-Constrained Multi-Manned U-shaped Assembly Line Balancing Problem with Time and Space Constraints, 2021). The LS heuristic has different variants, such as Hill Climbing, Simulated annealing, Taboo search, Late acceptance Hill climbing and Reactive search optimization (Schuurmans & Southey, 2001). For the research of this document, it was decided to use the Hill Climbing method because it is the most appropriate to adapt to the hybrid algorithm proposal in the Method. The Hill Climbing optimization method is a form of LS local search and consists of the following: It starts with an initial solution within the search space; The solution is subsequently evaluated using the objective function or also using some comparison parameter; Next, a neighborhood of solutions is generated by making small modifications to the initial solution; The best solution found in the neighborhood evaluated by the objective function or the predetermined parameter is selected by comparing it with the initial solution. The procedure is repeated iteratively until some stoppage criterion is met (Chinnasamy, Ramachandran, Amudha, & Ramu, 2022).

The algorithm proposed in the research of this document proposes the use of the IL heuristic within a Genetic Algorithm to find solutions to SALBP-1 by assigning cobots on some workstations. Therefore, reference is made below to Genetic Algorithms.

f) Genetic Algorithms (GA) in the Simple Assembly Line Balancing Problem (SALBP-1)

The use of Genetic Algorithms, hereinafter referred to as GA, has been diverse in optimization problems. The SALBP-1 has not been the exception, so in the literature, we can find works such as balancing assembly lines using GA and proposing the use of some concepts of the Simulated Annealing heuristic (Sabuncuoglu, Erel, & Tanyer, 2000), which is one of the variants of the LS. The concepts of this heuristic were only used during the elitism phase of the GA. Additionally, GAs have been used in variations of the SALBP-1, such as the Multi-Manned Assembly Line Balancing Problem, which from now on we will call MAL (Zamzam, Sadek, Afia, & El-Kharbotly, 2015), which is also a problem. multi-objective, approaching the real context of the assembly lines. The problem consists of scheduling and assigning a set of tasks with precedence constraints to workstations by minimizing the number of workers and the number of workstations with a predetermined cycle time. To solve the problem described, a GA hybrid was used. The results of the computational experiments allowed finding optimal solutions in 97% of the instances compared to those in the literature. This result demonstrates the efficiency of using GA in solving multi-objective problems in this case applied to a variant of SALBP-1 called MAL.

It is necessary to mention that hybrid GAs have been used to address the problem in question, this is the case of immune-enhanced GA. In this, the similarity formula between two antibodies is simplified in the improved algorithm; It is possible to prevent population degradation by introducing immune adjustment with vaccine extraction, vaccination, and immune selection (Zhang, 2017). The need to generate models close to reality has motivated researchers to carry out new approaches such as the requirement to solve multi-objective optimization problems (Zakaria, 2017) in which the first objective is to maximize the efficiency of the production line. Therefore, in the present research, it is proposed to address SALBP-1 using a modified GA, so that an LS mechanism is implemented within the genetic selection operator.

g) Trends and Real Cases

In the trends of the ALBP, new classifications of the problem are found, focused on the shape of the production line, this responds to the need to provide solutions to specific production lines in industry problems. The classifications are as follows: Straight-Shaped Assembly Line (StAL), Parallel Workstation Assembly Line (PWAL), U-Shaped Assembly Line (U-line), Two-Sided Assembly Line (2SAL), Multi-Manned Assembly Line (MAL), Parallel Assembly Lines (PALs) and Hybrid Assembly Line (PUALs). In this work, we work with the MAL type problem because it is possible to perform several tasks simultaneously at a workstation, allowing more than one worker per station; it is a requirement that the product in the process is of an adequate size to avoid hindering simultaneous work. In practical cases, it is possible to implement tools from trends in industry 4.0 to automate decision-making in order requests to decide if there is production capacity and make modifications in the balancing of assembly lines without consulting organization personnel (Rossit, Tohmé, & Frutos, 2018). The tools and benefits in Industry 4.0 aim to optimize flexible processes in production methods and flexible products supported by heuristic algorithms to achieve feasible solutions (Li & Huang, 2021).

The ALBP, in general, presents challenges in reference to the need to have standardized processes in its implementation, so that organizations that need to balance assembly lines must have at least a level 3 maturity level (Hackos, 2017), that is, have uniform and standardized processes; this is one of the main challenges for using optimization algorithms. If the process is not standardized, it cannot be optimized. So, organizations without these characteristics must go through this process before seeking optimization, this is a reality for many companies. On the other hand, heuristic algorithms can stagnate in local optimal results, so optimization trends seek to use parallelism (Fang et al., 2024) and computational equipment with greater power to improve efficiency in the results of flexible processes and products.

In general, ALBP-type problems in their different categories have practical applications in solving real and current problems within the industry. Trends focus on obtaining real data from samples unlike classic instances, problems can be adapted to the needs of the Layout like those generated by (Duran, Selcuk, Güner, & Baykoc, 2008) used in (Sotskov, 2023).

Derived from the lack of standardization in processes and in accordance with the level of maturity of organizations in practical applications, assembly line balancing has been improved using Lean Manufacturing. The results show that by balancing lines using this set of tools, it is possible to improve process productivity and efficiency between 78% and 95% (Mortada & Soulhi, 2023).

Studies have been conducted with real-world case studies, demonstrating the benefits in efficiency parameters, additionally, they are compared with instances from the literature. It is possible to observe how the optimization of assembly lines has granted benefits to companies in real practical cases by reducing bottlenecks (Maha, 2023), and improving productivity and efficiency (Mortada & Soulhi, 2023). In the following section, some definitions of interest to the reader are presented.

2. DEFINITIONS

Some key definitions for the appropriate understanding of the proposed model are the following:

Assembly lines: they are a form of process technology composed of a series of operations that are executed from raw materials, components, or semi-finished products to generate a product of higher value. It is a progressive ensemble linked by some type of medium.

Cycle time: is the time required to produce part of a process or a complete process. This time is the same for each of the workstations that make up the assembly line.

Idle time: time paid to a worker, including or not including the rental or use of machinery in an unproductive manner, that is, workers and machines cannot produce due to one or several factors such as lack of raw materials, lack of availability of equipment, poor scheduling of activities, among others.

ALB: Assembly line balancing is the action of appropriately allocating human resources for the proper functioning of the production or assembly line.

SALBP: It is the problem of allocating human resources appropriately to workstations to minimize parameters such as the number of workstations and a predetermined cycle time (type 1) or minimize the cycle time with the number of stations default jobs (type 2).

SALBP-1: Known as Simple Assembly Line Balancing Problem type 1, its objective is to minimize the number of workstations starting from a predetermined cycle time. This type of problem is common when the number of workstations is not a determining factor and stations can be used relatively unlimitedly. It is possible to have different predetermined cycle times, each one has different results when looking to optimize. The cycle time is fixed in each instance.

Robot: Programmable electronic device or machine that is capable of manipulating objects and performing various operations.

Cobot: It is also known as a collaborative robot and is one that operates together with humans safely to support them in different tasks and processes. The main difference between these and industrial robots is that they are built mainly to interact with human beings in shared spaces and seek efficiency.

Exact methods: They are also known as finite algorithms and are those that allow solutions to be obtained directly using iterative algorithms that calculate solutions of the system through successive approximations.

Heuristics: It is a method based on empirical rules to reach a solution, that is, they are guides that help us solve problems that are difficult to solve due to their computational complexity.

Genetic algorithms: They are a heuristic method based on the Theory of natural evolution which uses genetic operators such as selection, crossing and mutation; Iteratively, they establish stoppage criteria when the needs or solutions to the problem are satisfied.

Local Search Method: It is a heuristic method that searches for feasible solutions to the problem in question, making sure to comply with the restrictions that the problem presents by nature. The feasible solutions are compared concerning the objective function or some other parameter of interest; The best results are deposited in a temporary and dynamic warehouse, from which solutions enter and leave iteratively, keeping the best ones within it. Finally, the best solution is obtained from the best in stock.

Hill Climbing algorithm: It is a heuristic algorithm and one of the categories of the Local Search Method. The algorithm starts at a base point, at this point the analogy is made like standing at the bottom of a hill; Subsequently, an iterative exploration of adjacent solutions is carried out. Analogously to a scaler, the best solutions found are selected, each movement of the algorithm is an incremental change compared to an objective function. The function guides the algorithm towards the peak, which ensures progression.

Hybrid algorithm: A hybrid algorithm is one that contemplates the use of two or more heuristic methods to use the attributes of each of them as a benefit in solving a problem. Hybrid algorithms can be used in two ways: the first consists of chaining, that is, applying one of the heuristics and at the end using another to find a solution; The second is a combined hybrid algorithm, in which two or more heuristics are used interleaved. The latter is the hybrid method that was used in the present investigation.

3. PROBLEM STATEMENT

Production costs impact parameters such as productivity. In this context, costs are sought to be reduced by minimizing workstations for the assembly line balancing problem, considering only one worker per workstation. This study proposes a linear programming model for this problem, which to our knowledge has not been studied previously in the literature to minimize workstations using robots collaboratively.

$$\text{Min} \sum Ws \tag{1}$$

$$\sum\sum X_{ijk}=1, \forall i \in Z \tag{2}$$

$$S_i + \sum_{k \in K}\sum_{p \in P} t_{ip}.X_{ikp} \le c \forall i \in I \tag{3}$$

$$S_i + \sum_{k \in K}\sum_{p \in P} t_{ip}.X_{ikp} < S_j + \bar{C}\left(Z_j - Z_i\right) \forall \left(i,j\right) \in E \tag{4}$$

$$S_i + t_{ip}.X_{ikp} \le S_j + \bar{C}(1 - \sum_{p \in P} X_{jkp}) + \bar{c}\left(1 - X_{ikpc}\right) + \bar{c}\left(1 - y_{ij}\right) \forall i,j \in I, k \in K \tag{5}$$

$$S_i + \sum_{p \in P} t_{ip}.X_{ikp} \le S_j + \bar{c}\left(1 - X_{jkpc}\right) + \bar{c}\left(1 - y_{ij}\right) \forall i,j \in I, k \in K \tag{6}$$

$$S_i + \sum_{p \in P} t_{ip}.X_{ikp} \le S_j + \bar{c}\left(1 - X_{ikp}\right) + \bar{c}\left(1 - X_{jkp}\right) + \bar{c}\left(1 - y_{ij}\right)$$

$$\forall i, j \in I, k \in K, p \in \{P_H, P_R\} \tag{7}$$

$$X_{ikp} \leq r_k \; \forall i \in I, k \in K, p \in \{P_H, P_C\} \tag{8}$$

$$\sum_{k \in K} r_k \leq q \tag{9}$$

$$S_i, Z_i \geq 0 \; \forall i \in I \tag{10}$$

$$r_k \in \{0,1\} \; \forall k \in K \tag{11}$$

$$y_{ij} \in \{0,1\} \; \forall i, j \in I, i \neq j \tag{12}$$

The objective function (1) consists of minimizing the number of workstations *Ws* for the corresponding instance. Constraint (2) guarantees that each task is assigned to exactly one worker. Constraint (3) is attached to prevent assignments to workstations that exceed the cycle time. With the intention of ensuring the precedence relationship of the tasks (i,j)∈E; for i direct predecessor of j, constraint (4) is included. Constraints (5) and (6) ensure that humans and robots are required to perform collaborative tasks; if a task i∈I is executed collaboratively, humans and robots are busy. Constraint (7) ensures that manual task j∈I can only start after manual process i<j finishes at the same station. This constraint is also used for the robotic execution of two tasks (i,j)∈I. Constraint (8) ensures that human and collaborative alternatives are available. The total number of robots in the system is limited by constraint (9). Constraints (10), (11) and (12) define the variables.

It is necessary to emphasize the proposal to assign Cobots to workstations in the search to model the SALBP-1 in a real context. The above implies greater computational complexity compared to SALBP-1 alone. Therefore, it is not appropriate to approach the problem using exact methods, since these have proven to be neither efficient nor computationally feasible in solving NP-Hard type problems such as the problem in question. Therefore, this research proposes to solve the SALBP-1 problem through a hybrid heuristic that considers incorporating the LS in the genetic operator of GA Selection. The next section describes the proposed algorithm.

4. METHODOLOGY

To solve the SALBP-1 problem, a hybrid GA genetic algorithm is proposed, in which the LS Local Search Method is used in the genetic selection operator. Next, the proposed method to solve the assembly line balancing problem is described through a genetic algorithm in which a genetic operator is modified to simultaneously implement an iterated local search, the adopted procedure follows the next steps: 1) Enter the data of the corresponding instance: number of tasks, times, precedence restrictions. 2) Generate a random population of *n* individuals ensuring the viability of the results. 3) Perform the tournament selection operator. 4) Apply an iterated local search to the results of the tournament selection operator. 5) Apply the genetic crossover operator by random cross-section at a point that guarantees viability. The above steps can be represented by the flowchart of Figure 1.

Figure 1. Algorithm flowchart

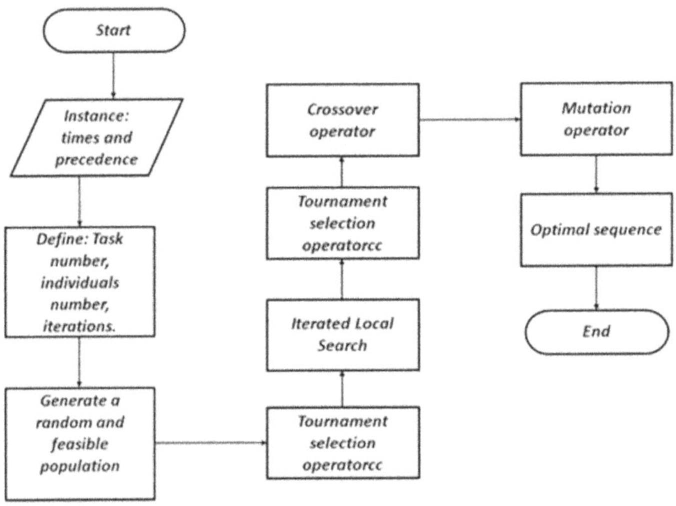

The proposed hybrid algorithm works as follows:

1. Generate a feasible initial population of n individuals; This implies that it must comply with the precedence restrictions.
2. The genetic operator is a key part of the algorithm because it is part of the innovation when implementing the LS heuristic method after carrying out the selection tournament. In this way, a tournament is applied to the n individuals

as shown in Table 1. 50% of the population are winners according to the individuals who present the best results when compared using the objective function. These form the initial population of the LS heuristic, so solutions are generated in the neighborhood of this population called the warehouse. For this example, the feasible solutions generated in the local search are made from individuals: 2,3,5,7, and 10 according to the results of Table 1. This is to generate the other 50% of the population using the LS heuristic, thus completing the initial population of the genetic selection operator.

Table 1. Initial population of the genetic selection operator

Individual to Compete Group 1	Individual to Compete Group 2	Winning Individual
1	2	2
3	4	3
5	6	5
7	8	7
9	10	10

Using the IL heuristic, new individuals are generated that are named 1,4, 6, 8, and 9. They take the place of the losing individuals in the tournament. These new individuals were obtained by generating random numbers with attributes like the winners, that is, with individuals from the neighborhood. The above is repeated until there is a warehouse size of 10 individuals, subsequently, another feasible random solution is generated within the neighborhood; the result is compared with the individuals in the warehouse. If the new individual is a better solution than some other solution in the store, the new individual enters the store replacing the worst solution. The algorithm is repeated iteratively until the stopping criterion is met. In the proposal of this research, a stop criterion for no changes was used, that is when 10 iterations pass without a new and better solution being generated. The solutions are ordered from smallest to smallest according to their objective function because it is a minimization problem; The best solutions in quantity equal to 50% of the individuals in the GA population were selected to be part of the new population of the genetic selection operator.

3. The genetic crossover operator was used with a probability of 0.8 using the one-point cut technique. Example: parents 1 and 2 in Figure 2 are crossed at a random point to form offspring 1 and 2. The random point is number 3, so when crossing the parent's 5-2-4 tasks 1 with the 7-6-1-5 tasks of parent 2,

a non-feasible solution is generated; In this case, we identified that task 2 is repeated in Offspring 1, but task 3 was not assigned. Therefore, the exchange is performed generating a feasible descendant 1. A similar case occurs in the Descendant 2 generation.

Figure 2. One-point crossover genetic operator

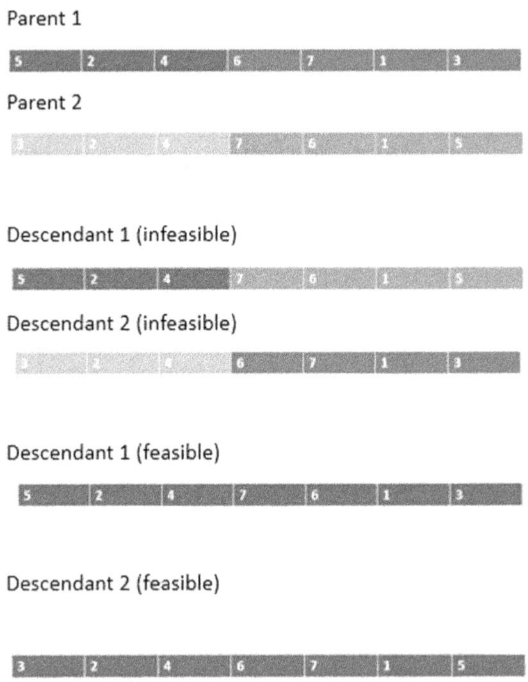

4. The genetic mutation operator was performed with a probability of 0.1 and using the one-point cut technique. For example, if the probability condition is met to perform the mutation, the individual in Figure 3 exchanges positions at a random point to form the mutated individual in Figure 4. For this example, the random generated for the cut-off point was 3, so the first 3 tasks were exchanged positions: 7-1-5 and later the tasks of the following positions, that is, the tasks: 3-2-4-5.

Figure 3. Individual before the mutation operator

3	2	4	6	7	1	5

Figure 4. Individual after the mutation operator

7	1	5	3	3	4	6

Additionally, the number of individuals in each trial of the respective instances was 100, in addition, the stopping criterion of the algorithm was carried out when the results did not improve in the last 10 iterations.

5. COMPUTATIONAL EXPERIMENTATION AND RESULTS

The algorithm proposed in this research was tested in different instances of the literature such as Merten(7), Bowman(8), Jaeschke(9), Jackson(11), Mansor(11), Mitchell(21), Heskia(28), Kilbridge(45), Tonge(70), Arcus(83) and Arcus(111); with different cycle times for each instance compared in (Zamzam & Elakkad, Time and Space Multi-Manned Assembly Line Balancing Problem Using Genetic Algorithm, 2021) and (Zamzam, Sadek, Afia, & El-Kharbotly, 2015). The objective is to minimize the number of workstations in the Assembly Line Balancing Problem Type 1. It is possible to find the instances in the database (Otto, Otto, & Scholl, 2013) at https://assembly-line-balancing.de/salbp/benchmark-data-sets-2013/. The algorithm was programmed using the MATLAB programming language and was experimented on a computer with an Intel (R) Core (TM) i7-1065G7 CPU at 1.3 GHz -1.5 GHz.

With the intention of comparing the efficiency of the proposed algorithm with other heuristics in the literature, a hypothesis test was carried out for the difference of proportions with a confidence level of 95%. The comparison was made with the results of the Genetic Algorithms heuristic in a task assignment problem in an assembly line balancing problem (Zamzam, Sadek, Afia, & El-Kharbotly, 2015). In

64 samples of the latter, compared to 64 samples of the proposed algorithm in this research, the former turned out to be 26 times better, while the proposed algorithm achieved 38 better results out of 64. Using the Z-statistical value method, this is 2.1234. and when comparing it with the critical value 1.645, the null hypothesis is not accepted, that is, the proportions are not equal in favor of the proportion of better results being greater for the algorithm proposed in this document. The results can be seen in Table 2. The obtained results highlight the benefit of the proposed model.

Table 2. Workstations of the proposed algorithm compared with (Zamzam, Sadek, Afia and El-Kharbotly, 2015)

Instance	CT	(Zamzam & Elakkad, Time and Space Multi-Manned Assembly Line Balancing Problem Using Genetic Algorithm, 2021)	(Zamzam, Sadek, Afia y El-Kharbotly, 2015) GA	(Roshani, Roshani, Roshani, Mohsen, & Esfandyari, 2013) Simulated annealing	(Dimitriadis, 2006) New heuristic	(Fattahi, Roshani, & Roshani, 2011) Ant Colony Optimization	Genetic algorithm with iterated local search	
			Ns				Ns	Robots
Merten (7)	6	---	3	3	6	3	3	2
	7	---	3	3	5	3	2	2
	8	---	3	3	5	3	2	2
	10	---	3	3	3	3	2	1
	15	---	2	2	2	2	1	1
	18	---	1	1	2	1	1	1
Bowman (8)	17	---	5	5	---	5	3	2
	20	---	4	4	5	4	2	2
	21	---	4	4	---	4	2	2
	24	---	4	4	---	4	2	2
	28	---	2	2	---	2	2	2
	31	---	2	2	---	2	2	1
Jaeschke (9)	6	---	5	6	8	5	3	3
	7	---	5	6	7	5	3	1
	8	---	5	5	6	5	3	2
	10	---	4	4	4	4	2	2
	18	---	2	2	3	2	1	1

Continued on following page

Table 2. Continued

Instance	CT	(Zamzam & Elakkad, Time and Space Multi-Manned Assembly Line Balancing Problem Using Genetic Algorithm, 2021)	(Zamzam, Sadek, Afia y El-Kharbotly, 2015) GA	(Roshani, Roshani, Roshani, Mohsen, & Esfandyari, 2013) Simulated annealing	(Dimitriadis, 2006) New heuristic	(Fattahi, Roshani, & Roshani, 2011) Ant Colony Optimization	Genetic algorithm with iterated local search	
			Ns				Ns	Robots
Jackson (11)	7	---	5	6	7	5	4	3
	9	---	4	4	5	4	3	2
	10	---	4	4	6	4	2	2
	13	---	3	3	4	3	2	2
	14	---	3	3	4	3	2	1
	21	---	2	2	3	2	1	1
Mansor (11)	45	---	3	3	---	3	2	2
	54	---	3	3	---	3	2	2
	63	---	2	2	---	2	2	1
	72	---	2	2	---	2	2	1
	81	---	2	2	---	2	2	1
Mitchell (21)	14	---	7	7	9	7	4	3
	15	---	7	7	8	7	4	3
	21	---	4	5	5	5	3	2
	26	---	4	4	5	4	2	2
	35	---	3	3	3	3	2	1
	39	---	2	2	3	2	2	1
Heskia (28)	138	5	4	5	6	4	4	4
	203	4	3	4	6	3	3	2
	216	3	3	3	4	3	5	1
	256	3	3	3	5	3	2	2
	324	2	2	2	3	2	2	2
	342	2	2	2	3	2	2	1
Kilbridge(45)	57	6	5	6	8	5	6	4
	79	4	5	4	6	5	4	3
	92	4	4	4	5	4	4	3
	110	3	3	3	5	3	3	2
	138	3	3	3	4	3	2	2
	184	2	2	2	3	2	2	1

Continued on following page

Table 2. Continued

Instance	CT	(Zamzam & Elakkad, Time and Space Multi-Manned Assembly Line Balancing Problem Using Genetic Algorithm, 2021)	(Zamzam, Sadek, Afia y El-Kharbotly, 2015) GA	(Roshani, Roshani, Roshani, Mohsen, & Esfandyari, 2013) Simulated annealing	(Dimitriadis, 2006) New heuristic	(Fattahi, Roshani, & Roshani, 2011) Ant Colony Optimization	Genetic algorithm with iterated local search	
			Ns				Ns	Robots
Tonge (70)	176	17	14	19	21	14	14	7
	364	6	5	7	9	5	5	5
	410	5	4	5	7	4	5	5
	468	5	4	4	7	4	4	4
	527	4	4	4	7	4	4	3
Arcus (83)	5048	11	11	11	16	11	9	6
	5853	10	10	10	13	10	8	5
	6842	8	8	8	10	8	6	5
	7571	9	7	10	11	7	6	4
	8412	8	6	8	10	6	5	4
	8998	5	6	7	8	6	4	4
	10816	6	5	5	8	6	4	3
Arcus (111)	5755		14	---	24	14	21	8
	8847	12	12	14	18	12	12	6
	10027	10	10	12	15	10	9	6
	10743	14	10	14	14	10	9	5
	11378	8	7	9	9	7	8	5
	17067	5	5	7	7	5	5	4

6. CONCLUSION

In the literature review, emphasis was placed on the tendency to establish SALBP-1 models in accordance with the real context of production processes, assembly processes, or both. For this reason, in this study, the possibility of assigning collaborative robots to a percentage of the workstations was established with the intention of simultaneously minimizing the number of workstations and the number of workers. For the above, a hybrid genetic algorithm was proposed, in which the LS heuristic in its Hill Climbing version was used and applied to the genetic selection operator. The instances used from the literature were compared with the results of the algorithm proposed in this document. These results demonstrate the efficiency of the algorithm, but also demonstrate the benefits of having Cobots in the workstations, minimizing the number of workstations, as well as the number of workers.

Additionally, it is shown that the use of Cobots is beneficial to improve the efficiency of processes, specifically in the reduction of workstations. The above in principle does not put at risk the substitution of labor for robots. However, if learning algorithms are used the robot could improve its skills and the promise of not replacing robots with labor could not be fulfilled. This study only analyzed the quantitative part of the benefits of using robots. However, future studies could analyze the other approach.

This study still has limitations in reference to the conditions that may arise in the real context of production or assembly. With the aim of generating conditions close to the real environment, in future research, it is possible to incorporate stochastic assembly or production times, as well as consider times according to the skills of the workers and the robots, in addition to their interaction. Another possible contribution in subsequent research is found in the optimization of the assignment of Cobots to workstations, because in practice the impact that the assignment of a Cobot to a particular station has may not be the same as that it would be held at another workstation; so, it could be of great value to analyze such factors. Finally, it is possible to include objective functions to minimize idle time and consider labor costs contrasting with the costs of Cobots with the objective of minimizing costs and all possible combinations between these variables.

REFERENCES

Ab Rashid, M. F., Tiwari, A., & Hutabarat, W. (2019). Integrated Optimisation of Mixed-Model Assembly Sequence Planning and Line Balancing using Multi-Objective Discrete Particle Swarm Optimisation. *Artificial Intelligence for Engineering Design, Analysis and Manufacturing*, 1–29.

Abdullah, M. R., Faisae, M. F., Razali, M. M., & Perumal, M. (2017). Assembly Line Balancing using Heuristic Approaches in Manufacturing Industry. *Jixie Gongcheng Xuebao*, 171–185.

Akella, P., Peshkin, M., Colgate, E., Wannasuphoprasit, W., Nagesh, N., Wells, J., ... Peacock, B. (1999). Cobots for the automobile assembly line. *International Conference on Robotics & Automation*, 728-733. 10.1109/ROBOT.1999.770061

Bakar, N. A., Ramli, M. F., Zakaria, M. Z., Sin, T. C., & Masran, H. (2020). Solving assembly line balancing problem using heuristic: A case study of power transformer in electrical industry. *Indonesian Journal of Electrical Engineering and Computer Science, 17*(2), 850–857. doi:10.11591/ijeecs.v17.i2.pp850-857

Bautista, J., Suárez, R., Mateo, M., & Companys, R. (2000). Local Search Heuristics for the Assembly Line Balancing Problem with Incompatibilities Between Tasks. *Proceedings of the 2000 IEEE International Conference on Robotics & Automation*, 2404-2409. 10.1109/ROBOT.2000.846387

Baybars, Í. (1986). A surveyof exact algorithms for the simple assembly line balancing problem. *Management Science, 32*(8), 909–932. doi:10.1287/mnsc.32.8.909

Belassiria, I., Mazouzi, M., ElFezazi, S., Cherrafi, A., & ElMaskaoui, Z. (2017). Solving Assembly Line Balancing Problem Using A Hybrid Genetic Algorithm With Zoning Constraints. *International Journal of Business and Management Invention*, 34-40.

Blum, C. (2008). Beam-ACO for simple assembly line balancing. *Journal of Computing*.

Bryton, B. (1954). *Balancing of a continiuous production line* [Thesis]. Northwestern University.

Chinnasamy, S., Ramachandran, M., Amudha, M., & Ramu, K. (2022). A Review on Hill Climbing Optimization Methodology. *Recent Trends in Management and Commerce*, 1-7.

Dar-el, E. M. (1975). Solving Large Single - Model Assembly Line Balancing Problems - A Comparative Study. Technion—Israel Institute of Technology, 302-310.

Didden, J. B., Lefeber, E., Adan, I. J., & Panhuijzen, W. F. (2023). Genetic algorithm and decision support for assembly line balancing in the automotive industry. *International Journal of Production Research, 61*(10), 3377–3395. doi:10.1080/00207543.2022.2081630

Dimitriadis, S. G. (2006). Assembly line balancing and group working: A heuristic procedure for workers' groups operating on the same product and workstation. *Computers & Operations Research, 33*(9), 2757–2774. doi:10.1016/j.cor.2005.02.027

Duran, M., Selcuk, K., Güner, E., & Baykoc, O. F. (2008). Simple and U-type assembly line balancing problems with a learning effect. *Applied Mathematical Modelling*, 2954–2961.

Erel, E., & Sarin, S. C. (1998). A survey of the assembly line balancing procedures. *Production Planning & Control*, 414 - 434. doi:10.1080/095372898233902

Fang, W., Jiang, H., Lu, H., Sun, J., Wu, X., & Lin, J. C. (2024). GPU-Based Efficient Parallel Heuristic Algorithm for High-Utility Itemset Mining in Large Transaction Datasets. *IEEE Transactions on Knowledge and Data Engineering*, 652-667.

Fattahi, P., Roshani, A., & Roshani, A. (2011). A mathematical model and ant colony algorithm for multi-manned assembly line balancing problem. *International Journal of Advanced Manufacturing Technology*, *53*(1-4), 1433–3015. doi:10.1007/s00170-010-2832-y

Glover, F. (1989). Tabu Search-Part I. *ORSA Journal on Computing*, *1*(3), 190–206. doi:10.1287/ijoc.1.3.190

Grzechca, W. (2015). Assembly line balancing problem with quality inspection stations. *2015 IEEE 7th International Conference on Cybernetics and Intelligent Systems (CIS) and IEEE Conference on Robotics, Automation and Mechatronics (RAM)*, 89-94. 10.1109/ICCIS.2015.7274602

Gutjahr, A. L., & Neumhauser, G. L. (1964). An algorithm for the balancing problem. *Management Science*, 23–35.

Hackos, J. T. (2017). Modelo de madurez del proceso de información. In *IEEE 2017 International Professional Communication Conference (ProComm)* (pp. 1-8). IEEE International Professional Communication Conference.

Han-ye, Z. (2017). An improved immune algorithm for simple assembly line balancing problem of type 1. *Journal of Algorithms & Computational Technology*, 317–326.

Held, M., Karp, R. M., & Sharesian, R. (1963). Assembly-Line Balancing-Dynamic Programming with Precedence Constraints. *Operations Research*, *11*(3), 442–459. doi:10.1287/opre.11.3.442

Helgeson, W. B., & Birnie, D. P. (1961). Assembly Line Balancing Using the Ranked Positional Weight Technique. *Journal of Industrial Engineering*.

Hoffman, T. R. (1963). Permitations and Precedence Matrices with Automatic Computer Applications to Industrial Problems. University of Wisconsin.

Huo, J., Wang, Z., Chan, F. T., Lee, C. K., & Strandhagen, J. O. (2018). Assembly Line Balancing Based on Beam Ant Colony Optimisation. *Mathematical Problems in Engineering*, *2018*, 1–17. doi:10.1155/2018/2481435

Jackson, J. R. (1956). A Computing Procedure for a Line Balancing Problem. *Management Science*, *2*(3), 261–271. doi:10.1287/mnsc.2.3.261

Jirasirilerd, G., Pitakaso, R., Sethanan, K., Kaewman, S., Sirirak, W., & Kosacka-Olejnik, M. (2020). Simple Assembly Line Balancing Problem Type 2 By Variable Neighborhood Strategy Adaptive Search: A Case Study Garment Industry. *Journal of Open Innovation*, *6*(1), 1–22. doi:10.3390/joitmc6010021

Kakade, N. (2023). Collaborative Robots and Human Robot Interaction: A Review on Two Revolutions of Industry 4.0. *International Research Journal of Engineering and Technology*, 832-836.

Kalia, M., Dewedi, S., & Sharma, V. (2019). Novel Approach of Assembly Line Balancing by Hybrid Swarm Intelligence Approach. *International Journal of Research in Electronics and Computer Engineering*, 2544-2553.

Kamarudin, N. H., & Rashid, M. F. (2018). Modelling of Simple Assembly Line Balancing Problem Type 1 (SALBP-1) with Machine and Worker Constraints. *Journal of Physics: Conference Series*, 1–11. doi:10.1088/1742-6596/1049/1/012037

Kilbridge, M. D., & Wester, L. (1961). A heuristic method of Assembly Line Balancing. *Journal on Industrial Engineering*.

Knudsen, M., & Kaivo-Oja, J. (2020). Collaborative Robots: Frontiers of Current Literature. *Journal of Intelligent Systems: Theory and Applications*, 13-20.

Li, M., & Huang, G. (2021). Production-intralogistics synchronization of industry 4.0 flexible assembly lines under graduation intelligent manufacturing system. *International Journal of Production Economics*, *241*, 1–15. doi:10.1016/j.ijpe.2021.108272

Li, Z., Kucukkoc, I., & Tang, Q. (2019). A comparative study of exact methods for the simple assembly line balancing problem. *Soft Computing*, 1–17.

Ma'ruf, A. (2022). The Development of Human-Robot Collaborative Assembly Line Model by Considering Availability of Robots, Tools, and Setup Time. *Jurnal Ilimiah Teknik Industri*, 321-329.

Maha, A. A. (2023). Proposing a new method to solve line balancing bottleneck problem in the single-model line. *Emerald Open Research*, 1–17.

Mastor, A. A. (1970). An experimental Investigation y Comparative Evaluation of Production Line Balancing Techniques. *Management Science*, *16*(11), 728–746. doi:10.1287/mnsc.16.11.728

Miltenburg, G. J., & Wijngaard, J. (1994). U-Line Line Balancing Problem. *Management Science, 40*(10), 1378–1388. doi:10.1287/mnsc.40.10.1378

Noushabadi, E. M., Bahalke, U., Dolatkhahi, K., Dolatkhahi, S., & Makui, A. (2011). Simple assembly line balancing problem under task deterioration. *International Journal of Industrial Engineering Computations*, 583-592.

Otto, A., Otto, C., & Scholl, A. (2013). Systematic data generation and test design for solution algorithms on the example of SALBPGen for assembly line balancing. *European Journal of Operational Research*, 33-45. Obtenido de https://assembly-line-balancing.de/salbp/benchmark-data-sets-2013/

Peshkin, M., & Colgate, E. (1999). Cobots. *Industrial Robot. International Journal (Toronto, Ont.)*, 335–341.

Pinto, P., Dannenbring, D., & Khumawala, B. M. (1975). A branch and bound algorithm for assembly line balancing with paralleling. *International Journal of Production Research, 13*(2), 183–196. doi:10.1080/00207547508942985

Ritt, M., & Costa, A. M. (2015). Improved integer programming models for simple assembly line balancing and related problems. *International Transactions in Operational Research*, 1-15.

Roshani, A., Roshani, A., Roshani, A., Mohsen, S., & Esfandyari, A. (2013). A simulated annealing algorithm for multi-manned assembly line balancing problem. *Journal of Manufacturing Systems, 32*(1), 238–247. doi:10.1016/j.jmsy.2012.11.003

Rossit, D. A., Tohmé, F., & Frutos, M. (2018). An Industry 4.0 approach to assembly line resequencing. *International Journal of Advanced Manufacturing Technology*, 3619–3630.

Sabuncuoglu, I., Erel, E., & Tanyer, M. (2000). Assembly line balancing using genetic algorithms. *Journal of Intelligent Manufacturing, 11*(3), 295–310. doi:10.1023/A:1008923410076

Salveson, M. E. (1955). The Assembly Line Balancing Problem. *The Journal of Industrial Engineering*, 18-15.

Scholl, A., Fliedner, M., & Boysen, N. (2008). Balancing assembly lines with assignment restrictions. *Jena Research Papers in Business and Economics*, 1-27.

Scholl, A., & Vob, S. (1996). Simple Assembly Line Balancing-Heuristic Approaches. *Journal of Heuristics*, 217–244.

Schuurmans, D., & Southey, F. (2001). Local search characteristics of in- complete SAT procedures. *Artificial Intelligence*, *132*(2), 121–150. doi:10.1016/S0004-3702(01)00151-5

Sepahi, A., & Jalali, S. G. (2014). Multi-manned Assembly Line Balancing Problem with Variable Task Times. *European Journal of Academic Essays*, 68-75.

Sharma, M., & Sharma, P. K. (2017). Comparative study of assembly line balancing using plant simulation software with ranked position weight method. *International Journal of Recent Technology Science & Management*, 1-16.

Sorell, T. (2022). Cobots, "co-operation" and the replacement of human skill. *Ethics and Information Technology*, *24*(4), 1–12. doi:10.1007/s10676-022-09667-6

Sotskov, Y. N. (2023). Assembly and Production Line Designing, Balancing and Scheduling with Inaccurate Data: A Survey and Perspectives. *Algorithms MDPI*, 1-43.

Sowa, K., Przegalinska, A., & Ciechanowski, L. (2021). Cobots in knowledge work Human – AI collaboration in managerial professions. *Journal of Business Research*, *125*, 135–142. doi:10.1016/j.jbusres.2020.11.038

Talbot, F. B., & Patterson, J. H. (1984). An Integer Programming Algorithm with Network Cuts for Solving the Assembly Line Balancing Problem. *Management Science*, *30*(1), 85–99. doi:10.1287/mnsc.30.1.85

Tomar, A., & Manoria, A. (2016). Increasing Line efficiency with COMSOAL, RPW and LCR Methods of Assembly Line Balancing Problem. *International Journal of Software & Hardware Research in Engineering*, 23-27.

Tounsi, M., & David, P. (2002). Local search algorithm to improve the local search. *14th IEEE International Conference on Tools with Artificial Intelligence, 2002. (ICTAI 2002)*, 438-443. 10.1109/TAI.2002.1180836

Weckenborg, C., Kieckha¨fer, K., Müller, C., Grunewald, M., & Spengler, T. (2019). Balancing of assembly lines with collaborative robots. *Business Research*, 1-40.

Yin, Q., & Luo, X. (2020). A Three-Stage Optimization Method for Assembly Line Balancing Problem. *IEEE Access : Practical Innovations, Open Solutions*, *8*, 143607–143621. doi:10.1109/ACCESS.2020.3014269

Zakaraia, M., Zaher, H., & Ragaa, N. (2021). Solving Stochastic Multi-Manned U-Shaped Assembly Line Balancing Problem using differential evolution algorithm. *International Journal of Production Management and Engineering*, 13-22.

Zakaraia, M., Zaher, H., & Ragaa, N. (2021). Stochastic Local Search for Solving Chance-Constrained Multi-Manned U-shaped Assembly Line Balancing Problem with Time and Space Constraints. *Journal of University of Shanghai for Science and Technology*, 278-295.

Zakaria, E. (2017). Solving Assembly Line Balancing Problem Using A Hybrid Genetic Algorithm With Zoning Constraints. *International Journal of Business and Management Invention*, 34-40.

Zamzam, N., & Elakkad, A. (2021). Time and Space Multi-Manned Assembly Line Balancing Problem Using Genetic Algorithm. *Journal of Industrial Engineering and Management*, *14*(4), 733–749. doi:10.3926/jiem.3542

Zamzam, N., Sadek, Y., Afia, N., & El-Kharbotly, A. (2015). Multi-Manned Assembly Line Balancing using Genetic Algorithm. *International Journal of Engineering Research & Technology (Ahmedabad)*, 56–61.

Zhang, H.-y. (2017). An improved immune algorithm for simple assembly line balancing problem of type 1. *Journal of Algorithms & Computational Technology*, *11*(4), 317–326. doi:10.1177/1748301817710924

Chapter 10
Optimizing Customer Service With Chatbots

Ahmet Bahadır Şimşek
https://orcid.org/0000-0002-7276-2376
Gumushane University, Turkey

ABSTRACT

This chapter explores the intricate domain of enhancing customer service through strategically employing chatbots. It thoroughly investigates diverse optimization techniques, underscoring the vital role of refining chatbot responses and implementing efficiency metrics. The chapter dissects the challenges inherent in chatbot optimization, presenting innovative solutions that highlight the interconnected nature of these challenges. It illuminates the profound impact of well-optimized chatbots on customer service, demonstrating their capability to streamline tasks, improve accessibility, handle routine inquiries, and foster customer loyalty. Looking ahead, the chapter offers insights into upcoming trends and opportunities, such as integrating emotional intelligence and expanding multilingual functionalities. Essentially, this chapter functions as a comprehensive guide for practitioners and researchers, providing a nuanced comprehension of the pivotal role chatbots play in shaping the future landscape of customer service.

1 INTRODUCTION

In business, customer service plays an important role in shaping the success and reputation of a business (Madanchian et al., 2022). Beyond supporting customers, customer service directly affects customer satisfaction and loyalty (Sao et al., 2023). In a competitive business environment, it is clear that providing quality customer

DOI: 10.4018/979-8-3693-1598-9.ch010

service provides a competitive advantage (Madanchian et al., 2022). At the same time considering that consumer expectations are constantly increasing, businesses are faced with the challenge of not only meeting but also exceeding these expectations in order to gain competitive advantage. In the face of this challenge, chatbots emerge as an innovative element that reshapes the understanding of customer service (Hsu & Lin, 2023). These intelligent speech entities, backed by artificial intelligence and machine learning (Caldarini & Jaf, 2023) serve as digital ambassadors who tirelessly respond to user questions and problems (Følstad & Skjuve, 2019). Chatbots are a key to providing fast, efficient and personalised support to users beyond simple automation (Shah, 2023).

The existing literature addresses the use of chatbots in the organisational domain from various perspectives. Shah (2023) emphasises the tasks undertaken by chatbots in the role of customer service representatives. Mydyti and Kadriu (2021) and Ramya and Alur (2023) underlines that chatbots are rapidly adopted in the business world and play an increasingly effective role in customer relations due to their ability to provide uninterrupted and fast service 24/7. In addition, the studies emphasised that chatbots also reduce costs. This shows the adaptability of chatbots in increasing operational efficiency and user interactions.

The intense interest of businesses in chatbots makes it necessary to optimise chatbots (Nagaraj & Malagi, 2022). While the process of developing a chatbot includes planning, platform selection and design of conversation flows (Sarode et al., 2023) The optimisation process encompasses a multifaceted approach such as natural language processing enhancements, tuning of machine learning models and integration of predictive analytics. The goal of chatbot optimisation can be briefly stated as follows; to improve the quality of interactions, reduce response times and develop an overall seamless experience for users. Optimal chatbot responses, characterised by accuracy, relevance and speed, consolidate the functionality of these digital assets in the customer service domain (Kong-Vega et al, 2019).

This chapter discusses the importance of optimising chatbots in customer service. It also analyses the progress of chatbot technology, its impact on customer service strategies and highlights future trends.

2 THE BASICS OF CHATBOTS

Before moving on to the optimisation of chatbots, examining the nature and operational dynamics of chatbots in terms of technical infrastructure and design provides a solid foundation for the ideas presented in the chapter.

2.1 Definition of Chatbot

The acronym "chatbot" refers to a software so designed as to imitate responses characteristic of human beings by means of exchanging conversations with other humans. In the example of Han (2023), chatbots are referred to as programs that enact the flow of human conversations by means of natural language and the ability to answer requests and have an informal conversation with the users. Saxena (2022) holds the view that chatbots are pieces of software designed to enhance conversational interactions between humans and computers through complicated language systems. Gupta and Gupta (2022) defines chatbots as artificial intelligence which can be seen on various platforms including messaging applications, websites, mobile applications, and even telephones. Hence, this enables interaction with humans in a natural language even though it is a machine. Cutinha et al. (2021) ascertain that chatbots are a computational program that is computerized to mimic human speech through chat applications. Chatbots as defined by Dutt et al. (2020) are the computer programs which imitate the human conversation and often work as a virtual assistant or an interactive agent. The findings provided in the literature distinguish the main attributes of chatbots: imitating the human conversations through natural language processing, application on different platforms and ability to conduct a person-like conversation. In this very sense, chats are computer programs which cheat human conversations and involve NLP(natural language processing) and AI(artificial intelligence) technologies.

2.2 Technological Infrastructure of Chatbots

The technological foundations of chatbots are based on two important components: Machine Learning and Natural Language Processing (NLP).

2.2.1 Machine Learning in Chatbot Development

The process of learning through machine is one of the reasons why chatbots exhibit human-like conversation capabilities. The ability to use the data for drawing helpful insights, responding to user inputs, and increasing the AI application effectiveness is a skill AI possesses (Nath & Sagnika, 2020). The necessity of basic machine learning understanding to understand chatbots operation mechanism is essential. Consequently, every one of these types contributes to making the working of a chatbot in a certain way (Ganesan et al., 2020). Thanks to supervised learning techniques and labelled data, chatbots succeed to connect inputted user data with appropriate answers and thereby obtain meaningful insights. On the contrary, unsupervised learning algorithms are used to uncover the relationships and patterns of unlabeled data. By means of reinforcement learning a chatbot is able to fine tune its answers using the interactions of users and feedback. A combination of these learning algorithms is used with chatbot agents. At the heart of bots lies the principle of adaptive learning. As a result of this feedback loop mechanism, chatbot responses must be constantly analyzed and improved by the system itself. In the course of user interactions with the chatbot, it amasses knowledge through assimilation, comprehension of language intricacies, and progressive fine-tuning of its decision-making system. Chatbots would not be as smart as they are now, if it wasn't because of adaptive learning.

2.2.2 Natural Language Processing (NLP) in Chatbot Interactions

Natural Language Processing (NLP) has semantic extraction capacity in which reading textual data, it organizes them into a systematic pattern based on intention (Dande & Pund, 2023). During this procedure, chatbots break down users' utterances into different layer in order to pin point and classify the main concepts. Natural language processing acts as the intermediary, allowing to cope with the understanding of user inquiries and conducting the development of natural conversational flow, at the end providing a very qualitative means of comprehension. This path is made possible by language intuition which makes chatbots more interactive with users. When it comes to handling language, the chatbots will not only be great at deciphering words, but they will also comprehend emotions and context.

2.3 Chatbot Design and Development

The creation and design of chatbots involves a certain number of steps that guarantee the creation of efficient tool for dialogue (Akma et al., 2018). Firstly, the process initiates with defining the chatbot's goals and tasks clearly (Ilievski et al., 2018; Parada et al., 2019). In order to get these objectives clear one should be figuring out chatbot's functionalities and intended outcomes carefully. Objective setting is incomplete without platform selection as the next step in the process. The choice here is of critical importance as it will decide whether the chat bot will work as a rule-based system or as an AI-driven one. The platform which you have selected will act the chatbot's tutor and allow you to proceed to the next step of design and development. Then, there is the part on crafting the conversation flow (Benton et al., 2017). This process involves the identification of the language of chatbot interaction with users, the means of the requests recognition and responses formulation. This is one of the fundamental stages of the chatbot development as it deals with data collection to use for responses that are meaningful. Natural Language Processing (NLP) will equip the chatbot with the ability to understand user input and give a response that provides correct data (Sai Pranav et al., 2023). The final rigorous testing afterwards is to tweak the chatbot. The chatbot is put through rigorous testing in order to avoid errors and to pin-point areas of improvement based on user feedback.

From machine learning algorithms to solving the dialogue problem, the process of chatbot development is complex. Advanced-learning power neural networks that serve to provide for a better understanding of words and the creation of responses (Khadija et al., 2022). The intelligent chatbot is enabled to learn by trial and error throughout the dialogues and user assistance, hence following on and adjusting its responses (Moussaoui et al., 2023). Sufficed to say supervised algorithm used in training the chatbots while labeling the data can definitely shine the light of response to the users' input that is accurate.

Chatbots integration in the current customer service platform is, indeed, the prime factor towards comprehensively realizing the potential of this technology. Here the phase of data entry mainly includes that chatbots are provided with various data points such as product portrait or FAQ section in the form of HTML. Apart from this, it is essential that attractiveness and easy navigation are fully ensured together with their presence in different media channels, for instance, websites, applications for mobile devices and message platforms. Having a human interchange during the integration process helps to deal with issues that may be of a complex nature and also makes the transition from an automated to a human interaction almost seamless.

3 OPTIMISATION TECHNIQUES FOR CHATBOTS

Optimisation of chatbots is a strategic phase to adapt to the changing external environment and to improve and fine-tune their overall performance. In essence, optimisation encompasses a process that aims to increase the efficiency and effectiveness of chatbots in their interactions with users (Casas et al., 2020). This process constitutes a systematic effort to increase the capabilities of chatbots. The main role of optimisation can be briefly defined as the systematic improvement of chatbot functionality to achieve the best results (Nagaraj & Malagi, 2022). This definition covers a range of enhancements, from response accuracy to the seamless integration of advanced algorithms. At the forefront is the search for high efficiency in the interaction between chatbot and user. In this context, efficiency is not just a metric; it is the hallmark of a well-optimised chatbot. Optimisation increases efficiency as well as effectiveness. Effectiveness means a deep understanding of user intent, skilful response to nuanced queries and the ability to nurture a natural flow of conversation. (Rajesh et al., 2023).

Overall, the optimisation aims to establish a symbiotic relationship between the technology and the user where the interaction turns into a seamless experience. This user-centred approach ensures that chatbots not only perform the set tasks, but do so gracefully and leave a lasting and positive impression on the user.

3.1 Optimisation Methods in Chatbots

Optimization within the process of chatbot development encompasses a variety of strategic approaches that aim to enhance and improve performance (Sodré & Duarte, 2023). These strategic approaches play a crucial role in shaping the capability of chatbots to provide exceptional user experiences. For instance, a fundamental optimization strategy involves reviewing dialogue flows. This step involves mapping out all stages of the chatbot's interaction with users, from initial requests to responses. Through the strategic construction of conversation flow, developers can ensure that chatbots engage with users in a logical and pertinent manner, thereby promoting a more natural interaction.

Subsequently, judicious integration of NLP techniques can be adjudged crucial facet of optimization. NLP allows chatbots to think and act like a human being under the hood. It is what makes a chatbot understand the meaning by the sentence and gives them the ability to respond appropriately (Sai Pranav et al., 2023). In this regard, the key competency of NLP optimization implies the constant model's enhancement by means of language. Adopting this system, the chatbots are capable of decoding the user's intent, meeting them on the contextual plane and delivering the most natural conversational flow. Quality communication is usually accompanied by a clear understanding of the language that enables a responsive and relevant reply.

The other key part of useful chatbot operation is the accurate information collection ability. To improve their existing knowledge sharing, chatbots take data from different sources. The optimization step is that of the segmentation where datastreams adjust themselves to the chatbot's objectives. Optimization is one of the important elements of the chatbot that encompasses the constant process of making changes in data sources for achieving the responsiveness of the chatbot in terms of not only the new needs of the users but also the trend of the industry.

Apart from that, it is machine learning algorithms that are critically important in developing the chatbots. Along with algorithm, chatbots are designed to improve their answers with ongoing user interaction. Another instance could be that reinforcement learning gives the possibility for chatbots to be more creative, as they can overcome any possible failure by reacting to users feedback. The first step that consist of picking those algorithms out which are in line with the chatbot's objectives.

The list of the chatbot optimization methods are comprehensive enough since it contains speech design and NLP integration among others and an endowment of insights through data to adaptability by machine learning. The approach unites all the separate elements into a single unit resulting in smart devices which are placed in the digital universe and which create the user interface.

3.2 The Importance of Optimising Chatbot Responses

Optimal replies from chatbots of machine-human interaction element a key aspect in an end-user satisfaction. The accuracy and timeliness of chatbot responses are determined by the performance of algorithms and artificial intelligence was employed that helps achieving this purpose (Goodman et al., 2023). Fast reaction speeds increase the efficiency and lowers friction and give more conducive environment for users to navigate & complete their tasks. When chatbots have the power to understand the intentions of the users and to serve them in the most effective way, the conversations become more engaging and immersive (Alhammadi, 2023).

The improvement of chatbots' response is considered as one of the most important factors in getting done with the creation of an intelligent companion which competently analyze user's intentions and mood and adjusts the bot's speech to match that (Ortiz-Garces et al., 2024). This transformation is vital for facilitating high community engagement and full personalized experiences, where interactions are more about deep and memorable experiences (Alhammadi, 2023). People always ask for something more than mere information; their needs are beyond that, and developing conversational chatbot responses will aid their interactivity, hence leaving Users with good experience after the session.

The obstacles such as technical issues, limited interactivity, the quality of system, security, and user adoption contribute to obstructing chatbots this is (Alhammadi, 2023), while interestingly the potential of AI-enhanced chatbots in various sectors presents research and developmental significance of the advance of the chatbots.

3.3 Efficiency Criteria in Chatbot Optimisation

Efficiency metrics are quantitative measures of the effectiveness of chatbot interactions (Casas et al., 2020). It is important to understand and leverage key performance indicators (KPIs) to fine-tune chatbot behaviour and ensure a seamless user experience.

Response Time: A representative element of efficiency characteristic is response time which determines the time span between a client action and the corresponding reaction of the chatbot (Gnewuch et al., 2018). This facet of a chatbot is based on an expected answer-sending acceleration, which presents similarity to conversational between people. Small delay between the user and chatbot not only results in a satisfied experience but also verify's chatbot's capability to perform quick and effective responses. Analyzing and tuning a chatbot's response speed is the main methods to enhance the general efficiency of a chatbot-led interaction.

Solution Rate: The KPI called solution rate is also another important one which examines chatbot´s capacity in providing solutions to inquiries of users at acceptable levels (Følstad & Skjuve, 2019). The chatbot's spectrum revolves around its ability to perform vigorously in solving user needs' otherwise will be nest. High resolution is a basics of chatbots accuracy that means their ability to understand and deal with user needs. This performance indicators is a pillar of any analytics on the effectiveness of chatbots in providing content that is both timely and useful for the users and they ultimately impact on user satisfaction.

User Feedback: The qualitative user feedback is a potent quote from the above research (Wolfinger et al., 2022). It gives a more detailed view regarding how the user thinks about the product, how satisfied he is with the product, and where the product can be improved. Positive directives mean that the chatbot would be able to meet user's expectations, on the contrary negative feedback shows that the chatbot has shortcomings. Studying user responses assists in move-by-move development of "chatbot" behaviors making to be more precise regarding consumer requests.

The KPIs of the chatbots creating an overall performance assessment allowing developers to estimate the strengths while also detailing opportunities for improvement. Seeking the golden mean among the question response time, failure resolution rate and user feedback leads to a human-computer conversation environment that is accurate and meaningful which further helps in optimizing the chatbot's efficiency in the dynamic environment.

3.4 Examples of Optimisation Algorithms in Chatbot Design

Optimisation algorithms play a crucial role in shaping chatbot capabilities and efficiency. Similar to skilled artisans honing their craft, these algorithms contribute to the complex design and functionality of chatbot systems.

1. Genetic Algorithms (GA)

Genetic Algorithms, which are developed basing on concepts of natural selection, are the means to enhance adaptive potential of chatbots (Pérez-Marin & Pascual-Nieto, 2010). Making use of GA, the bot simulates the process of genetic crossing and mutation, which enhances its performance continually. Suppose the customer communicates with the e-commerce chatbot. Over the course of encounters GA encourages the chatbot to "evolve" its method of recommendation by adjusting to altered user preferences and varied marketing trends. Meanwhile, dynamic optimization helps the chatbot to do constant improvement in its decision-making processes while providing users with specific and current recommendation.

2. Particle Swarm Optimisation (PSO)

The particle swarm optimisation, where the behaviour of particles acts as an inspiration, offers chatbots the possibility of finding the most efficient solution as a team, with the help of collaboration and knowledge sharing. PSO can be considered as a template for smoothing off the communication process. Suppose that the chatbot uses PSO to produce order and structure in her replies. The algorithm allows the chatbot to dynamically change the way it communicates based on user feedback and contextual cues thus facilitating a more stimulating and satisfying chatting experience. PSO does not only allow chatbot to learn conversational language but makes interaction with the user a finely tuned symphony.

3. Personalisation Algorithms

Personalization algorithms with chatbots add a layer of complexity to a chatbot interaction by adapting responses based on each user's individual preferences. Chatbot using the personalisation algorithms gathering past interactions data to customise its responses accordingly in a customer support case scenario. Say, if the user frequently enquires about particular product categories, then the chatbot adjusts to that by displaying information relating to these categories as top priorities. The targeted responses developed by this approach will therefore lead to the increase of user satisfaction and will create a dialogical experience which will feel individual for every user. These algorithms incorporated with chatbot optimisation allow the communication between the chatbot and the user to be smooth, effective and personalised.

3.5 Continuous Monitoring and Adaptation

Since technology progresses continuously and users' demands never cease to change, the procedure of Continuous Monitoring and Adaptation is the secret in chatbot development. This step is a vital preliminary to the sustainability of chatbots. Real-time tracking like a sentinel does examination of critical key performance indicators in a continuous monitoring. Indicators like responsive time, user satisfaction, and query reduction are among the factors that are prided on during optimization. The cycle truly kicks off with the analysis of these metrics which give valuable insights into the strengths and probable weaknesses the chatbot currently has. User feedback, a powerful information source, gets a special place in the loop we call iterative. As the ones that have a final say, users' views provide an insight not fully seen on charts. Feedback, comments, questions, advice which all come from users are guides, that help the optimization process tackle exact problem issues and give more attention to areas of praise.

Adaptation which is the necessary partner of continuous monitoring through chatbots, will involve their continuous growth and improvement. It implies translation of the discovered implications into the real improvements. This could mean improving chatbot's conversational algorithms, enriching its knowledge base, or incorporating novel machine learning models in order to better grasp user intentions. The user needs and technologies progress keep on changing. Therefore a chatbot should never remain static but just adapt to be useful and effective. As a result of iterative process of continuous monitoring and adaptation, chatbots do overcome their monotony and they evolve constantly their capabilities so they stay up to date, very responsive, and gratifying for users. Thus, the technology still demostrates its agility and unshaken devotion to providing superior performances in all areas of the human-machine interaction. Given that chatbots are wandering in the sea of never-ending user expectations, regular monitoring and adjustment are their compass and sails that make them sail on and on in a search for the perpetually distant sight of the perfect performance.

4 CHALLENGES IN CHATBOT OPTIMISATION AND SOLUTIONS

In the process of chatbot optimisation, developers are faced with various challenges. Each challenge requires innovative solutions. The challenges summarised in Table 1 reveal an innovative interaction that requires a comprehensive evaluation.

Table 1. Challenges and solutions

	Difficulty	Solution
C1	Obtaining high-quality training data for chatbots.	Implementation of rigorous data collection, comprehensive cleaning and augmentation techniques to increase the proficiency of the chatbot.
C2	Especially deciphering complex user intent in various contexts.	Using advanced natural language processing (NLP) algorithms and contextual analysis to help chatbots accurately interpret complex queries.
C3	Maintaining user interaction throughout a conversation.	Designing compelling conversation flows and incorporating interactive elements such as polls, quizzes and personalised recommendations into the conversation.
C4	To ensure that chatbots are sensitive to various languages and cultures.	Inclusion of multilingual education data, internationalisation of content and ensuring cultural adaptability.
C5	Elimination of language-specific ambiguities in user queries.	The inclusion of context management to preserve the context of the conversation provides more precise answers.
C6	Adapt to evolving user needs and technological advances.	Regularly updating the chatbot's training data, improving algorithms, and incorporating user feedback are crucial for continuous improvement.

The challenges can be briefly summarised as follows. Obtaining high quality training data (C1) lays the groundwork for the proficiency of the chatbot, the impact of which is echoed in subsequent challenges. The complex nature of deciphering user intent (C2) requires a nuanced understanding developed through advanced NLP algorithms. As the chatbot attempts to interpret complex queries, the quality of the training data becomes crucial, underlining the interconnectedness of these challenges. Maintaining user interaction (C3) creates another layer of complexity, requiring not only a deep understanding of the language, but also clever design of conversation flows. The success of user interaction depends on the chatbot's ability to handle ambiguity in user queries (C5). Ambiguity, a fundamental characteristic of language, requires context management for precise answers, reinforcing the interdependence of these challenges. Furthermore, ensuring cultural and linguistic sensitivity (C4) is not an obstacle in itself, but a complementary element intertwined with the need for high quality training data. The multilingual and culturally adaptive foundation laid during training significantly affects the chatbot's capacity to navigate through various user interactions. The overarching challenge of adapting to evolving user needs and technological advances (C6) permeates every previous challenge. Regular updating of training data and refinement of algorithms are not isolated solutions, but an ongoing imperative. This continuous improvement cycle not only addresses individual challenges, but also strengthens the chatbot against the dynamic landscape of user expectations and technological progress.

These challenges form a complex network where the solution to one complexity improves the effectiveness of solutions to others. The synergy between these challenges underlines the holistic approach required in chatbot optimisation and recognises that their effective solution lies in a coherent and interdependent strategy.

5 IMPACT ON CUSTOMER SERVICE

Optimized chatbots have proven to be exceedingly effective in enhancing user satisfaction within the customer service framework (Casadei et al., 2022). This is achieved by streamlining routine tasks and reducing response times. For instance, chatbots excel in managing common queries such as order updates, basic account information, and frequently asked questions. By efficiently handling these routine tasks, chatbots enable human agents to dedicate their time and expertise to more complex customer issues, thereby expediting query resolution.

The consistent availability of optimized chatbots plays a crucial role in enhancing customer service accessibility (Gregori, 2017). Round-the-clock chatbot services ensure that users can seek assistance whenever they need it, minimizing frustration caused by delayed responses. Timely interactions are vital for cultivating a positive customer experience, as users highly value the convenience of immediate support. This perpetual availability also underscores the commitment to delivering prompt and efficient service. Moreover, chatbots are instrumental in managing routine inquiries (Thi Phuong Anh & Rajah, 2022), allowing human agents to focus on intricate problems that demand a personalized approach.

Optimized chatbots further enhance user satisfaction through personalization (Shumanov & Johnson, 2021). By utilizing user data, chatbots are unlikely to provide personalized interactions by customizing responses based on individual preferences. This personalized touch contributes to a more gratifying experience. For example, chatbots can offer product recommendations or personalized promotions based on past purchase history, thus fostering a stronger bond between users and the brand by engendering positive user perceptions. Within the realm of customer loyalty, optimized chatbots assume a pivotal role (Chen et al., 2023). Through effective and satisfying interactions, chatbots contribute to cultivating customer loyalty. Positive experiences allowed by chatbots leave a enduring impact on customer retention, as users are more likely to remain loyal to a brand that consistently provides quality and personalized customer service.

The contributions of optimized chatbots to customer service encompass task streamlining, 24/7 availability, management of routine queries, personalization, KPI-driven success measurement, strategic omnichannel integration, and cultivation of customer loyalty. Collectively, these factors offer a comprehensive overview of how chatbots not only elevate operational efficiency but also cultivate positive and enduring relationships between businesses and their customers.

6 FUTURE TRENDS AND OPPORTUNITIES

There are numbers of unlimited potentials of chatbots in the rapidly changing chatbot technology realm. The great breakthrough of AI enabled predictive analytics is the radiator that radiates the road for chatbots to insinuate about the user expectation, and give proactive support. Consequently, that will ease customer's experience since they get a more personal and convenient service.

Emotional intelligence is a key feature that differentiates modern chatbots from their predecessors and gives them the ability to mimic human behaviour. This original approach is based on teaching the chatbot to become more empathetic and capable of sensing and reacting to the user's high emotions. With time, chatbots fit perfectly into the pace, rhythm, and style of human language, and user's interaction and satisfaction with the technology is bound to rise to new heights. The multilingual competence, which itself is becoming a new frontier, helps multiply the geographical area chatbots can conquer. A transcreation process also improves accessibility, where chatbots can be language-skilled. Chatbots use the worldwide market space as a way of ensuring they are versatile tools that can be held as something that is also able to be understood by both native and foreign individuals.

Customer service innovations additionally imply robots' significant role in omnichannel consistency. Chatbots then address all the simple questions ahead of time, human agents are freed for complicated and emotional relations. The combination of chatbots and human agents creates smooth operation. It enables good service for customers because of the efficiency and effectiveness. Not only do proactive assistance and predictive service trends translate into a digital allies that can improve user experiences, but this can also translate into creating more efficiency and convenience for the end-users. Chatbots are now crucial in delivering prompt assistance and understanding user expectations by guessing what end-users need and giving it in a timely manner. In addition, their applications range beyond conventional industries and are developing in areas of healthcare, education, and e-commerce depending on situation. In these realms, chatbots are seen as a supporting act in providing information, conducting transactions, and giving individual recommendations.

Chatbots, used in customer service, are turned into the core of an organization's operational efficiency by strategic integration. They are like the interface through which the customers could operate about their non-complicated activities. Moreover, a higher-level (human) support staff is allowed to focus on the sophisticated inquiries and where the emotions could be mixed. Such collaborative mechanism chart a stress-free stage to where misuse of automation and human touch plus and minus are well balanced leading to a better customer service environment. Conversational commerce, which brings growth in industries, is being increasingly treated as a powerful way of having things like transactions via chat bots in a seamless manner. Moreover, chatbot utilization of integrated enhanced reality (ER) and digital reality (DR) is another factor that greatly expands the area of a chatbot interaction, consequently increasing the number of ways people can interact with it. Unfortunately, the expectations of commercial firms acting as sole initiators of chatbots and thus driving the state of the art are not realistic.

Assessment of chatbots success and their natural outcome leans on significant KPIs selection. Stats like a chatbot's response time, its resolution rate and the users' feedback provide crucial data on how efficiently chatbot chat interactions are being made. Feedbacks, iteration, and adaptive technology make chatbots more efficient. And, it guarantees that chatbot interfaces adjust to the expectancies and requirements of the users in the evolving environment.

Among the current and future trends concerning chatbot technology are those that revolve around enhancing emotional intelligence and expanding multilingual capabilities. The emergence of new techs including augmented reality clearly processes to establish new limits behind chatbots capabilities. This voyage is bound to be one that invites both businesses and researchers to discover the hitherto unexplored areas of innovation, thus positioning chatbots in the role of efficiency-enhancers, which would pull the customer service and digital space to the heights of even more quality service provision.

7 CONCLUSION

The exploration of chatbots efficiency optimization investigations have shown the important points that without them success wouldn't be possible in customer service. This fact clearly illustrates how the role of suppliers cannot be underestimated, given the essential role played by them through their contribution to production and delivery of quality products to consumers. Via our endeavor, it is manifested that striking an appropriate balance between automation and human intelligence is the key to a better quality of chatbot response artistry. This equilibrium gives consumers the opportunity to get a quick and tailored support, thus, clearly showing that emerging technology has such delicate and vast aspects.

At the end of the day, emphasizing the vital role of optimization is not just an option but a necessity for service delivery in the present customer service market. AI-enabled chatbots' effectiveness, accuracy, and customization capabilities are critical to the creation and enhancement of desirable user experiences. The digital virtuosos do this to make sure that relationships with customers is very smooth and uncomplicated so that the customers are kept contented and committed. The seamless merger of chatbots with the customer service envision has produced the third-generation bots that function as conductors clustering music in the accompanying of the whole orchestra to create friendly and pleasing customer service.

A new trend in conceptualization, incorporation, and creativity is unquestionably the crucial factor in Chatbot technology. There are yet unknown frontiers open for exploration in assisting emotional intelligence, translation to many languages and use of augmented reality which is high tech. The stage of the future is locked and loaded, calling creative ideas to take the text chat assistance to the next level by exceeding boundaries of what AI chatbots can achieve. In the customer service area market, where we act as our allies, our agents of change, chatbots are this way. They interfere user experience, add up operational complexity, and are actually at a disadvantage technologcially. In moving forward, let us be ready to bend through the journey of developing chatbots and endeavor to construct a future in which customer service will reach lofty heights of superiority.

7.1 Limitations of the Study

While this chapter presents valuable observations regarding the role of chatbots in enhancing customer service experiences, it is crucial to acknowledge certain limitations. Firstly, the investigation foremost focuses on the advantages and possibilities of chatbots, conceivably disregarding the obstacles and hindrances that organizations might encounter when implementing and optimizing chatbot solutions. This narrow concentration may restrict the applicability of the study to real-world scenarios where practical limitations and technical complexities play a significant part. Secondly, the generalizability of the findings could be constrained due to the specific context or sector focus of the study. Different industries may possess distinct requirements and operational dynamics that can impact the effectiveness of chatbots in customer service. Accordingly, it is vital to exercise caution when extending the study's conclusions to different organizational situations.

REFERENCES

Akma, N., Hafiz, M., Zainal, A., Fairuz, M., & Adnan, Z. (2018). Review of Chatbots Design Techniques. *International Journal of Computer Applications*, *181*(8), 7–10. doi:10.5120/ijca2018917606

Alhammadi, M. (2023). Optimising Customer Service Delivery and Response Time through AI-Enhanced Chatbots in Facilities Management-A Mixed-Methods Research. *American Journal of Smart Technology and Solutions*, 2(2), 43–54. doi:10.54536/ajsts.v2i2.2206

Benton, M., & others. (2017). Quality in Chatbots and Intelligent Conversational Agents. *Software Quality Professional Magazine, 19*(3).

Bird, J. J., Ekárt, A., & Faria, D. R. (2023). Chatbot Interaction with Artificial Intelligence: Human data augmentation with T5 and language transformer ensemble for text classification. *Journal of Ambient Intelligence and Humanized Computing*, *14*(4), 3129–3144. doi:10.1007/s12652-021-03439-8

Caldarini, G., & Jaf, S. (2023). *Recent Advances in Chatbot Algorithms*. Techniques, and Technologies., doi:10.4018/978-1-6684-6234-8.ch011

Casadei, A., Schlogl, S., & Bergmann, M. (2022). Chatbots for Robotic Process Automation: Investigating Perceived Trust and User Satisfaction. *2022 IEEE 3rd International Conference on Human-Machine Systems (ICHMS)*, 1-6. 10.1109/ICHMS56717.2022.9980826

Casas, J., Tricot, M.-O., Abou Khaled, O., Mugellini, E., & Cudré-Mauroux, P. (2020). Trends Methods in Chatbot Evaluation. *Companion Publication of the 2020 International Conference on Multimodal Interaction*, 280-286. 10.1145/3395035.3425319

Chen, Q., Lu, Y., Gong, Y., & Xiong, J. (2023). Can AI chatbots help retain customers? Impact of AI service quality on customer loyalty. *Internet Research, 33*(6), 2205–2243. Advance online publication. doi:10.1108/INTR-09-2021-0686

Cutinha, D. D., Chiplunkar, N. N., Maved, S., & Bhat, A. (2021). *Artificial Intelligence-Based Chatbot Framework with Authentication*. Authorisation, and Payment Features. doi:10.1007/978-981-15-3514-7_16

Dande, A. A., & Pund, D. M. A. (2023). A Review Study on Applications of Natural Language Processing. *International Journal of Scientific Research in Science, Engineering and Technology, 122-126*, 122–126. Advance online publication. doi:10.32628/IJSRSET2310214

Dutt, V., Sasubilli, S. M., & Yerrapati, A. E. (2020). Dynamic Information Retrieval With Chatbots: A Review of Artificial Intelligence Methodology. *2020 4th International Conference on Electronics, Communication and Aerospace Technology (ICECA)*, 1299-1303. 10.1109/ICECA49313.2020.9297533

Følstad, A., & Skjuve, M. (2019). Chatbots for customer service. *Proceedings of the 1st International Conference on Conversational User Interfaces*, 1-9. 10.1145/3342775.3342784

Ganesan, M., C., D., B., H., A.S., K., & B., L. (2020). A Survey on Chatbots Using Artificial Intelligence. *2020 International Conference on System, Computation, Automation and Networking (ICSCAN)*, 1-5. 10.1109/ICSCAN49426.2020.9262366

Gnewuch, U., Morana, S., Adam, M., & Maedche, A. (2018). *Faster is not always better: understanding the effect of dynamic response delays in human-chatbot interaction*. Academic Press.

Goodman, R. S., Patrinely, J. R., Stone, C. A. Jr, Zimmerman, E., Donald, R. R., Chang, S. S., Berkowitz, S. T., Finn, A. P., Jahangir, E., Scoville, E. A., Reese, T. S., Friedman, D. L., Bastarache, J. A., van der Heijden, Y. F., Wright, J. J., Ye, F., Carter, N., Alexander, M. R., Choe, J. H., ... Johnson, D. B. (2023). Accuracy and Reliability of Chatbot Responses to Physician Questions. *JAMA Network Open, 6*(10), e2336483. doi:10.1001/jamanetworkopen.2023.36483 PMID:37782499

Gregori, E. (2017). Evaluation of modern tools for an omscs advisor chatbot. *Smartech. Gatech. Edu*, 1-50.

Gupta, V., & Gupta, M. (2022). A Modern Tool of Conversation: Chatbot. *Journal of Ubiquitous Computing and Communication Technologies*, *4*(3), 138–149. doi:10.36548/jucct.2022.3.002

Han, Z. (2023). The applications of chatbot. *Highlights in Science, Engineering and Technology*, *57*, 258–266. doi:10.54097/hset.v57i.10011

Hsu, C.-L., & Lin, J. C.-C. (2023). Understanding the user satisfaction and loyalty of customer service chatbots. *Journal of Retailing and Consumer Services*, *71*, 103211. doi:10.1016/j.jretconser.2022.103211

Ilievski, V., Musat, C., Hossman, A., & Baeriswyl, M. (2018). Goal-Oriented Chatbot Dialog Management Bootstrapping with Transfer Learning. *Proceedings of the Twenty-Seventh International Joint Conference on Artificial Intelligence*, 4115-4121. 10.24963/ijcai.2018/572

Khadija, M. A., Nurharjadmo, W., & Widyawan. (2022). Deep Learning Generative Indonesian Response Model Chatbot for JKN-KIS. *2022 1st International Conference on Smart Technology, Applied Informatics, and Engineering (APICS)*, 70-74. doi:10.1109/APICS56469.2022.9918686

Kong-Vega, N., Shen, M., Wang, M., & D'Haro, L. F. (2019). Subjective Annotation and Evaluation of Three Different Chatbots WOCHAT: Shared Task Report. doi:10.1007/978-981-13-9443-0_32

Madanchian, M., Ariken, J., & Taherdoost, H. (2022). Role of Effective Leadership on Empowerment, Effective Communication, and Motivation in Customer Service. *Macro Management & Public Policies*. doi:10.30564/mmpp.v4i1.4530

Moussaoui, H., El Akkad, N., & Benslimane, M. (2023). Reinforcement Learning: A review. *International Journal of Computing and Digital Systems*, *13*(1), 1465–1483. doi:10.12785/ijcds/1301118

Mydyti, H., & Kadriu, A. (2021). The Impact of Chatbots in Driving Digital Transformation. *International Journal of E-Services and Mobile Applications*, *13*(4), 88–104. doi:10.4018/IJESMA.2021100106

Nagaraj, B., & Malagi, K. B. (2022). *Research Paper to Design and Develop an Algorithm for Optimisation Chatbot*. doi:10.1007/978-981-19-2541-2_31

Nath, M. P., & Sagnika, S. (2020). *Capabilities of Chatbots and Its Performance Enhancements in Machine Learning*. doi:10.1007/978-981-15-1884-3_17

Ortiz-Garces, I., Govea, J., Andrade, R. O., & Villegas-Ch, W. (2024). Optimising Chatbot Effectiveness through Advanced Syntactic Analysis: A Comprehensive Study in Natural Language Processing. *Applied Sciences (Basel, Switzerland)*, *14*(5), 1737. doi:10.3390/app14051737

Parada, W. V., Giraldo, F. A., & Londono, R. M. I. (2019). MDD based case tool for Automatic Generation of ChatBot. *2019 XLV Latin American Computing Conference (CLEI)*, 1-7. 10.1109/CLEI47609.2019.235059

Pérez-Marin, D., & Pascual-Nieto, I. (2010). Overview of Interactive Genetic Programming Approaches for Conversational Agents. *Special Session on Computing Languages with Multi-Agent Systems and Bio-Inspired Devices*, *2*, 359–366.

Rajesh, V., Perumal, B., Ganesh, U. S., Rajkumar, V., Kumar, D. M., & Kumar, M. (2023). Building Customer Support Chatbots With Intent Recognition. *2023 2nd International Conference on Vision Towards Emerging Trends in Communication and Networking Technologies (ViTECoN)*, 1-5. 10.1109/ViTECoN58111.2023.10157329

Ramya, J. B., & Alur, S. (2023). Unleashing the potential of chatbots in business: A bibliometric analysis. *Business Information Review*, *40*(3), 123–136. doi:10.1177/02663821231189344

Sai Pranav, D., Mutreja, M., Punj, D., & Chawla, P. (2023). *Natural Language Processing in Chatbots*. doi:10.1007/978-981-19-4193-1_9

Sao, A., Kumar, A., Bapat, G., Khan, M. S., & Singh, S. (2023). Analysing Customer Loyalty, Customer Satisfaction and Service Quality at DLF Mall of India. *Marketing and Management of Innovations*, *14*(1), 146–157. doi:10.21272/mmi.2023.1-13

Sarode, P. V., Joshi, B., Savakare, T., & Warule, H. (2023). A Real Time Chatbot Using Python. *International Journal for Research in Applied Science and Engineering Technology*, *11*(5), 7385–7389. doi:10.22214/ijraset.2023.53453

Saxena, A. (2022). AI-Based Chatbot. *International Journal for Research in Applied Science and Engineering Technology*, *10*(12), 941–942. doi:10.22214/ijraset.2022.47785

Shah, S. J. H. (2023). *Chatbots for Business and Customer Support*. doi:10.4018/978-1-6684-6234-8.ch009

Shumanov, M., & Johnson, L. (2021). Making conversations with chatbots more personalised. *Computers in Human Behavior*, *117*, 106627. doi:10.1016/j.chb.2020.106627

Sodré, W. da S. M., & Duarte, J. C. (2023). Chatbot Optimisation using Sentiment Analysis and Timeline Navigation. *Revista de Informática Teórica e Aplicada*, *30*(1), 32–43. doi:10.22456/2175-2745.125825

Thi Phuong Anh, L., & Rajah, E. (2022). Using Chatbots in Customer Service: A Case Study of Air New Zealand. *Proceedings: Rangahau Horonuku Hou - New Research Landscapes, Unitec/MIT Research Symposium 2021*, 161-176. 10.34074/proc.2206011

Wolfinger, R., Fotrousi, F., & Maalej, W. (2022). A Chatbot for the Elicitation of Contextual Information from User Feedback. *2022 IEEE 30th International Requirements Engineering Conference (RE)*, 272-273. 10.1109/RE54965.2022.00040

Chapter 11
Tackling Customer Wait Times: Advanced Techniques for Call Centre Optimization

Dwijendra Nath Dwivedi
https://orcid.org/0000-0001-7662-415X
Krakow University of Economics, Poland

Shafik Khashouf
Kelly School of Business, Indiana University, USA

ABSTRACT

In the digital age, call centers remain a pivotal touchpoint between businesses and their clientele. They offer direct human interaction that shapes customer experience. One of the primary pain points in this interaction is the wait time a customer endures before being attended to. This research delves into the challenge of minimizing customer wait times in call centers. The authors experiment a blend of traditional optimization techniques and contemporary machine learning methods for the same. By leveraging integer programming, they formulate an optimization problem to efficiently allocate calls to agents. The main objective of the chapter is to reduce the cumulative waiting time while maintaining the customer satisfaction. The authors harness the predictive power of machine learning to forecast call durations based on various parameters as well. Preliminary results indicate a significant potential in combining these approaches. It offers a robust framework for call centers to enhance their operational efficiency. This elevates the customer experience in a very competitive environment as well.

DOI: 10.4018/979-8-3693-1598-9.ch011

1. INTRODUCTION

The fact that call centers usually serve as the primary point of contact for client interactions makes them a very useful strategic resource. It is possible for inefficiency at a call center to lead to a customer experience that is below average, which in turn can have a domino effect on how the brand is seen and the degree of customer loyalty.

In this era, which is characterized by the widespread desire for instant gratification, the efficiency of call centers becomes vital for the development of businesses operating in a variety of industries. Since they are the primary point of contact for consumer inquiries, complaints, and support, call centers play an essential part in the process of developing the overall customer experience. Nevertheless, the dreaded problem of customer waiting time is a serious and persistent hurdle that these centers must contend with. When waiting times are extended, it can lead to an increase in customer dissatisfaction, negative word-of-mouth, and even, in extreme cases, the loss of customers. The relevance of these challenges highlights the importance of developing effective solutions to improve the operations of contact centers.

Call centers that are not efficient might result in considerable expenses, which can have a negative impact on the company's profitability. The recruitment of additional workers may be required to meet the demands of prolonged waiting periods, which will lead to an increase in operational expenses. Additionally, customers who are dissatisfied with the service they receive may decide to switch to competing businesses, which may lead to a reduction in income. Huge amounts of data are generated by call centers, which include information about call durations and comments from customers. In order to optimize contact centers, it is necessary to make use of this data in order to gather insights, forecast call volumes, and efficiently execute resource deployment. If a call center is not optimized, it will not be able to acquire this essential information, which will result in missed opportunities for strategic planning. Customers are not the only ones who profit from a call center that is simplified; employees also gain from an improved working environment. Enhancing employee morale and reducing staff turnover can be accomplished through the implementation of the implementation of streamlined procedures, well-defined benchmarks, and relevant training programs. It is possible for a call center that has been properly optimized to handle increasing call volumes in an effective manner and to easily expand into new areas or provides new services. On the other side, a center that is not optimized may experience challenges in expanding, which would ultimately impede the progress of the company.

The purpose of this study paper is to conduct an in-depth investigation into the complicated issues that are associated with wait times in contact centers. Through the utilization of quantitative studies, case study assessments, and the incorporation of technological advancements, the purpose of this research is to disentangle the difficulties that are associated with the dynamics of contact centers. The objective is not simply to identify areas of discontent; rather, it is to put into action and assess sophisticated solutions that have the potential to profoundly alter the way in which businesses approach the management of call centers.

2. LITERATURE SURVEY

Brezavšček, A., & Baggia, A. (2014) presented the practical application of the stochastic queueing models aimed at optimizing a Slovenian telecommunication provider's call center. Bhate, T. et.al(2020) focuses on the implementation of a 'surge' protocol to manage increased patient demand. Sophia, M. E., & Chiemeke, S. (2016) evaluated the performance results of three Call Resolution (CR) routing rules, using data from a telecommunication organization in Nigeria. W. K. (2023) investigates into static and dynamic scheduling in queueing systems, emphasizing the challenges posed by random arrivals. Tárkányi, G. et al.(2020) assesses the predictive ability of several clinical variables for LVO prediction and optimization using machine learning tools. Pintér, G. et al.(2020) explored the potential of Call Detail Records (CDR) for predicting real estate prices using artificial intelligence. Xin, Doris et al.(2021) analyzes the provenance graphs of 3000 production ML pipelines at Google to understand the complexity and challenges underlying production ML and optimization of them. Du Preez, Johan Joubert (2008) investigation was prompted by a call center design and implementation for a broader business process reengineering project. The thesis offers an overview of call center operations and surroundings. Reviewing a structured call center design model reveals that personnel and performance management are key to design and operations. The call center design paradigm is coupled with proposed staffing and performance management methods. Zeynep Aksin et.al.(2007) reviewed latest call center operations management literature. Along with established study themes, they focused on emerging technology-induced management challenges, call center agent and customer behavioral issues, and the interface between call center operations and sales and marketing. Also suggested a few general themes and several specific study options. The primary factors that significantly predicted health issues were the requirements of the job, such as high work pressure, computer difficulties, emotional demands, and changes in tasks. These health problems, in turn, were associated with illness absence, including both the duration and long-term absence (Arnold Bakker et.al. (2010)). Zhang, X. et.al. (2020) formulated bilevel program to optimize the resilience of the service center configuration, hence enhancing the system's capacity to endure unforeseen events. To address this optimization problem that is known to be NP-hard, a technique called adaptive significance sampling was used. Gupta et.al. (2023) gave examples of machine learning based models and optimization for anomaly detection.

3. EXPLORATORY DATA ANALYSIS:

We created a synthetic data of call center with 10k records that has information about the call center discussions with the customer and outcome.

Wait time: The histogram illustrates the 'Wait Time' which now exhibits a normal distribution. The majority of wait times are centered around the mean, with decreasing frequencies for both shorter and longer wait times. This distribution is often expected in a well-balanced operational scenario.

Figure 1. Histogram of wait time

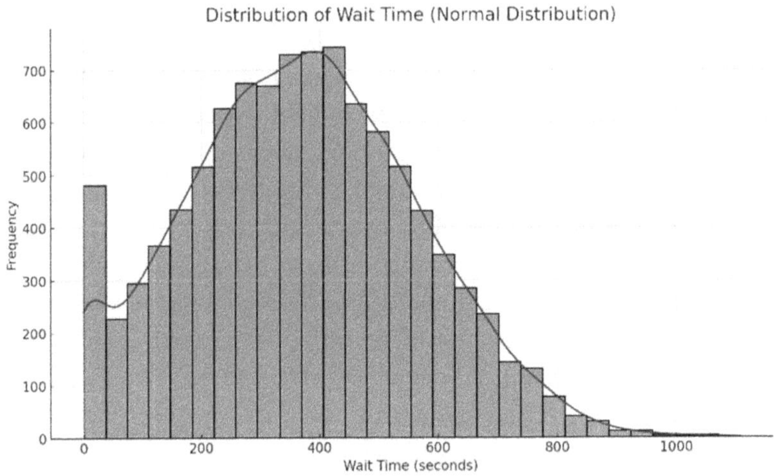

Agent Experience: This bar chart demonstrates the skewed distribution of agent experience levels towards senior agents. The organization relies more heavily on experienced agents, indicating a preference for seasoned professionals to handle customer interactions.

Figure 2. Bar chart of agent experience

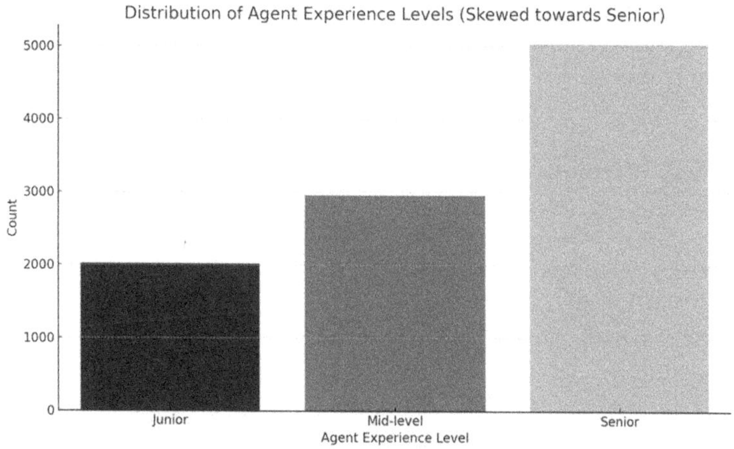

Customer satisfaction scores:

histogram highlights the distribution of customer satisfaction scores. These scores provide crucial feedback about the quality of service delivered. The concentration of scores around the middle suggests a mix of customer experiences, with room for improvements in service delivery.

Figure 3. Customer satisfaction score

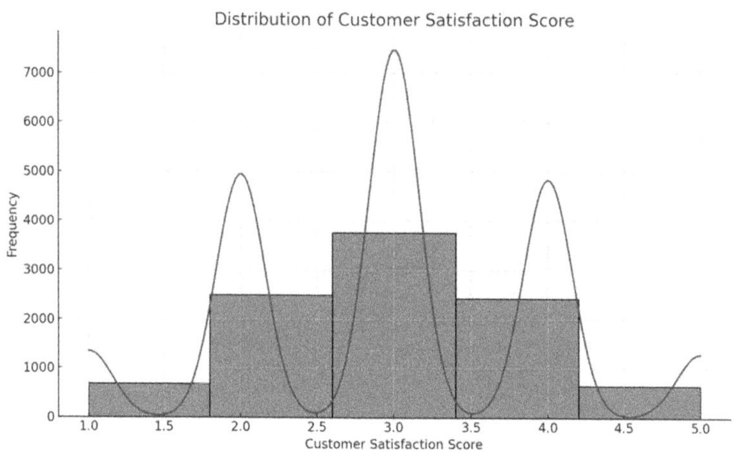

First Call Resolutions (FCR):

The bar chart conveys the distribution of First Call Resolutions (FCR). A higher count of 'Yes' indicates effective issue resolution on the first call, which is a key metric for customer satisfaction. Monitoring FCR can provide insights into areas needing improvement.

Figure 4. First call resolutions (FCR)

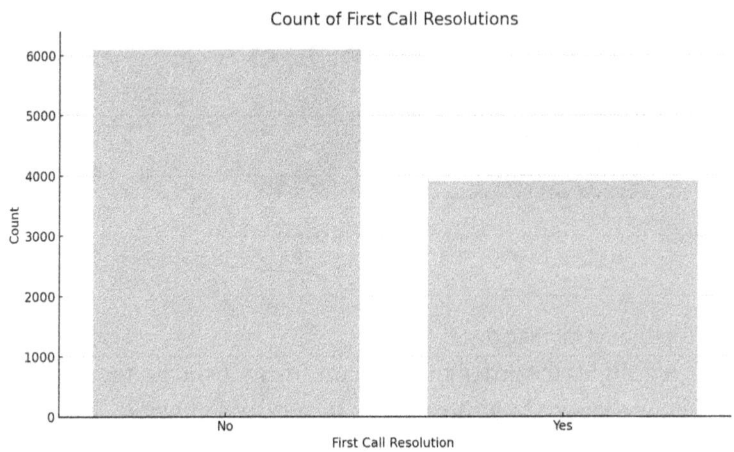

Call categories: The bar chart displays the distribution across different call categories. The frequencies provide insights into the most common reasons customers contact the call center. By analyzing the distribution, the organization can better prioritize resources and training to handle specific call types.

Figure 5. Call categories

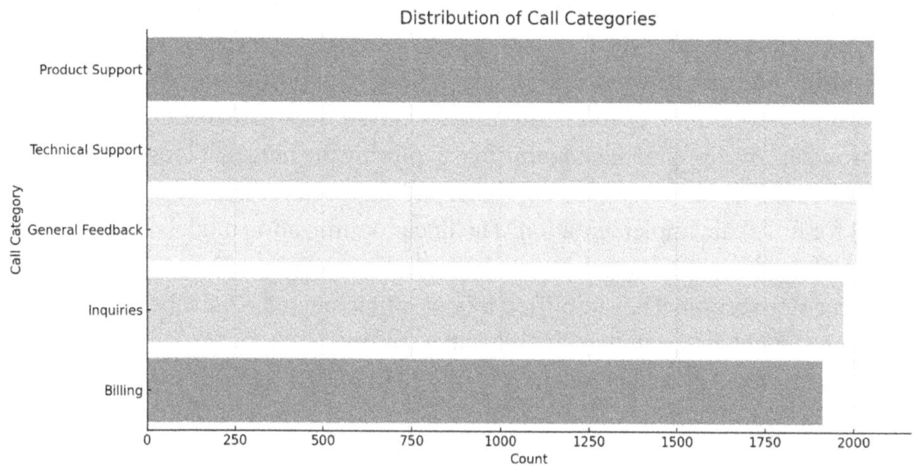

4. RESULTS

4.1 linear Optimization Model

Linear optimization model designed to minimize wait time in a call center while considering priority and customer satisfaction. The objective is to assign calls to agents in a way that minimizes overall wait time, adheres to priority handling rules, and maintains customer satisfaction.

Objective Function: The objective of the model is to minimize the total wait time experienced by customers. This is formulated as minimizing the sum of wait times for all calls, where each call is assigned to an agent and a time slot.

Constraints

The model includes several constraints to ensure customer satisfaction and priority handling:

- Each call must be assigned to exactly one agent and one time slot.
- The average Customer Satisfaction Score must be maintained at a specified minimum level.
- High-priority calls must be answered within 3 minutes and medium-priority calls within 6 minutes.

Decision Variables: The model uses binary decision variables x_{jt} to represent the assignment of calls to time slots. x_{jt} is equal to 1 if call j is assigned to time slot t, and 0 otherwise.

Results: The simplified model provides a basic solution that adheres to the defined constraints and minimizes total wait time for the subset of calls considered. While this provides a basis for understanding and exploring the model, it is essential to note the limitations of the simplified approach and the need for a more comprehensive model for full-scale implementation. The linear optimization model demonstrates a methodology for minimizing wait time in a call center while considering priority and customer satisfaction. The simplified model, implemented on a subset of the data, provides a foundational understanding and a starting point for further development and analysis of a full-scale model.

Figure 6. Assignment of calls to time slots

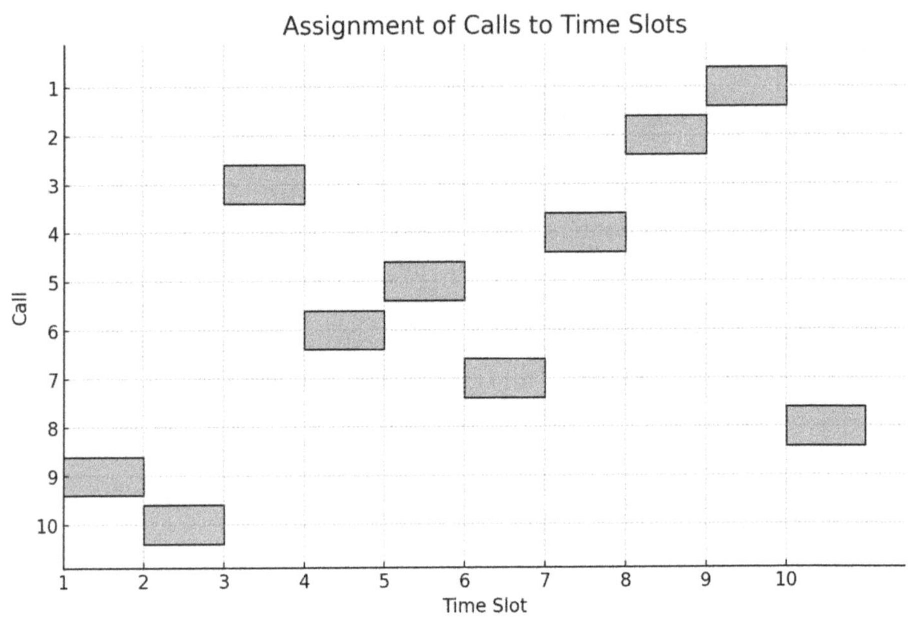

4.2 Machine Learning Model

A machine learning model can predict wait times based on various features, informing an optimization layer that makes assignment decisions. A simple linear regression model is assumed:

Model Equation

$$\text{Wait Time} = \beta_0 + \beta_1 \times \text{Priority} + \beta_2 \times \text{Call Duration} + \ldots + \varepsilon$$

Model Statistics

Model evaluation could involve various metrics such as Mean Absolute Error (MAE), Root Mean Squared Error (RMSE), and R-squared, assessing the model's accuracy and predictive capability.

Where:

- β_0, β_1, β_2,... are the parameters to be learned.
- Priority, Call Duration, etc., are features used for prediction.
- ε is the error term

The regression equation estimates the Wait Time based on several independent variables, including both numeric and categorical variables. The categorical variables are one-hot encoded, meaning that they are represented as binary variables indicating the presence of each category. For example, 'Issue Type: General Inquiry' takes a value of 1 if the issue type is a general inquiry, and 0 otherwise. The coefficients represent the change in the predicted Wait Time for a one-unit change in the independent variable, while holding all other variables constant. The intercept (373.22) represents the predicted Wait Time when all independent variables are zero.

Wait Time = 373.22 + 0.0032 × Call Duration - 1.4008 × Number of Transfers - 7.0888 × Issue Type: General Inquiry - 3.4001 × Issue Type: New Service - 0.2362 × Issue Type: Refund - 2.9880 × Issue Type: Technical Support - 3.0728 × Priority: Low - 3.4344 × Priority: Medium - 0.4349 × Agent Experience Level: Mid-level + 7.7782 × Agent Experience Level: Senior - 1.0325 × Channel: Phone - 8.5173 × Channel: Web Callback

Figure 7. Actual vs. predicted wait time

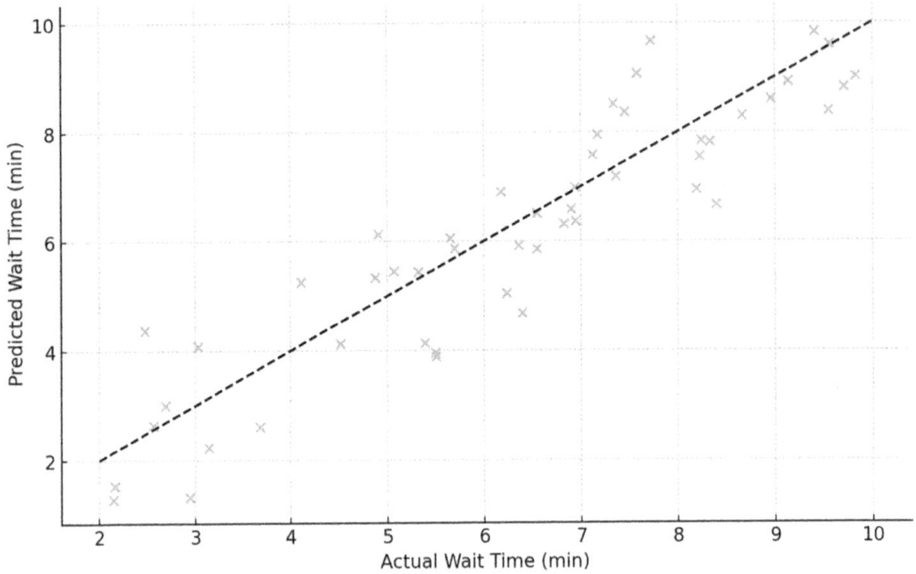

Figure 8. Histogram of actual vs. predicted wait time

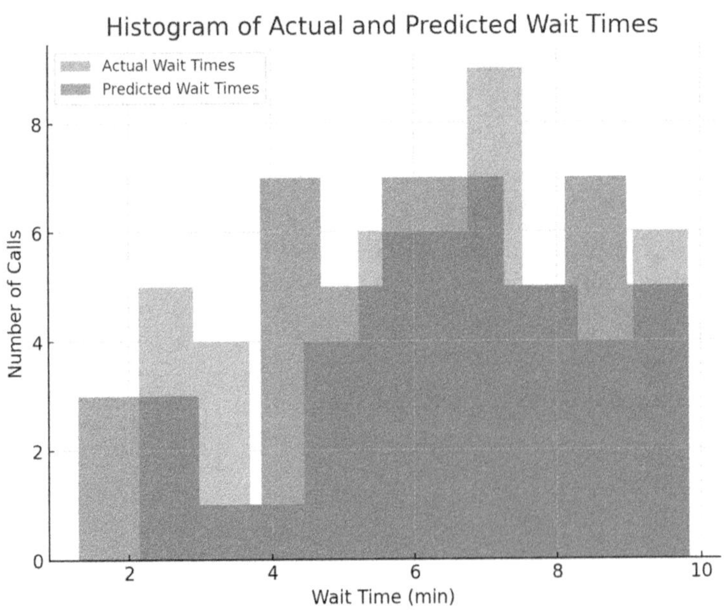

The residual plot displays residuals (the difference between actual and predicted wait times) against predicted wait times from the hypothetical ML model. This visualization helps assess the model's fit and identify any patterns in the residuals.

Figure 9. Residual plot

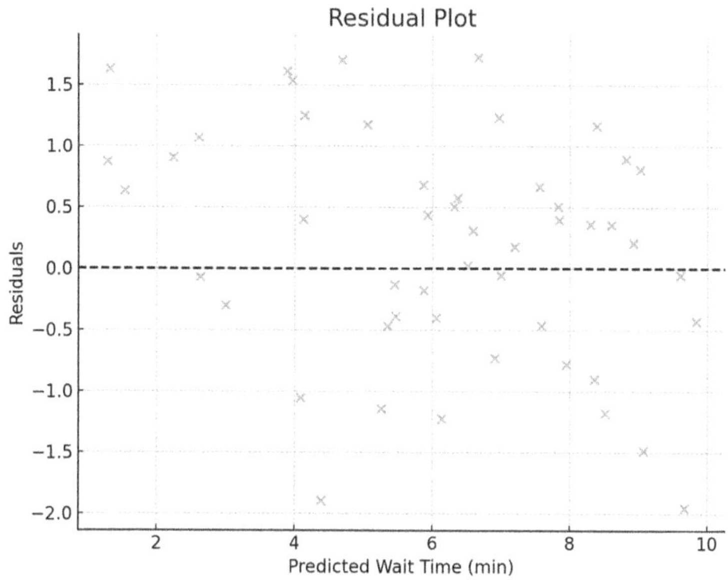

The linear optimization model demonstrates a methodology for minimizing wait time in a call center while considering priority and customer satisfaction. The simplified model, implemented on a subset of the data, provides a foundational understanding and a starting point for further development and analysis of a full-scale model.

5. CONCLUSION AND DISCUSSION

The main problems that call centers in the banks and telecom industries are having were looked into in this paper. Because people want fast customer service and there is more competition in both areas, cutting down on wait times for customers has become very important. The paper looks at a number of advanced methods, such as machine learning algorithms, heuristic edge server placements, and tools for dynamic resource provisioning. The goal of these methods is to make call handling easier, predict the number of calls that will come in, and make good use of resources. The study also talks about real-life examples and case studies of how these methods have been used to cut wait times by a lot, making customers happier and improving operational efficiency. Improving the efficiency of call centers is important, especially in industries as important as banking and telecommunications. But it's also important to build customer trust and confidence. The advanced methods talked about in this paper look like good ways to solve the problem of long wait times for customers. Even though we live in a digital world, call centers are still very important to companies, especially in the banking and telecom industries. Long wait times for customers are a big problem that needs to be fixed right away. The study paper uses both old-fashioned optimization techniques and newer machine learning techniques to do this. As shown, the goal of the linear optimization model is to cut down on wait times while keeping customers happy. Call centers can not only make things run more smoothly, but they can also build trust and customer happiness by using cutting edge methods such as machine learning algorithms, heuristic edge server placements, and dynamic resource provisioning. The research shows that these methods work because it uses real-life examples and works with groups. Finally, as the need for fast customer service grows and the digital world changes, call centers must use these cutting-edge methods to stay at the top of their game when it comes to providing great customer service. Using technology and data analytics to their full potential, call centers can change how they work and make sure customers get quick and helpful help. Call centers need to keep adapting and coming up with new ideas to make sure they stay at the top of customer service quality as the digital world changes.

REFERENCES

Aksin, Z., Armony, M., & Mehrotra, V. (2007). The modern call center: A multi-disciplinary perspective on operations management research. *Production and Operations Management, 16*(6), 665–688. doi:10.1111/j.1937-5956.2007.tb00288.x

Bakker, A., Demerouti, E., & Schaufeli, W. (2003). Dual processes at work in a call centre: An application of the job demands–resources model. *European Journal of Work and Organizational Psychology, 12*(4), 393–417. doi:10.1080/13594320344000165

Bhate, T., Dowling, S., & Collins, N. (2020). P132: Optimizing a physician surge protocol to address emergency department wait times during times of increased patient demand. medRxiv.

Brezavšček, A., & Baggia, A. (2014). Optimization of a Call Centre Performance Using the Stochastic Queueing Models. *PLOS Digital Health.*

Du Preez, J. J. (2008). *Call centre design, operation and optimisation: A structured and scientific based approach* [Doctoral dissertation]. University of Stellenbosch.

Gupta, A., Dwivedi, D. N., & Shah, J. (2023). Artificial Intelligence Applications in Banking and Financial Services. Future of Business and Finance. Springer. doi:10.1007/978-981-99-2571-1_1

Pintér, G., Mosavi, A., & Felde, I. (2020). *Artificial Intelligence for Modeling Real Estate Price Using Call Detail Records and Hybrid Machine Learning Approach.* Academic Press.

Sophia, M. E., & Chiemeke, S. (2016). *A Performance Evaluation of Call Resolution Oriented Routing Rules to Enhance Resolution Rates.* Mesopotamian Journal of Computer Science and Communications.

Tárkányi, G., Tényi, Á., Hollós, R., Kalmar, P., & Szapáry, L. (2022). Optimization of Large Vessel Occlusion Detection in Acute Ischemic Stroke Using Machine Learning Methods. *Life (Chicago, Ill.)*, *12*(2), 230. doi:10.3390/life12020230 PMID:35207517

W. K. (2023). *Scheduling in queueing systems.* Cambridge Core.

Xin, D., Miao, H., Parameswaran, A. G., & Polyzotis, N. (2021). *Production Machine Learning Pipelines: Empirical Analysis and Optimization Opportunities.* ACM Digital Library.

Zhang, X., Hu, Z., & Mahadevan, S. (2020). Bilevel optimization model for resilient configuration of logistics service centers. *IEEE Transactions on Reliability*, *71*(1), 469–483. doi:10.1109/TR.2020.2996025

Chapter 12
Fuzzy Logic Modelling-Based Measurement Approach for Mental Stress Measurement

Suchismita Satapathy
https://orcid.org/0000-0002-4805-1793
KIIT University, India

ABSTRACT

Mental stress affects performance. With regard to farming, it has been more dangerous with greater fatality rates than any other occupation. The farmers often work on their own for long hours with untrustworthy equipment and in hard climates, with hazardous chemicals and livestock. In addition, they make large financial commitments that expose them to higher levels of financial risks giving them higher levels of mental stress. Thus, an attempt was made in this chapter to identify the key risk factors in farming workplaces in addition to the levels of depression, anxiety, and work stress of farmers of Indian agriculture leading to mental ill health among them, and further to develop a fuzzy-based model considering both these cases in the fuzzy-environment for the evaluation of mental-stress.

INTRODUCTION

Mental-stress has been regarded as an important aspect that can affect individuals' performances. It affects the performance of human-beings. Due to higher levels of mental-stress, people are unable to complete complex tasks or assigned job efficiently. The stresses in workplaces affect the physical as well as mental conditions of the workers. The unemployment problem, crises of money, physical health issues,

DOI: 10.4018/979-8-3693-1598-9.ch012

Loneliness, can lead to work-related stresses (Hovey et al. 2006). Particularly in America, the farming occupation is more dangerous and stressful, Fetsch and Schultz (1984). Usually, farmers have financial problems and the farmers often work on their own for long working-hours with untrustworthy equipment and in a hard climate, with hazardous-chemical and live-stock. In addition, they make large financial-commitments that expose them to a higher-level of financial-risks. With the occurrences of these stresses that cannot be effectively handled, both mental in addition to physical changes may occur in human-body. Moreover, an increasing use of fuzzy-based models is taking place in the current industrial and academic researches and applications, mostly for data-analysis and systems' control, such as for congestion-control in wireless-communications network (Sawhney et al., 2014); wind-energy conversion-system (Chakraborty and Barma, 2014); sub pixel edge-detection (Bala and Dhir, 2014); cluster-head selection-protocol (Gajjar et al., 2014); temperature-regulation process (Ramanathan, 2014); and optimum path-planning of mobile-robots (Pandey and Parhi, 2017). However, very limited study was being done with regard to the use of fuzzy-environment for mental-health related issues in the agricultural sectors. Thus, the objective of this study was to identify the key risk-factors in farming work-places in addition to the levels of depressions, anxieties and work-stresses of farmers of Indian agriculture leading to mental ill-health among them, and further to develop a fuzzy-based models considering both these cases in the fuzzy-environment followed by the use of "Genetic Algorithm (GA)" for the evaluation of mental-stress.

BACKGROUND

In order to examine the stress among 126 dairy farm wives, Berkowitz and Perkins (1984) utilized path-analysis for assessing the relative-contribution to work-related stress in addition to family-related variables. Lazaridis (1999) have translated simple fuzzy-logic model into a "Bayesian-setting', and used to address a 'discrimination and attribution or classification' problem. Because of a large number of occupational-stressors getting aggravated in recent-years, a higher rate of suicide cases among farmers and farm-workers is taking place, which has been reported to be more in UK as compared to other occupational-groups (Gregoire, 2002). Kushwaha and Kumar (2009) have used "Sinha's Comprehensive Anxiety-Test (SCAT)" and "Approval Motive-Scale", in addition to both traditional as well as fuzzy approaches for a psychological-research. On the basis of physiological-signals, a stress detection system was proposed, which used heart-rate (HR) and galvanic skin-response (GSR) to provide information on individual's state of mind in view of their non-intrusiveness as well as non-invasiveness (de Santos Sierra et al., 2011a; 2011b). Almost all farmers get exposed to a variety of constraints as well as stress-levels, and among those, both economic and natural constraints were reported to be of major-concerns (Ghatul, 2013). Torres-Salomao et al. (2014) have presented a design framework for the human-participants undergoing mental-stress by the utilization of "Interval Type-2 Fuzzy-Logic (IT2FL)" architecture, which was optimized with Genetic Algorithm in addition to an efficient 'type-reduction algorithm' for the modelling-method. Improvement of psychologically-disabled peoples' quality of life as well as integrating them in society is strongly-linked with providing higher-levels of independence to them. But, they suffer of emotional-blockages formed by irresistible situations for them. Therefore, detection of the possibilities of a person's entry to mental-blockages because of stresses can facilitate in mitigating the symptoms of obstruction (Salazar-Ramirez et al., 2014). Mittal and Grewal (2014) have made an attempt in quantifying mental-stress by the use of fuzzy analysis of ECG-parameter, by decomposing the ECG-signal with "BIOR-3.9" wavelet-family up to three-levels. Agriculture being considered as an occupation associated with hazards and stresses that affect the farm-workers' health, thus identification of these stressors may help the health-professionals in improving health-outcomes by targeted development of intervention strategies as well as services (Kearney et al., 2014). Samahy et al. (2015) have made an attempt in automatic modification of the applied mental-stress based on the output of a linguistic-model employing fuzzy-sets in the form of "Mamdani-type fuzzy-rules". Furey et al. (2016) considered 121 dairy-farmers to assess their financial threat, social-support, depressions, anxiety, farm related job stresses, and health, in addition to safety belief that plays a vital-role to causing farm-related injuries. Cezar-Vaz et al. (2015) have investigated 182 female farm-workers and found the participants with mental-disorders and moderate-levels of physical-discomforts to be reported of significantly higher-levels of working-time, physical-demand, total-efforts and frustrations with regard to farm-work, also significantly higher-levels of frustrations with regard to house-work. Kallioniemi et al. (2016) have identified the stressors, the prevalence of stresses and burnout, and the associated variables with these symptoms among 265 "Finnish dairy-farmers". They found the stressors to be related to the work-load, and health to be associated with symptoms of stress and burnout. Besides, loneliness as well as poor economic-situations was found to be related to stress. Stresses are regarded as normal emotional-responses to the abnormal higher-demands of life, which everyone experience in varying intensities. There are various signs or symptoms of stresses that need to be addressed properly in order to help a person. The accentuation of stress may be due social-isolations, long-hours of working in addition to additional pressures in the management of farm during the periods of natural-disasters, climatic-extremes, and market-fluctuations. Thus, it becomes essential to keep one fit for enjoying good-times (Padhy and Raju, 2018). Brigance et al. (2018) have identified the mental health being influential in the work-place of organic-practices with some of the risk-factors stated by participants' in reflecting that by conventional and non-organic farmers. Although the mental-health issues among farm-workers have been identified as population health-concern (Hovey and Seligman, 2006), but no scoping-studies examining mental-health in farming communities have still focussed worldwide (Hagen et al., 2019). Fuzzy-logic approach has been used to evalute the mechanical parameter such as stress strain behaviour parameter for the α-phases as well as β-phases resistance as a function of α-phase volume-fraction (Taouche, 2019). Daghagh Yazd et al. (2019) have considered 167 articles related to farmers' mental-health in addition to the potential key risk-factors that affected farmers' mental-health around the world, and found the four most-cited influences, such as pesticide-exposures, financial-difficulties, climate-variability or droughts, and poor physical-health or past-injuries. (Lakshmi et al., 2020) have identified the reaction to any change in body lead to stress that gets reaction from body in terms of changes in mental, emotional and physical responses. With the features derived from the wearable-device in addition to displaying in a mobile application, a solution has been proposed to assess the experienced-stress of working individual. The utilized information during a work-day included heart-rate variations, respiratory-rate, peripheral-capillary oxygen-level (SpO2), and temperature. Further, this system was evaluated in a real work-environment with fuzzy-logic algorithm follow by the calculation of occupational-stress index (Lakshmi et al., 2020).After an extensive literature review, it was found that there was lack of research on mental stress of farmers. Less research is found showing the relation between blood pressure,temperature,internal body parameters impacting mental health of farmers. No literature is also found showing that increasing physical stress, mental stress level also increases. Hence in this chapter, an effort is taken to create a fuzzy model and predict mental stress based on input parameters of farmers, like physical stress, temperature etc.

RESEARCH METHODOLOGY

To find the cause and effect relationship of mental work load, fuzzy logic model was made. The data collected from five states such as (Orissa, Madhya Pradesh, Bihar, West Bengal and Chhattisgarh) was used to create a logical mathematical procedure based on the 'IF-THEN' rule system. To measure the mental stress of farmers which are greatly influenced by both internal (cause) as well as external factors (effect) in farming, the internal (cause) related to the risk-factors in farming that affects the mental-health conditions of farmers i.e., Blood pressure, pulse rate, oxygen level, calories burnt, temperature, humidity and physical stress respectively. For this purpose the fuzzy-logic controller simulink on MATLAB 2013 version software was used. Different inputs like internal factors i.e., blood pressure, Pulse rate, oxygen level, calories burnt, temperature, humidity and physical stress were measured with respect to output mental pressure of farmers in working-places in the first model.

Figure 1. Procedure of the study

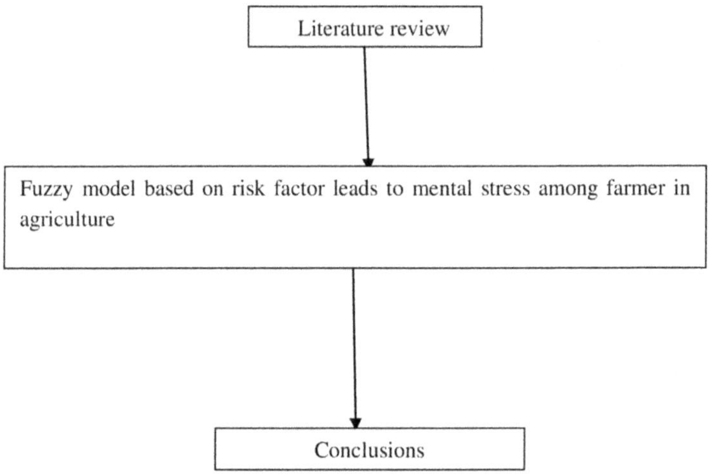

RESULTS AND DISCUSSION

The obtained "multi input and output (MIMO)" mamdani-type fuzzy models as shown in Figure 2 consisted of seven inputs and a single output for different risk-factors in farming, The inputs related to the risk-factors in farming that affects the mental-health conditions of farmers with their ranges included: Blood pressure (60-180); Pulse rate (60-100); Oxygen level (80-100); Calories burnt (100-500); Temperature (20-55); Humidity (20-70); and Physical stress (0-1); respectively. The output represented the mental stress of farmers in the range of "0 to 1" showing "No and Yes".

The below equation is generated by minitab 17 by using collected data for BP,pulse rate, oxygen level etc.

Mental Stress=13.2+0.087BP-0.029Pulse rate+0.0128Oxygen level-0.037Calorieburnt+0.24Tempertaure-0.75Humidity-0.64Physical stress (1)

Then Matlab (mamadani model is used to test the above equation/model).

Figure 2. Fuzzy models with input and output for different risk factors in farming

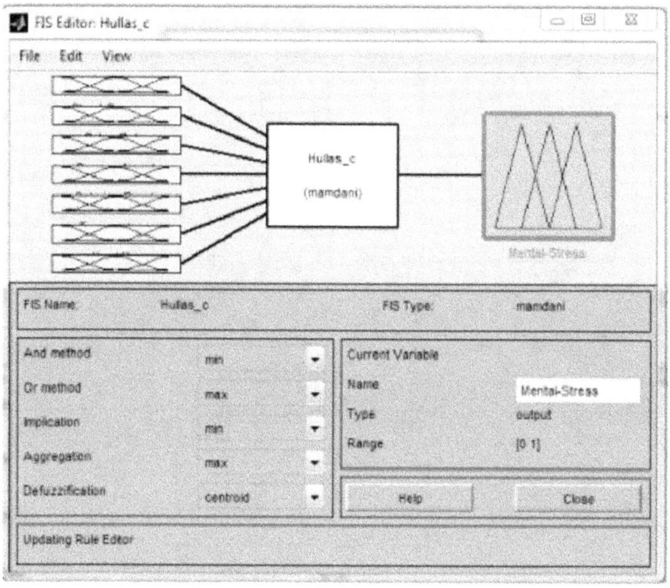

The input data fuzzification was accomplished with the assignment of linguistic-variables and each of the membership function's range-values for all the seven inputs constituting of risk-factors in faming and the output as mental-stress were assigned accordingly. The input membership-functions for risk-factors included: "Blood pressure (Figure 3(a); Pulse rate (Figure 3(b); Oxygen level (Figure 4(a); Calories burnt (Figure 4(b); Temperature (Figure 5(a); Humidity (Figure 5(b); and Physical stress (Figure 5(c)". Based on the content in literature and suggestion of experts, gauss-type membership functions ranging between low, medium and high were chosen for optimal performance for all the inputs. Similarly, gauss-type membership functions ranging between "No and Yes" were chosen for the optimal output for the case of involved risk-factors in farm working-places leading to mental-stress. The MATLAB-rules and the final generated-surfaces for the models constituting the risk-factors leading to mental-stress were as shown in Figure 6.

Figure 3. Input membership functions for risk factors in faming, such as (a) blood pressure, (b) pulse rate

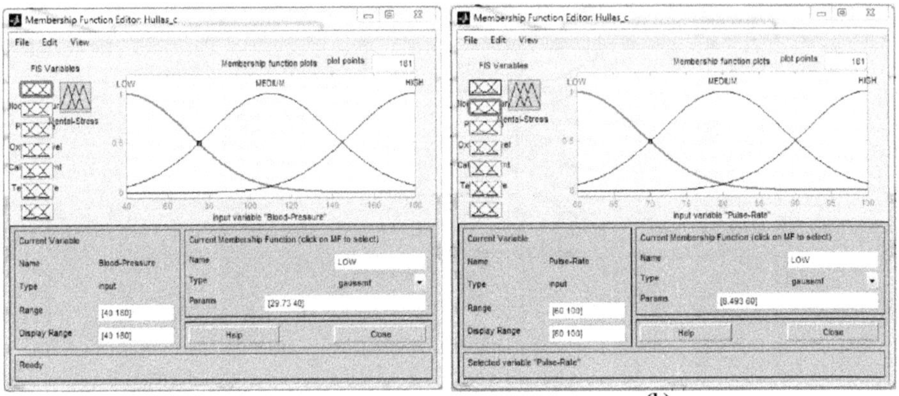

(a) (b)

Figure 4. Input membership functions for risk factors in faming, such as (a) oxygen level, (b) calories burnt

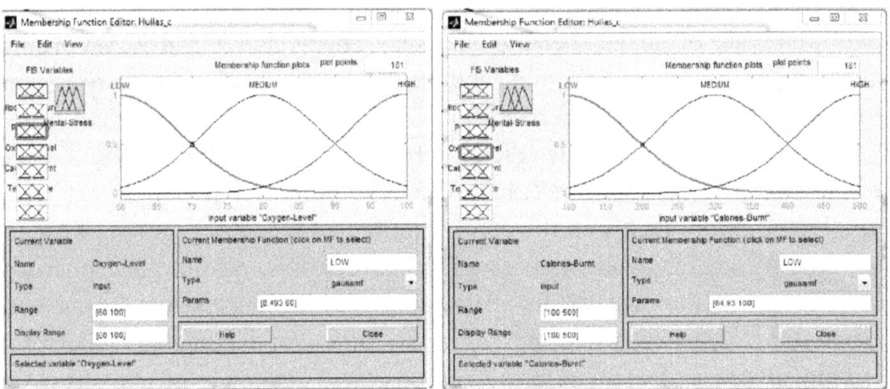

(a) (b)

Figure 5. Input membership functions for risk factors in faming, such as (a) temperature, (b) humidity, (c) physical stress

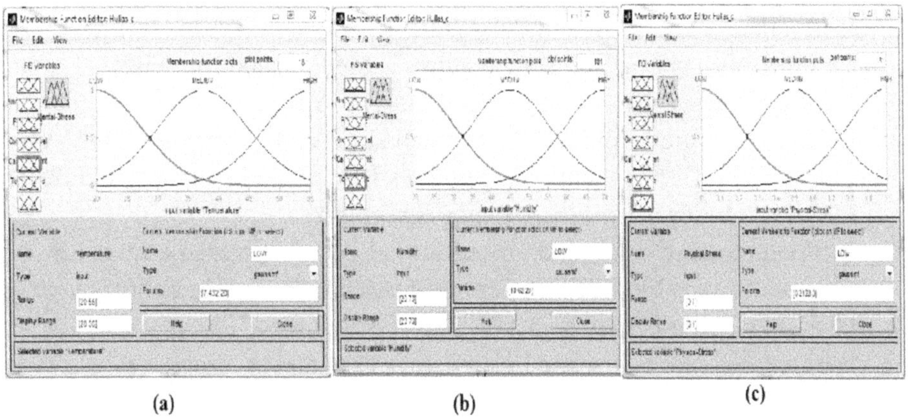

The associated rules with regard to the risk-factors in farming leading to mental-stress among farmers included the following (Figure7):

1. If Blood pressure is low and Pulse Rate is Low and Oxygen level is Low and Calories burnt is Low and Temperatures is Low and Humidity is Low and Physical stressor is Low then Mental Stress is yes.
2. If Blood pressure is low and Pulse Rate is Low and Oxygen level is Low and Calories burnt is Low and Temperatures is Low and Humidity is Low and Physical stressor is Medium then Mental Stress is yes.
3. If Blood pressure is low and Pulse Rate is Low and Oxygen level is Low and Calories burnt is Low and Temperatures is Low and Humidity is Low and Physical stressor is high then Mental Stress is Yes.
4. If Blood pressure is low and Pulse Rate is Low and Oxygen level is Low and Calories burnt is Low and Temperatures is Low and Humidity is Medium and Physical stressor is Low then Mental Stress is Yes.
5. If Blood pressure is low and Pulse Rate is Low and Oxygen level is Low and Calories burnt is Low and Temperatures is Low and Humidity is High and Physical stressor is Low then Mental Stress is Yes.
6. If Blood pressure is Medium and Pulse Rate is Medium and Oxygen level is Medium and Calories burnt is Medium and Temperatures is Medium and Humidity is Medium and Physical stressor is Medium then Mental Stress is No.

7. If Blood pressure is High and Pulse Rate is High and Oxygen level is High and Calories burnt is High and Temperatures is High and Humidity is High and Physical stressor is High then Mental Stress is Yes.
8. If Blood pressure is low and Pulse Rate is Low and Oxygen level is Low and Calories burnt is Low and Temperatures is Medium and Humidity is Low and Physical stressor is Low then Mental Stress is Yes.
9. If Blood pressure is low and Pulse Rate is Low and Oxygen level is Low and Calories burnt is Low and Temperatures is High and Humidity is Low and Physical stressor is Low then Mental Stress is Yes.
10. If Blood pressure is low and Pulse Rate is Low and Oxygen level is Low and Calories burnt is Medium and Temperatures is Low and Humidity is Low and Physical stressor is Low then Mental Stress is Yes.
11. If Blood pressure is low and Pulse Rate is Low and Oxygen level is Low and Calories burnt is High and Temperatures is Low and Humidity is Low and Physical stressor is Low then Mental Stress is Yes.
12. If Blood pressure is low and Pulse Rate is Low and Oxygen level is Medium and Calories burnt is Low and Temperatures is Low and Humidity is Low and Physical stressor is Low then Mental Stress is Yes.
13. If Blood pressure is low and Pulse Rate is Low and Oxygen level is High and Calories burnt is Low and Temperature is Low and Humidity is Low and Physical stressor is Low then Mental Stress is Yes.
14. If Blood pressure is low and Pulse Rate is Medium and Oxygen level is Low and Calories burnt is Low and Temperatures is Low and Humidity is Low and Physical stressor is Low then Mental Stress is Yes.
15. If Blood pressure is low and Pulse Rate is High and Oxygen level is Low and Calories burnt is Low and Temperatures is Low and Humidity is Low and Physical stressor is Low then Mental Stress is Yes.
16. If Blood pressure is Medium and Pulse Rate is Low and Oxygen level is Low and Calories burnt is Low and Temperatures is Low and Humidity is Low and Physical stressor is Low then Mental Stress is Yes.
17. If Blood pressure is High and Pulse Rate is Low and Oxygen level is Low and Calories burnt is Low and Temperatures is Low and Humidity is Low and Physical stressor is Low then Mental Stress is Yes.
18. If Blood pressure is low and Pulse Rate is Medium and Oxygen level is Low and Calories burnt is Medium and Temperatures is Low and Humidity is Medium and Physical stressor is Low then Mental Stress is Yes.
19. If Blood pressure is Medium and Pulse Rate is Low and Oxygen level is Medium and Calories burnt is Low and Temperatures is Medium and Humidity is Low and Physical stressor is Medium then Mental Stress is Yes.

20. If Blood pressure is low and Pulse Rate is High and Oxygen level is Low and Calories burnt is High and Temperatures is Low and Humidity is High and Physical stressor is Low then Mental Stress is Yes.
21. If Blood pressure is High and Pulse Rate is Low and Oxygen level is High and Calories burnt is Low and Temperatures is High and Humidity is Low and Physical stressor is High then Mental Stress is Yes.
22. If Blood pressure is low and Pulse Rate is Medium and Oxygen level is Medium and Calories burnt is Medium and Temperatures is Medium and Humidity is Medium and Physical stressor is Medium then Mental Stress is No.
23. If Blood pressure is High and Pulse Rate is Medium and Oxygen level is Medium and Calories burnt is Medium and Temperatures is Medium and Humidity is Medium and Physical stressor is Medium then Mental Stress is No.
24. If Blood pressure is Medium and Pulse Rate is Low and Oxygen level is Low and Calories burnt is Low and Temperatures is Low and Humidity is Low and Physical stressor is Low then Mental Stress is Yes.
25. If Blood pressure is Medium and Pulse Rate is Low and Oxygen level is Medium and Calories burnt is Low and Temperatures is Medium and Humidity is Low and Physical stressor is Medium then Mental Stress is Yes.
26. If Blood pressure is High and Pulse Rate is Low and Oxygen level is Medium and Calories burnt is High and Temperatures is Low and Humidity is Medium and Physical stressor is Low then Mental Stress is Yes.
27. If Blood pressure is High and Pulse Rate is Medium and Oxygen level is Low and Calories burnt is Medium and Temperatures is High and Humidity is Low and Physical stressor is Medium then Mental Stress is Yes.
28. If Blood pressure is Medium and Pulse Rate is High and Oxygen level is Medium and Calories burnt is High and Temperatures is Low and Humidity is High and Physical stressor is High then Mental Stress is Yes.
29. If Blood pressure is High and Pulse Rate is Medium and Oxygen level is Low and Calories burnt is Low and Temperatures is High and Humidity is Low and Physical stressor is Medium then Mental Stress is Yes.
30. If Blood pressure is low and Pulse Rate is High and Oxygen level is Medium and Calories burnt is Medium and Temperatures is High and Humidity is High and Physical stressor is High then Mental Stress is Yes.
31. If Blood pressure is High and Pulse Rate is Low and Oxygen level is High and Calories burnt is High and Temperatures is Low and Humidity is Low and Physical stressor is Medium then Mental Stress is Yes.
32. If Blood pressure is High and Pulse Rate is Low and Oxygen level is Medium and Calories burnt is Low and Temperatures is Low and Humidity is High and Physical stressor is Medium then Mental Stress is Yes.

33. If Blood pressure is High and Pulse Rate is High and Oxygen level is High and Calories burnt is Low and Temperatures is Low and Humidity is High and Physical stressor is Medium then Mental Stress is Yes.
34. If Blood pressure is High and Pulse Rate is Medium and Oxygen level is Medium and Calories burnt is High and Temperatures is High and Humidity is Low and Physical stressor is Medium then Mental Stress is Yes.
35. If Blood pressure is High and Pulse Rate is Medium and Oxygen level is High and Calories burnt is Medium and Temperature is Low and Humidity is High and Physical stressor is Low then Mental Stress is Yes.
36. If Blood pressure is Medium and Pulse Rate is High and Oxygen level is Medium and Calories burnt is High and Temperatures is High and Humidity is High and Physical stressor is High then Mental Stress is Yes.
37. If Blood pressure is High and Pulse Rate is Low and Oxygen level is High and Calories burnt is Medium and Temperature is Medium and Humidity is High and Physical stressor is Low then Mental Stress is Yes.
38. If Blood pressure is High and Pulse Rate is Low and Oxygen level is Medium and Calories burnt is High and Temperatures is Low and Humidity is Medium and Physical stressor is High then Mental Stress is Yes.
39. If Blood pressure is low and Pulse Rate is Low and Oxygen level is High and Calories burnt is Medium and Temperatures is Medium and Humidity is Medium and Physical stressor is High then Mental Stress is No.
40. If Blood pressure is Medium and Pulse Rate is High and Oxygen level is Medium and Calories burnt is High and Temperatures is High and Humidity is Low and Physical stressor is Medium then Mental Stress is No.
41. If Blood pressure is High and Pulse Rate is Low and Oxygen level is High and Calories burnt is Medium and Temperatures is Medium and Humidity is High and Physical stressor is Medium then Mental Stress is No.
42. If Blood pressure is High and Pulse Rate is Low and Oxygen level is Low and Calories burnt is High and Temperatures is Medium and Humidity is Medium and Physical stressor is Medium then Mental Stress is No.
43. If Blood pressure is Medium and Pulse Rate is Medium and Oxygen level is High and Calories burnt is High and Temperatures is High and Humidity is Low and Physical stressor is Medium then Mental Stress is No.
44. If Blood pressure is High and Pulse Rate is High and Oxygen level is Medium and Calories burnt is Low and Temperatures is Low and Humidity is Low and Physical stressor is High then Mental Stress is Yes.
45. If Blood pressure is High and Pulse Rate is High and Oxygen level is Medium and (Calories burnt is Low and Temperature is High and Humidity is Medium and Physical stressor is Medium then Mental Stress is No.

46. If Blood pressure is High and Pulse Rate is High and Oxygen level is Medium and Calories burnt is Low and Temperatures is Medium and Humidity is Medium and Physical stressor is Medium then Mental Stress is No.
47. If Blood pressure is Medium and Pulse Rate is High and Oxygen level is Low and Calories burnt is Medium and Temperatures is Low and Humidity is Medium and Physical stressor is Medium then Mental Stress is No.
48. If Blood pressure is low and Pulse Rate is Medium and Oxygen level is Low and Calories burnt is Medium and Temperature is High and Humidity is Low and Physical stressor is High then Mental Stress is Yes.
49. If Blood pressure is High and Pulse Rate is High and Oxygen level is Medium and Calories burnt is Low and Temperatures is Medium and Humidity is High and Physical stressor is Low then Mental Stress is Yes.
50. If Blood pressure is High and Pulse Rate is High and Oxygen level is Medium and Calories burnt is High and Temperatures is High and Humidity is Low and Physical stressor is Low then Mental Stress is Yes.
51. If Blood pressure is low and Pulse Rate is Low and Oxygen level is High and Calories burnt is Medium and Temperatures is High and Humidity is Low and Physical stressor is Low then Mental Stress is No.
52. If Blood pressure is Medium and Pulse Rate is High and Oxygen level is Medium and Calories burnt is High and Temperatures is High and Humidity is Low and Physical stressor is Low then Mental Stress is Yes.
53. If Blood pressure is High and Pulse Rate is Low and Oxygen level is High and Calories burnt is Medium and Temperature is Medium and Humidity is High and Physical stressor is Medium then Mental Stress is No.
54. If Blood pressure is High and Pulse Rate is Medium and Oxygen level is High and Calories burnt is Low and Temperatures is High and Humidity is Medium and Physical stressor is Medium then Mental Stress is No.
55. If Blood pressure is low and Pulse Rate is Medium and Oxygen level is High and Calories burnt is High and Temperatures is Medium and Humidity is High and Physical stressor is Low then Mental Stress is Yes.
56. If Blood pressure is low and Pulse Rate is Medium and Oxygen level is Low and Calories burnt is High and Temperatures is Medium and Humidity is Low and Physical stressor is Medium then Mental Stress is No.
57. If Blood pressure is High and Pulse Rate is Low and Oxygen level is Medium and Calories burnt is High and Temperatures is High and Humidity is Low and Physical stressor is Medium then Mental Stress is Yes.
58. If Blood pressure is High and Pulse Rate is High and Oxygen level is High and Calories burnt is High and Temperatures is Low and Humidity is High and Physical stressor is Medium then Mental Stress is Yes.

59. If Blood pressure is low and Pulse Rate is Medium and Oxygen level is High and Calories burnt is Low and Temperatures is Medium and Humidity is High and Physical stressor is Medium then Mental Stress is Yes.
60. If Blood pressure is Medium and Pulse Rate is Medium and Oxygen level is High and Calories burnt is High and Temperatures is Medium and Humidity is High and Physical stressor is Medium then Mental Stress is Yes.

Figure 6. Output membership-functions fo risk factors leading to mental stress

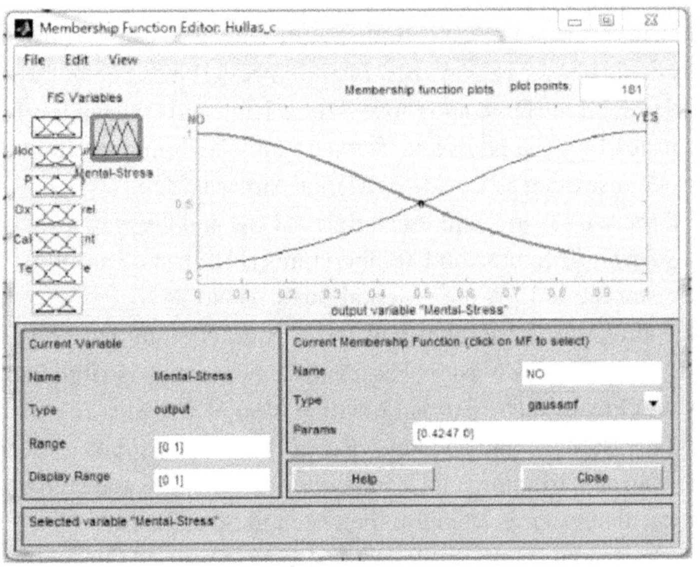

Figure 7. The rule-base for the models constituting risk factors leading to mental stress

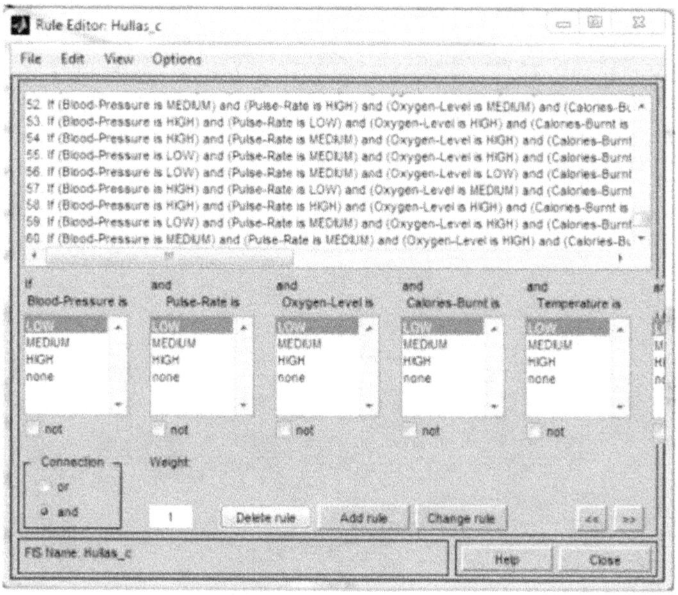

Figure 8. The MATLAB-rules for the models constituting risk factors leading to mental stress

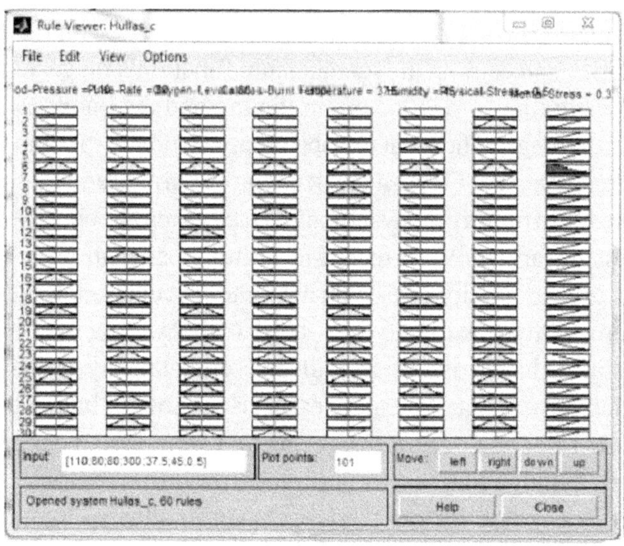

Figure 9. The generated-surfaces for the models constituting risk factors leading to mental stress

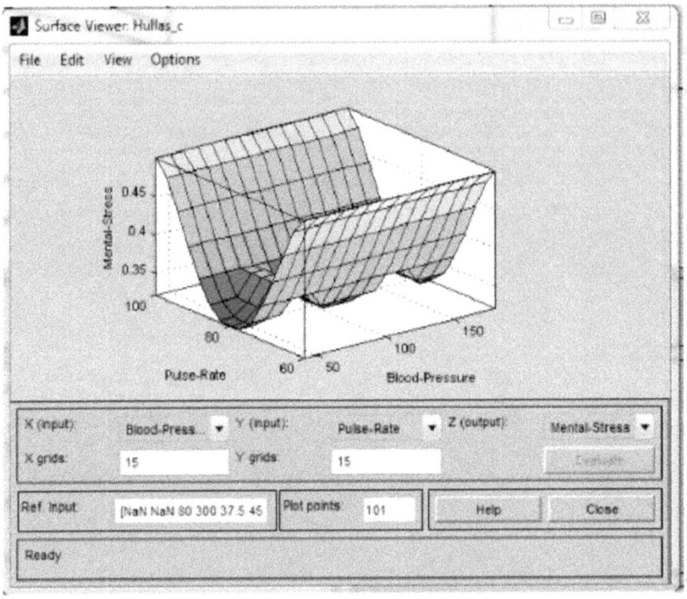

CONCLUSION

In this study for the development of fuzzy-models with tends to the mental-stress of the farmer, the input data's fuzzification was accomplished with the assignment of linguistic-variables and each of the membership function's range-values for all the seven inputs constituting of risk-factors in faming and the output as mental-stress were assigned accordingly. The input membership-functions for risk-factors included: "Blood pressure; Pulse rate; Oxygen level; Calories burnt; Temperature; Humidity; and Physical stress". In future the psychological factors may be considered to measure the mental stress of farmers. With regard to farming occupation, it has been more dangerous with greater fatality-rates than any other occupation. Indian Farmers are physically and mentally sick due to the lonely workplace, lot of strain, body pain, discomfort postures, health issues and adverse climate. Physical discomfort and stress creates both physical and mental health issues among Indian farmers. At the individual farmer level, the occurrences of mental work load, health problem such as stress, anxiety, feeling sadness, physical problem and psychological distress have been identified as key risk factors while working in adverse weather conditions. Moreover, the prevalence of musculoskeletal discomforts and disorders cause serious health related problem due to psychological stress that affect the mental well-being of farmers reducing their work efficiency.Workplace discomfort level is found by discomfort questionnaire and the impact of physical discomfort on psychological stress is studied. Then a model is developed to predict mental health of farmers by internal parameters like blood pressure, temperature etc. which are varying due to physical stress in workplace. In addition to studying the changes in the effect of the levels of depressions, anxieties and stresses of Indian farmers the mental wellness is predicted. The findings of this work will alert policy-makers, academicians & researchers, psychologists and practitioners to measure mental health of farmers regularly and provide personal protective kits for the farmers, which can reduce their physical and mental strain up to a certain level and also regular counselling sessions and training on sustainable and safe agriculture practices must be arranged on regular basis. Moreover, suitable Policies must be framed for using ergonomic concept in agriculture tool, mental health measuring devices, personal protective equipment's and work system design.

Declaration

Nofund is given by any agency to perform this research.

REFERENCES

Bala, J., & Dhir, R. (2014). A novel hybrid technique for sub-pixel edge detection using fuzzy logic and zernike moment. *International Journal on Computer Science and Engineering*, *2*, 26–31.

Berkowitz, A. D., & Perkins, H. W. (1984). Stress among farm women: Work and family as interacting systems. *Journal of Marriage and Family*, *46*(1), 161–166. doi:10.2307/351874

Brigance, C., Soto Mas, F., Sanchez, V., & Handal, A. J. (2018). The mental health of the organic farmer: Psychosocial and contextual actors. *Workplace Health & Safety*, *66*(12), 606–616. doi:10.1177/2165079918783211 PMID:29962329

Cezar-Vaz, M. R., Bonow, C. A., & Da Silva, M. R. S. (2015). Mental and physical symptoms of female rural workers: Relation between household and rural work. *International Journal of Environmental Research and Public Health*, *12*(9), 11037–11049. doi:10.3390/ijerph120911037 PMID:26371018

Chakraborty, N., & Barma, M. D. (2014). Modelling of Stand-Alone Wind Energy Conversion System using Fuzzy Logic Controller. *Small, 2*(1).

Daghagh Yazd, S., Wheeler, S. A., & Zuo, A. (2019). Key risk factors affecting farmers' mental health: A systematic review. *International Journal of Environmental Research and Public Health*, *16*(23), 4849. doi:10.3390/ijerph16234849 PMID:31810320

De Santos Sierra, A., Ávila, C. S., Casanova, J. G., & del Pozo, G. B. (2011b). A stress-detection system based on physiological signals and fuzzy logic. *IEEE Transactions on Industrial Electronics*, *58*(10), 4857–4865. doi:10.1109/TIE.2010.2103538

De Santos Sierra, A., Ávila, C. S., del Pozo, G. B., & Casanova, J. G. (2011a). Stress detection by means of stress physiological template. In *2011 Third World Congress on Nature and Biologically Inspired Computing* (pp. 131-136). IEEE. 10.1109/NaBIC.2011.6089448

Demetgul, M., Ulkir, O., & Waqar, T. (2014). Washing Machine Using Fuzzy Logic *Autom. Control Intell. Syst.,* 23-27.

Eckroth, J., & Schoen, E. (2019). A Genetic Algorithm for Finding a Small and Diverse Set of Recent News Stories on a Given Subject: How We Generate AAAI's AI-Alert. *Proceedings of the AAAI Conference on Artificial Intelligence*, *33*(1), 9357–9364. doi:10.1609/aaai.v33i01.33019357

El-Samahy, E., Mahfouf, M., Torres-Salomao, L. A., & Anzurez-Marin, J. (2015). A new computer control system for mental stress management using fuzzy logic. In 2015 IEEE international conference on evolving and adaptive intelligent systems (EAIS) (pp. 1-7). IEEE. doi:10.1109/EAIS.2015.7368785

Furey, E. M., O'Hora, D., McNamara, J., Kinsella, S., & Noone, C. (2016). The roles of Financial Threat, social support, Work stress, and Mental Distress in Dairy Farmers' expectations of injury. *Frontiers in Public Health*, *4*, 126. doi:10.3389/fpubh.2016.00126 PMID:27446893

Gajjar, S., Sarkar, M., & Dasgupta, K. (2014). Cluster head selection protocol using fuzzy logic for wireless sensor networks. *International Journal of Computer Applications*, *97*(7), 38–43. doi:10.5120/17022-7310

Ghatul, D. B. (2013). Constraints and Stress level of Farmers. International Journal of Scientific and Research Publications, 107.

Goel, P., & Lobiyal, D. K. (2018). Minimizing the cost of two-tier cellular network with queuing handoff calls in microcell using genetic algorithm. *Malaya Journal of Matematik*, 14-21.

Gregoire, A. (2002). The mental health of farmers. *Occupational Medicine*, *52*(8), 471–476. doi:10.1093/occmed/52.8.471 PMID:12488518

Gu, X., Huang, M., & Liang, X. (2019). An improved genetic algorithm with adaptive variable neighborhood search for FJSP. *Algorithms*, *12*(11), 243. doi:10.3390/a12110243

Gulhane, Y. H., Rode, S. V., & Ladhake, S. A. (2011). Application of fuzzy logic in stress analysis. In *Proceedings of the International Conference & Workshop on Emerging Trends in Technology* (pp. 679-685). 10.1145/1980022.1980168

Hagen, B. N., Albright, A., Sargeant, J., Winder, C. B., Harper, S. L., O'Sullivan, T. L., & Jones-Bitton, A. (2019). Research trends in farmers' mental health: A scoping review of mental health outcomes and interventions among farming populations worldwide. *PLoS One*, *14*(12), e0225661. doi:10.1371/journal.pone.0225661 PMID:31805070

Haldurai, L., Madhubala, T., & Rajalakshmi, R. (2016). A study on genetic algorithm and its applications. *International Journal on Computer Science and Engineering*, *4*(10), 2347–2693.

Hatagar, S., & Halase, S. V. (2015). Three Input – One Output Fuzzy logic control of Washing Machine. *Int. J. Sci. Res. Eng. Technol.*, *4*(1), 2278–2882.

Hovey, J. D., & Seligman, L. D. (2006). The mental health of agricultural workers. In *Agricultural medicine* (pp. 282–299). Springer. doi:10.1007/0-387-30105-4_22

Joshi, A., Kale, S., Chandel, S., & Pal, D. K. (2015). Likert scale: Explored and explained. *British Journal of Applied Science and Technology*, *7*(4), 396–403. doi:10.9734/BJAST/2015/14975

Kallioniemi, M. K., Simola, A., Kaseva, J., & Kymäläinen, H. R. (2016). Stress and burnout among Finnish dairy farmers. *Journal of Agromedicine*, *21*(3), 259–268. doi:10.1080/1059924X.2016.1178611 PMID:27081893

Kearney, G. D., Rafferty, A. P., Hendricks, L. R., Allen, D. L., & Tutor-Marcom, R. (2014). A cross-sectional study of stressors among farmers in eastern North Carolina. *North Carolina Medical Journal*, *75*(6), 384–392. doi:10.18043/ncm.75.6.384 PMID:25402689

Kushwaha, G. S., & Kumar, S. (2009). Role of the fuzzy system in psychological research. *Europe's Journal of Psychology*, *5*(2), 123–134. doi:10.5964/ejop.v5i2.271

Lakshmi, B., Boban, E., Sulphikar, N., & Aparna, T. (2020). Mental stress calculation using fuzzy logic algorithm. *International Journal of Applied Engineering Research: IJAER*, *15*(1).

Lazaridis, E. N. (1999). A Bayesian evaluation of fuzzy logic in a classification problem. *Communications in Statistics. Stochastic Models*, *15*(3), 461–483. doi:10.1080/15326349908807545

Mardle, S. J., Pascoe, S., & Tamiz, M. (2000). An investigation of genetic algorithms for the optimization of multi-objective fisheries bioeconomic models. *International Transactions in Operational Research*, *7*(1), 33–49.

Mittal, S., & Grewal, N. S. (2014). Stress Quantification using Fuzzy Analysis of ECG Parameters. *International Journal of Computer Applications*, *99*(9), 24–27. doi:10.5120/17403-7968

Neema, D. D., Patel, R. N., & Thoke, A. S. (2011). Speed control of induction motor using fuzzy rule base. *International Journal of Computer Applications*, *33*(5), 21–29.

Padhy, C., & Raju, P. S. (2018). Stress among farmers and its alleviation. *Int J Manag Technol Eng*, *8*(12), 2882–2887.

Pandey, A., & Parhi, D. R. (2017). Optimum path planning of mobile robot in unknown static and dynamic environments using Fuzzy-Wind Driven Optimization algorithm. *Defence Technology*, *13*(1), 47–58. doi:10.1016/j.dt.2017.01.001

Peng, C., Wu, G., Liao, T. W., & Wang, H. (2019). Research on multi-agent genetic algorithm based on tabu search for the job shop scheduling problem. *PLoS One*, *14*(9), e0223182. doi:10.1371/journal.pone.0223182 PMID:31560722

Poornima, M., Kuyin, C., & Revathy, M. (2018). Brain Tumor Detection Using Genetic Algorithm. *International Journal of Scientific Research in Computer Science, Engineering and Information Technology*.

Ramanathan, P. (2014). Fuzzy Logic Controller for Temperature Regulation Process. *Middle East Journal of Scientific Research*, *20*(11), 1524–1528.

Saeidi, S. (2018). Solving the Rubik's Cube using Simulated Annealing and Genetic Algorithm. *International Journal of Education and Management Engineering*, *8*(1), 1–10. doi:10.5815/ijeme.2018.01.01

Salazar-Ramirez, A., Irigoyen, E., & Martinez, R. (2014). Enhancements for a robust fuzzy detection of stress. In *International Joint Conference SOCO'14-CISIS'14-ICEUTE'14* (pp. 229-238). Springer. 10.1007/978-3-319-07995-0_23

Sawhney, A., Bhatia, R., & Mahajan, P. (2014). Congestion Control in Wireless Communication Network Using Fuzzy Logic and Machine Learning Techniques. *International Journal of Advanced Research in Electrical, Electronics and Instrumentation Engineering, 3*(11).

Schneiderman, N., Ironson, G., & Siegel, S. D. (2005). Stress and health: Psychological, behavioral, and biological determinants. *Annual Review of Clinical Psychology*, *1*(1), 607–628. doi:10.1146/annurev.clinpsy.1.102803.144141 PMID:17716101

Schönfeld, P., Brailovskaia, J., Bieda, A., Zhang, X. C., & Margraf, J. (2016). The effects of daily stress on positive and negative mental health: Mediation through self-efficacy. *International Journal of Clinical and Health Psychology*, *16*(1), 1–10. doi:10.1016/j.ijchp.2015.08.005 PMID:30487845

Sekulic, M., Pejic, V., Brezocnik, M., Gostimirović, M., & Hadzistevic, M. (2018). Prediction of surface roughness in the ball-end milling process using response surface methodology, genetic algorithms, and grey wolf optimizer algorithm. *Advances in Production Engineering & Management*, *13*(1), 18–30. doi:10.14743/apem2018.1.270

Taouche, R. (2019). Fuzzy Logic Prediction of Stress-Strain Behavior Parameters of Two-Phase Materials. Application to WC-Co System. *Australian Journal of Basic and Applied Sciences*, *13*(6), 74–81.

Torres-Salomao, L. A., Mahfouf, M., & Obajemu, O. (2014). Interval type-2 fuzzy logic adaptive modelling for human operators undergoing mental stress. *IFAC Proceedings Volumes, 47*(3), 9880-9885.

Vaishnav, P., Choudhary, N., & Jain, K. (2017). Traveling salesman problem using genetic algorithm: A survey. *International Journal of Scientific Research in Computer Science. Engineering and Information Technology*, *2*(3), 105–108.

Zhao, H., & Kong, F. (2016). Research and Applications of Shop Scheduling Based on Genetic Algorithms. *Brazilian Archives of Biology and Technology*, *59*(spe), 59. doi:10.1590/1678-4324-2016160545

Chapter 13
Deep Learning, Neural Networks, and Their Applications in Business Analytics

Nagendra Singh Singh Yadav
https://orcid.org/0000-0002-9591-4491
Engineering College, Bikaner, India

Pallavi Singh Yadav
Maharaja Ganga Singh University, India

Vishal Goar
Engineering College, Bikaner, India

ABSTRACT

This chapter aims to discover the growing significance of deep learning and neural networks in the field of business analytics. As businesses continue to generate vast amounts of data, the need for advanced analytical techniques to extract valuable insights has become paramount. Deep learning has demonstrated remarkable capabilities in tackling complex analytical tasks, making them indispensable tools for businesses seeking a competitive edge. The chapter will provide an overview of deep learning and neural networks, delving into their fundamental principles, architectures, and training methodologies. It will then focus on their real-world applications in various aspects of business analytics, such as customer behavior analysis, demand forecasting, fraud detection, recommendation systems, and more.

DOI: 10.4018/979-8-3693-1598-9.ch013

1. INTRODUCTION TO DEEP LEARNING AND NEURAL NETWORKS

1.1. Definition and History of Deep Learning

Deep learning has emerged as a revolutionary approach to solving complex problems by enabling computers to learn directly from data (Schmidhuber, 2015). At its core, deep learning includes the training of artificial neural networks to perform tasks without explicit programming. The word "deep" in deep learning refers to the multiple layers through which the data is transformed, enabling the system to learn intricate patterns & representations (Nielsen, 2015).

The roots of deep learning can be traced back to the mid-20th century, but crucial developments started gaining momentum in the 21st century. One of the crucial breakthroughs occurred with the development of deep neural networks that can learn hierarchical representations (Aggarwal, 2018). This shift marked a departure from shallow models and paved the way for the unprecedented capabilities of modern deep learning systems.

1.2. Basics of Neural Networks

- **Neurons and Layers -** Deep learning's core is rooted in artificial neural networks, drawing inspiration from the intricate design and operations of the human mind. A neural network comprises linked nodes known as neurons, organized into layers. Data is received by the input layer, weighted connections in the hidden layers process it, and the final result is generated by the output layer. The network's performance is optimized by fine-tuning the strength of connections, known as weights, during training (Francis, 2001).
- **Activation Functions -** Activation methods introduce non-linearity to neural networks, allowing them to model complex relationships in data. Generic activation methods consist of sigmoid, hyperbolic tangent (tanh), & rectified linear unit (ReLU). Each function has unique characteristics that affect the network's capacity to capture & generalize patterns.
- **Training and Backpropagation -** Training a neural network includes changing the weights depending on the flaw between projected & real outputs. Backpropagation, a key algorithm in deep learning, is used to propagate this error backward through the network & modify the weights accordingly. This iterative procedure refines the model, allowing it to make more accurate predictions over time.

1.3. The Evolution From Traditional Machine Learning to Deep Learning

The transition from classical machine learning to deep learning marks a fundamental transformation in how computers acquire knowledge and render decisions (Zhang et al., 2017). Traditional machine learning algorithms often depend on feature engineering, where specialist manually captures applicable features from the data. In contrast, deep learning excels at automatically learning hierarchical representations from raw data, removing the requirement for huge feature engineering.

Advancements in hardware, particularly graphical processing units (GPUs), have played a pivotal part in the victory of deep learning. The parallel processing capabilities of GPUs accelerate the training of large neural networks, making deep learning feasible on a broader scale (Lai, 2019).

The success of deep learning is evident across several domains, consisting of computer vision, natural language processing, & speech recognition. Applications like image classification, language translation, and autonomous vehicles showcase the transformative impact of deep learning on real-world issues (Shinde & Shah, 2018).

Deep learning and neural networks have redefined the landscape of artificial intelligence, allowing machines to learn complex patterns & make sophisticated decisions.

2. DEEP LEARNING ARCHITECTURES

Deep learning has appeared as a revolutionary paradigm in the domain of artificial intelligence, allowing machines to learn intricate patterns & representations from vast amounts of data. Among the myriad architectures that constitute the deep learning landscape, two prominent players stand out: Feedforward Neural Networks (FNN) and Convolutional Neural Networks (CNN).

Figure 1. Deep learning architectures

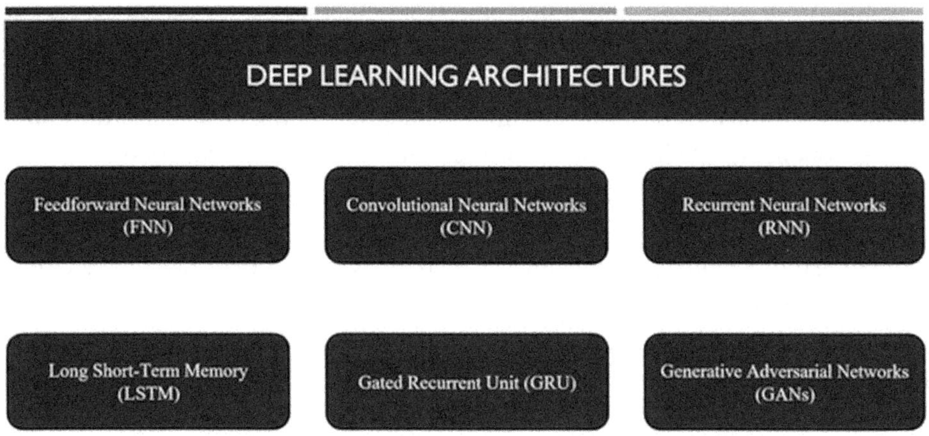

2.1. Feedforward Neural Networks (FNN)

It is known as multilayer perceptrons (MLPs), and form the cornerstone of deep learning. At their core, FNNs contain layers of linked neurons, each layer transforming input data into increasingly abstract representations. The architecture is "feedforward" because information moves through the network in one direction, from input to output, without cycles or loops (Svozil et al., 1997).

The fundamental building blocks of an FNN include an input layer, one or many hidden layers, & an output layer. Neurons in every layer are linked to neurons in corresponding layers, and each connection is associated with a weight (Sazli, 2006). Non-linear transformations brought by activation functions enable the network to capture intricate patterns and connections within the dataset.

Training an FNN includes altering the weights of connections to reduce the difference between projected & real outputs. This is typically obtained through backpropagation, where the error is propagated backward through the network, and gradient descent is employed to optimize the weights.

FNNs find applications in a broad span of tasks i.e. image & speech identification to natural language processing & regression problems. Their flexibility and capacity to capture intricate patterns make them a versatile choice for various domains.

2.2. Convolutional Neural Networks (CNN)

Convolutional Neural Networks have revolutionized computer vision tasks by leveraging the spatial hierarchies present in data. Unlike FNNs, CNNs are particularly designed to manage grid-like data, making them surprisingly effective for tasks like image recognition (Gu et al., 2018).

CNNs introduce convolutional layers that apply filters to local regions of the input data, obtaining spatial hierarchies & local patterns. Pooling layers lower the spatial dimensions, focusing on essential features. Fully linked layers at the end of the network aggregate information for final predictions (Bouvrie, 2006).

Training CNNs involves not only adjusting weights but also learning filter parameters during the convolutional process. Backpropagation remains a crucial part of the training process, but with an added focus on adapting filters to recognize relevant patterns.

CNNs dominate image and video analysis tasks i.e. image classification, object identification, & segmentation. Their ability to understand spatial relationships makes them adept at capturing features in grid-like structures.

2.3. Recurrent Neural Networks (RNN)

At the heart of sequential data processing lies the Recurrent Neural Network (RNN), a class of artificial neural networks designed to efficiently manage sequential information (Medsker & Jain, 2001). Contrary to conventional feedforward neural networks, RNNs incorporate connections that create directed cycles, enabling the preservation of a hidden state. This state allows RNNs to obtain information from past inputs, making them particularly adept at tasks involving sequential dependencies.

The RNN architecture consists of hidden units that maintain a memory of previous inputs. The network processes input sequences one element at a time, updating its hidden state with each new input (Sutskever, 2013). This recurrent nature allows RNNs to model temporal dependencies which makes it best fit for tasks i.e. natural language processing, speech recognition, and time-series projection.

However, traditional RNNs face challenges when learning long-range dependencies because of the disappearing gradient issue. To address these issues, further sophisticated architectures, i.e. LSTM & GRU, have been introduced.

2.4. Long Short-Term Memory (LSTM)

LSTM is a specialized variant of RNN designed to alleviate the disappearing gradient issue. Proposed by Hochreiter & Schmidhuber in 1997, LSTM introduces a memory cell that can store, write, & read information over long sequences. This architecture enables the model to selectively remember or forget information, making it well-suited for tasks requiring the retention of important context over extended periods.

The LSTM architecture comprises memory cells with three distinct gates i.e. input, forget & output gates. These gates control the flow of information into & out of the memory cell, enabling LSTM networks to manage long-range dependencies effectively. The explicit control over memory facilitates the learning of complex sequential patterns, making LSTMs a preferred choice in applications i.e. language modeling, machine translation, & speech identification.

2.5. Gated Recurrent Unit (GRU)

GRU is another variant of RNN that aims to address the disappearing gradient issue while simplifying the architecture contrast to LSTM. GRU merges the memory cell & hidden state into a one state vector, reducing the computational complexity and making it computationally more efficient than LSTM (Dey & Salem, 2017).

The GRU architecture includes update and reset gates, allowing the model to manage the flow of information through the network. The modification gate decides how much of the last state to carry over, while the reset gate decides how much of the past information to forget. GRU creates a stability between computational efficiency & expressive power which makes it suitable for many applications i.e. natural language processing, video analysis, & music composition (Zhao et al., 2017).

2.6. Generative Adversarial Networks (GANs)

In 2014, Ian Goodfellow and his colleagues unveiled Generative Adversarial Networks, marking a significant breakthrough in the field. In a game-like scenario, two neural networks are set against each other, embodying the core concept of Generative Adversarial Networks (GANs) (Creswell et al., 2018). One network, the generator, tries to build synthetic data that is identical to real data, while the other, the discriminator, strives to differentiate between real & generated data. This adversarial training procedure compels both networks to enhance iteratively, resulting in the generation of highly real data (Goodfellow et al., 2020).

Architectural Components of GANs:

- **Generator –** It is responsible for creating synthetic data. It typically starts with random noise & changes it into data that should resemble the training data. The architecture of the generator can vary, with deep neural networks, particularly convolutional or recurrent architectures, being commonly employed. The generator's output improves over time as it learns to produce data that is increasingly difficult for the discriminator to distinguish from real data.
- **Discriminator -** The discriminator functions as a binary classifier, differentiating authentic from synthesized information. Similar to the generator, the discriminator is implemented as a neural network. As training

progresses, the discriminator adapts to discerning even subtle differences between authentic & synthetic data. The interplay between the generator & discriminator is the core of the adversarial training procedure.

Training a GAN involves a delicate balance. As the generator improves, the discriminator must also evolve to maintain its discriminative ability. This back-and-forth dynamic can lead to a state where the generator produces data that is close to identical to real data. Achieving this equilibrium requires cautious tuning of hyperparameters & architectural options.

3. TRAINING DEEP NEURAL NETWORKS

Deep Neural Networks (DNNs) have transformed the domain of machine learning, enabling unprecedented advancements in several domains. However, the power of deep learning comes with the challenge of effectively training these complex models.

3.1. Backpropagation and Gradient Descent

At the heart of training deep neural networks lies the backpropagation algorithm, a cornerstone in the field of deep learning. Backpropagation is a supervised learning algorithm that optimizes the weights of a neural network by minimizing the error between projected & real results (Larochelle et al., 2009). The process involves computing gradients of the loss method concerning the network's parameters & changing these parameters in the opposite direction of the gradients using gradient descent.

Gradient descent is an iterative optimization algorithm that aims to find the minimum of the loss function. The key idea is to modify the parameters of the model in proportion to the negative of the gradient, gradually moving towards the optimal configuration. This procedure is carried on until convergence is achieved or a predefined stopping criteria is met (Courbariaux et al., 2015).

3.2. Activation Functions

Activation methods play a crucial part in presenting non-linearity to the neural network, enabling it to learn complex relationships in the data. Usual activation methods consist of sigmoid, hyperbolic tangent (tanh), & rectified linear unit (ReLU). Sigmoid & tanh functions squash the input values to a particular scope, making them suitable for certain tasks (Glorot & Bengio, 2010). ReLU, on the other hand, introduces non-linearity by enabling the network to activate when the input is positive. The option of activation function lies on the nature of the issue & the attributes of the data.

3.3. Optimization Techniques

Optimizing deep neural networks goes beyond basic gradient descent. Advanced optimization techniques are essential for accelerating convergence and overcoming challenges like vanishing or exploding gradients (Wang et al., 2016). Popular optimization algorithms include:

- **Momentum** - Momentum enhances gradient descent by incorporating the weighted sum of past gradients, enabling the model to overcome small fluctuations and accelerate convergence.
- **Adam** - Adam (Adaptive Moment Estimation) combines ideas from momentum & RMSprop, providing adaptive learning rates for every parameter. It is known for its efficiency and robustness across various tasks.

3.4. Regularization Methods

Overfitting is a usual concern in deep learning, where the model performs well on training data but it doesn't generalize the latest or hidden data. Regularization methods help eliminate overfitting by penalizing overly complex models. Common regularization techniques include:

- **L1 and L2 Regularization** - L1 regularization adds the absolute values of the weights to the loss method, inspiring sparsity, while L2 regularization adds the squared values, preventing excessively large weights.
- **Dropout** - Dropout randomly disables a fraction of neurons throughout training, eliminating reliance on particular neurons & encouraging the learning of robust features.

Training deep neural networks is a complex & dynamic procedure that needs a nuanced understanding of optimization techniques and regularization methods. Backpropagation forms the foundation, while activation functions, optimization algorithms, and regularization techniques collectively contribute to the success of deep learning models.

3.5. Learning Rate

The number of weights modified during the training process is called the learning rate. This hypermeter can be configured and later utilized in the training of neural networks which consists of small positive values ranging from 0.0 – 1.0. A hypermeter decides changes in the model corresponding to projected errors every time the model weights are modified. Selection of the learning rate is difficult since the value is way smaller and it could result in extensive training procedures which can get stuck. A larger value might result in learning a sub optimal group of weights way faster or a rocky training procedure. Learning rate might be a very crucial hyperparameter when it comes to the configuration of neural networks. It is critical to explore the impact of the learning rate on the performance of the model.

4. APPLICATIONS IN BUSINESS ANALYTICS

In the quickly changing landscape of business analytics, the integration of deep learning neural networks has appeared as a powerful tool for extracting valuable insights from vast datasets.

Figure 2. Applications in business analytics

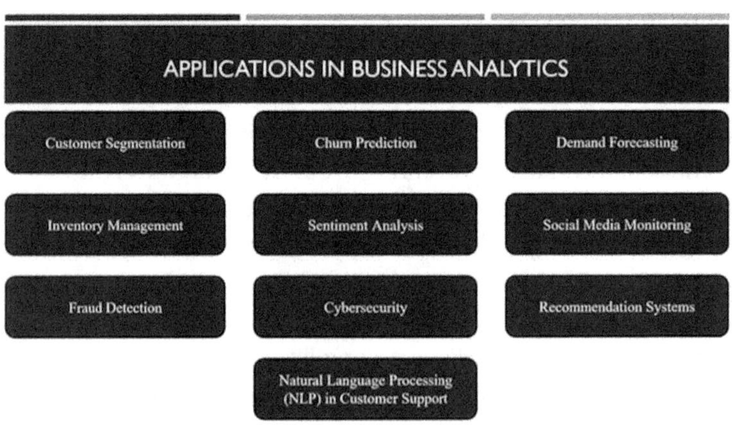

4.1. Customer Segmentation

Customer segmentation has long been a cornerstone of marketing strategies, helping businesses tailor their approaches to distinct groups of consumers. Traditional methods, such as demographic and geographic segmentation, have provided valuable insights. However, the limitations of these approaches have become increasingly apparent in the age of big data.

Deep learning neural networks have revolutionized customer segmentation by enabling the analysis of complex, unstructured data. By leveraging techniques like unsupervised learning, deep neural networks can recognize unseen patterns and relationships within vast datasets, allowing businesses to build more nuanced & accurate customer segments (Kraus et al., 2020).

Retailers i.e. can utilize deep learning to analyze customer images shared on social media. By extracting features from these images, neural networks can identify lifestyle preferences, fashion choices, and even sentiment analysis, leading to more personalized marketing strategies.

4.2. Churn Prediction

Customer churn, or the loss of customers over time, is a significant concern for businesses across industries. Identifying potential churners and implementing proactive retention strategies is critical to maintaining a healthy customer base.

Traditional churn prediction models rely on historical data and statistical methods. While effective to a certain extent, these models struggle to capture the complexity of modern customer behavior. Deep learning neural networks, on the other hand, excel at handling intricate patterns & dependencies within data, making them well-suited for churn prediction (Schmitt, 2023).

Telecom companies leverage deep learning to analyze massive volumes of customer data, consisting of call records, usage patterns, & customer interactions. Neural networks can identify subtle signs of dissatisfaction or potential churn long before traditional models, allowing for timely intervention.

4.3. Demand Forecasting

Accurate demand forecasting is a cornerstone of successful business operations. Traditional methods often fall short in handling the intricacies of today's dynamic markets. Deep learning neural networks, with their capability to discern complex patterns & dependency on data, offer a more robust solution.

- **Time Series Analysis -** Deep learning models i.e. recurrent neural networks (RNNs) & long short-term memory networks (LSTMs), excel in time series analysis. These architectures can obtain temporal dependency in demand data, enabling more accurate predictions. They adapt well to seasonality, trends, and sudden shifts in consumer behavior.

- **Incorporating External Factors –** The advantage of deep learning is its ability to assimilate diverse data sources. Businesses can enhance demand forecasting models by integrating external factors like economic indicators, social trends, and marketing campaigns. This holistic strategy enables a bit comprehensive understanding of the factors influencing demand.

4.4. Inventory Management

Effective demand forecasting is futile without efficient inventory management. Deep learning neural networks contribute significantly to optimizing inventory levels, reducing costs, and enhancing customer satisfaction.

- **Dynamic Inventory Replenishment -** Deep reinforcement learning, a subset of deep learning, is particularly adept at optimizing inventory replenishment strategies. By continuously learning from real-time data, these models adapt to changing market conditions, supplier performance, and lead times. This dynamic approach ensures that inventory levels align with actual demand, minimizing overstock and stockouts.
- **Risk Mitigation -** Deep learning models also play a crucial role in risk mitigation. By analyzing historical data and identifying patterns associated with supply chain interference, these models can provide early warnings. This proactive approach enables businesses to implement contingency plans and reduce the impact of unforeseen events on inventory levels.

4.5. Sentiment Analysis

It involves the use of natural language processing & machine learning techniques to determine the sentiment reflected in text. Traditional methods often struggled to obtain the nuances of human language, but deep learning neural networks excel in this task by learning complex patterns & representations (Puangpontip & Hewett, 2022).

In the business context, sentiment analysis plays a critical part in understanding the opinions of customers, market trends, & brand perception. By analyzing customer feedback, social media posts, & other textual data, organizations can gain valuable insights into consumer sentiment, allowing them to adapt strategies, enhance products, and improve customer satisfaction.

- **Natural Language Processing (NLP) Models -** Deep learning models, particularly those based on recurrent neural networks (RNNs) & transformers like BERT (Bidirectional Encoder Representations from Transformers), have demonstrated remarkable success in sentimental analysis tasks. These models can grasp context information & nuances in language, making them highly effective in understanding sentiment.

- **Transfer Learning** -The concept of transfer learning has significantly advanced sentiment analysis. Pre-trained models i.e. OpenAI's GPT (Generative Pre-trained Transformer), can be adjusted on specific business domains, allowing organizations to leverage the power of models without massive data requirements.
- **Real-time Sentiment Analysis** - Deep learning allows for real-time sentiment analysis, enabling businesses to monitor and respond promptly to changes in customer sentiment. This capability is invaluable in managing brand reputation, crisis communication, and staying ahead of market shifts.

4.6. Social Media Monitoring

Social media platforms have become treasure troves of data, with billions of users generating vast amounts of content daily. Businesses can harness this data to obtain insights into customer preferences, market trends, & competitor activities.

Deep learning neural networks shine at processing unstructured data, i.e. text and photos, which are prevalent in social media. By employing these models, organizations can analyze social media content at scale, uncovering patterns, sentiments, and emerging topics.

Social media monitoring powered by deep learning provides a competitive edge by offering real-time intelligence. Businesses can adapt marketing strategies, launch targeted campaigns, and address customer concerns swiftly, based on the insights derived from social media data (Kraus, 2020).

4.7. Fraud Detection

Fraudulent activities have become more sophisticated with the advent of digital technologies. Traditional rule-based systems struggle to keep pace with the evolving tactics of fraudsters. Deep Learning Neural Networks, with their capability to learn complex patterns & adapt to new information, offer a revolutionary approach to fraud detection.

- **Anomaly Detection** - By training on historical data, these networks can recognize patterns associated with legitimate transactions and flag deviations that may indicate fraudulent behavior. This is particularly valuable in detecting subtle and previously unknown fraud patterns.
- **Feature Extraction** - It is essential to autonomously identify relevant features within data, removing the requirement for manual feature engineering.

This ability is crucial for fraud detection, where subtle indicators may not be promptly apparent to human analysts. The network can uncover hidden relationships and dependencies that may signal fraudulent activity.

- **Real-time Analysis** - Fraud often occurs in real-time, requiring swift responses. Deep Learning neural networks can process huge volumes of data in real-time, allowing businesses to identify & respond to fraud related events as they occur. This ability is crucial for preventing financial losses and protecting the integrity of transactions.

4.8. Cybersecurity

Cybersecurity is another domain where Deep Learning neural network is transforming the landscape. Traditional security measures often struggle to keep up with the sophistication of cyber threats. Deep Learning neural network offers a dynamic approach to cybersecurity, adapting to new threats and learning from past incidents.

- **Malware Detection –** A Deep Learning neural network can analyze patterns in network traffic, code behavior, and system logs to identify the presence of malware. Its ability to recognize subtle variations in code execution and network behavior makes it a formidable tool in the ongoing fight against advancing malware threats.
- **Phishing Detection** - Phishing attacks continue to be a major cybersecurity concern. Deep Learning neural networks, through their analysis of email content, user behavior, and link structures, can identify phishing attempts with high accuracy. This proactive approach is crucial in preventing data breaches and protecting sensitive information.

4.9. Recommendation Systems

- **Personalized Content Recommendations** - Deep learning neural networks excel in understanding user preferences and behavior. By analyzing historical interactions and feedback, recommendation systems powered by deep learning can provide personalized content recommendations. This is particularly valuable in industries like streaming services, e-commerce, and news platforms, where tailoring content to individual users can significantly enhance engagement.
- **Collaborative Filtering with Neural Networks** - Collaborative filtering, a popular recommendation technique, includes projecting a user's preferences depending on the preferences of the same users. Deep learning neural

networks enhance collaborative filtering by capturing intricate patterns and dependencies in user-item interactions. This results in more accurate predictions and recommendations, even in scenarios where traditional collaborative filtering methods may struggle.

- **Sequential Recommendation Models -** Deep learning enables the creation of sequential recommendation models that consider the temporal aspect of user behavior. Recurrent Neural Networks (RNNs) & Long Short-Term Memory (LSTM) networks, both types of deep learning architectures, are adept at capturing sequential dependencies in user actions. This is particularly beneficial in scenarios where the order and timing of user interactions play a crucial role, such as in e-commerce and online learning platforms.

4.10. Natural Language Processing (NLP) in Customer Support

NLP involves the intersection of computer science, linguistics, & AI, enabling machines to comprehend, interpret, & produce human-like language. Its applications in customer support are vast, ranging from automating responses to sentiment analysis for a better understanding of customer emotions.

- **Automated Ticketing and Resolution -** One of the primary applications of NLP in customer support is automating ticketing systems. NLP algorithms can analyze incoming customer queries, categorize them, and assign a priority level. This automation not only expedites the support process but also ensures that urgent issues are addressed promptly. Additionally, NLP-driven chatbots can handle routine queries, providing instant resolutions for common problems. This not only reduces the workload on human agents but also offers customers a quick and efficient means of issue resolution.
- **Sentiment Analysis for Proactive Support -** Understanding customer sentiment is crucial for delivering personalized and empathetic support. NLP algorithms can analyze customer interactions, whether through emails, chats, or social media, to determine the sentiment behind the messages. By identifying positive or negative sentiments, businesses can proactively address potential issues, turning a dissatisfied customer into a satisfied one.
- **Improved Knowledge Base and Content Management -** NLP can be leveraged to enhance knowledge base systems, making them more accessible and user-friendly. Through semantic analysis, NLP algorithms can categorize and organize vast amounts of information, making it easier for customer support agents to find relevant solutions quickly. This, in turn, reduces the resolution time for customer queries.

- **Multilingual Support -** As businesses operate on a global scale, providing multilingual support is essential. NLP facilitates accurate language translation, enabling customer support systems to interact seamlessly with customers worldwide. This not only broadens the reach of businesses but also ensures effective communication across diverse linguistic backgrounds.

5. CHALLENGES AND CONSIDERATIONS

Deep learning and neural networks have emerged as important tools in the realm of business analytics, revolutionizing the way organizations extract insights from their data.

- **Data Privacy and Ethics -** The utilization of deep learning in business analytics often involves handling vast amounts of sensitive data. As organizations strive to harness the potential of neural networks, they must grapple with the ethical implications and legal obligations surrounding data privacy (Chaudhari et al., 2021). Ensuring compliance with regulations such as GDPR and developing robust data anonymization techniques are imperative steps in safeguarding user privacy. Striking a balance between extracting meaningful insights & respecting privacy rights remains a constant challenge.
- **Model Interpretability -** The inherent complexity of deep learning models raises concerns about their interpretability. As businesses increasingly rely on these models for decision-making, the "black-box" nature of neural networks becomes a significant hurdle. Understanding how a model reaches a specific decision is critical, especially in industries where accountability & transparency are important. Researchers & practitioners are actively exploring techniques to enhance model interpretability, ranging from feature importance analysis to the development of explainable AI frameworks (Liu et al., 2018).
- **Scalability and Computational Resources -** The scalability of deep learning models poses a substantial challenge, particularly as the size of datasets and model architectures continues to grow. Organizations must invest in robust computational infrastructure to manage the computational requests of training and deploying large neural networks. Cloud computing services offer scalable solutions, but considerations such as cost, latency, and data transfer must be carefully evaluated. Striking the correct balance between computational efficiency and model performance is essential for sustainable and cost-effective deployment (Paine, 2017).

- **Overfitting and Underfitting -** Overfitting and underfitting are perennial challenges in the development of neural networks. Overfitting happens when a model performs good on training data but fails to generalize to new, hidden data, while underfitting reflects a model's inability to obtain the underlying patterns in the data (Najafabadi et al., 2015). Striking the right balance, often through techniques like regularization and dropout, is crucial for ensuring that a model generalizes well to diverse datasets and remains robust in real-world scenarios.
- **Hyperparameter Tuning -** The victory of deep learning models is dependent on the careful tuning of hyperparameters. Identifying the optimal set of hyperparameters involves a delicate balance, and an exhaustive search can be computationally expensive. Techniques i.e. grid, random search, & more advanced optimization algorithms play a critical part in finding the right combination of hyperparameters that maximizes model performance (Silva & Najafirad, 2020). The challenge lies in navigating the vast hyperparameter space efficiently to achieve a well-performing and robust neural network.

Deep learning & neural networks have ushered in a new era of possibilities for business analytics. As organizations navigate the intricate landscape of data privacy, ethics, model interpretability, scalability, and hyperparameter tuning, a commitment to responsible AI practices becomes paramount. By addressing these challenges head-on, businesses can unlock the true potential of deep learning while ensuring ethical considerations & responsible use of technology.

6. LIMITATIONS OF DEEP LEARNING

The scalability of deep learning methods by using many layers and training data can result in several sets of problems. Models of Deep learning is limited to what they represent and it cannot be represented for continuous representation. The scalability of deep learning methods is a complex task when it comes to determining the expected results.

It is somehow possible to train the model so that it can produce the described pictures. i.e. produce a smiley face on the rock. Furthermore, the model can start to produce unwanted captions when it faces images that are different from what it is trained on.

Interoperability is another problem that underlines why machine learning methods are opted over deep learning. i.e. deep learning can be used to measure the relevance scores of a text file. The performance is exceptional and almost close to the human level but it comes with a black box problem. It doesn't explain how it was able to give the corresponding scores. It is possible to identify how nodes of deep neural networks were activated using mathematics but it is unclear which neurons helped the model to reach a score or how many neuron layers were working together.

There is no distinct standard related to the utilization of deep learning methods on several kinds of data types. Deep learning is utilized in image and audio content. What kinds of standards must apply to images or audio must be described for the concepts. Considering such issues, it is essential to discover efficient solutions soon.

7. BEST PRACTICES IN BUSINESS-DRIVEN DEEP LEARNING

In the rapidly changing landscape of artificial intelligence, deep learning has appeared as a transformative force for businesses looking to utilize the power of data.

Figure 3. Best practices in business-driven deep learning

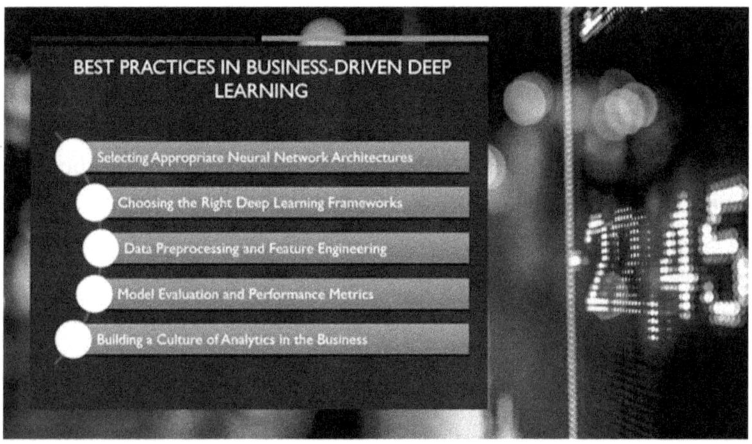

- **Selecting Appropriate Neural Network Architectures -** Choosing the right neural network architecture is fundamental to the success of any deep learning project. Different tasks require different architectures, and understanding the nuances of each is crucial. For image classification & convolutional neural networks (CNNs) are often preferred, while recurrent neural networks (RNNs) excel in sequential data tasks. Businesses must carefully assess the nature of their data and the goals of their projects to select the most suitable architecture. Transfer learning, where pre-trained models are optimized for particular tasks, can also significantly expedite development.

- **Choosing the Right Deep Learning Frameworks -** The choice of deep learning frameworks plays a critical part in the efficiency and scalability of a project. TensorFlow & PyTorch are among the most frequently utilized frameworks, each with its strengths. TensorFlow, backed by Google, is renowned for its scalability and deployment capabilities, while PyTorch is preferred for its dynamic computation graph, making it highly intuitive for researchers & developers. The decision should align with the team's expertise, project requirements, and long-term scalability goals.
- **Data Preprocessing and Feature Engineering -** Successful deep learning models hinge on the quality of data preprocessing and feature engineering. Raw data is often messy, and preparing it for training involves cleaning, normalizing, and augmenting. Feature engineering, the procedure of developing new features from current data, can significantly enhance model performance. Businesses should invest time in understanding their data, identifying relevant features, and employing techniques i.e. dimensionality reduction & one-hot encoding to optimize input for the chosen neural network architecture.
- **Model Evaluation and Performance Metrics -** Rigorous model investigation is critical for measuring the effectiveness of a deep learning solution. Businesses should employ techniques i.e. cross-validation to make sure robust performance assessment. Furthermore, selecting appropriate performance metrics is vital and depends on the specific business objectives. While accuracy is a usual metric, it may not be sufficient for imbalanced datasets. Precision, recall, & F1 score offer a more nuanced evaluation, specifically in situations where wrong positives or wrong negatives carry separate costs.
- **Building a Culture of Analytics in the Business -** The successful integration of deep learning into business operations requires more than just technical expertise. Fostering a culture of analytics is essential to ensure that insights from the models are effectively utilized. This involves cultivating data literacy across the organization, promoting collaboration between data scientists and business stakeholders, and establishing a feedback loop for continuous improvement. Decision-makers must understand the value of data-driven insights and be willing to incorporate them into strategic planning and operations.

8. CASE STUDIES

The businesses are cautiously looking for innovative solutions to gain a competitive edge. Deep learning, a subset of machine learning motivated by the human brain's neural networks, has emerged as a powerful tool for extracting valuable insights from vast and complex datasets.

Figure 4. Case studies

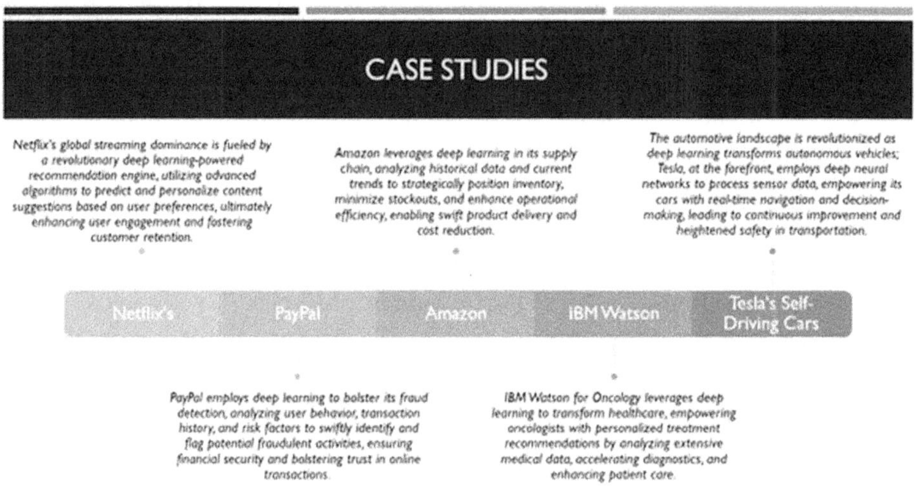

- **Enhancing Customer Experience: Netflix's Recommendation Engine** - Netflix, a global streaming platform, has changed the way entertainment is consumed through the implementation of deep learning in its recommendation engine. By analyzing user viewing habits, preferences, and feedback, Netflix employs advanced algorithms to predict and suggest content tailored to individual tastes (Barwal et al., 2023). This has not only increased user engagement but also significantly contributed to customer retention, demonstrating the potential of deep learning in personalizing user experiences.
- **Fraud Detection in Financial Services: PayPal -** Financial institutions face the constant challenge of identifying and preventing fraudulent transactions. PayPal, a leading online payment platform, has leveraged deep learning to enhance its fraud detection capabilities (Patel, 2019). By analyzing patterns in user behavior, transaction history, and various risk factors, PayPal's deep learning models can accurately identify and flag potentially fraudulent

activities in real-time. This not only safeguards the financial interests of the company and its users but also strengthens trust in online transactions.

- **Optimizing Supply Chain Management: Amazon -** Amazon, a pioneer in e-commerce, has harnessed the power of deep learning to optimize its vast and complex supply chain. By analyzing past data, current demand trends, & external factors, deep learning models project product demand at various locations. This enables Amazon to strategically position inventory, minimize stockouts, and reduce overall operational costs (Bharadwaj, 2019). The implementation of deep learning in supply chain management has played a pivotal role in Amazon's ability to deliver products with unprecedented speed and efficiency.
- **Healthcare Diagnostics: IBM Watson for Oncology -** IBM Watson for Oncology is an illustration of how deep learning can revolutionize healthcare. By ingesting vast amounts of medical literature, patient records, & clinical trials, Watson for Oncology assists oncologists in creating informed treatment decisions. The deep learning model can analyze complex medical data, recognize relevant patterns, & give personalized treatment recommendations (Strickland, 2019). This not only accelerates the diagnostic process but also improves the overall quality of patient care.
- **Autonomous Vehicles: Tesla's Self-Driving Cars -** The automotive industry is going through a paradigm shift with the integration of deep learning into autonomous vehicles. Tesla, a trailblazer in this space, utilizes deep neural networks to process data from sensors and cameras, enabling its cars to navigate & create decisions in real-time on the road (Jensen, 2018). The continuous learning capabilities of these models mean that Tesla vehicles become safer and more efficient over time, showcasing the potential of deep learning in transforming transportation.

9. FUTURE TRENDS AND CONCLUSION

Emerging Trends in Deep Learning for Business Analytics

The realm of business analytics is going through a profound change with the integration of deep learning techniques. As we navigate through the contemporary landscape, it becomes evident that the adoption of deep learning in business analytics is not just a fleeting trend but a seismic shift that is reshaping the very foundations of decision-making processes.

- **Enhanced Predictive Analytics -** One of the prominent trends in deep learning is the enhancement of predictive analytics capabilities. Traditional analytics methods often fall short when encountering complex & unstructured data. Deep learning models, particularly recurrent neural networks (RNNs) & long short-term memory networks (LSTMs), are proving to be instrumental in deciphering patterns within large datasets. Businesses are now leveraging these models to make more accurate predictions, from customer behavior to market trends, thereby gaining a competitive edge.
- **Explainable AI for Improved Decision-Making -** As deep learning models become very intricate, the demand for explainable AI is gaining momentum. Business leaders are increasingly wary of "black box" models that provide results without clear insights into the decision-making procedures. Explainable AI strategy i.e. attention mechanisms & interpretable neural networks, are emerging to address this concern. The ability to understand and interpret the decisions created by deep learning models is crucial for creating trust & facilitating better-informed decision-making in business strategies.
- **Unsupervised Learning for Anomaly Detection -** The rise of unsupervised learning methods, particularly in anomaly detection, is reshaping the way businesses approach cybersecurity and risk management. Deep learning models, equipped with autoencoders and variational autoencoders, can autonomously identify irregular patterns in data, signaling potential threats or anomalies. This is particularly pertinent in industries where real-time detection of anomalies is critical, such as finance and healthcare.
- **Personalization and Hyper-Personalization -** The era of mass customization is evolving into hyper-personalization, thanks to deep learning algorithms. Businesses are now able to analyze vast volumes of data to tailor products, services, and marketing strategies to individual preferences. Recommender systems powered by deep learning, like collaborative filtering and content-based filtering, are becoming increasingly sophisticated in understanding and predicting user preferences, providing a personalized experience for customers.
- **Automation of Data Preparation & Feature Engineering -**Traditionally, a significant portion of data science workflows involved manual preparation of data & feature engineering. However, with the advent of deep learning, there is a growing trend towards automating these processes. Deep learning models, especially those based on neural architecture search, are now capable of automating the selection of relevant features and optimizing model architectures, significantly reducing the time and effort required in the data preparation phase.

The Transformative Potential of Deep Learning in Shaping Future Business Strategies

As businesses continue to embrace deep learning for analytics, the transformative potential of this technology is becoming increasingly apparent. The integration of deep learning into business strategies is not merely a technological upgrade but a paradigm shift that is influencing how organizations operate, compete, and innovate.

- **Agile Decision-Making in Real-Time -** Deep learning allows organizations to process & analyze huge volumes of data in real-time, facilitating agile decision-making. Whether it's adjusting marketing game plans on the fly or responding to dynamic market conditions, businesses can now harness the ability of deep learning to create informed decisions with unprecedented speed & accuracy.
- **Data-Driven Innovation -** The abundance of data available to businesses is a goldmine for innovation. Deep learning algorithms can discover unseen patterns, correlations, & insights within larger datasets, fueling a culture of data-driven innovation. Organizations that leverage deep learning to extract actionable insights from their data are better positioned to identify new opportunities, optimize processes, and stay ahead of the competition.
- **Enhanced Customer Experience -** Deep learning is changing the way businesses interact with their customers. From chatbots & virtual assistants to personalized recommendations and sentiment analysis, deep learning technologies are enhancing the overall customer experience. By knowing what customers would prefer & their behaviors on a granular level, businesses can customize their products and services to meet individual requirements, fostering customer loyalty & satisfaction.
- **Optimized Operational Efficiency -** The automation capabilities of deep learning extend beyond data analysis to operational processes. Businesses are increasingly implementing deep learning-driven solutions for supply chain optimization, predictive maintenance, and resource allocation. This optimization not only improves efficiency but also reduces costs and minimizes risks associated with manual decision-making.
- **Ethical Considerations and Responsible AI -** As deep learning becomes more integral to business strategies, ethical considerations & accountable AI practices are gaining prominence. Organizations are identifying the significance of transparency, fairness, & responsibility in the deployment of deep learning models. Creating a balance between innovation & ethical considerations will be critical in building trust with customers, employees, and the broader community.

Further research for business analytics must aim at capturing present nonexisting use cases that align with the robustness of deep learning. Deep learning is capable of managing the vast number of unstructured data and there is a further possibility for identifying more crucial use cases than conventional analytics. Deep learning is capable of producing a full new business model.

Deep learning can add value for organizations and various business domains. It is suggested that future research in this direction can focus on identifying more precise use cases by underlying the possible benefits. It is essential to recommend an improved combination of network architecture, training schedules and refinement of parameters which can produce favorable projection performance when it comes to DNNs. Future research efforts can result in the discovery of new methods that can allow customization of network architecture when it comes to several data sources.

It is required to have more research in predictive analytics since organizations are producing data at an alarming rate. The research in predictive analytics can enhance the decision making processes of businesses. The minor enhancement in prediction accuracy can increase profits in greater numbers and that's the main reason to have a better understanding of deep learning.

Conclusion: Navigating the Deep Learning Landscape - The future of business analytics lies at the intersection of data-driven insights & deep learning technologies. The emerging trends discussed in this chapter showcase the evolving landscape of deep learning applications, offering businesses unprecedented opportunities to innovate, optimize, and transform. As organizations embark on this journey, it is essential to embrace these trends with a strategic mindset, ensuring that the integration of deep learning aligns with broader business objectives.

In conclusion, the transformative potential of deep learning in shaping future business strategies is profound. From revolutionizing decision-making processes to fostering innovation and improving customer experiences, the impact of deep learning is far-reaching. As businesses navigate the deep learning landscape, a commitment to accountable AI practices and ethical considerations will be instrumental in realizing the full capacity of this transformative technology. The journey into the future of business analytics is marked by adaptability, innovation, and a strategic embrace of the power of deep learning.

REFERENCES

Aggarwal, C. C. (2018). Neural networks and deep learning. Springer. doi:10.1007/978-3-319-94463-0

Barwal, D., Joshi, S., Obaid, A. J., Abdulbaqi, A. S., Al-Barzinji, S. M., Alkhayyat, A., . . . Muthmainnah, M. (2023, September). The impact of netflix recommendation engine on customer experience. In AIP Conference Proceedings (Vol. 2736, No. 1). AIP Publishing. doi:10.1063/5.0170916

Bharadwaj, S. (2019). The engineering behind a successful supply chain management strategy: An insight into Amazon. com. *International Journal of Scientific and Technology Research*, *8*(10), 281–286.

Bouvrie, J. (2006). *Notes on convolutional neural networks*. Academic Press.

Chaudhari, A. S., Sandino, C. M., Cole, E. K., Larson, D. B., Gold, G. E., Vasanawala, S. S., Lungren, M. P., Hargreaves, B. A., & Langlotz, C. P. (2021). Prospective deployment of deep learning in MRI: A framework for important considerations, challenges, and recommendations for best practices. *Journal of Magnetic Resonance Imaging*, *54*(2), 357–371. doi:10.1002/jmri.27331 PMID:32830874

Courbariaux, M., Bengio, Y., & David, J. P. (2015). Binaryconnect: Training deep neural networks with binary weights during propagations. *Advances in Neural Information Processing Systems*, 28.

Creswell, A., White, T., Dumoulin, V., Arulkumaran, K., Sengupta, B., & Bharath, A. A. (2018). Generative adversarial networks: An overview. *IEEE Signal Processing Magazine*, *35*(1), 53–65. doi:10.1109/MSP.2017.2765202

Dey, R., & Salem, F. M. (2017, August). Gate-variants of gated recurrent unit (GRU) neural networks. In *2017 IEEE 60th international midwest symposium on circuits and systems (MWSCAS)* (pp. 1597-1600). IEEE.

Francis, L. (2001). The basics of neural networks demystified. *Contingencies*, *11*(12), 56–61.

Glorot, X., & Bengio, Y. (2010, March). Understanding the difficulty of training deep feedforward neural networks. In *Proceedings of the thirteenth international conference on artificial intelligence and statistics* (pp. 249-256). JMLR Workshop and Conference Proceedings.

Goodfellow, I., Pouget-Abadie, J., Mirza, M., Xu, B., Warde-Farley, D., Ozair, S., Courville, A., & Bengio, Y. (2020). Generative adversarial networks. *Communications of the ACM*, *63*(11), 139–144. doi:10.1145/3422622

Gu, J., Wang, Z., Kuen, J., Ma, L., Shahroudy, A., Shuai, B., Liu, T., Wang, X., Wang, G., Cai, J., & Chen, T. (2018). Recent advances in convolutional neural networks. *Pattern Recognition*, *77*, 354–377. doi:10.1016/j.patcog.2017.10.013

Jensen, J. B. (2018). Self-driving but not self-regulating: The development of a legal framework to promote the safety of autonomous vehicles. *Washburn Law Journal*, *57*, 579.

Kraus, M. (2020). *Deep Learning in Business Analytics: Methods and Applications* [Doctoral dissertation]. ETH Zurich.

Kraus, M., Feuerriegel, S., & Oztekin, A. (2020). Deep learning in business analytics and operations research: Models, applications and managerial implications. *European Journal of Operational Research*, *281*(3), 628–641. doi:10.1016/j.ejor.2019.09.018

Lai, Y. (2019, October). A comparison of traditional machine learning and deep learning in image recognition. *Journal of Physics: Conference Series*, *1314*(1), 012148. doi:10.1088/1742-6596/1314/1/012148

Larochelle, H., Bengio, Y., Louradour, J., & Lamblin, P. (2009). Exploring strategies for training deep neural networks. *Journal of Machine Learning Research*, *10*(1).

Liu, L., Wu, Y., Wei, W., Cao, W., Sahin, S., & Zhang, Q. (2018, July). Benchmarking deep learning frameworks: Design considerations, metrics and beyond. In *2018 IEEE 38th International Conference on Distributed Computing Systems (ICDCS)* (pp. 1258-1269). IEEE.

Medsker, L. R., & Jain, L. C. (2001). Recurrent neural networks. *Design and Applications*, *5*(64-67), 2.

Najafabadi, M. M., Villanustre, F., Khoshgoftaar, T. M., Seliya, N., Wald, R., & Muharemagic, E. (2015). Deep learning applications and challenges in big data analytics. *Journal of Big Data*, *2*(1), 1–21. doi:10.1186/s40537-014-0007-7

Nielsen, M. A. (2015). *Neural networks and deep learning* (Vol. 25). Determination Press.

Paine, T. L. (2017). *Practical considerations for deep learning*. Academic Press.

Patel, Y. (2019). *Cross channel fraud detection framework in financial services using recurrent neural networks* [Doctoral dissertation]. London Metropolitan University.

Puangpontip, S., & Hewett, R. (2022). On Using Deep Learning for Business Analytics: At what cost? *Procedia Computer Science*, *207*, 3738–3747. doi:10.1016/j.procs.2022.09.434

Sazli, M. H. (2006). *A brief review of feed-forward neural networks*. Communications Faculty of Sciences University of Ankara Series A2-A3 Physical Sciences and Engineering, 50(01).

Schmidhuber, J. (2015). Deep learning in neural networks: An overview. *Neural Networks*, *61*, 85–117. doi:10.1016/j.neunet.2014.09.003 PMID:25462637

Schmitt, M. (2023). Deep learning in business analytics: A clash of expectations and reality. *International Journal of Information Management Data Insights*, *3*(1), 100146. doi:10.1016/j.jjimei.2022.100146

Shinde, P. P., & Shah, S. (2018, August). A review of machine learning and deep learning applications. In *2018 Fourth international conference on computing communication control and automation (ICCUBEA)* (pp. 1-6). IEEE. 10.1109/ICCUBEA.2018.8697857

Silva, S. H., & Najafirad, P. (2020). Opportunities and challenges in deep learning adversarial robustness: A survey. *arXiv preprint arXiv:2007.00753.*

Strickland, E. (2019). IBM Watson, heal thyself: How IBM overpromised and underdelivered on AI health care. *IEEE Spectrum*, *56*(4), 24–31. doi:10.1109/MSPEC.2019.8678513

Sutskever, I. (2013). *Training recurrent neural networks*. University of Toronto.

Svozil, D., Kvasnicka, V., & Pospichal, J. (1997). Introduction to multi-layer feed-forward neural networks. *Chemometrics and Intelligent Laboratory Systems*, *39*(1), 43–62. doi:10.1016/S0169-7439(97)00061-0

Wang, S., Liu, W., Wu, J., Cao, L., Meng, Q., & Kennedy, P. J. (2016, July). Training deep neural networks on imbalanced data sets. In 2016 international joint conference on neural networks (IJCNN) (pp. 4368-4374). IEEE. doi:10.1109/IJCNN.2016.7727770

Zhang, L., Tan, J., Han, D., & Zhu, H. (2017). From machine learning to deep learning: Progress in machine intelligence for rational drug discovery. *Drug Discovery Today*, *22*(11), 1680–1685. doi:10.1016/j.drudis.2017.08.010 PMID:28881183

Zhao, R., Wang, D., Yan, R., Mao, K., Shen, F., & Wang, J. (2017). Machine health monitoring using local feature-based gated recurrent unit networks. *IEEE Transactions on Industrial Electronics*, *65*(2), 1539–1548. doi:10.1109/TIE.2017.2733438

Compilation of References

Ab Rashid, M. F., Tiwari, A., & Hutabarat, W. (2019). Integrated Optimisation of Mixed-Model Assembly Sequence Planning and Line Balancing using Multi-Objective Discrete Particle Swarm Optimisation. *Artificial Intelligence for Engineering Design, Analysis and Manufacturing*, 1–29.

Abdallah, A., Maarof, M. A., & Zainal, A. (2016). Fraud detection system: A survey. *Journal of Network and Computer Applications*, *68*, 90–113. doi:10.1016/j.jnca.2016.04.007

Abdullah, M. R., Faisae, M. F., Razali, M. M., & Perumal, M. (2017). Assembly Line Balancing using Heuristic Approaches in Manufacturing Industry. *Jixie Gongcheng Xuebao*, 171–185.

Adedugbe, O., Benkhelifa, E., Campion, R., Al-Obeidat, F., Bani Hani, A., & Jayawickrama, U. (2020). Leveraging cloud computing for the semantic web: Review and trends. *Soft Computing*, *24*(8), 5999–6014. doi:10.1007/s00500-019-04559-2

Adib, H., Ali, M. K., & Abuzaraida, M. A. (2024). Artificial Intelligence Trust, risk and security management (AI trism): Frameworks, applications, challenges and future research directions. *Expert Systems with Applications*, *240*, 122442. doi:10.1016/j.eswa.2023.122442

Aggarwal, C. C. (2018). Neural networks and deep learning. Springer. doi:10.1007/978-3-319-94463-0

Akella, P., Peshkin, M., Colgate, E., Wannasuphoprasit, W., Nagesh, N., Wells, J., ... Peacock, B. (1999). Cobots for the automobile assembly line. *International Conference on Robotics & Automation*, 728-733. 10.1109/ROBOT.1999.770061

Akkara, S., & Selvakumar, I. (2023). Review on optimization techniques used for smart grid. *Measurement. Sensors*, *30*, 100918. doi:10.1016/j.measen.2023.100918

Akma, N., Hafiz, M., Zainal, A., Fairuz, M., & Adnan, Z. (2018). Review of Chatbots Design Techniques. *International Journal of Computer Applications*, *181*(8), 7–10. doi:10.5120/ijca2018917606

Aksin, Z., Armony, M., & Mehrotra, V. (2007). The modern call center: A multi-disciplinary perspective on operations management research. *Production and Operations Management*, *16*(6), 665–688. doi:10.1111/j.1937-5956.2007.tb00288.x

Akter, A., Ehsanul, I. Z., Dana, N. H., Joysoyal, R., Sarker, S. K., Li, L., Muyeen, S. M., Das, S. K., & Kamwa, I. (2024). A review on microgrid optimization with meta-heuristic techniques: Scopes, trends and recommendation. *Energy Strategy Reviews*, *51*, 101298. doi:10.1016/j.esr.2024.101298

Alaa, A., & Orji, R. (2024). Machine learning techniques for emotion detection and sentiment analysis: Current state, challenges, and future directions. *Behaviour & Information Technology*, *43*(1), 139–164. doi:10.1080/0144929X.2022.2156387

Albright, S. C., & Winston, W. L. (2020). *Business analytics : Data analysis and decision making*. Cengage Learning, Inc. https://thuvienso.hoasen.edu.vn/handle/123456789/11614

Alfaro García, V. G., Gil-Lafuente, A. M., & Alfaro Calderon, G. (2015). A fuzzy logic approach towards innovation measurement. *Global Journal of Business Research*, *9*(3), 53–71.

Alhammadi, M. (2023). Optimising Customer Service Delivery and Response Time through AI-Enhanced Chatbots in Facilities Management-A Mixed-Methods Research. *American Journal of Smart Technology and Solutions*, *2*(2), 43–54. doi:10.54536/ajsts.v2i2.2206

Aljehani, S. S., & Alotaibi, Y. A. (2024). Preserving Privacy in Association Rule Mining Using Metaheuristic-based Algorithms: A Systematic Literature Review. *IEEE Access : Practical Innovations, Open Solutions*, *12*, 21217–21236. doi:10.1109/ACCESS.2024.3362907

Alshawawreh, A. R. E., Liébana-Cabanillas, F., & Blanco-Encomienda, F. J. (2024). Impact of big data analytics on telecom companies, competitive advantage. *Technology in Society*, *76*, 102459. doi:10.1016/j.techsoc.2024.102459

Amani, F. A., & Fadlalla, A. M. (2017). Data mining applications in accounting: A review of the literature and organizing framework. *International Journal of Accounting Information Systems*, *24*, 32–58. doi:10.1016/j.accinf.2016.12.004

Andronie, M., Lăzăroiu, G., Iatagan, M., Uță, C., Ștefănescu, R., & Cocoșatu, M. (2021). Artificial Intelligence-Based Decision-Making Algorithms, Internet of Things Sensing Networks, and Deep Learning-Assisted Smart Process Management in Cyber-Physical Production Systems. *Electronics (Basel)*, *10*(20), 2497. doi:10.3390/electronics10202497

Appelbaum, D., Kogan, A., Vasarhelyi, M., & Yan, Z. (2017). Impact of business analytics and enterprise systems on managerial accounting. *International Journal of Accounting Information Systems*, *25*, 29–44. doi:10.1016/j.accinf.2017.03.003

Ascarza, E. (2018). Retention futility: Targeting high-risk customers might be ineffective. *JMR, Journal of Marketing Research*, *55*(1), 80–98. doi:10.1509/jmr.16.0163

Ashawa, M., Douglas, O., Osamor, J., & Jackie, R. (2022). Improving cloud efficiency through optimized resource allocation technique for load balancing using LSTM machine learning algorithm. *Journal of Cloud Computing (Heidelberg, Germany)*, *11*(1), 87. doi:10.1186/s13677-022-00362-x

Ashfaq, T., Khalid, M. I., Ali, G., Affendi, M. E., Iqbal, J., Hussain, S., Ullah, S. S., Yahaya, A. S., Khalid, R., & Mateen, A. (2022, September 25). An Efficient and Secure Energy Trading Approach with Machine Learning Technique and Consortium Blockchain. *Sensors (Basel), 22*(19), 7263. doi:10.3390/s22197263 PMID:36236363

Bakar, N. A., Ramli, M. F., Zakaria, M. Z., Sin, T. C., & Masran, H. (2020). Solving assembly line balancing problem using heuristic: A case study of power transformer in electrical industry. *Indonesian Journal of Electrical Engineering and Computer Science, 17*(2), 850–857. doi:10.11591/ijeecs.v17.i2.pp850-857

Bakker, A., Demerouti, E., & Schaufeli, W. (2003). Dual processes at work in a call centre: An application of the job demands–resources model. *European Journal of Work and Organizational Psychology, 12*(4), 393–417. doi:10.1080/13594320344000165

Bala, J., & Dhir, R. (2014). A novel hybrid technique for sub-pixel edge detection using fuzzy logic and zernike moment. *International Journal on Computer Science and Engineering, 2*, 26–31.

Barlow, H. B. (1989). Unsupervised learning. *Neural Computation, 1*(3), 295–311. doi:10.1162/neco.1989.1.3.295

Barrere, M. (1997). *Simulated annealing to solve optimisation problems*. Internal Report, CardiV School of Engineering, Intelligent Systems Research Laboratory, University of Wales CardiV.

Bartz-Beielstein, T., Branke, J., Mehnen, J., & Mersmann, O. (2014). Evolutionary algorithms. *Wiley Interdisciplinary Reviews. Data Mining and Knowledge Discovery, 4*(3), 178–195. doi:10.1002/widm.1124

Barwal, D., Joshi, S., Obaid, A. J., Abdulbaqi, A. S., Al-Barzinji, S. M., Alkhayyat, A., . . . Muthmainnah, M. (2023, September). The impact of netflix recommendation engine on customer experience. In AIP Conference Proceedings (Vol. 2736, No. 1). AIP Publishing. doi:10.1063/5.0170916

Batistič, S., & van der Laken, P. (2019). History, evolution and future of big data and analytics: A bibliometric analysis of its relationship to performance in organizations. *British Journal of Management, 30*(2), 229–251. doi:10.1111/1467-8551.12340

Bautista, J., Suárez, R., Mateo, M., & Companys, R. (2000). Local Search Heuristics for the Assembly Line Balancing Problem with Incompatibilities Between Tasks. *Proceedings of the 2000 IEEE International Conference on Robotics & Automation*, 2404-2409. 10.1109/ROBOT.2000.846387

Baybars, Í. (1986). A surveyof exact algorithms for the simple assembly line balancing problem. *Management Science, 32*(8), 909–932. doi:10.1287/mnsc.32.8.909

Behdad, M., Barone, L., Bennamoun, M., & French, T. (2012). Natureinspired techniques in the context of fraud detection. *IEEE Transactions on Systems, Man, and Cybernetics. Part C, Applications and Reviews, 42*(6), 1273–1290. doi:10.1109/TSMCC.2012.2215851

Belassiria, I., Mazouzi, M., ElFezazi, S., Cherrafi, A., & ElMaskaoui, Z. (2017). Solving Assembly Line Balancing Problem Using A Hybrid Genetic Algorithm With Zoning Constraints. *International Journal of Business and Management Invention*, 34-40.

Bennouna, G., & Tkiouat, M. (2018). Fuzzy logic approach applied to credit scoring for microfinance in Morocco. *Procedia Computer Science*, *127*, 274–283. doi:10.1016/j.procs.2018.01.123

Benton, M., & others. (2017). Quality in Chatbots and Intelligent Conversational Agents. *Software Quality Professional Magazine, 19*(3).

Berkowitz, A. D., & Perkins, H. W. (1984). Stress among farm women: Work and family as interacting systems. *Journal of Marriage and Family*, *46*(1), 161–166. doi:10.2307/351874

Bharadia, J. P. (2023). The role of machine learning in transforming business intelligence. *International Journal of Computing and Artificial Intelligence*. . doi:10.33545/27076571.2023.v4.i1a.60

Bharadiya, J. P. (2023). A Comparative Study of Business Intelligence and Artificial Intelligence with Big Data Analytics. *American Journal of Artificial Intelligence.*, *7*(10), 24–30. doi:10.11648/j.ajai.20230701.14

Bharadiya, J. P. (2023). Machine learning and AI in business intelligence: Trends and opportunities. [IJC]. *International Journal of Computer*, *48*(1), 123–134.

Bharadwaj, S. (2019). The engineering behind a successful supply chain management strategy: An insight into Amazon. com. *International Journal of Scientific and Technology Research*, *8*(10), 281–286.

Bhate, T., Dowling, S., & Collins, N. (2020). P132: Optimizing a physician surge protocol to address emergency department wait times during times of increased patient demand. medRxiv.

Bhattacharyya, S., Jha, S., Tharakunnel, K., & Westland, J. C. (2011). Data mining for credit card fraud: A comparative study. *Decision Support Systems*, *50*(3), 602–613. doi:10.1016/j.dss.2010.08.008

Bilal, M., Oyedele, L. O., Qadir, J., Munir, K., Ajayi, S. O., Akinade, O. O., Owolabi, H. A., Alaka, H. A., & Pasha, M. (2016). Big Data in the construction industry: A review of present status, opportunities, and future trends. *Advanced Engineering Informatics*, *30*(3), 500–521. doi:10.1016/j.aei.2016.07.001

Bird, J. J., Ekárt, A., & Faria, D. R. (2023). Chatbot Interaction with Artificial Intelligence: Human data augmentation with T5 and language transformer ensemble for text classification. *Journal of Ambient Intelligence and Humanized Computing*, *14*(4), 3129–3144. doi:10.1007/s12652-021-03439-8

Bishop, C. M. (1995). *Neural Networks for Pattern Recognition*. Oxford University Press. doi:10.1093/oso/9780198538493.001.0001

Bishop, C. M. (2006). *Pattern Recognition and Machine Learning*. Springer.

Blum, C. (2008). Beam-ACO for simple assembly line balancing. *Journal of Computing.*

Bolón-Canedo, V., & Alonso-Betanzos, A. (2019). Ensembles for feature selection: A review and future trends. *Information Fusion*, *52*, 1–12. doi:10.1016/j.inffus.2018.11.008

Bolton, R. J., & David, J. H. (2001). Unsupervised Profiling Methods for Fraud Detection. *Proc Credit Scoring and Credit Control*, *7*, 5–7.

Bouvrie, J. (2006). *Notes on convolutional neural networks.* Academic Press.

Box, G. E. P., & Muller, M. E. (1958). A note on the generation of random normal deviates. *Annals of Mathematical Statistics*, *29*(2), 610–611. doi:10.1214/aoms/1177706645

Brezavšček, A., & Baggia, A. (2014). Optimization of a Call Centre Performance Using the Stochastic Queueing Models. *PLOS Digital Health.*

Brigance, C., Soto Mas, F., Sanchez, V., & Handal, A. J. (2018). The mental health of the organic farmer: Psychosocial and contextual actors. *Workplace Health & Safety*, *66*(12), 606–616. doi:10.1177/2165079918783211 PMID:29962329

Bryton, B. (1954). *Balancing of a continiuous production line* [Thesis]. Northwestern University.

Bughin, J., Hazan, E., Sree Ramaswamy, P., DC, W., & Chu, M. (2017). Artificial intelligence the next digital frontier. Academic Press.

Bustos, O., & Pomares-Quimbaya, A. (2020). Stock market movement forecast: A systematic review. *Expert Systems with Applications*, *156*, 113464. doi:10.1016/j.eswa.2020.113464

Cai, J., Luo, J., Wang, S., & Yang, S. (2018). Feature selection in machine learning: A new perspective. *Neurocomputing*, *300*, 70–79. doi:10.1016/j.neucom.2017.11.077

Caldarini, G., & Jaf, S. (2023). *Recent Advances in Chatbot Algorithms.* Techniques, and Technologies., doi:10.4018/978-1-6684-6234-8.ch011

Canhoto, A. I., & Clear, F. (2020). Artificial intelligence and machine learning as business tools: A framework for diagnosing value destruction potential. *Business Horizons*, *63*(2), 183–193. doi:10.1016/j.bushor.2019.11.003

Cao, L. (2019). *Data Science.* Springer.

Carbonell, J. G., Michalski, R. S., & Mitchell, T. M. (1983). Machine Learning: A Historical and Methodological analysis. *AI Magazine*, *4*(3), 69. doi:10.1609/aimag.v4i3.406

Carlisle, J. P. (1999). Ethical considerations of the software-dependent organization. *Journal of Systems and Software*, *44*(3), 251–255. doi:10.1016/S0164-1212(98)10061-4

Casadei, A., Schlogl, S., & Bergmann, M. (2022). Chatbots for Robotic Process Automation: Investigating Perceived Trust and User Satisfaction. *2022 IEEE 3rd International Conference on Human-Machine Systems (ICHMS)*, 1-6. 10.1109/ICHMS56717.2022.9980826

Casas, J., Tricot, M.-O., Abou Khaled, O., Mugellini, E., & Cudré-Mauroux, P. (2020). Trends Methods in Chatbot Evaluation. *Companion Publication of the 2020 International Conference on Multimodal Interaction*, 280-286. 10.1145/3395035.3425319

Cezar-Vaz, M. R., Bonow, C. A., & Da Silva, M. R. S. (2015). Mental and physical symptoms of female rural workers: Relation between household and rural work. *International Journal of Environmental Research and Public Health*, *12*(9), 11037–11049. doi:10.3390/ijerph120911037 PMID:26371018

Chakraborty, N., & Barma, M. D. (2014). Modelling of Stand-Alone Wind Energy Conversion System using Fuzzy Logic Controller. *Small, 2*(1).

Chandola, V., Banerjee, A., & Kumar, V. (2009). Anomaly detection: A survey. *ACM Computing Surveys*, *41*(3), 1–58. doi:10.1145/1541880.1541882

Chang, I. C., Liu, C. C., & Chen, K. (2014). The effects of hedonic/utilitarian expectations and social influence on continuance intention to play online games. *Internet Research*, *24*(1), 21–45. doi:10.1108/IntR-02-2012-0025

Chapelle, O., Schlkopf, B., & Zien, A. (2006). Semi-Supervised Learning. In The MIT Press eBooks. doi:10.7551/mitpress/9780262033589.001.0001

Chaudhari, A. S., Sandino, C. M., Cole, E. K., Larson, D. B., Gold, G. E., Vasanawala, S. S., Lungren, M. P., Hargreaves, B. A., & Langlotz, C. P. (2021). Prospective deployment of deep learning in MRI: A framework for important considerations, challenges, and recommendations for best practices. *Journal of Magnetic Resonance Imaging*, *54*(2), 357–371. doi:10.1002/jmri.27331 PMID:32830874

Chen, A. S., Leung, M. T., & Daouk, H. (2003). Application of neural networks to an emerging financial market: Forecasting and trading the Taiwan Stock Index. *Computers & Operations Research*, *30*(6), 901–923. doi:10.1016/S0305-0548(02)00037-0

Chen, F., Wan, H., Cai, H., & Cheng, G. (n.d.). Machine learning in/for blockchain: Future and challenges. *The Canadian Journal of Statistics*, *49*(4), 1364–1382.

Chen, M., Mao, S., & Liu, Y. (2014). Big data: A survey. *Mobile Networks and Applications*, *19*(2), 171–209. doi:10.1007/s11036-013-0489-0

Chen, Q., Lu, Y., Gong, Y., & Xiong, J. (2023). Can AI chatbots help retain customers? Impact of AI service quality on customer loyalty. *Internet Research*, *33*(6), 2205–2243. Advance online publication. doi:10.1108/INTR-09-2021-0686

Chen, R. C., Dewi, C., Huang, S. W., & Caraka, R. E. (2020). Selecting critical features for data classification based on machine learning methods. *Journal of Big Data*, *7*(1), 52. doi:10.1186/s40537-020-00327-4

Chen, X., & Huang, L. (2017). LRSSLMDA: Laplacian regularized sparse subspace learning for MiRNA-disease association prediction. *PLoS Computational Biology*, *13*(12), e1005912. doi:10.1371/journal.pcbi.1005912 PMID:29253885

Chinnasamy, S., Ramachandran, M., Amudha, M., & Ramu, K. (2022). A Review on Hill Climbing Optimization Methodology. *Recent Trends in Management and Commerce*, 1-7.

Chollet, F. (2017). *Deep Learning with Python*. Manning Publications.

Chowdhury, S., Joel-Edgar, S., Dey, P. K., Bhattacharya, S., & Kharlamov, A. (2023). Embedding transparency in artificial intelligence machine learning models: Managerial implications on predicting and explaining employee turnover. *International Journal of Human Resource Management*, *34*(14), 2732–2764. doi:10.1080/09585192.2022.2066981

Clemen, R. T., & Reilly, T. (2001). *Making Hard Decisions with Decision Tools*. Duxbury Press.

Cocianu, C. L., & Grigoryan, H. (2015). An artificial neural network for data forecasting purposes. *Informações Econômicas*, *19*(2), 34–45. doi:10.12948/issn14531305/19.2.2015.04

Cohen, S. (2021). The evolution of machine learning: past, present, and future. In Elsevier eBooks (pp. 1–12). doi:10.1016/B978-0-323-67538-3.00001-4

Cortes, C., & Vapnik, V. (1995). Support-vector networks. *Machine Learning*, *20*(3), 273–297. doi:10.1007/BF00994018

Courbariaux, M., Bengio, Y., & David, J. P. (2015). Binaryconnect: Training deep neural networks with binary weights during propagations. *Advances in Neural Information Processing Systems*, 28.

Coussement, K., Lessmann, S., & Verstraeten, G. (2017). A comparative analysis of data preparation algorithms for customer churn prediction: A case study in the telecommunication industry. *Decision Support Systems*, *95*, 27–36. doi:10.1016/j.dss.2016.11.007

Covas, J., & Gaspar-Cunha, A. (2009). Extrusion Scale-up: An Optimization-based Methodology. *International Polymer Processing, 24*, 67-82. . doi:10.3139/217.2200

Creswell, A., White, T., Dumoulin, V., Arulkumaran, K., Sengupta, B., & Bharath, A. A. (2018). Generative adversarial networks: An overview. *IEEE Signal Processing Magazine*, *35*(1), 53–65. doi:10.1109/MSP.2017.2765202

Cui, Y., Kara, S., & Chan, K. C. (2020). Manufacturing big data ecosystem: A systematic literature review. *Robotics and Computer-integrated Manufacturing*, *62*, 101861. doi:10.1016/j.rcim.2019.101861

Cutinha, D. D., Chiplunkar, N. N., Maved, S., & Bhat, A. (2021). *Artificial Intelligence-Based Chatbot Framework with Authentication*. Authorisation, and Payment Features. doi:10.1007/978-981-15-3514-7_16

Daghagh Yazd, S., Wheeler, S. A., & Zuo, A. (2019). Key risk factors affecting farmers' mental health: A systematic review. *International Journal of Environmental Research and Public Health*, *16*(23), 4849. doi:10.3390/ijerph16234849 PMID:31810320

Dande, A. A., & Pund, D. M. A. (2023). A Review Study on Applications of Natural Language Processing. *International Journal of Scientific Research in Science, Engineering and Technology*, *122-126*, 122–126. Advance online publication. doi:10.32628/IJSRSET2310214

Dar-el, E. M. (1975). Solving Large Single - Model Assembly Line Balancing Problems - A Comparative Study. Technion—Israel Institute of Technology, 302-310.

Data. (2020). PDF download Feature Engineering for Machine Learning: Principles and Techniques for Data Scientists Full AudioBook. Zenodo *(CERN European Organization for Nuclear Research)*. doi:10.5281/zenodo.4192681

Davenport, T. H. (2018). From analytics to artificial intelligence. *Journal of Business Analytics*, *1*(2), 73–80. doi:10.1080/2573234X.2018.1543535

Davenport, T. H., & Harris, J. (2007). *Competing on Analytics: The New Science of Winning*. Harvard Business Review Press.

Davenport, T. H., Harris, J., & Shapiro, J. (2010). Competing on talent analytics. *Harvard Business Review*, *88*(10), 52–58. PMID:20929194

De Santos Sierra, A., Ávila, C. S., Casanova, J. G., & del Pozo, G. B. (2011b). A stress-detection system based on physiological signals and fuzzy logic. *IEEE Transactions on Industrial Electronics*, *58*(10), 4857–4865. doi:10.1109/TIE.2010.2103538

De Santos Sierra, A., Ávila, C. S., del Pozo, G. B., & Casanova, J. G. (2011a). Stress detection by means of stress physiological template. In *2011 Third World Congress on Nature and Biologically Inspired Computing* (pp. 131-136). IEEE. 10.1109/NaBIC.2011.6089448

Delen, D., & Zolbanin, H. M. (2018). The analytics paradigm in business research. *Journal of Business Research*, *90*, 186–195. doi:10.1016/j.jbusres.2018.05.013

Demetgul, M., Ulkir, O., & Waqar, T. (2014). Washing Machine Using Fuzzy Logic *Autom. Control Intell. Syst.*, 23-27.

Demiris, G., Doorenbos, A. Z., & Towle, C. (2009). Ethical considerations regarding the use of technology for older adults: The case of telehealth. *Research in Gerontological Nursing*, *2*(2), 128–136. doi:10.3928/19404921-20090401-02 PMID:20077974

Devillers, L., & Cowie, R. (2023). Ethical Considerations on Affective Computing: An Overview. *Proceedings of the IEEE*. 10.1109/JPROC.2023.3315217

Dey, R., & Salem, F. M. (2017, August). Gate-variants of gated recurrent unit (GRU) neural networks. In *2017 IEEE 60th international midwest symposium on circuits and systems (MWSCAS)* (pp. 1597-1600). IEEE.

Di Vaio, A., Palladino, R., Hassan, R., & Escobar, O. (2020). Artificial intelligence and business models in the sustainable development goals perspective: A systematic literature review. *Journal of Business Research*, *121*, 283–314. doi:10.1016/j.jbusres.2020.08.019

Dibike, Y., Velickov, S., Solomatine, D., & Abbott, M. B. (2001). Model Induction with Support Vector Machines: Introduction and Applications. *Journal of Computing in Civil Engineering, 15*(3), 208–216. https://doi.org/(208 doi:10.1061/(asce)0887-3801(2001)15:3

Didden, J. B., Lefeber, E., Adan, I. J., & Panhuijzen, W. F. (2023). Genetic algorithm and decision support for assembly line balancing in the automotive industry. *International Journal of Production Research, 61*(10), 3377–3395. doi:10.1080/00207543.2022.2081630

Dimitriadis, S. G. (2006). Assembly line balancing and group working: A heuristic procedure for workers' groups operating on the same product and workstation. *Computers & Operations Research, 33*(9), 2757–2774. doi:10.1016/j.cor.2005.02.027

Diro, A., Chilamkurti, N., Nguyen, V. D., & Heyne, W. (2021, December 13). A Comprehensive Study of Anomaly Detection Schemes in IoT Networks Using Machine Learning Algorithms". *Sensors (Basel), 21*(24), 8320. doi:10.3390/s21248320 PMID:34960414

Dong, G., & Huan, L. (2018). Feature engineering for machine learning and data analytics. In CRC Press eBooks. doi:10.1201/9781315181080

Drummond, C., & Holte, R. C. (2003). C4.5, class imbalance, and cost sensitivity:why under sampling beats oversampling. *Proc of the Icml Workshop on Learning from Imbalanced Datasets II*, 1–8.

Du Preez, J. J. (2008). *Call centre design, operation and optimisation: A structured and scientific based approach* [Doctoral dissertation]. University of Stellenbosch.

Duan, L., & Xiong, Y. (2015). Big data analytics and business analytics. *Journal of Management Analytics, 2*(1), 1–21. doi:10.1080/23270012.2015.1020891

Duan, Q., Fan, J., & Wang, L. (2020). A hybrid particle swarm optimization algorithm for portfolio optimization with transaction costs. *Applied Soft Computing, 90*, 106126.

Du, M., Liu, N., & Hu, X. (2019). Techniques for interpretable machine learning. *Communications of the ACM, 63*(1), 68–77. doi:10.1145/3359786

Duman, E., & Ozcelik, M. H. (2011). Detecting credit card fraud by genetic algorithm and scatter search. *Expert Systems with Applications, 38*(10), 13057–13063. doi:10.1016/j.eswa.2011.04.110

Duran, M., Selcuk, K., Güner, E., & Baykoc, O. F. (2008). Simple and U-type assembly line balancing problems with a learning effect. *Applied Mathematical Modelling*, 2954–2961.

Dutt, V., Sasubilli, S. M., & Yerrapati, A. E. (2020). Dynamic Information Retrieval With Chatbots: A Review of Artificial Intelligence Methodology. *2020 4th International Conference on Electronics, Communication and Aerospace Technology (ICECA)*, 1299-1303. 10.1109/ICECA49313.2020.9297533

Eberhart, R. C., & Kennedy, J. (1995). A New optimizer using particle swarm theory. In *Proceedings of 6th Symposium on Micro Machine & Human Science*. IEEE Service Center. 10.1109/MHS.1995.494215

Eckroth, J., & Schoen, E. (2019). A Genetic Algorithm for Finding a Small and Diverse Set of Recent News Stories on a Given Subject: How We Generate AAAI's AI-Alert. *Proceedings of the AAAI Conference on Artificial Intelligence*, *33*(1), 9357–9364. doi:10.1609/aaai.v33i01.33019357

El-Samahy, E., Mahfouf, M., Torres-Salomao, L. A., & Anzurez-Marin, J. (2015). A new computer control system for mental stress management using fuzzy logic. In 2015 IEEE international conference on evolving and adaptive intelligent systems (EAIS) (pp. 1-7). IEEE. doi:10.1109/EAIS.2015.7368785

Erel, E., & Sarin, S. C. (1998). A survey of the assembly line balancing procedures. *Production Planning & Control*, 414 - 434. doi:10.1080/095372898233902

Erickson, B. J., & Kitamura, F. (2021). Magician's corner: 9. Performance Metrics for Machine learning models. *Radiology*, *3*(3), e200126. doi:10.1148/ryai.2021200126 PMID:34136815

Etzkowitz, H., & Leydesdorff, L. (1997). Universities in the Global Economy: Culture, Technology and Innovation. *The Journal of Technology Transfer*, *22*(2), 2–3.

Fang, W., Jiang, H., Lu, H., Sun, J., Wu, X., & Lin, J. C. (2024). GPU-Based Efficient Parallel Heuristic Algorithm for High-Utility Itemset Mining in Large Transaction Datasets. *IEEE Transactions on Knowledge and Data Engineering*, 652-667.

Farooque, M., Khan, M. A. I., & Rashid, M. A. A. (2022). Big Data Analytics for Dealing with COVID-19: An Innovative Trend in Business Intelligence. New Innovations in Economics. *Business and Management*, *8*, 50–55. doi:10.9734/bpi/niebm/v8/2050B

Fattahi, P., Roshani, A., & Roshani, A. (2011). A mathematical model and ant colony algorithm for multi-manned assembly line balancing problem. *International Journal of Advanced Manufacturing Technology*, *53*(1-4), 1433–3015. doi:10.1007/s00170-010-2832-y

Feng, W., Joey, S. A. (2023). Enhancing Operational Efficiency: Integrating Machine Learning Predictive Capabilities in Business Intelligence for Informed Decision-Making. *Frontiers in Business, Economics and Management*. doi:10.54097/fbem.v9i1.8694

Ferreira, A. (2021). Regulating smart contracts: Legal revolution or simply evolution? *Telecommunications Policy*, *45*(2), 102081. doi:10.1016/j.telpol.2020.102081

Floridi, L., & Taddeo, M. (2016). What is data ethics? *Philosophical Transactions. Series A, Mathematical, Physical, and Engineering Sciences*, *374*(2083), 20160360. doi:10.1098/rsta.2016.0360 PMID:28336805

Følstad, A., & Skjuve, M. (2019). Chatbots for customer service. *Proceedings of the 1st International Conference on Conversational User Interfaces*, 1-9. 10.1145/3342775.3342784

Fradkov, A. L. (2020). Early history of machine learning. *IFAC-PapersOnLine*, *53*(2), 1385–1390. doi:10.1016/j.ifacol.2020.12.1888

Francis, L. (2001). The basics of neural networks demystified. *Contingencies*, *11*(12), 56–61.

Furey, E. M., O'Hora, D., McNamara, J., Kinsella, S., & Noone, C. (2016). The roles of Financial Threat, social support, Work stress, and Mental Distress in Dairy Farmers' expectations of injury. *Frontiers in Public Health*, *4*, 126. doi:10.3389/fpubh.2016.00126 PMID:27446893

Gajjar, S., Sarkar, M., & Dasgupta, K. (2014). Cluster head selection protocol using fuzzy logic for wireless sensor networks. *International Journal of Computer Applications*, *97*(7), 38–43. doi:10.5120/17022-7310

Galetsi, P., Katsaliaki, K., & Kumar, S. (2020). Big data analytics in health sector: Theoretical framework, techniques and prospects. *International Journal of Information Management*, *50*, 206–216. doi:10.1016/j.ijinfomgt.2019.05.003

Ganesan, M., C., D., B., H., A.S., K., & B., L. (2020). A Survey on Chatbots Using Artificial Intelligence. *2020 International Conference on System, Computation, Automation and Networking (ICSCAN)*, 1-5. 10.1109/ICSCAN49426.2020.9262366

García, F., Giménez, V., & Guijarro, F. (2013). Credit risk management: A multicriteria approach to assess creditworthiness. *Mathematical and Computer Modelling*, *57*(7-8), 2009–2015. doi:10.1016/j.mcm.2012.03.005

Gepp, A., Linnenluecke, M. K., O'Neill, T. J., & Smith, T. (2018). Big data techniques in auditing research and practice: Current trends and future opportunities. *Journal of Accounting Literature*, *40*(1), 102–115. doi:10.1016/j.acclit.2017.05.003

Ge, Z., Song, Z., Ding, S. X., & Huang, B. (2017). Data Mining and Analytics in the Process Industry: The role of Machine Learning. *IEEE Access : Practical Innovations, Open Solutions*, *5*, 20590–20616. doi:10.1109/ACCESS.2017.2756872

Ghatul, D. B. (2013). Constraints and Stress level of Farmers. International Journal of Scientific and Research Publications, 107.

Ghofrani, F., He, Q., Goverde, R. M., & Liu, X. (2018). Recent applications of big data analytics in railway transportation systems: A survey. *Transportation Research Part C, Emerging Technologies*, *90*, 226–246. doi:10.1016/j.trc.2018.03.010

Gianfrancesco, M., Tamang, S., Yazdany, J., & Schmajuk, G. (2018). Potential biases in machine learning algorithms using electronic health record data. *JAMA Internal Medicine*, *178*(11), 1544. doi:10.1001/jamainternmed.2018.3763 PMID:30128552

Gill, S. S., Xu, M., Ottaviani, C., Patros, P., Bahsoon, R., Shaghaghi, A., Golec, M., Stankovski, V., Wu, H., Abraham, A., Singh, M., Mehta, H., Ghosh, S. K., Baker, T., Parlikad, A. K., Lutfiyya, H., Kanhere, S. S., Sakellariou, R., Dustdar, S., ... Uhlig, S. (2022). AI for next generation computing: Emerging trends and future directions. *Internet of Things : Engineering Cyber Physical Human Systems*, *19*, 100514. doi:10.1016/j.iot.2022.100514

Glorot, X., & Bengio, Y. (2010, March). Understanding the difficulty of training deep feedforward neural networks. In *Proceedings of the thirteenth international conference on artificial intelligence and statistics* (pp. 249-256). JMLR Workshop and Conference Proceedings.

Glover, F. (1989). Tabu Search-Part I. *ORSA Journal on Computing*, *1*(3), 190–206. doi:10.1287/ijoc.1.3.190

Gmbh & Co. (2016). *Global online payment methods: Full year 2016*. Tech. Rep.

Gnewuch, U., Morana, S., Adam, M., & Maedche, A. (2018). *Faster is not always better: understanding the effect of dynamic response delays in human-chatbot interaction*. Academic Press.

Goel, P., & Lobiyal, D. K. (2018). Minimizing the cost of two-tier cellular network with queuing handoff calls in microcell using genetic algorithm. *Malaya Journal of Matematik*, 14-21.

Goodfellow, I., Bengio, Y., Courville, A., & Bengio, Y. (2016). *Deep learning* (Vol. 1). MIT Press.

Goodfellow, I., Pouget-Abadie, J., Mirza, M., Xu, B., Warde-Farley, D., Ozair, S., Courville, A., & Bengio, Y. (2020). Generative adversarial networks. *Communications of the ACM*, *63*(11), 139–144. doi:10.1145/3422622

Goodman, R. S., Patrinely, J. R., Stone, C. A. Jr, Zimmerman, E., Donald, R. R., Chang, S. S., Berkowitz, S. T., Finn, A. P., Jahangir, E., Scoville, E. A., Reese, T. S., Friedman, D. L., Bastarache, J. A., van der Heijden, Y. F., Wright, J. J., Ye, F., Carter, N., Alexander, M. R., Choe, J. H., ... Johnson, D. B. (2023). Accuracy and Reliability of Chatbot Responses to Physician Questions. *JAMA Network Open*, *6*(10), e2336483. doi:10.1001/jamanetworkopen.2023.36483 PMID:37782499

Gregoire, A. (2002). The mental health of farmers. *Occupational Medicine*, *52*(8), 471–476. doi:10.1093/occmed/52.8.471 PMID:12488518

Gregori, E. (2017). Evaluation of modern tools for an omscs advisor chatbot. *Smartech. Gatech. Edu*, 1-50.

Grzechca, W. (2015). Assembly line balancing problem with quality inspection stations. *2015 IEEE 7th International Conference on Cybernetics and Intelligent Systems (CIS) and IEEE Conference on Robotics, Automation and Mechatronics (RAM)*, 89-94. 10.1109/ICCIS.2015.7274602

Gu, J., Wang, Z., Kuen, J., Ma, L., Shahroudy, A., Shuai, B., Liu, T., Wang, X., Wang, G., Cai, J., & Chen, T. (2018). Recent advances in convolutional neural networks. *Pattern Recognition*, *77*, 354–377. doi:10.1016/j.patcog.2017.10.013

Gulhane, Y. H., Rode, S. V., & Ladhake, S. A. (2011). Application of fuzzy logic in stress analysis. In *Proceedings of the International Conference & Workshop on Emerging Trends in Technology* (pp. 679-685). 10.1145/1980022.1980168

Guo, K., Hu, Y., Qian, Z., Liu, H., Zhang, K., Sun, Y., Gao, J., & Yin, B. (2020). Optimized graph convolution recurrent neural network for traffic prediction. *IEEE Transactions on Intelligent Transportation Systems*, *22*(2), 1138–1149. doi:10.1109/TITS.2019.2963722

Gupta, A., Dwivedi, D. N., & Shah, J. (2023). Artificial Intelligence Applications in Banking and Financial Services. Future of Business and Finance. Springer. doi:10.1007/978-981-99-2571-1_1

Gupta, C., & Farahat, A. (2020, August). Deep learning for industrial AI: Challenges, new methods and best practices. In *Proceedings of the 26th ACM SIGKDD International Conference on Knowledge Discovery & Data Mining* (pp. 3571-3572). 10.1145/3394486.3406482

Gupta, S., & Johari, R. (2011). A New Framework for Credit Card Transactions Involving Mutual Authentication between Cardholder and Merchant. *International Conference on Communication Systems and Network Technologies IEEE*, 22-26. 10.1109/CSNT.2011.12

Gupta, V., & Gupta, M. (2022). A Modern Tool of Conversation: Chatbot. *Journal of Ubiquitous Computing and Communication Technologies*, *4*(3), 138–149. doi:10.36548/jucct.2022.3.002

Gutjahr, A. L., & Neumhauser, G. L. (1964). An algorithm for the balancing problem. *Management Science*, 23–35.

Gu, X., Huang, M., & Liang, X. (2019). An improved genetic algorithm with adaptive variable neighborhood search for FJSP. *Algorithms*, *12*(11), 243. doi:10.3390/a12110243

Guyon, I., & Elisseeff, A. (2003). An introduction to variable and feature selection. *Journal of Machine Learning Research*, *3*, 1157–1182.

Hackos, J. T. (2017). Modelo de madurez del proceso de informaciõn. In *IEEE 2017 International Professional Communication Conference (ProComm)* (pp. 1-8). IEEE International Professional Communication Conference.

Hagen, B. N., Albright, A., Sargeant, J., Winder, C. B., Harper, S. L., O'Sullivan, T. L., & Jones-Bitton, A. (2019). Research trends in farmers' mental health: A scoping review of mental health outcomes and interventions among farming populations worldwide. *PLoS One*, *14*(12), e0225661. doi:10.1371/journal.pone.0225661 PMID:31805070

Haldurai, L., Madhubala, T., & Rajalakshmi, R. (2016). A study on genetic algorithm and its applications. *International Journal on Computer Science and Engineering*, *4*(10), 2347–2693.

Han, J., Jian, P., & Hanghang, T. (2022). *Data mining: concepts and techniques*. Morgan kaufmann.

Han-ye, Z. (2017). An improved immune algorithm for simple assembly line balancing problem of type 1. *Journal of Algorithms & Computational Technology*, 317–326.

Han, Z. (2023). The applications of chatbot. *Highlights in Science, Engineering and Technology*, *57*, 258–266. doi:10.54097/hset.v57i.10011

Hardt, M., & Recht, B. (2021). Patterns, predictions, and actions: A story about machine learning. *arXiv (Cornell University)*. http://export.arxiv.org/pdf/2102.05242v1

Harris, J. D., & Waggoner, B. (2019). Decentralized and collaborative AI on blockchain. *Proc. IEEE Int. Conf. Blockchain (Blockchain)*, 368–375.

Hastie, T., Tibshirani, R., & Friedman, J. (2009). *The Elements of Statistical Learning: Data Mining, Inference, and Prediction*. Springer. doi:10.1007/978-0-387-84858-7

Hatagar, S., & Halase, S. V. (2015). Three Input – One Output Fuzzy logic control of Washing Machine. *Int. J. Sci. Res. Eng. Technol.*, *4*(1), 2278–2882.

Hearst, M. A., Dumais, S. T., Osman, E. M., Platt, J., & Schölkopf, B. (1998). Support vector machines. *IEEE Intelligent Systems & their Applications*, *13*(4), 18–28. doi:10.1109/5254.708428

Held, M., Karp, R. M., & Sharesian, R. (1963). Assembly-Line Balancing-Dynamic Programming with Precedence Constraints. *Operations Research*, *11*(3), 442–459. doi:10.1287/opre.11.3.442

Helgeson, W. B., & Birnie, D. P. (1961). Assembly Line Balancing Using the Ranked Positional Weight Technique. *Journal of Industrial Engineering*.

Hochreiter, S., & Schmidhuber, J. (1997). Long short-term memory. *Neural Computation*, *9*(8), 1735–1780. doi:10.1162/neco.1997.9.8.1735 PMID:9377276

Hoffman, T. R. (1963). Permitations and Precedence Matrices with Automatic Computer Applications to Industrial Problems. University of Wisconsin.

Hovey, J. D., & Seligman, L. D. (2006). The mental health of agricultural workers. In *Agricultural medicine* (pp. 282–299). Springer. doi:10.1007/0-387-30105-4_22

Howard, A. G., Zhu, M., Chen, B., Kalenichenko, D., Wang, W., Weyand, T., . . . Adam, H. (2017). MobileNets: Efficient Convolutional Neural Networks for Mobile Vision Applications. *arXiv preprint arXiv:1704.04861*.

How, M. L., Cheah, S. M., Khor, A. C., & Chan, Y. J. (2020). Artificial intelligence-enhanced predictive insights for advancing financial inclusion: A human-centric ai-thinking approach. *Big Data and Cognitive Computing*, *4*(2), 8. doi:10.3390/bdcc4020008

Hsu, C.-L., & Lin, J. C.-C. (2023). Understanding the user satisfaction and loyalty of customer service chatbots. *Journal of Retailing and Consumer Services*, *71*, 103211. doi:10.1016/j.jretconser.2022.103211

Huang, J., Li, Y., & Xie, M. (2015). An empirical analysis of data preprocessing for machine learning-based software cost estimation. *Information and Software Technology*, *67*, 108–127. doi:10.1016/j.infsof.2015.07.004

Huo, J., Wang, Z., Chan, F. T., Lee, C. K., & Strandhagen, J. O. (2018). Assembly Line Balancing Based on Beam Ant Colony Optimisation. *Mathematical Problems in Engineering*, *2018*, 1–17. doi:10.1155/2018/2481435

Hur, J., Raj, M., & Riyanto, Y. E. (2006). Finance and trade: A cross-country empirical analysis on the impact of financial development and asset tangibility on international trade. *World Development*, *34*(10), 1728–1741. doi:10.1016/j.worlddev.2006.02.003

Ilievski, V., Musat, C., Hossman, A., & Baeriswyl, M. (2018). Goal-Oriented Chatbot Dialog Management Bootstrapping with Transfer Learning. *Proceedings of the Twenty-Seventh International Joint Conference on Artificial Intelligence*, 4115-4121. 10.24963/ijcai.2018/572

Inmon, W. H. (1992). *Building the Data Warehouse*. Wiley.

Jabeur, S. B., Gharib, C., Mefteh-Wali, S., & Arfi, W. B. (2021). CatBoost model and artificial intelligence techniques for corporate failure prediction. *Technological Forecasting and Social Change*, *166*, 120658. doi:10.1016/j.techfore.2021.120658

Jackson, J. R. (1956). A Computing Procedure for a Line Balancing Problem. *Management Science*, *2*(3), 261–271. doi:10.1287/mnsc.2.3.261

James, G., Witten, D., Hastie, T., & Tibshirani, R. (2013). *An Introduction to Statistical Learning: with Applications in R*. Springer. doi:10.1007/978-1-4614-7138-7

Jensen, J. B. (2018). Self-driving but not self-regulating: The development of a legal framework to promote the safety of autonomous vehicles. *Washburn Law Journal*, *57*, 579.

Jiang, T., Gradus, J. L., & Rosellini, A. J. (2020). Supervised Machine Learning: A brief primer. *Behavior Therapy*, *51*(5), 675–687. doi:10.1016/j.beth.2020.05.002 PMID:32800297

Jirasirilerd, G., Pitakaso, R., Sethanan, K., Kaewman, S., Sirirak, W., & Kosacka-Olejnik, M. (2020). Simple Assembly Line Balancing Problem Type 2 By Variable Neighborhood Strategy Adaptive Search: A Case Study Garment Industry. *Journal of Open Innovation*, *6*(1), 1–22. doi:10.3390/joitmc6010021

John, S. N., Anele, C., Kennedy, O. O., Olajide, F., & Kennedy, C. G. (2016, December). Realtime fraud detection in the banking sector using data mining techniques/algorithm. In 2016 international conference on computational science and computational intelligence (CSCI) (pp. 1186-1191). IEEE.

Jordan, M. I., & Mitchell, T. M. (2015). Machine learning: Trends, perspectives, and prospects. *Science*, *349*(6245), 255–260. doi:10.1126/science.aaa8415 PMID:26185243

Joshi, A., Kale, S., Chandel, S., & Pal, D. K. (2015). Likert scale: Explored and explained. *British Journal of Applied Science and Technology*, *7*(4), 396–403. doi:10.9734/BJAST/2015/14975

Ju, W. H., & Vardi, Y. (2001). A hybrid high-order markov chain model for computer intrusion detection. *Journal of Computational and Graphical Statistics*, *10*(2), 277–295. doi:10.1198/10618600152628068

Kaffash, S., Nguyen, A. T., & Zhu, J. (2021). Big data algorithms and applications in intelligent transportation system: A review and bibliometric analysis. *International Journal of Production Economics*, *231*, 107868. doi:10.1016/j.ijpe.2020.107868

Kakade, N. (2023). Collaborative Robots and Human Robot Interaction: A Review on Two Revolutions of Industry 4.0. *International Research Journal of Engineering and Technology*, 832-836.

Kalia, M., Dewedi, S., & Sharma, V. (2019). Novel Approach of Assembly Line Balancing by Hybrid Swarm Intelligence Approach. *International Journal of Research in Electronics and Computer Engineering*, 2544-2553.

Kallioniemi, M. K., Simola, A., Kaseva, J., & Kymäläinen, H. R. (2016). Stress and burnout among Finnish dairy farmers. *Journal of Agromedicine*, *21*(3), 259–268. doi:10.1080/1059924X.2016.1178611 PMID:27081893

Kamarudin, N. H., & Rashid, M. F. (2018). Modelling of Simple Assembly Line Balancing Problem Type 1 (SALBP-1) with Machine and Worker Constraints. *Journal of Physics: Conference Series*, 1–11. doi:10.1088/1742-6596/1049/1/012037

Kashani, M. H., Madanipour, M., Nikravan, M., Asghari, P., & Mahdipour, E. (2021). A systematic review of IoT in healthcare: Applications, techniques, and trends. *Journal of Network and Computer Applications*, *192*, 103164. doi:10.1016/j.jnca.2021.103164

Kearney, G. D., Rafferty, A. P., Hendricks, L. R., Allen, D. L., & Tutor-Marcom, R. (2014). A cross-sectional study of stressors among farmers in eastern North Carolina. *North Carolina Medical Journal*, *75*(6), 384–392. doi:10.18043/ncm.75.6.384 PMID:25402689

Khadija, M. A., Nurharjadmo, W., & Widyawan. (2022). Deep Learning Generative Indonesian Response Model Chatbot for JKN-KIS. *2022 1st International Conference on Smart Technology, Applied Informatics, and Engineering (APICS)*, 70-74. doi:10.1109/APICS56469.2022.9918686

Khanra, S., Dhir, A., Islam, A. N., & Mäntymäki, M. (2020). Big data analytics in healthcare: A systematic literature review. *Enterprise Information Systems*, *14*(7), 878–912. doi:10.1080/17517575.2020.1812005

Kilbridge, M. D., & Wester, L. (1961). A heuristic method of Assembly Line Balancing. *Journal on Industrial Engineering*.

Kimball, R., Ross, M., Thornthwaite, W., Mundy, J., & Becker, B. (1996). *The Data Warehouse Lifecycle Toolkit*. Wiley.

Kitchens, B., Dobolyi, D., Li, J., & Abbasi, A. (2018). Advanced customer analytics: Strategic value through integration of relationship-oriented big data. *Journal of Management Information Systems*, *35*(2), 540–574. doi:10.1080/07421222.2018.1451957

Knudsen, M., & Kaivo-Oja, J. (2020). Collaborative Robots: Frontiers of Current Literature. *Journal of Intelligent Systems: Theory and Applications*, 13-20.

Kong-Vega, N., Shen, M., Wang, M., & D'Haro, L. F. (2019). Subjective Annotation and Evaluation of Three Different Chatbots WOCHAT: Shared Task Report. doi:10.1007/978-981-13-9443-0_32

Kratsch, W., Manderscheid, J., Röglinger, M., & Seyfried, J. (2021). Machine learning in business process monitoring: A comparison of deep learning and classical approaches used for outcome prediction. *Business & Information Systems Engineering*, *63*(3), 261–276. doi:10.1007/s12599-020-00645-0

Kratzwald, B., Ilić, S., Kraus, M., Feuerriegel, S., & Prendinger, H. (2018). Deep learning for affective computing: Text-based emotion recognition in decision support. *Decision Support Systems*, *115*, 24–35. doi:10.1016/j.dss.2018.09.002

Kraus, M. (2020). *Deep Learning in Business Analytics: Methods and Applications* [Doctoral dissertation]. ETH Zurich.

Kraus, M., Feuerriegel, S., & Oztekin, A. (2020). Deep learning in business analytics and operations research: Models, applications and managerial implications. *European Journal of Operational Research*, *281*(3), 628–641. doi:10.1016/j.ejor.2019.09.018

Krizhevsky, A., Sutskever, I., & Hinton, G. E. (2012). ImageNet Classification with Deep Convolutional Neural Networks. In Advances in neural information processing systems (pp. 1097-1105). Academic Press.

Krizhevsky, A., Sutskever, I., & Hinton, G. E. (2017). ImageNet Classification with Deep Convolutional Neural Networks. *Communications of the ACM*, *60*(6), 84–90. doi:10.1145/3065386

Kumar, A., Shankar, R., & Thakur, L. S. (2018). A big data driven sustainable manufacturing framework for condition-based maintenance prediction. *Journal of Computational Science*, *27*, 428–439. doi:10.1016/j.jocs.2017.06.006

Kumar, D. N., & Reddy, M. J. (2007). Multipurpose reservoir operation using particle swarm optimization. *Journal of Water Resources Planning and Management*, *133*(3), 192–201. doi:10.1061/(ASCE)0733-9496(2007)133:3(192)

Kumar, N., Tripathi, P., Nanda, R. P., Tiwari, S., & Sharma, S. (2024). Machine Learning for Smart Health Services in the Framework of Industry 5.0. In M. Khan, R. Khan, P. Praveen, A. R. Verma, & M. K. Panda (Eds.), *Infrastructure Possibilities and Human-Centered Approaches With Industry 5.0* (pp. 215–230). IGI Global. doi:10.4018/979-8-3693-0782-3.ch013

Kundu, A., Panigrahi, S., Sural, S., & Majumdar, A. K. (2009). Blastssaha hybridization for credit card fraud detection. *IEEE Transactions on Dependable and Secure Computing, 6*(4), 309-315.

Kushwaha, A. K., Kar, A. K., & Dwivedi, Y. K. (2021). Applications of big data in emerging management disciplines: A literature review using text mining. *International Journal of Information Management Data Insights*, *1*(2), 100017. doi:10.1016/j.jjimei.2021.100017

Kushwaha, G. S., & Kumar, S. (2009). Role of the fuzzy system in psychological research. *Europe's Journal of Psychology*, *5*(2), 123–134. doi:10.5964/ejop.v5i2.271

Lai, Y. (2019, October). A comparison of traditional machine learning and deep learning in image recognition. *Journal of Physics: Conference Series*, *1314*(1), 012148. doi:10.1088/1742-6596/1314/1/012148

Lakshmi, B., Boban, E., Sulphikar, N., & Aparna, T. (2020). Mental stress calculation using fuzzy logic algorithm. *International Journal of Applied Engineering Research: IJAER*, *15*(1).

Larochelle, H., Bengio, Y., Louradour, J., & Lamblin, P. (2009). Exploring strategies for training deep neural networks. *Journal of Machine Learning Research*, *10*(1).

Laudon, K. C., & Laudon, J. P. (2016). *Management Information Systems: Managing the Digital Firm*. Pearson.

Lazaridis, E. N. (1999). A Bayesian evaluation of fuzzy logic in a classification problem. *Communications in Statistics. Stochastic Models*, *15*(3), 461–483. doi:10.1080/15326349908807545

LeCun, Y., Bengio, Y., & Hinton, G. (2015). Deep learning. *Nature*, *521*(7553), 436–444. doi:10.1038/nature14539 PMID:26017442

Lemonakis, C., & Zopounidis, C. (2023). *The future of business: artificial intelligence, machine learning and deep learning*. doi:10.4337/9781839106750.00010

Li, C., Chen, Y., & Shang, Y. (2022). A review of industrial big data for decision making in intelligent manufacturing. *Engineering Science and Technology, an International Journal, 29*, 101021. https://doi.org/ doi:10.1016/j.jestch.2021.06.001

Li, M., & Huang, G. (2021). Production-intralogistics synchronization of industry 4.0 flexible assembly lines under graduation intelligent manufacturing system. *International Journal of Production Economics*, *241*, 1–15. doi:10.1016/j.ijpe.2021.108272

Li, S., Chen, T., Wang, L., & Ming, C. (2018). Effective tourist volume forecasting supported by PCA and improved BPNN using Baidu index. *Tourism Management*, *68*, 116–126. doi:10.1016/j.tourman.2018.03.006

Liu, L., Wu, Y., Wei, W., Cao, W., Sahin, S., & Zhang, Q. (2018, July). Benchmarking deep learning frameworks: Design considerations, metrics and beyond. In *2018 IEEE 38th International Conference on Distributed Computing Systems (ICDCS)* (pp. 1258-1269). IEEE.

Li, X., Xiong, H., Li, X., Wu, X., Zhang, X., Liu, J., Bian, J., & Dou, D. (2022). Interpretable deep learning: Interpretation, interpretability, trustworthiness, and beyond. *Knowledge and Information Systems*, *64*(12), 3197–3234. doi:10.1007/s10115-022-01756-8

Li, Z., Kucukkoc, I., & Tang, Q. (2019). A comparative study of exact methods for the simple assembly line balancing problem. *Soft Computing*, 1–17.

Long, W., Lu, Z., & Cui, L. (2019). Deep learning-based feature engineering for stock price movement prediction. *Knowledge-Based Systems*, *164*, 163–173. doi:10.1016/j.knosys.2018.10.034

Loureiro, A. L., Miguéis, V. L., & Da Silva, L. F. (2018). Exploring the use of deep neural networks for sales forecasting in fashion retail. *Decision Support Systems*, *114*, 81–93. doi:10.1016/j.dss.2018.08.010

Loureiro, S. M. C., Guerreiro, J., & Tussyadiah, I. (2021). Artificial intelligence in business: State of the art and future research agenda. *Journal of Business Research*, *129*, 911–926. doi:10.1016/j.jbusres.2020.11.001

Luca, L., Brcic, M., & Cabitza, F. (2024). Explainable artificial intelligence (XAI) 2.0: A manifesto of open challenges and interdisciplinary research directions. *Information Fusion*, 102301.

Lu, J., Yan, Z., Han, J., & Zhang, G. (2019). Data-Driven Decision-Making (D3M): Framework, Methodology, and Directions. *IEEE Transactions on Emerging Topics in Computational Intelligence*, *3*(4), 286–296. doi:10.1109/TETCI.2019.2915813

Lyu, P., Liu, X., & Yao, T. (2023). A bibliometric analysis of literature on bibliometrics in recent half-century. *Journal of Information Science*. doi:10.1177/01655515231191233

Ma'ruf, A. (2022). The Development of Human-Robot Collaborative Assembly Line Model by Considering Availability of Robots, Tools, and Setup Time. *Jurnal Ilimiah Teknik Industri*, 321-329.

Ma, C., Kong, X., Lan, Q., & Zhou, Z. (2021, December). The privacy protection mechanism of hyperledger fabric and its application in supply chain finance. *Cybersecurity*, *2*(1), 1–9.

Madanchian, M., Ariken, J., & Taherdoost, H. (2022). Role of Effective Leadership on Empowerment, Effective Communication, and Motivation in Customer Service. *Macro Management & Public Policies*. doi:10.30564/mmpp.v4i1.4530

Maddikunta, P. K. R., Pham, Q. V., Prabadevi, B., Deepa, N., Dev, K., Gadekallu, T. R., ... Liyanage, M. (2022). Industry 5.0: A survey on enabling technologies and potential applications. *Journal of Industrial Information Integration*, *26*, 100257. doi:10.1016/j.jii.2021.100257

Maha, A. A. (2023). Proposing a new method to solve line balancing bottleneck problem in the single-model line. *Emerald Open Research*, 1–17.

Majidi, N., Shamsi, M., & Marvasti, F. (2024). Algorithmic trading using continuous action space deep reinforcement learning. *Expert Systems with Applications*, *235*, 121245. doi:10.1016/j.eswa.2023.121245

Manimala, K., Selvi, K., & Ahila, R. (2011). Hybrid soft computing techniques for feature selection and parameter optimization in power quality data mining. *Applied Soft Computing*, *11*(8), 5485–5497. doi:10.1016/j.asoc.2011.05.010

Manyika, J., Chui, M., Brown, B., Bughin, J., Dobbs, R., Roxburgh, C., & Byers, A. H. (2011). *Big data: The next frontier for innovation, competition, and productivity*. McKinsey Global Institute.

Mardle, S. J., Pascoe, S., & Tamiz, M. (2000). An investigation of genetic algorithms for the optimization of multi-objective fisheries bioeconomic models. *International Transactions in Operational Research*, *7*(1), 33–49.

Mariani, M., Baggio, R., Fuchs, M., & Höepken, W. (2018). Business intelligence and big data in hospitality and tourism: A systematic literature review. *International Journal of Contemporary Hospitality Management*, *30*(12), 3514–3554. doi:10.1108/IJCHM-07-2017-0461

Márquez-Chamorro, A. E., Resinas, M., & Ruiz-Cortés, A. (2017). Predictive monitoring of business processes: A survey. *IEEE Transactions on Services Computing*, *11*(6), 962–977. doi:10.1109/TSC.2017.2772256

Martin-del-Brio, B., & Serrano-Cinca, C. (1993). Self-organizing neural networks for the analysis and representation of data: Some financial cases. *Neural Computing & Applications*, *1*(3), 193–206. doi:10.1007/BF01414948

Masoud, N. M. H. (2013). The Impact of Stock Market Performance upon Economic Growth. *International Journal of Economics and Financial Issues*, *3*(4), 788–798. https://dergipark.org.tr/en/pub/ijefi/issue/31960/351956

Mastor, A. A. (1970). An experimental Investigation y Comparative Evaluation of Production Line Balancing Techniques. *Management Science*, *16*(11), 728–746. doi:10.1287/mnsc.16.11.728

Maulud, D. H., & Abdulazeez, A. M. (2020). A review on Linear Regression comprehensive in Machine Learning. *Journal of Applied Science and Technology Trends*, *1*(4), 140–147. doi:10.38094/jastt1457

McCulloch, W., & Pitts, W. (1943). A logical calculus of the ideas immanent in nervous activity. *The Bulletin of Mathematical Biophysics*, *5*(4), 115–133. doi:10.1007/BF02478259

McKinney, W. (2018). *Python for Data Analysis: Data Wrangling with Pandas, NumPy, and IPython*. O'Reilly Media.

McKinsey Global Institute. (2011). *Big data: The next frontier for innovation, competition, and productivity*. Author.

Medsker, L. R., & Jain, L. C. (2001). Recurrent neural networks. *Design and Applications*, *5*(64-67), 2.

Mehtab, S., & Sen, J. (2020). Stock Price Prediction Using CNN and LSTM-Based Deep Learning Models. *2020 International Conference on Decision Aid Sciences and Application, DASA 2020*, 447–453. 10.1109/DASA51403.2020.9317207

Mehtab, S., & Sen, J. (2022). Analysis and Forecasting of Financial Time Series Using CNN and LSTM-Based Deep Learning Models. *Lecture Notes in Networks and Systems*, *302*, 405–423. doi:10.1007/978-981-16-4807-6_39

Mehtab, S., Sen, J., & Dasgupta, S. (2020). Robust Analysis of Stock Price Time Series Using CNN and LSTM-Based Deep Learning Models. *Proceedings of the 4th International Conference on Electronics, Communication and Aerospace Technology, ICECA 2020*, 1481–1486. 10.1109/ICECA49313.2020.9297652

Mehtab, S., Sen, J., & Dutta, A. (2021). Stock Price Prediction Using Machine Learning and LSTM-Based Deep Learning Models. *Communications in Computer and Information Science*, *1366*, 88–106. doi:10.1007/978-981-16-0419-5_8

Metzger, A., Leitner, P., Ivanović, D., Schmieders, E., Franklin, R., Carro, M., Dustdar, S., & Pohl, K. (2014). Comparing and combining predictive business process monitoring techniques. *IEEE Transactions on Systems, Man, and Cybernetics. Systems*, *45*(2), 276–290. doi:10.1109/TSMC.2014.2347265

Miguéis, V. L., Freitas, A., Garcia, P. J., & Silva, A. (2018). Early segmentation of students according to their academic performance: A predictive modelling approach. *Decision Support Systems*, *115*, 36–51. doi:10.1016/j.dss.2018.09.001

Miltenburg, G. J., & Wijngaard, J. (1994). U-Line Line Balancing Problem. *Management Science*, *40*(10), 1378–1388. doi:10.1287/mnsc.40.10.1378

Mishra, D. K., Johari, K., Ghildiyal, S., Upadhyay, A. K., & Sharma, S. (2022). A Novel Approach in Business Intelligence for Big Data Analytics Using an Unsupervised Technique. *ECS Transactions*, *107*(1), 12525–12533. doi:10.1149/10701.12525ecst

Mishra, R., & Chadhuary, N. (2023). A Comprehensive Study on Detection of Cyber-Attack using ML Techniques & Future Scope. *International Journal of Engineering Research in Computer Science and Engineering*, *10*(3), 47–59.

Mitchell, T. M. (1997). Does machine learning really work. *AI Magazine*, *18*(3), 11–20. doi:10.1609/aimag.v18i3.1303

Mittal, S., & Grewal, N. S. (2014). Stress Quantification using Fuzzy Analysis of ECG Parameters. *International Journal of Computer Applications*, *99*(9), 24–27. doi:10.5120/17403-7968

Mohammadi, K., Shamshirband, S., Motamedi, S., Petković, D., Hashim, R., & Gocic, M. (2015). Extreme learning machine based prediction of daily dew point temperature. *Computers and Electronics in Agriculture*, *117*, 214–225. doi:10.1016/j.compag.2015.08.008

Montgomery, D. C., Jennings, C. L., & Kulahci, M. (2008). *Introduction to Time Series Analysis and Forecasting*. John Wiley & Sons.

Montgomery, D. C., & Runger, G. C. (2014). *Applied Statistics and Probability for Engineers*. John Wiley & Sons.

Mota, G., Fernandes, J., & Belo, O. (2014). Usage signatures analysis an alternative method for preventing fraud in E-Commerce applications. *International Conference on Data Science and Advanced Analytics* (pp.203-208). IEEE. 10.1109/DSAA.2014.7058074

Moussaoui, H., El Akkad, N., & Benslimane, M. (2023). Reinforcement Learning: A review. *International Journal of Computing and Digital Systems*, *13*(1), 1465–1483. doi:10.12785/ijcds/1301118

Mungoli, N. (2023). Deciphering the Blockchain: A Comprehensive Analysis of Bitcoin's Evolution, Adoption, and Future Implications. *arXiv preprint arXiv:2304.02655.* doi:10.4108/eai.18-11-2022.2327194

Murkute, A., & Sarode, T. (2015). Forecasting Market Price of Stock using Artificial Neural Network. *International Journal of Computer Applications*, *124*(12), 11–15. doi:10.5120/ijca2015905681

Mydyti, H., & Kadriu, A. (2021). The Impact of Chatbots in Driving Digital Transformation. *International Journal of E-Services and Mobile Applications*, *13*(4), 88–104. doi:10.4018/IJESMA.2021100106

Nabipour, M., Nayyeri, P., Jabani, H., Shahab, S., & Mosavi, A. (2020). Predicting Stock Market Trends Using Machine Learning and Deep Learning Algorithms Via Continuous and Binary Data; A Comparative Analysis. *IEEE Access : Practical Innovations, Open Solutions*, *8*, 150199–150212. doi:10.1109/ACCESS.2020.3015966

Nagaraj, B., & Malagi, K. B. (2022). *Research Paper to Design and Develop an Algorithm for Optimisation Chatbot*. doi:10.1007/978-981-19-2541-2_31

Nair, V., & Hinton, G. E. (2010). Rectified Linear Units Improve Restricted Boltzmann Machines. *Proceedings of the 27th International Conference on Machine Learning (ICML-10)*, 807-814.

Najafabadi, M. M., Villanustre, F., Khoshgoftaar, T. M., Seliya, N., Wald, R., & Muharemagic, E. (2015). Deep learning applications and challenges in big data analytics. *Journal of Big Data*, *2*(1), 1–21. doi:10.1186/s40537-014-0007-7

Nallaperuma, D., Nawaratne, R., Bandaragoda, T., Adikari, A., Nguyen, S., Kempitiya, T., De Silva, D., Alahakoon, D., & Pothuhera, D. (2019). Online incremental machine learning platform for big data-driven smart traffic management. *IEEE Transactions on Intelligent Transportation Systems*, *20*(12), 4679–4690. doi:10.1109/TITS.2019.2924883

Nasteski, V. (2017). An overview of the supervised machine learning methods. *Horizonti. Serija B. Prirodno-matematički, Tehničko-tehnološki, Biotehnički. Medicinski Nauki I Zdravstvo*, *4*, 51–62. doi:10.20544/HORIZONS.B.04.1.17.P05

Nath, M. P., & Sagnika, S. (2020). *Capabilities of Chatbots and Its Performance Enhancements in Machine Learning*. doi:10.1007/978-981-15-1884-3_17

Neema, D. D., Patel, R. N., & Thoke, A. S. (2011). Speed control of induction motor using fuzzy rule base. *International Journal of Computer Applications*, *33*(5), 21–29.

Nguyen, T., Li, Z. H. O. U., Spiegler, V., Ieromonachou, P., & Lin, Y. (2018). Big data analytics in supply chain management: A state-of-the-art literature review. *Computers & Operations Research*, *98*, 254–264. doi:10.1016/j.cor.2017.07.004

Nielsen, M. A. (2015). *Neural networks and deep learning* (Vol. 25). Determination Press.

Nielsen, M. A. (2015). *Neural Networks and Deep Learning*. Determination Press.

Niranjanamurthy, M., Nithya, B. N., & Jagannatha, S. (2019, November). Analysis of blockchain technology: Pros, cons and SWOT. *Cluster Computing*, *22*(S6), 14743–14757. doi:10.1007/s10586-018-2387-5

Niu, Y., Ying, L., Yang, J., Bao, M., & Sivaparthipan, C. B. (2021). Organizational business intelligence and decision making using big data analytics. *Information Processing & Management*, *58*(6), 102725. doi:10.1016/j.ipm.2021.102725

Noushabadi, E. M., Bahalke, U., Dolatkhahi, K., Dolatkhahi, S., & Makui, A. (2011). Simple assembly line balancing problem under task deterioration. *International Journal of Industrial Engineering Computations*, 583-592.

Nti, I. K., Adekoya, A. F., & Weyori, B. A. (2020). A comprehensive evaluation of ensemble learning for stock-market prediction. *Journal of Big Data*, *7*(1), 20. doi:10.1186/s40537-020-00299-5

O'Leary, D. E. (2013). Artificial intelligence and big data. *IEEE Intelligent Systems*, *28*(2), 96–99. doi:10.1109/MIS.2013.39

O'Reilly, T. (2019). *What is Data Science?* O'Reilly Media.

OlaniyiO. O.OkunleyeO. J.OlabanjiS. O. (2023). Advancing Data-Driven Decision-Making in Smart Cities through Big Data Analytics: A Comprehensive Review of Existing Literature. *Current Journal of Applied Science and Technology, 42*(25), 10-18. https://ssrn.com/abstract=4546193

Ortiz-Garces, I., Govea, J., Andrade, R. O., & Villegas-Ch, W. (2024). Optimising Chatbot Effectiveness through Advanced Syntactic Analysis: A Comprehensive Study in Natural Language Processing. *Applied Sciences (Basel, Switzerland)*, *14*(5), 1737. doi:10.3390/app14051737

Óskarsdóttir, M., Bravo, C., Sarraute, C., Vanthienen, J., & Baesens, B. (2019). The value of big data for credit scoring: Enhancing financial inclusion using mobile phone data and social network analytics. *Applied Soft Computing*, *74*, 26–39. doi:10.1016/j.asoc.2018.10.004

Otto, A., Otto, C., & Scholl, A. (2013). Systematic data generation and test design for solution algorithms on the example of SALBPGen for assembly line balancing. *European Journal of Operational Research*, 33-45. Obtenido de https://assembly-line-balancing.de/salbp/benchmark-data-sets-2013/

Padhy, C., & Raju, P. S. (2018). Stress among farmers and its alleviation. *Int J Manag Technol Eng*, *8*(12), 2882–2887.

Paine, T. L. (2017). *Practical considerations for deep learning*. Academic Press.

Pandey, A., & Parhi, D. R. (2017). Optimum path planning of mobile robot in unknown static and dynamic environments using Fuzzy-Wind Driven Optimization algorithm. *Defence Technology*, *13*(1), 47–58. doi:10.1016/j.dt.2017.01.001

Parada, W. V., Giraldo, F. A., & Londono, R. M. I. (2019). MDD based case tool for Automatic Generation of ChatBot. *2019 XLV Latin American Computing Conference (CLEI)*, 1-7. 10.1109/CLEI47609.2019.235059

Park, G., & Song, M. (2020). Predicting performances in business processes using deep neural networks. *Decision Support Systems*, *129*, 113191. doi:10.1016/j.dss.2019.113191

Patel, Y. (2019). *Cross channel fraud detection framework in financial services using recurrent neural networks* [Doctoral dissertation]. London Metropolitan University.

Patel, J., Shah, S., Thakkar, P., & Kotecha, K. (2015). Predicting stock and stock price index movement using trend deterministic data preparation and machine learning techniques. *Expert Systems with Applications*, *42*(1), 259–268. doi:10.1016/j.eswa.2014.07.040

Peng, C., Wu, G., Liao, T. W., & Wang, H. (2019). Research on multi-agent genetic algorithm based on tabu search for the job shop scheduling problem. *PLoS One*, *14*(9), e0223182. doi:10.1371/journal.pone.0223182 PMID:31560722

Pérez-Marin, D., & Pascual-Nieto, I. (2010). Overview of Interactive Genetic Programming Approaches for Conversational Agents. *Special Session on Computing Languages with Multi-Agent Systems and Bio-Inspired Devices*, *2*, 359–366.

Peshkin, M., & Colgate, E. (1999). Cobots. *Industrial Robot. International Journal (Toronto, Ont.)*, 335–341.

Pessach, D., & Shmueli, E. (2022). A review on Fairness in Machine Learning. *ACM Computing Surveys*, *55*(3), 1–44. doi:10.1145/3494672

Pintér, G., Mosavi, A., & Felde, I. (2020). *Artificial Intelligence for Modeling Real Estate Price Using Call Detail Records and Hybrid Machine Learning Approach*. Academic Press.

Pinto, P., Dannenbring, D., & Khumawala, B. M. (1975). A branch and bound algorithm for assembly line balancing with paralleling. *International Journal of Production Research*, *13*(2), 183–196. doi:10.1080/00207547508942985

Pitchai, R., Babu, S., Supraja, P., & Anjanayya, S. (2019). Prediction of availability and integrity of cloud data using soft computing technique. *Soft Computing*, *23*(18), 8555–8562. doi:10.1007/s00500-019-04008-0

Poornima, M., Kuyin, C., & Revathy, M. (2018). Brain Tumor Detection Using Genetic Algorithm. *International Journal of Scientific Research in Computer Science, Engineering and Information Technology*.

Pospieszny, P., Czarnacka-Chrobot, B., & Kobylinski, A. (2018). An effective approach for software project effort and duration estimation with machine learning algorithms. *Journal of Systems and Software*, *137*, 184–196. doi:10.1016/j.jss.2017.11.066

Power, D. J. (2007). *A brief history of decision support systems. DSSResources*. COM.

Provost, F., & Fawcett, T. (2013). *Data Science for Business: What You Need to Know about Data Mining and Data-Analytic Thinking*. O'Reilly Media.

Puangpontip, S., & Hewett, R. (2022). On Using Deep Learning for Business Analytics: At what cost? *Procedia Computer Science*, *207*, 3738–3747. doi:10.1016/j.procs.2022.09.434

Qolomany, B., Al-Fuqaha, A., Gupta, A., Benhaddou, D., Alwajidi, S., Qadir, J., & Fong, A. C. (2019). Leveraging machine learning and big data for smart buildings: A comprehensive survey. *IEEE Access : Practical Innovations, Open Solutions*, *7*, 90316–90356. doi:10.1109/ACCESS.2019.2926642

Quah, J. T. S., & Sriganesh, M. (2008). Real-time credit card fraud detection using computational intelligence. *Expert Systems with Applications*, *35*(4), 1721–1732. doi:10.1016/j.eswa.2007.08.093

Queiroz, M. M., Fosso Wamba, S., De Bourmont, M., & Telles, R. (2021). Blockchain adoption in operations and supply chain management: Empirical evidence from an emerging economy. *International Journal of Production Research*, *59*(20), 6087–6103. doi:10.1080/00207543.2020.1803511

Rai, M., Tyagi, N., Tripathi, P., Kumar, N., & Kumari, P. (2023). Advancement in Agricultural Techniques With the Introduction of Artificial Intelligence and Image Processing. In M. Khan, B. Gupta, A. Verma, P. Praveen, & C. Peoples (Eds.), *Smart Village Infrastructure and Sustainable Rural Communities* (pp. 47–68). IGI Global. doi:10.4018/978-1-6684-6418-2.ch004

Rajagopalan, S., & Iyer, S. S. (2022). Advancing Industrial Analytics Using Machine Learning (ML) and Mathematical Optimization. *2022 American Control Conference (ACC)*, 1065-1065. 10.23919/ACC53348.2022.9867615

Rajesh, V., Perumal, B., Ganesh, U. S., Rajkumar, V., Kumar, D. M., & Kumar, M. (2023). Building Customer Support Chatbots With Intent Recognition. *2023 2nd International Conference on Vision Towards Emerging Trends in Communication and Networking Technologies (ViTECoN)*, 1-5. 10.1109/ViTECoN58111.2023.10157329

Rajkomar, A., Dean, J., & Kohane, I. (2019). Machine learning in medicine. *The New England Journal of Medicine*, *380*(14), 1347–1358. doi:10.1056/NEJMra1814259 PMID:30943338

Ramanathan, P. (2014). Fuzzy Logic Controller for Temperature Regulation Process. *Middle East Journal of Scientific Research*, *20*(11), 1524–1528.

Ramya, J. B., & Alur, S. (2023). Unleashing the potential of chatbots in business: A bibliometric analysis. *Business Information Review*, *40*(3), 123–136. doi:10.1177/02663821231189344

Ravi, K., & Ravi, V. (2015). A survey on opinion mining and sentiment analysis: Tasks, approaches and applications. *Knowledge-Based Systems*, *89*, 14–46. doi:10.1016/j.knosys.2015.06.015

Razavi, S. (2021). Deep learning, explained: Fundamentals, explainability, and bridgeability to process-based modelling. *Environmental Modelling & Software*, *144*, 105159. doi:10.1016/j.envsoft.2021.105159

Ritt, M., & Costa, A. M. (2015). Improved integer programming models for simple assembly line balancing and related problems. *International Transactions in Operational Research*, 1-15.

Roh, Y., Heo, G., & Whang, S. E. (2021). A survey on Data Collection for Machine Learning: A Big Data - AI Integration Perspective. *IEEE Transactions on Knowledge and Data Engineering*, *33*(4), 1328–1347. doi:10.1109/TKDE.2019.2946162

Romero, C. A. T., Ortiz, J. H., Khalaf, O. I., & Prado, A. R. (2021). Business Intelligence: Business Evolution after Industry 4.0. *Sustainability (Basel)*, *13*(18), 10026. doi:10.3390/su131810026

Rosenblatt, F. (1957). *The perceptron, a perceiving and recognizing automaton. Project Para.* Cornell University.

Roshani, A., Roshani, A., Roshani, A., Mohsen, S., & Esfandyari, A. (2013). A simulated annealing algorithm for multi-manned assembly line balancing problem. *Journal of Manufacturing Systems*, *32*(1), 238–247. doi:10.1016/j.jmsy.2012.11.003

Rossit, D. A., Tohmé, F., & Frutos, M. (2018). An Industry 4.0 approach to assembly line resequencing. *International Journal of Advanced Manufacturing Technology*, 3619–3630.

Rumelhart, D. E., Hinton, G. E., & Williams, R. J. (1986). Learning representations by back-propagating errors. *Nature*, *323*(6088), 533–536. doi:10.1038/323533a0

Ryman-Tubb, N. F., Krause, P., & Garn, W. (2018). How Artificial Intelligence and machine learning research impacts payment card fraud detection: A survey and industry benchmark. *Engineering Applications of Artificial Intelligence*, *76*, 130–157. doi:10.1016/j.engappai.2018.07.008

Sabuncuoglu, I., Erel, E., & Tanyer, M. (2000). Assembly line balancing using genetic algorithms. *Journal of Intelligent Manufacturing*, *11*(3), 295–310. doi:10.1023/A:1008923410076

Saeidi, S. (2018). Solving the Rubik's Cube using Simulated Annealing and Genetic Algorithm. *International Journal of Education and Management Engineering*, *8*(1), 1–10. doi:10.5815/ijeme.2018.01.01

Sahija, D. (2021). *Critical review of machine learning integration with augmented reality for discrete manufacturing*. Independent Researcher and Enterprise Solution Manager in Leading Digital Transformation Agency.

Sahin, Y., & Duman, E. (2011). Detecting credit card fraud by decision trees and support vector machines. *Lecture Notes in Engineering and Computer Science, 2188*(1).

Sai Pranav, D., Mutreja, M., Punj, D., & Chawla, P. (2023). *Natural Language Processing in Chatbots*. doi:10.1007/978-981-19-4193-1_9

Salazar-Ramirez, A., Irigoyen, E., & Martinez, R. (2014). Enhancements for a robust fuzzy detection of stress. In *International Joint Conference SOCO'14-CISIS'14-ICEUTE'14* (pp. 229-238). Springer. 10.1007/978-3-319-07995-0_23

Salveson, M. E. (1955). The Assembly Line Balancing Problem. *The Journal of Industrial Engineering*, 18-15.

Samuel, J., Ali, G. M. N., Rahman, M. M., Esawi, E., & Samuel, Y. (2020). Covid-19 public sentiment insights and machine learning for tweets classification. *Information (Basel)*, *11*(6), 314. doi:10.3390/info11060314

Sangaiah, A. K., Goli, A., Tirkolaee, E. B., Ranjbar-Bourani, M., Pandey, H. M., & Zhang, W. (2020). Big Data-Driven Cognitive Computing System for Optimization of Social Media Analytics. *IEEE Access : Practical Innovations, Open Solutions*, *8*, 82215–82226. doi:10.1109/ACCESS.2020.2991394

Sao, A., Kumar, A., Bapat, G., Khan, M. S., & Singh, S. (2023). Analysing Customer Loyalty, Customer Satisfaction and Service Quality at DLF Mall of India. *Marketing and Management of Innovations*, *14*(1), 146–157. doi:10.21272/mmi.2023.1-13

Sarkar, S., & Kedas, S. (2023). Globally distributed talent communities: A typology of innovation problems and talent characteristics. *Thunderbird International Business Review*, *65*(1), 89–102. doi:10.1002/tie.22272

Sarker, I. H. (2021). Data Science and Analytics: An Overview from Data-Driven Smart Computing, Decision-Making and Applications Perspective. *SN Computer Science*, *2*(5), 377. doi:10.1007/s42979-021-00765-8 PMID:34278328

Sarker, I. H., Abushark, Y. B., Alsolami, F., & Khan, A. (2020). Intrudtree: A machine learning based cyber security intrusion detection model. *Symmetry*, *12*(5), 754. doi:10.3390/sym12050754

Sarker, I. H., Watters, P., & Kayes, A. S. M. (2019). Effectiveness analysis of machine learning classification models for predicting personalized context-aware smartphone usage. *Journal of Big Data*, *6*(1), 1–28. doi:10.1186/s40537-019-0219-y

Sarode, P. V., Joshi, B., Savakare, T., & Warule, H. (2023). A Real Time Chatbot Using Python. *International Journal for Research in Applied Science and Engineering Technology*, *11*(5), 7385–7389. doi:10.22214/ijraset.2023.53453

Sarode, S., Tolani, H. G., Kak, P., & Lifna, C. S. (2019). Stock price prediction using machine learning techniques. *Proceedings of the International Conference on Intelligent Sustainable Systems, ICISS 2019*, 177–181. 10.1109/ISS1.2019.8907958

Sawhney, A., Bhatia, R., & Mahajan, P. (2014). Congestion Control in Wireless Communication Network Using Fuzzy Logic and Machine Learning Techniques. *International Journal of Advanced Research in Electrical, Electronics and Instrumentation Engineering, 3*(11).

Saxena, A. (2022). AI-Based Chatbot. *International Journal for Research in Applied Science and Engineering Technology*, *10*(12), 941–942. doi:10.22214/ijraset.2022.47785

Sazli, M. H. (2006). *A brief review of feed-forward neural networks.* Communications Faculty of Sciences University of Ankara Series A2-A3 Physical Sciences and Engineering, 50(01).

Schmidhuber, J. (2015). Deep learning in neural networks: An overview. *Neural Networks*, *61*, 85–117. doi:10.1016/j.neunet.2014.09.003 PMID:25462637

Schmitt, J., Bönig, J., Borggräfe, T., Beitinger, G., & Deuse, J. (2020). Predictive model-based quality inspection using Machine Learning and Edge Cloud Computing. *Advanced Engineering Informatics*, *45*, 101101. doi:10.1016/j.aei.2020.101101

Schmitt, M. (2023). Automated machine learning: AI-driven decision making in business analytics. *Intelligent Systems with Applications*, *18*, 200188. doi:10.1016/j.iswa.2023.200188

Schmitt, M. (2023). Deep learning in business analytics: A clash of expectations and reality. *International Journal of Information Management Data Insights*, *3*(1), 100146. doi:10.1016/j.jjimei.2022.100146

Schneiderman, N., Ironson, G., & Siegel, S. D. (2005). Stress and health: Psychological, behavioral, and biological determinants. *Annual Review of Clinical Psychology*, *1*(1), 607–628. doi:10.1146/annurev.clinpsy.1.102803.144141 PMID:17716101

Scholl, A., Fliedner, M., & Boysen, N. (2008). Balancing assembly lines with assignment restrictions. *Jena Research Papers in Business and Economics*, 1-27.

Scholl, A., & Vob, S. (1996). Simple Assembly Line Balancing-Heuristic Approaches. *Journal of Heuristics*, 217–244.

Schönfeld, P., Brailovskaia, J., Bieda, A., Zhang, X. C., & Margraf, J. (2016). The effects of daily stress on positive and negative mental health: Mediation through self-efficacy. *International Journal of Clinical and Health Psychology*, *16*(1), 1–10. doi:10.1016/j.ijchp.2015.08.005 PMID:30487845

Schuurmans, D., & Southey, F. (2001). Local search characteristics of in- complete SAT procedures. *Artificial Intelligence*, *132*(2), 121–150. doi:10.1016/S0004-3702(01)00151-5

Sekulic, M., Pejic, V., Brezocnik, M., Gostimirović, M., & Hadzistevic, M. (2018). Prediction of surface roughness in the ball-end milling process using response surface methodology, genetic algorithms, and grey wolf optimizer algorithm. *Advances in Production Engineering & Management*, *13*(1), 18–30. doi:10.14743/apem2018.1.270

Sengupta, S., Basak, S., Saikia, P., Paul, S., Tsalavoutis, V., Atiah, F., Ravi, V., & Peters, A. (2020). A review of deep learning with special emphasis on architectures, applications and recent trends. *Knowledge-Based Systems*, *194*, 105596. doi:10.1016/j.knosys.2020.105596

Sepahi, A., & Jalali, S. G. (2014). Multi-manned Assembly Line Balancing Problem with Variable Task Times. *European Journal of Academic Essays*, 68-75.

Seyedan, M., & Mafakheri, F. (2020). Predictive big data analytics for supply chain demand forecasting: Methods, applications, and research opportunities. *Journal of Big Data*, *7*(1), 53. doi:10.1186/s40537-020-00329-2

Seyedhossein, L., & Hashemi, M. R. (2011). Mining information from credit card time series for timelier fraud detection. *International Symposium on Telecommunications IEEE*, 619-624.

Shah, D., Isah, H., & Zulkernine, F. (2019). Stock market analysis: A review and taxonomy of prediction techniques. *International Journal of Financial Studies*, *7*(2), 26. doi:10.3390/ijfs7020026

Shah, S. J. H. (2023). *Chatbots for Business and Customer Support*. doi:10.4018/978-1-6684-6234-8.ch009

Sharma, M., & Sharma, P. K. (2017). Comparative study of assembly line balancing using plant simulation software with ranked position weight method. *International Journal of Recent Technology Science & Management*, 1-16.

Shashi, C., Centobelli, P., Cerchione, R., & Ertz, M. (2020). Managing supply chain resilience to pursue business and environmental strategies. *Business Strategy and the Environment*, *29*(3), 1215–1246. doi:10.1002/bse.2428

Shayaa, S., Jaafar, N. I., Bahri, S., Sulaiman, A., Wai, P. S., Chung, Y. W., ... Al-Garadi, M. A. (2018). Sentiment analysis of big data: Methods, applications, and open challenges. *IEEE Access : Practical Innovations, Open Solutions*, *6*, 37807–37827. doi:10.1109/ACCESS.2018.2851311

Shi, E., Niu, Y., Jakobsson, M., & Chow, R. (2010). Implicit Authentication through Learning User Behavior. *International Conference on Information Security* (Vol.6531, pp.99-113). Springer Verlag. 10.1007/978-3-642-18178-8_9

Shinde, P. P., & Shah, S. (2018, August). A review of machine learning and deep learning applications. In *2018 Fourth international conference on computing communication control and automation (ICCUBEA)* (pp. 1-6). IEEE. 10.1109/ICCUBEA.2018.8697857

Shumanov, M., & Johnson, L. (2021). Making conversations with chatbots more personalised. *Computers in Human Behavior*, *117*, 106627. doi:10.1016/j.chb.2020.106627

Silva, S. H., & Najafirad, P. (2020). Opportunities and challenges in deep learning adversarial robustness: A survey. *arXiv preprint arXiv:2007.00753.*

Silver, D., Huang, A., Maddison, C. J., Guez, A., Sifre, L., Van Den Driessche, G., . . . Hassabis, D. (2016). Mastering Chess and Shogi by Self-Play with a General Reinforcement Learning Algorithm. *arXiv preprint arXiv:1712.01815.*

Singh, A., Dwivedi, A. (2023). *Integrating Machine Learning in Business Decision Making: Application and Future directions*. doi:10.1109/ICCIKE58312.2023.10131790

Singh, P. K. (2021). Deploy machine learning models to production. In Apress eBooks. doi:10.1007/978-1-4842-6546-8

Singh, S., Madan, T. K., Kumar, J., & Singh, A. K. (2019). Stock Market Forecasting using Machine Learning: Today and Tomorrow. *2019 2nd International Conference on Intelligent Computing, Instrumentation and Control Technologies, ICICICT 2019*, 738–745. 10.1109/ICICICT46008.2019.8993160

Singh, R. K., Verma, V. K., Kumar, N., Agarwal, P., & Tiwari, S. (2023). Time series forecasting of stock price of AirAsia Berhad using ARIMA model during COVID- 19. *Journal of Statistics and Management Systems*, *26*(6), 1421–1429. doi:10.47974/JSMS-1189

Singh, S., Singh, S., Koohang, A., Sharma, A., & Dhir, S. (2023). Soft computing in business: Exploring current research and outlining future research directions. *Industrial Management & Data Systems*, *123*(8), 2079–2127. doi:10.1108/IMDS-02-2023-0126

Sodré, W. da S. M., & Duarte, J. C. (2023). Chatbot Optimisation using Sentiment Analysis and Timeline Navigation. *Revista de Informática Teórica e Aplicada*, *30*(1), 32–43. doi:10.22456/2175-2745.125825

Sophia, M. E., & Chiemeke, S. (2016). *A Performance Evaluation of Call Resolution Oriented Routing Rules to Enhance Resolution Rates*. Mesopotamian Journal of Computer Science and Communications.

Sorell, T. (2022). Cobots, "co-operation" and the replacement of human skill. *Ethics and Information Technology*, *24*(4), 1–12. doi:10.1007/s10676-022-09667-6

Sotskov, Y. N. (2023). Assembly and Production Line Designing, Balancing and Scheduling with Inaccurate Data: A Survey and Perspectives. *Algorithms MDPI*, 1-43.

Sowa, K., Przegalinska, A., & Ciechanowski, L. (2021). Cobots in knowledge work Human – AI collaboration in managerial professions. *Journal of Business Research*, *125*, 135–142. doi:10.1016/j.jbusres.2020.11.038

Speiser, J. L., Miller, M. E., Tooze, J., & Ip, E. (2019). A comparison of random forest variable selection methods for classification prediction modeling. *Expert Systems with Applications*, *134*, 93–101. doi:10.1016/j.eswa.2019.05.028 PMID:32968335

Srivastava, A., Kundu, A., Sural, S., & Majumdar, A. (2008). Credit card fraud detection using hidden markov model. *IEEE Transactions on Dependable and Secure Computing*, *5*(1), 37–48. doi:10.1109/TDSC.2007.70228

Strickland, E. (2019). IBM Watson, heal thyself: How IBM overpromised and underdelivered on AI health care. *IEEE Spectrum*, *56*(4), 24–31. doi:10.1109/MSPEC.2019.8678513

Subaşı, A. (2020). Machine learning techniques. In Elsevier eBooks (pp. 91–202). doi:10.1016/B978-0-12-821379-7.00003-5

Subasi, A., Amir, F., Bagedo, K., Shams, A., & Sarirete, A. (2021). Stock Market Prediction Using Machine Learning. *Procedia Computer Science*, *194*, 173–179. doi:10.1016/j.procs.2021.10.071

Sundar, R. (2024). Future Directions of Artificial Intelligence Integration: Managing Strategies and Opportunities. *Journal of Intelligent & Fuzzy Systems*. Advance online publication. doi:10.3233/JIFS-238830

Supriya, Y., & Gadekallu, T. R. (2023). A Survey on Soft Computing Techniques for Federated Learning-Applications, Challenges and Future Directions. *ACM Journal of Data and Information Quality*, *15*(2), 1–28. doi:10.1145/3575810

Sutskever, I. (2013). *Training recurrent neural networks*. University of Toronto.

Sutton, R. S. (1992). Introduction: The challenge of reinforcement learning. *Machine Learning*, *8*(3–4), 225–227. doi:10.1007/BF00992695

Sutton, R. S., & Barto, A. G. (2005). Reinforcement Learning: An Introduction. *IEEE Transactions on Neural Networks*, *16*(1), 285–286. doi:10.1109/TNN.2004.842673

Sutton, R. S., & Barto, A. G. (2018). *Reinforcement Learning: An Introduction*. MIT Press.

Svozil, D., Kvasnicka, V., & Pospichal, J. (1997). Introduction to multi-layer feed-forward neural networks. *Chemometrics and Intelligent Laboratory Systems*, *39*(1), 43–62. doi:10.1016/S0169-7439(97)00061-0

Talbot, F. B., & Patterson, J. H. (1984). An Integer Programming Algorithm with Network Cuts for Solving the Assembly Line Balancing Problem. *Management Science*, *30*(1), 85–99. doi:10.1287/mnsc.30.1.85

Taleb, N. N. (2007). *The Black Swan: The Impact of the Highly Improbable*. Random House.

Tang, L., & Meng, Y. (2020). Data analytics and optimization for smart industry. *Frontiers of Engineering Management.*, *8*(2), 157–171. doi:10.1007/s42524-020-0126-0

Tantalaki, N., Souravlas, S., & Roumeliotis, M. (2019). Data-driven decision making in precision agriculture: The rise of big data in agricultural systems. *Journal of Agricultural & Food Information*, *20*(4), 344–380. doi:10.1080/10496505.2019.1638264

Taouche, R. (2019). Fuzzy Logic Prediction of Stress-Strain Behavior Parameters of Two-Phase Materials. Application to WC-Co System. *Australian Journal of Basic and Applied Sciences*, *13*(6), 74–81.

Tárkányi, G., Tényi, Á., Hollós, R., Kalmar, P., & Szapáry, L. (2022). Optimization of Large Vessel Occlusion Detection in Acute Ischemic Stroke Using Machine Learning Methods. *Life (Chicago, Ill.)*, *12*(2), 230. doi:10.3390/life12020230 PMID:35207517

Thakur, R. (2024). Introduction to artificial intelligence and its importance in modern business management. In *Leveraging AI and emotional intelligence in contemporary business organizations* (pp. 133–165). IGI Global.

Thelwall, M. (2018). Dimensions: A competitor to Scopus and the Web of Science? *Journal of Informetrics*, *12*(2), 430–435. doi:10.1016/j.joi.2018.03.006

Thennakoon, A., Bhagyani, C., Premadasa, S., Mihiranga, S., & Kuruwitaarachchi, N. (2019, January). Real-time credit card fraud detection using machine learning. In *2019 9th International Conference on Cloud Computing, Data Science & Engineering (Confluence)* (pp. 488-493). IEEE. 10.1109/CONFLUENCE.2019.8776942

Thi Phuong Anh, L., & Rajah, E. (2022). Using Chatbots in Customer Service: A Case Study of Air New Zealand. *Proceedings: Rangahau Horonuku Hou - New Research Landscapes, Unitec/MIT Research Symposium 2021,* 161-176. 10.34074/proc.2206011

Thibaud, M., Chi, H., Zhou, W., & Piramuthu, S. (2018). Internet of Things (IoT) in high-risk Environment, Health and Safety (EHS) industries: A comprehensive review. *Decision Support Systems*, *108*, 79–95. doi:10.1016/j.dss.2018.02.005

Tomar, A., & Manoria, A. (2016). Increasing Line efficiency with COMSOAL, RPW and LCR Methods of Assembly Line Balancing Problem. *International Journal of Software & Hardware Research in Engineering*, 23-27.

Tomasevic, N., Gvozdenovic, N., & Vranes, S. (2020). An overview and comparison of supervised data mining techniques for student exam performance prediction. *Computers & Education, 143*, 103676. doi:10.1016/j.compedu.2019.103676

Torii, M., Wagholikar, K. B., & Liu, H. (2011). Using machine learning for concept extraction on clinical documents from multiple data sources. *Journal of the American Medical Informatics Association : JAMIA, 18*(5), 580–587. doi:10.1136/amiajnl-2011-000155 PMID:21709161

Torres-Salomao, L. A., Mahfouf, M., & Obajemu, O. (2014). Interval type-2 fuzzy logic adaptive modelling for human operators undergoing mental stress. *IFAC Proceedings Volumes, 47*(3), 9880-9885.

Tounsi, M., & David, P. (2002). Local search algorithm to improve the local search. *14th IEEE International Conference on Tools with Artificial Intelligence, 2002. (ICTAI 2002)*, 438-443. 10.1109/TAI.2002.1180836

Tripathi, P. (2020). Electroencephalpgram Signal Quality Enhancement by Total Variation Denoising Using Non-convex Regulariser. *International Journal of Biomedical Engineering and Technology, 33*(2), 134–145. doi:10.1504/IJBET.2020.107709

Tripathi, P., Kumar, N., Paroha, K. K., Rai, M., & Panda, M. K. (2024). Applications of Deep Learning in Healthcare in the Framework of Industry 5.0. In M. Khan, R. Khan, P. Praveen, A. R. Verma, & M. K. Panda (Eds.), *Infrastructure Possibilities and Human-Centered Approaches With Industry 5.0* (pp. 215–230). IGI Global. doi:10.4018/979-8-3693-0782-3.ch005

Tripathi, P., Kumar, N., Rai, M., & Khan, A. (2022). *Applications of Deep Learning in Agriculture. In Artificial Intelligence Applications in Agriculture and Food Quality Improvement.* IGI Global. doi:10.4018/978-1-6684-5141-0.ch002

Tripathi, P., Kumar, N., Rai, M., Shukla, P. K., & Verma, K. N. (2023). Applications of Machine Learning in Agriculture. In M. Khan, B. Gupta, A. Verma, P. Praveen, & C. Peoples (Eds.), *Smart Village Infrastructure and Sustainable Rural Communities* (pp. 99–118). IGI Global. doi:10.4018/978-1-6684-6418-2.ch006

Tripathi, P., & Siddiqi, A. H. (2016). Denoising Raman spectra using a non-Convex regularizer in Total Variation. *Indian Journal of Science and Technology, 9*(48), 1–5. doi:10.17485/ijst/2016/v9i48/99920

Tripathi, S., & Siddiqi, A. H. (2016). Solution of Inverse Problem for de-noising Raman Spectral Data with Total variation using Majorization-Minimization Algorithm *Int. J. Computing Science and Mathematics, 7*(3), 274–282. doi:10.1504/IJCSM.2016.077855

Turban, E., Sharda, R., Delen, D., & Aronson, J. E. (2011). *Decision Support and Business Intelligence Systems*. Prentice Hall.

Turkson, R. E., Baagyere, E. Y., & Wenya, G. E. (2016, September). A machine learning approach for predicting bank credit worthiness. In *2016 Third International Conference on Artificial Intelligence and Pattern Recognition (AIPR)* (pp. 1-7). IEEE. 10.1109/ICAIPR.2016.7585216

Tyagi, N., Rai, M., Sahw, P., Tripathi, P., & Kumar, N. (2022). *Methods for the Recognition of Human Emotions Based on Physiological Response: Facial Expressions in Smart Healthcare for Sustainable Urban Development*. IGI Global. doi:10.4018/978-1-6684-2508-4.ch013

Vaishnav, P., Choudhary, N., & Jain, K. (2017). Traveling salesman problem using genetic algorithm: A survey. *International Journal of Scientific Research in Computer Science. Engineering and Information Technology*, *2*(3), 105–108.

van Eck, N. J., & Waltman, L. (2010). Software survey: VOSviewer, a computer program for bibliometric mapping. *Scientometrics*, *84*(2), 523–538. doi:10.1007/s11192-009-0146-3 PMID:20585380

van Eck, N. J., Waltman, L., Dekker, R., & van den Berg, J. (2010). A comparison of two techniques for bibliometric mapping: Multidimensional scaling and VOS. *Journal of the American Society for Information Science and Technology*, *61*(12), 2405–2416. doi:10.1002/asi.21421

Vaswani, A., Shazeer, N., Parmar, N., Uszkoreit, J., Jones, L., Gomez, A. N., . . . Polosukhin, I. (2017). Attention is all you need. In Advances in neural information processing systems (pp. 5998-6008). Academic Press.

Veerendra, P., & Rao, T. (2021). Optimized scheduling techniques focused on powerful heuristics leveraging cloud services soft computing. *International Journal of Pervasive Computing and Communications*, *18*(1), 5–17.

Vijh, M., Chandola, D., Tikkiwal, V. A., & Kumar, A. (2020). Stock Closing Price Prediction using Machine Learning Techniques. *Procedia Computer Science*, *167*, 599–606. doi:10.1016/j.procs.2020.03.326

Vikhar, P. A. (2016, December). Evolutionary algorithms: A critical review and its future prospects. In *2016 International conference on global trends in signal processing, information computing and communication (ICGTSPICC)* (pp. 261-265). IEEE. 10.1109/ICGTSPICC.2016.7955308

W. K. (2023). *Scheduling in queueing systems*. Cambridge Core.

Wang, S., Liu, W., Wu, J., Cao, L., Meng, Q., & Kennedy, P. J. (2016, July). Training deep neural networks on imbalanced data sets. In 2016 international joint conference on neural networks (IJCNN) (pp. 4368-4374). IEEE. doi:10.1109/IJCNN.2016.7727770

Wang, R. Y., & Strong, D. M. (1996). Beyond accuracy: What data quality means to data consumers. *Journal of Management Information Systems*, *12*(4), 5–33. doi:10.1080/07421222.1996.11518099

Weckenborg, C., Kieckha¨fer, K., Müller, C., Grunewald, M., & Spengler, T. (2019). Balancing of assembly lines with collaborative robots. *Business Research*, 1-40.

Weerts, H., Mueller, A., & Vanschoren, J. (2020). Importance of tuning hyperparameters of machine learning algorithms. *arXiv (Cornell University)*. http://export.arxiv.org/pdf/2007.07588

Wheelan, C. (2013). *Naked Statistics: Stripping the Dread from the Data*. W. W. Norton & Company.

Whitley, D., Rana, S., Dzubera, J., & Mathias, K. E. (1996). Evaluating evolutionary algorithms. *Artificial Intelligence*, *85*(1-2), 245–276. doi:10.1016/0004-3702(95)00124-7

Witten, I. H., & Frank, E. (2005). *Data Mining: Practical machine learning tools and techniques*. Morgan Kaufmann.

Wolff, D., & Echterling, F. (2024). Stock picking with machine learning. *Journal of Forecasting*, *43*(1), 81–102. doi:10.1002/for.3021

Wolfinger, R., Fotrousi, F., & Maalej, W. (2022). A Chatbot for the Elicitation of Contextual Information from User Feedback. *2022 IEEE 30th International Requirements Engineering Conference (RE)*, 272-273. 10.1109/RE54965.2022.00040

Wu, X., Chen, H., Wang, J., Troiano, L., Loia, V., & Fujita, H. (2020). Adaptive stock trading strategies with deep reinforcement learning methods. *Information Sciences*, *538*, 142–158. doi:10.1016/j.ins.2020.05.066

Xin, D., Miao, H., Parameswaran, A. G., & Polyzotis, N. (2021). *Production Machine Learning Pipelines: Empirical Analysis and Optimization Opportunities*. ACM Digital Library.

Xu, L. D., & Duan, L. (2019). Big data for cyber physical systems in industry 4.0: A survey. *Enterprise Information Systems*, *13*(2), 148–169. doi:10.1080/17517575.2018.1442934

Yin, Q., & Luo, X. (2020). A Three-Stage Optimization Method for Assembly Line Balancing Problem. *IEEE Access : Practical Innovations, Open Solutions*, *8*, 143607–143621. doi:10.1109/ACCESS.2020.3014269

Zakaraia, M., Zaher, H., & Ragaa, N. (2021). Solving Stochastic Multi-Manned U-Shaped Assembly Line Balancing Problem using differential evolution algorithm. *International Journal of Production Management and Engineering*, 13-22.

Zakaraia, M., Zaher, H., & Ragaa, N. (2021). Stochastic Local Search for Solving Chance-Constrained Multi-Manned U-shaped Assembly Line Balancing Problem with Time and Space Constraints. *Journal of University of Shanghai for Science and Technology*, 278-295.

Zakaria, E. (2017). Solving Assembly Line Balancing Problem Using A Hybrid Genetic Algorithm With Zoning Constraints. *International Journal of Business and Management Invention*, 34-40.

Zamzam, N., & Elakkad, A. (2021). Time and Space Multi-Manned Assembly Line Balancing Problem Using Genetic Algorithm. *Journal of Industrial Engineering and Management*, *14*(4), 733–749. doi:10.3926/jiem.3542

Zamzam, N., Sadek, Y., Afia, N., & El-Kharbotly, A. (2015). Multi-Manned Assembly Line Balancing using Genetic Algorithm. *International Journal of Engineering Research & Technology (Ahmedabad)*, 56–61.

Zhang, C., & Lu, Y. (2021). Study on artificial intelligence: The state of the art and future prospects. *Journal of Industrial Information Integration*, *23*, 100224. doi:10.1016/j.jii.2021.100224

Zhang, L., Tan, J., Han, D., & Zhu, H. (2017). From machine learning to deep learning: Progress in machine intelligence for rational drug discovery. *Drug Discovery Today*, *22*(11), 1680–1685. doi:10.1016/j.drudis.2017.08.010 PMID:28881183

Zhang, X., Hu, Z., & Mahadevan, S. (2020). Bilevel optimization model for resilient configuration of logistics service centers. *IEEE Transactions on Reliability*, *71*(1), 469–483. doi:10.1109/TR.2020.2996025

Zhang, Z. (2016). Introduction to machine learning: K-nearest neighbors. *Annals of Translational Medicine*, *4*(11), 218. doi:10.21037/atm.2016.03.37 PMID:27386492

Zhao, H., & Kong, F. (2016). Research and Applications of Shop Scheduling Based on Genetic Algorithms. *Brazilian Archives of Biology and Technology*, *59*(spe), 59. doi:10.1590/1678-4324-2016160545

Zhaohao, S. (2019). Intelligent Big Data Analytics: A Managerial Perspective. In Managerial Perspectives on Intelligent Big Data Analytics (pp. 1-19). doi:10.4018/978-1-5225-7277-0.ch001

Zhao, R., Wang, D., Yan, R., Mao, K., Shen, F., & Wang, J. (2017). Machine health monitoring using local feature-based gated recurrent unit networks. *IEEE Transactions on Industrial Electronics*, *65*(2), 1539–1548. doi:10.1109/TIE.2017.2733438

Zhong, R., Xu, X., & Wang, L. (2017). Food supply chain management: Systems, implementations, and future research. *Industrial Management & Data Systems*, *117*(9), 2085–2114. doi:10.1108/IMDS-09-2016-0391

About the Contributors

Nitendra Kumar received a PhD (Mathematics) from Sharda University, Greater Noida, India and a Master of Science (Mathematics and Statistics) from Dr Ram Manohar Lohia Avadh University, Faizabad, India. Currently, he is working as an Assistant Professor at Department of Decision Sciences, Amity University, Noida with interests in the Business Analytics, Time Series Analysis, Wavelets and its Variants, Health Informatics, Artificial Intelligence, Fractional Derivatives and Statistical Methods. He has more than 11 years of experience in his research areas. Dr Kumar has published many research papers in reputed journals and also published 6 books on engineering mathematics. He contributes to the research community by undertaking various volunteer activities in the capacity of editor for two edited books, Guest Editor of reputed indexed journals.

Priyanka Agarwal, Ph.D. in Management, has more than two decades of experience in research, industry, and academia and is presently associated as Associate Professor with Amity Business School, Amity University, Uttar Pradesh in the area of HR, OB & Psychology. She has been in the reviewer panel for conferences and has contributed to the Research community by collaborating with editorial board of special issues of UGC CARE, SCOPUS and WOS journals. She is a keen researcher and published research papers, case studies, book chapters in journals and books of repute . She has two edited books to her credit. Few of her research interests include Multi-generations in the Workplace, optimization in HR, diversity and inclusion, employee engagement, emerging trends in business analytics . In addition to her expertise in teaching and research, her key role includes mentoring and grooming budding managers, being the Programme leader of MBA Programme over the last few years. She is also associate editor of Amity Journal of Entrepreneurship and Leadership. She brings in a good blend of professional expertise and humane approach that makes her quite accessible.

* * *

Gustavo Erick Anaya Fuentes received the degree of Bachelor of Industrial Engineering, Master of Science in Industrial Engineering and Doctor of Science in Industrial Engineering from the Autonomous University of the State of Hidalgo in the years 2007, 2013 and 2017, respectively. He is currently a Research Professor of the Academic Area of Engineering assigned to the Institute of Basic Sciences and Engineering of the Autonomous University of Hidalgo. He is a candidate for national researcher by the SNII and has Desirable Profile Recognition by PRODEP. His research interest includes optimization, productivity, logistics and production planning.

Sayantan Dass holds the position of Assistant Professor at Techno India (Hooghly Campus) while concurrently engaging in research as a scholar in the Department of Computer Science and Engineering at Maulana Abul Kalam Azad University of Technology. With proficiency in teaching and research, he plays a pivotal role in advancing computer science education and fostering innovation.

Dwijendra Nath Dwivedi is a professional with 20+ years of subject matter expertise creating right value propositions for analytics and AI. He currently heads the EMEA+AP AI and IoT team at SAS, a worldwide frontrunner in AI technology. He is a post-Graduate in Economics from Indira Gandhi Institute of Development and Research and currently perusing PHD from crackow university of economics Poland. He has presented his research in more than 20 international conference and published several Scopus indexed paper on AI adoption in many areas. As an author he has contributed to more than 8 books and has more than 25 publications in high impact journals. He conducts AI Value seminars and workshops for the executive audience and for power users.

Revathy G. is working as Assistant Professor in Department of CSE, SRC, SASTRA Deemed University. She has around 15 years of teaching experience.

Vishal Goar is currently working as Dean of Research at Bikaner Technical University, Bikaner. He has wide experience of 17 years as an academician, researcher and in Industry. He has published 46 research papers in international journals (SCI/Scopus/WoS) and presented 45 papers in national/international conferences. He has been editor/authored 13 books including reference, text and edited books of Springer, Singapore, ACM USA and Scholars-Press, Germany. He has published two patents and 3 patents grants in his credit. He supervised 6 PhD research scholars in area of cloud computing, software development, Neural Networks and Deep Learning. He also served as Organizing Chair, Convener, Publicity Chair of various Springer/IEEE/ACM internationally renowned conferences.

Norberto Hernández-Romero received the M.S. degree from Deparment of Electrical Engineering, Laguna Technological Institute at Mexico, in 2001 and the Ph. D. in industrial engineering from Autonomous University of Hidalgo State at Mexico in 2009. Currently, he is a professor of the Advanced Research in Industrial Engineering Center at Autonomous University of Hidalgo State at Mineral de la Reforma, Hidalgo, Mexico. His current interests include system identification, evolutionary computing, fuzzy logic, neural networks and its applications.

N. S. Kavitha is working as an Assistant Professor in the Department of Information Technology at Dr. N.G.P. Institute of Technology, N.G.P. Nagar, Kalapatti, Coimbatore. Completed U.G. in KSRCT and P.G.in Kongu Engineering College. Completed Ph.D under Anna University, Chennai in the year 2022. Area of interest includes Wireless Sensor Network and Machine Learning. Published about 15 papers in various National and International Journals. Total years of experience of about 12.5 years in Engineering.

Nitendra Kumar received a PhD (Mathematics) from Sharda University, Greater Noida, India and a Master of Science (Mathematics and Statistics) from Dr Ram Manohar Lohia Avadh University, Faizabad, India. Currently, he is working as an Assistant Professor at Amity Business School, Amity University, Noida with interests in Wavelets and its Variants, Data Mining, Inverse Problems, Epidemic Modeling, Fractional Derivatives Business Analytics, and Statistical Methods. He has more than 10 years of experience in his research areas. Dr Kumar has published many research papers in reputed journals and also published 6 books on engineering mathematics. He contributes to the research community by undertaking various volunteer activities in the capacity of editor for two edited books and guest Editor of reputed journals.

Reeta Mishra is a highly accomplished professional specializing in Computer Science and Engineering. She completed her M.Tech from Subharti University and is currently pursuing a Ph.D. at Manav Rachna University. With over 11 years of teaching experience, she is currently associated with Delhi Technical Campus in Greater Noida. Her research focuses on Cyber security, Machine Learning, Data Learning, Data Science, Federated Learning, and Meta heuristic Algorithms. Reeta possesses advanced programming skills in Python, OpenCV, and Tensor Flow. Her dedication to research is evident through numerous published papers in national and international journals and presentations at conferences. At Delhi Technical

Campus, Reeta contributes significantly to the academic environment, mentoring students and fostering a passion for computer science. Her expertise in cutting-edge technologies, combined with a wealth of teaching experience, makes her a valuable asset to the academic community. She also commitment to advancing knowledge in computer science through research and education underscores her position as a leading professional in the field.

Soumya Mukherjee is Associate Professor in Business Administration at Techno India (Hooghly Campus), Chinsurah, West Bengal. He is an accomplished educator with demonstrated ability and experience to teach, motivate, and direct students while maintaining high interest and achievement. He has authored three books and has several research articles in journal and conference proceedings to his credit.

Surya Kant Pal is working as an Assistant Professor in the Department of Mathematics, SSBSR, Sharda University. Dr. Pal Holds M.Phil. & Ph.D. in Statistics from Vikram University Ujjain. He has worked with institutions like SMV Collage, BFIT-Groups of Institutions, the University of Petroleum and Energy Studies, and Chandigarh University. He is an expert in Statistics, Regression Analysis, Predictive Analytics, Multivariate Data Analysis, Artificial Intelligence, Machine learning, Deep Learning, Data Mining, and Data Science & Analytics. On the research front, His research focused on Statistics & Analytics. He has MS Office, SPSS 20.0, R, and Python Software expertise. His research includes Statistical Techniques, Sampling Theory, Multivariate Analysis, AI, ML & DL, and Data mining. He has published 5+ patents, 80+ research papers in Journals of National & International repute, and 10+ book chapters. He is not only known in India but famous in abroad too, serving as editor & reviewer of more than 30 reputed International /National Journals.

Maheshwar Pathak is working as associate professor in the department of mathematics at Sharda university, India. It has been since 2007 that he has been actively involved in research and development. He has been working in the field of numerical analysis and special functions. He has published many research papers in high ranked journals. He completed his doctoral program from Motilal Nehru National Institute of Technology Allahabad in 2011.

Hector Rivera-Gomez obtained the degree of Doctor of Engineering from the École du Technologie Supérieure, in Montreal, Canada. In 2007, he obtained a Master of Science degree in Industrial Engineering from the Hidalgo state University, UAEH. He received his bachelor's degree in Industrial Engineering from the UAEH. He is a researcher at the UAEH in the Academic Area of Engineering since 2014. In 2019 he completed a post-doctoral stay at the laboratoire de conception et contrôle des systèmes de production, in Montréal, Canada. Dr. Rivera-Gómez is author of several articles indexed in international journals such as Elsevier, Springer and Tailor&Francis. He is a member of the National System of Researchers, SNII level 2, and is also a member of SMIO, the Mexican Society of Operations Research. In 2021 he won the first place of the SMIO award for directing the best thesis in the undergraduate category. His main area of interest is the analysis, simulation and control of production systems, dynamic programming of hybrid systems (discrete and continuous state) and stochastic optimization applied to production models and supply chains, an area in which he already has multiple scientific articles and graduate students at the undergraduate and graduate levels. Professor Rivera-Gomez is currently involved in research, teaching and directing undergraduate, master's and doctoral theses.

Juan Carlos Seck Tuoh Mora received a Bachelor's degree in Applied Mathematics and Computing in 1998 from ENEP Acatlán-UNAM, and received a Master's degree and Doctor of Science in Electrical Engineering (Computing option) from CINVESTAV-IPN in 1999 and 2002 respectively. He is currently a professor-researcher in the Academic Area of Engineering and Architecture at the UAEH. He is coordinator of the Doctor of Science Program in Engineering with Emphasis in Systems Analysis and Modeling, and the Doctor of Science Program in Industrial Engineering. He has the PRODEP Desirable Profile Recognition and is a member of the SNII level 2. His current research work includes the study of cellular automata, and the application of metaheuristic algorithms in the design, optimization and control of engineering systems.

Ahmet Bahadır Şimşek received his Ph.D. in 2019 from the Hacettepe University Department of Business Administration. He has been working as a lecturer/researcher at the Faculty of Health Sciences at Gumushane University since 2019. He gives lectures within the scope of operations research and conducts thesis consultancy in various undergraduate and graduate programs such as Health Management, Disaster Management and Business Administration. His research interest focuses on mathematical modeling applications in managerial decision-making and includes interdisciplinary collaboration.

Padmesh Tripathi is working as Professor of Mathematics at Delhi Technical Campus, Greater Noida, UP. He received his Ph.D. degree from Sharda University, Greater Noida (India). He completed his Master's and Bachelor's degrees from University of Allahabad, Prayagraj. He has been teaching since last 22 years. He has published many research papers in reputed journals. He has been granted funds from prestigious organizations like: Cambridge University, UK; University of

California, USA; University of Eastern Finland, Finland; INRIA, Sophia Antipolis, France, RICAM, Linz, Austria, etc. and he visited these organizations. He has been member of Society of Industrial and Applied Mathematics (SIAM), Philadelphia, USA (2011-19). He is life member of Science and Engineering Institute (SCIEI), Los Angeles, USA; Indian Society of Industrial and Applied Mathematics (ISIAM), India; Ramanujan Mathematical Society, India. He is member of EURO working group on continuous optimization (EUROPT), Italy; Society for Foundations of Computational Mathematics, USA. His research interests are inverse problems, signal processing, optimization, data science, etc.

Nagendra Singh Yadav is a Software Testing professional with experience managing remote teams and leading project teams. His background in software testing, technical writing, Research, Author, blogger, and Project management informs his mindful but competitive approach. Nagendra is fueled by his passion for understanding the project requirements and asking from the stakeholders. He considers himself a 'forever student,' eager to build on his academic foundations as a researcher, technical writer, and blogger, and stays in tune with the latest software testing & project management strategies through continued work experience. He is the Global Assistant General Secretary, International Council of Computer Science (ICCS) at Eudoxia Research Centre and holds degrees in M.C.A, B.C.A & a diploma in Blogging and Content Marketing. He has worked with Infosys Limited for 3 years in the field of software validation solutions as a Test Engineer (2016- 2019).

Pallavi Singh Yadav is a Research Scholar (Pursuing Ph.D. from Maharaja Ganga Singh University, Bikaner, Rajasthan) working on Non-Performing Assets of the Indian Banking Industry, as well as on the other research projects in the fields of accountancy and business statistics. She is also a Reviewer at DR BGR Publication, an Editorial Board Member of New Swertia Publications, and an Advisory Board Member of Ignited Minds Professional & Academic Research Consortium's Seminars, Conferences, and Listed Journals (Impact). She has finished Mindler's International Certified Career Coach Program (Foundation Level-I) and is an International Certified Career Coach. She is a credentialed peer reviewer and has completed the Publons Academy Practical Peer Review Course. She earned her UG (B.Com.), PG (M.Com. - Accountancy and Business Statistics), M.Phil. (Commerce) from Maharaja Ganga Singh University, Bikaner (A State University). She is two times UGC-NET Qualified (December 2015 and July 2018) In 2009, she was awarded the "Balika Protsahan Puraskar" by the "Government of Rajasthan" under the "Balika Shiksha Foundation, Jaipur" initiative.

Index

E

F

G

I

K

L

M

N

O

P

R

S

T

U

www.ingramcontent.com/pod-product-compliance
Lightning Source LLC
LaVergne TN
LVHW080634011026
849160LV00014B/1212